Readings in Caribbean History and Culture

Readings in Caribbean History and Culture

Breaking Ground

Edited by
D. A. Dunkley

LEXINGTON BOOKS
Lanham • Boulder • New York • Toronto • Plymouth, UK

Published by Lexington Books
A wholly owned subsidiary of The Rowman & Littlefield Publishing Group, Inc.
4501 Forbes Boulevard, Suite 200, Lanham, Maryland 20706
www.lexingtonbooks.com

Estover Road, Plymouth PL6 7PY, United Kingdom

British Library Cataloguing in Publication Information Available

Library of Congress Cataloging-in-Publication Data

Readings in Caribbean history and culture : breaking ground / edited by Daive A.
Dunkley.
    p. cm.
Includes bibliographical references and index.
ISBN 978-0-7391-6846-2 (cloth : alk. paper) — ISBN 978-0-7391-6847-9 (electronic)
    1. Caribbean Area—Civilization. 2. Caribbean Area—History. 3. Caribbean
Area—Colonial influence. 4. Caribbean Area—Intellectual life. 5. Caribbean
fiction—History and criticism. I. Dunkley, Daive A., 1973–
    F2169.R43 2011
    972.9—dc23   2011030550

Printed in the United States of America

For my mother, Shirley Joy Thompson,
and my stepfather, Maurice Washington Thompson

CONTENTS

List of Illustrations

Preface

Caribbean history and culture is entering both an exciting time but also a challenging period, where old certitudes seem less plausible than they previously did. That the history and culture of the various countries that make up the English- and French-speaking West Indies is undergoing considerable change is not surprising, given that the region itself is at a new stage of development. It is now getting close to half a century since the largest islands in the British West Indies gained independence. Few people below the age of retirement have much experience of life directly under colonial rule. Indeed, the mostly young contributors to this thought-provoking and wide-ranging set of essays are very distant in their own lives from the experiences that shaped a pioneering generation of investigators into West Indian history and culture. The old paradigms of national identity and creolization no longer make much sense in societies struggling with a set of issues often far removed from those that animated the intellectual predecessors of these contributors. How do we make sense of societies that are bewildering in their cultural diversity, often unsecure of their place in a world that seldom thinks them very important, and beset by major problems, such as crime, educational underachievement, and continuing endemic poverty?

The new concerns of the present can help to shape new responses to the past. For Raymond Ramcharitar, in the lead chapter in this collection, the task of historians just entering into the profession is to unsettle established notions of the past, especially a version of West Indian historiography that is essentially celebratory. Perhaps reflecting a more somber mood in the Caribbean as it enters the second decade of the twenty-first century, Ramcharitar insists that we should see Caribbean history in a much more negative, less positive light. For him, and for many other contributors, the history of the West Indies and even more so West Indian historiography is disturbing, challenging, and distinctly un-heroic.

Critiquing master narratives is a theme in this deliberately non-prescriptive volume. The editor has deliberately not chosen to shoehorn essays into a predetermined pattern, except to divide them into the subject categories of history and culture, in large degree because he doesn't want readers to think that the patterns of the past and present in the Caribbean are all that clear. What he suggests is that this is a period of intellectual flux, when lots of the master narratives that shaped a previous generation's understanding of West Indian history and culture no longer pertain. Thus, many of the chapters in this book question received knowledge. Michael Niblett challenges the utility of creolization as an organizing device by pointing out how the concept was systematically misused by French imperial thinkers when writing on Martinique. Shivani Sivagurunathan and Claudia Hucke also question received wisdom in their penetrating essays on important West Indian cultural figures, David Dabydeen and Karl Parboosingh. Eldon Birthwright similarly looks at the art form of Reggae through new eyes, while Dennis Gill examines West Indian plays through the prism of masculinity. What is clear is that old narratives that prioritize race and the legacy of slavery are insufficient to explain the diversity of experiences that make up the contemporary Caribbean, and which were just as present in the past.

The point of this volume is to showcase new researchers. This aim is splendidly met. The contributors, who live in the United States, the United Kingdom, Malaysia, and various countries in the Caribbean, are examples of how a new generation is challenging old ideas and shaping new perspectives. For those of us brought up on older orthodoxies, the experience is an occasionally unsettling one. It is difficult for many of us to see that old defender of proslavery, George Wilson Bridges, treated not just as a symbol of a retrogressive plantocractic sensibility, but also as someone with important things to say about the Jamaican past in a chapter written by the editor and in the following one by Russell Lord. Similarly, the chapters by Benita Thompson and her collaborators, and by Dalea Bean, tell us important new things about the interplay between gender and class in both the present and the past. The editor rightly thinks that the many challenges presented to us in the essays in this book say something about the multiple perspectives that one needs to take in order to understand the complex and always fascinating if often disturbing Caribbean. What that 'something' is should be left to you, the reader, on taking up this volume.

Trevor Burnard

University of Warwick, August 2010

Acknowledgments

Many people contributed to the production of this book from the time that it was just an idea to the moment it became a reality. I would like to thank, firstly, the contributors, who kindly consented to have their essays appear as chapters in this volume. They all share my desire to promote new ideas and to take on this challenge in spite of the difficulties.

I would like to thank Professors Verene Shepherd and Trevor Burnard as well for their encouragement and support. Professor Burnard also kindly agreed to write the preface for this volume, as an expression of his own view that new perspectives should indeed be encouraged and supported, however much they might seem to depart from and challenge accepted views.

I developed the idea for this book while I was still a doctoral student under the supervision of historian Gad Heuman at the University of Warwick. His advice and good guidance were instrumental in my intellectual development as a budding historian. I wish to thank him for helping me to fashion and grow my ideas, some of which, of course, appear in my own contributions to this volume.

Finally, I wish to express my gratitude to the editor and staff of Lexington Press, who agreed with me that these new voices (and some not so new ones) should indeed be heard.

Introduction*
by D. A. Dunkley

When I first thought of putting together this volume of essays, I had a completely different plan in mind, one that included essays on the history of the Caribbean and nothing more. As you can see, this is not the way that things turned out in the end. This collection of eleven essays cover both history and culture, and these matters are addressed through different lenses. The collection contains essays on social history, art history, education, literature, and music. It is my view that this mosaic is a reflection of the complexity of the problems facing the Caribbean, which in turn require a multidisciplinary approach wherein all subject areas can make a contribution to finding relevant solutions for the future of the region. Of course, this collection is also a valuable teaching tool at the university level and particularly in courses which examine Caribbean society, both past and present.

Part I, which contains six chapters under the heading of history, commences with a challenging essay by Raymond Ramcharitar on the forbidden subject of the "Freemasons" in Trinidad and Tobago (p. 13). Ramcharitar argues that the Freemasons of the nineteenth and early twentieth centuries belonged to what he has called the "underground history" of Trinidad and Tobago (p. 3, see title). This history has been systematically neglected in the history-writing on the Caribbean. Ramcharitar argues that the neglect has been part of the nationalist agenda since independence in the Anglophone Caribbean, which has been trying to rewrite and sanitize the history of non-white groups such as the Indo- and Afro-Trinidadians—this has meant eliminating unsavory and unceremonious aspects of their histories. These characteristics do not fit in with the attempt being made to present these groups as victims who had to

*All references appear in brackets (p.) and refer to page numbers in this volume.

struggle against colonialism, slavery, and indentured servitude. Groups such as the Freemasons, whose practices were shrouded in secrecy and which raised suspicions and serious criticisms that they were involved in illicit and unchristian activities, are inconvenient realities with which historians would rather not have to contend. The reconfigurations of "murderous rebellion, criminality, and nihilism into resistance or some other convenient trope of moral acceptability," as Ramcharitar asserts, is viewed generally as almost impossible if groups such as the Freemasons are to be involved, whose membership also ironically included many prominent members of the Indo-Trinidadian community (p. 5).

In the second chapter, D. A. Dunkley examines the early attempts to create an education system in the British colony of Jamaica. Dunkley argues that this system evolved during slavery and out of the decision by the Anglican Church to prioritize slave instruction and conversion in the church. The essay shows how through instruction, the church was established as the main provider of a fledgling system of education which, of course, was heavily influenced by the church's doctrines and principles. Since most of the teachers were also clergymen and later catechists employed by the Church Missionary Society, which had close ties to the Anglican Church, it was not surprising that the Christian religion was the main means through which tuition was delivered to the slaves. But Dunkley also makes a largely speculative attempt to explain the ways in which the slaves under instruction were able to influence the teaching that they received. This helped in the transformation of slavery, as slaves began to gravitate in larger numbers towards the church, viewing the opportunity to gain some form of literacy as part of their longstanding struggle for freedom. Even though the intention of the church was to use instruction to produce conformity among the slaves and to prolong slavery, the view taken by the slaves appears to have been in the opposite direction, where instruction was an investment that they could make in their psychological and perhaps physical liberation at some future date.

Chapter 3, which contains an analysis of the education systems in the English-speaking Caribbean during and after colonialism, can be seen as providing a challenge to the presentation in the previous chapter. The three authors of chapter 3 are education specialists Benita P. Thompson, S. Joel Warrican, and Coreen J. Leacock, who have been observing developments in education in the region and have done research on problems related to access to education, unfair testing, teacher selection and training, and teaching practices. The authors argue that many of these problems are "relics of the colonial past," which have been continued even to the present day (p. 62). The leaders in education across the region seem to be trapped in the colonial mind-set, which encourages the perpetuation of British practices which the British themselves have long abandoned. The issue of the churches' involvement in education is presented as a major cause of many of the problems still plaguing education. Rather than facilitating the liberation of Caribbean students, as Dunkley asserted in chapter 3, church control over education has left a legacy in which access to education is still limited based on socioeconomic circumstances. Testing practices have established hierarchies within the system between the schools, and within schools themselves in which students are streamed according to questionable perceptions about their abilities. Certainly both chapters 2 and 3 establish as a fact that there have always been problems in education, and that these are linked to the motives of the colonizers who saw educating the 'masses' as a way to establish conformity to British rule, rather than to unlock the potential of the students so that they could all move up on the social ladder.

Chapters 4 and 5 are also linked by their examinations of the Anglican clergyman George Wilson Bridges, who had arrived in Jamaica in 1816 and remained a resident of the island until his permanent departure in 1837. After this, as Russell Lord shows in chapter 5, Bridges abandoned his proslavery advocacy, developed a passion for photography, and went on tours of Canada, the Mediterranean, and the Middle East, on an unsuccessful venture to use photographs to prove the "truths" in the Bible (p. 109). Dunkley's assessment of Bridges in chapter 4 is largely about his advocacy of the social order that had created the institution of slavery, and which Bridges supported because he considered slavery crucial to the maintenance of the society which had given him status and economic prosperity. The chapter presents Bridges as a vicious advocate of the social order, having been influenced by enlightenment thinkers such as Jean Jacques Rousseau, whose work Bridges interpreted in a way that supported his own preconceived notions about the hierarchies of race and ethnicity. Dunkley argues that to continue to simply reject what Bridges had to say because of his insalubrious views is also, ironically, to miss opportunities to better understand why slavery survived for such a long time, and how the slaves made inroads into the system which eventually resulted in its abolition in the British colonies in 1834. Lord shows too that Bridges was an important figure in the development of photography in the nineteenth century, even interacting with prominent persons such as William Henry Fox Talbot, who is regarded as the inventor of photography and one of its pioneers. These chapters are not meant to celebrate Bridges but to do precisely what Ramcharitar suggests in chapter 1: to engage with the most unpleasant parts of the history of the region, however unsettling and upsetting the activities of the characters involved.

Dalea Bean, who authors chapter 6, the last chapter in Part I, examines yet another neglected subject: prostitution by women of color. Bean explains that these women who were trapped by poverty decided that they would raise themselves up from that situation by resorting to the sale of their sexuality. The money that they earned must have been quite attractive because prostitution flourished to the point that it became a concern for the authorities. Bean draws her examples from an assessment of the reactions of the military authorities in Jamaica during the early to mid-twentieth century, which includes the World War I era, the interwar years, and the immediate post-World War II period. The leadership of the military linked prostitution to the spread of venereal diseases, but they did almost nothing to stem this practice by addressing the other cause of the problem: the men, mainly military personnel, who sought out the services of prostitutes. It is certainly quite intriguing how gender bias played out even in the effort to deal with prostitution and the problem of disease. This just goes to show, as Bean suggests, that gender bias was a prominent feature of the colonial period of the Anglophone Caribbean, which drew its ideas about women from Victorian England, where women were not only regarded as inferior, but their inferiority was supported by notions that women were the causes of major social problems, including the practice of prostitution and spread of venereal diseases. The Caribbean continues to grapple with some of these harsh views about women, and unraveling how they were played out in the past is surely a contribution to identifying ways to overcome them in the present.

In chapter 7, Michael Niblett takes us into the French-speaking Caribbean to commence Part II of the book, which examines the culture of the region. Niblett uses Martinique to reconsider the concept of creolization, which he also does through an analysis of the 1998 novel *Solibo Magnifique* by the Martiniquan writer, Patrick Chamoiseau. Niblett presents this novel as a continuation of Chamoiseau's work on localizing the Créolité Movement, which had appeared in a previous nonfiction work, *Éloge de la Créolité,* published in 1989 and coauthored by Chamoiseau and fellow Martiniquan writers, Jean Bernabé and Raphaël Confiant. Niblett argues that *Solibo Magnifique* contains ample evidence of the deeply problematical nature of creolization, exemplified by its reconfiguration by metropolitan scholars into the destructive idea of "hybridity" (p. 157). This concept provided some of the epistemological justifications on which France based its decision to deepen its connection with Martinique through a process known as departmentalization that started in 1946. Since then, Martinique has been the injured party in the attempts by French capitalists to further impose on the island products Made-in-France to the detriment of locally made goods which are part of Martinique's folk culture. The destruction of the "manioc" trade is used by Niblett to show how French consumer items, sold as substitutes, have led to the replacement of this local product. One of the important points Niblett makes is the urgent need for Caribbean countries to force their own interpretations of the origins and characteristics of creolization upon the discourse advocating hybridity. Creolization has to remain a Caribbean phenomenon, since it has the potential to expose Caribbean countries to more insidious forms of domination through hegemony, or the conscious renewal of colonization through a seemingly innocent process of accidental consent.

Dennis Gill's contribution in chapter 8 is also concerned with colonialism and includes an examination of another French-speaking territory, Haiti, along with two others from the English-speaking Caribbean. In an era when it has become rather too common to explain issues related to Caribbean masculinity using present-day formations such as the Jamaican dancehall and its music, it is refreshing to see that Gill has not excluded the influence of "the persistent, un-heroic past," as Ramcharitar would put it (p. 3, see title). Gill insists that Caribbean masculinity is still tied very closely to the structures of the past which gained currency through the powerful influence of colonialism, which has in turn resulted in the survival of severe, problematical features such as the "patriarchal mind-set" of our men, their "race hatred," and their "moral relativism" (p. 183). These are very serious issues which have had graver consequences than the sexual ambiguity of often undereducated and often unemployed men who flirt with the opposite gender in the ways that they dress and dance in temporary existential settings such as the dancehall. Gill shows, through his examination of four Caribbean plays by C. L. R. James, Derek Walcott, and Errol John, that the Eurocentric ideas that Caribbean men have embraced continue to affect not only them but also their children and women folk. These problems are played out through the exercise of power or through absenteeism in the case of fatherhood and relationships with spouses, placing Caribbean societies in imperiled situations that continue to setback social maturity and further social growth.

Chapter 9 by Shivani Sivagurunathan is an intriguing departure into a still largely unheard-of phenomenon: "Coolitude" (p. 204). This is an interesting idea since it shows how the grossness of the past can be embraced without sanitization and used as a form of empowerment for Caribbean people. The word *coolie* is still seen as a derogatory term in countries such as Trinidad and Tobago, Guyana, and Jamaica where large communities of Indo-Caribbean nationals exist, and the term is used widely in other settings in the region to deride Indo-Caribbean people and to suggest that they are somehow inferior to other inhabitants of the region. This is precisely why Sivagurunathan is interested in rehabilitating the notion of the coolie using the concept of Coolitude, a term coined by the Indo-Mauritian poet Khal Torabully "to reposition the coolie in the national imaginary be it in the Caribbean, Africa, or Asia" (p. 204). Sivagurunathan explains how coolitude is already present in the

Caribbean in her analysis of the 2004 novel *Our Lady of Demerara* by literary icon David Dabydeen, himself a displaced Indian of Guyanese birth and British upbringing. This novel, according to Sivagurunathan, is both a Coolitudian and Caribbean text that explores the intricacies of post-emancipation indentureship, which was responsible for the introduction of Indian laborers into the Caribbean. The novel shows that in order to survive and improve their condition, Indians in the Caribbean had to manipulate their new environment through a tough, "never-ending" process of identity creation and a "web of relationships" aimed at "perpetual reassessment," "constant movement," and "constant possibilities" (p. 214). Indians engineered their successful adaptation through coolitude, which suggests that the coolie identity is not something for them to be ashamed of, but rather to be proud about.

In chapter 10, Claudia Hucke uses the metropolitan idea of "hybridity" to analyze the post-independence art movement and particularly the visual art of Jamaican painter Karl Parboosingh. Niblett, who might find it interesting that Hucke herself is of German origin, though she has been working in Jamaica for several years, would find many reasons to criticize Hucke's assessment in chapter 10. This is because Hucke uses the very same notion of hybridity that Niblett sees as a manipulation of the concept of creolization to integrate postcolonial societies of the Caribbean into the global capitalist system in order to facilitate the exploitation through hegemonic controls. However, Hucke stresses that hybridity in the hands of Caribbean artistes, such as Parboosingh, was instead an attempt by them to control the very same process of creolization, which as Niblett himself admits, is open to external reconfiguration and exploitation. The point Hucke makes is quite important given that these artists had to struggle even against people from the academy in the Caribbean, who had complained that they were painting not for society but for themselves. Parboosingh, who had received exposure to art movements in Panama, Mexico, New York, and Paris, chose to integrate all of these influences into his art, viewing this process as his own demonstration of personal independence, rather than succumbing to nationalist agendas that tried to control the creativity of artists. Parboosingh showed that in the hands of Caribbean people, hybridity can be a useful tool to establish one's identity and independence. It is only a problem when it is controlled by outsiders, especially those from metropolitan countries who, of course, have in mind their own self-interest.

The final chapter in the book, chapter 11, which also closes the part on culture, provides an examination of the poetic musical genre known as Reggae, which, according to the author of the chapter, Eldon V. Birthwright, has been heavily influenced by the Rastafari Movement. It is certainly well known that Rastafari, which was formed in Jamaica in the 1930s, was established as much more than a theological movement. It advocated a political discourse that was aimed at improving the social and economic condition of the poorest people in Jamaica and across the Caribbean. This is no doubt why Rastafari's influence spread to other Caribbean countries and the wider world, aided, of course, by the musical form known as Reggae, which had attracted and continues to attract artistes who adhere to Rastafari ideas, either partially or entirely. Birthwright knows that music is a powerful tool that drives fear into political establishments, and he communicates this by showing how even Plato, while writing his famous *Republic,* warned about the power of music. In Jamaica, especially during the 1970s and 1980s, Reggae music went through periods of suppression and exploitation by political parties vying for power. Some musicians were even forced into exile out of the fear of repercussions for songs they had written or sung. And, as Birthwright explains, a major part of the reason for the powerful message in Reggae is the influence of Rastafari, which has helped to infuse the musical form with its poetics of resistance. Reggae is thus a medium through which the poor has been demanding social justice, economic opportunity, and responsible political representation. It also suggests ways in which these improvements can be manifested by simply adopting the principle of equity, which sends a more powerful message that the plight of the poor is caused by a crisis of leadership—a leadership unwilling or unable to implement ideas that seem to be not too challenging to embrace.

As a final note, I wish to reiterate my hope that this book provides some useful ideas that will help the Caribbean people in their developmental goals in the coming years. I also hope that, as a teaching tool, this book will inspire and provoke serious thought and discussion among students. I hope, too, that academics will find within this book ideas which are worthy of their attention and contemplation. The contributors and I certainly welcome any challenges that they might have.

PART I

HISTORY

Chapter 1

Underground History

The Persistent, Unheroic Past

Raymond Ramcharitar

INTRODUCTION: OTHER HISTORIES

Many of Charles Dickens' novels show a Victorian England that scandalized the respectable sensibilities of his time: side by side with sneering peers, middle class social climbers, and the virtuous poor was an array of disquieting, dangerous, and evil characters and dystopian institutions. From the glacial, corrupt judiciary of *Bleak House,* to the satanic factories and their human cogs of *Hard Times,* to the myopic Victorian bureaucracy and its Podsnaps of *Our Mutual Friend,* Dickens juxtaposes the macabre and the magnificent of Victorian England.

However much its depiction unsettled the moral certainties of Victorian Imperialism, the macabre aspect of British society was a crucial element of the era's constitution and depiction in historical and creative works. In describing leisure and entertainment in Britain in the preindustrial period, historian Eric Evans notes that

> the recreations of the lower orders in preindustrial Britain were either violent, drunken, cruel or all three. Crowds flocked to cock-fights, bull-baitings, prize fights, public executions and fairs. These last usually had rowdy undertones and [were] . . . debauched by the presence of prostitutes and by other opportunities for illicit sexual liaison.[1]

Donald Thomas in *The Victorian Underworld,* wrote of a London where the poor lived in misery and vice, sometimes within a stone's throw of the Victorian moralists. The divisions were so stark, that "there were areas of

London as uninstructed by Christianity as the remotest corners of empire.
. . . The Christian doctrine of forgiving one's enemies was regarded with
skepticism, if not scorn."[2]

A similar vision of the United States was immortalized by Upton Sinclair
in his 1905 novel *The Jungle,* which painted a dark, factual picture of labor
conditions among immigrants in Chicago at the end of the nineteenth century.
More recently, Martin Scorsese in his 2003 film *The Gangs of New York,*
and other contemporary metropolitan filmmakers, writers, and journalists,
like Guy Ritchie, Thomas Pynchon, Quentin Tarantino, Don DeLillo, Eric
Schlosser, and Greg Palast have made careers out of fictional, scholarly, and
journalistic depictions of past and contemporary *underworlds.*

Significantly, these narratives are continuously roiled in a dialectical
engagement with counter-narratives—political, fictional, and religious—
reflecting the materiality of mainstream-underworld relations. The results are
complex, ever-evolving conceptions and re-conceptions of those societies and
the re-formation of the societies themselves, and the enlarging of the collective memory and moral imagination.

Just as French libertinism, American frontier *laissez faire,* and Victorian
brothels contributed to shaping the worldviews of their time, gangsta rap,
Internet pornography, and the popular cult of marijuana continuously, and
in tandem with an array of other forces, shape and re-shape contemporary
Western society in their confrontations with fundamentalist Christianity on
the nature of freedom and sexuality, and capitalist sponsored discourses on
issues as variegated as education and mental health.

In this continuous reshaping, the Caribbean/West Indies contributes almost
involuntarily (primary commodities, images, and landscapes of primitivist
fantasias), but is not itself central to the discourses of re-creation, and is a
discourse taker, rather than a discourse maker. I propose that it is, crucially,
an *absence* of the heteroglossic conflict of ideas and worldviews described
above that has led to the stasis or retrograde trajectories of many contemporary West Indian nations and nationalisms. A major reason the necessary
creative/discursive conflict is absent is the epistemological and political
orientation of the West Indian academe and political institutions, and specifically because accounts, and the *idea,* of the West Indian underworld, whether
fictional or factual, do not seem to exist in the artistic, social science, or
historical repertoire of the West Indies academe and, the West Indian social
and civil imaginaries. I propose that this absence, or its withholding by the
institutional gate keepers, has deprived Caribbean and West Indian discursive agents of a valuable theatre or factory of self-knowledge: to paraphrase
Bakhtin, the moral dialogic imagination remains underdeveloped, its conclusions and dialectical processes replaced by edict, slogan, and commandment.

Morality, intellect, and sophistication in the conduct of material affairs remain rhetorical, disconnected from the brutish praxis.

To be sure, there are a few accounts of subcultures, cultural interactions, and artistic representations of the criminal underworld and alternative cultural dialectics, like Perry Henzel's film *The Harder They Come,* Laurie Gunst's book *Born Fi Dead,* and Kamau Brathwaite's study *The Development of Creole Society in Jamaica,* and the contemporary texts of dancehall "gangsta" lyrics and popular movies, like Cess Silvera's 2006 film, *Shottas.* But these texts, inhibited by politics, do not cohere into a social or cultural discourse or counter-discourse. Indeed, the general orientation of studies of phenomena which might constitute an underworld is to appropriate them into mainstream discourse, or rehabilitate them: to turn murderous rebellion, criminality, and nihilism into resistance or some other convenient trope of moral acceptability. The best example of this is the rewriting of Obeah practices in the twenty-first century by metropolitan scholars as cultural retention and resistance.[3] More pervasively, the discourse of Creolization, and the counter discourse of Carnival (in Trinidad and throughout the Caribbean) have been appropriated into nationalistic narratives, and reframed and bowdlerized in works like, *inter alia,* John Cowley's 1996 *Carnival Canboulay and Calypso;* Hollis Liverpool's *Rituals of Power and Rebellion* which appeared in 2003, Milla Riggio's 2004 collection *Carnival: Culture in Action: The Trinidad Experience,* and Gordon Rohlehr's 1990 *Calypso and Society in pre-Independence Trinidad.*[4]

The reason for this discursive anomaly is that post-independence histories, and prevailing West Indian conceptions of history, have tended to enact what in communications theory is labeled as "perception management."[5] This has meant revising and re-visioning the past to fit contemporary exigencies of moral repudiation for centuries of European racism, and a monotonous, one-dimensional response to echoes (or mirages) of the Eurocentric conceptions of the inferiority of the colored races.

B.W. Higman points out that even though "the detachment, objectivity, and scientific method of the professional historian seem to leave little room for emotional approaches to the past, little opportunity for celebration of moral indignation," the "black West Indian history-writers wrote . . . with a moral right to express resentment in anger, to expect apologies for wrongs done, and to dispense and withhold forgiveness." The results are the "heroizing" and "villainizing" of history, and the consequent recourse to the narratives of the victim and the inversion of standards like the creation of heroes from anti-heroes.[6]

Laënnec Hurbon, in discussing "Ideology" as it relates to Caribbean historiography, puts an optimistic "spin" on the creation of heroes, writing that in resistance to the imposition of Western values, "we have managed to develop the ideologies of negritude and cultural nationalism, and to show that the history of the Caribbean distinguishes itself by the creation of new cultures." But Hurbon recognizes that "the process of alienation resulting from the teaching of history has led new Caribbean historians to a veritable nationalist "overkill.""[7]

This "overkill" has drawn many critics. Higman cites late Jamaican Prime Minister Michael Manley's decrying the paucity of historical scholarship, much of which he described as "journalism masquerading as history," which creates a kind of "self-inflicted disability" more suited to propaganda.[8] Similarly, historian William Green points out that in the writing of the history of the post-emancipation era, "the struggle assumes a moral cast," and that "Emancipation history is uniformly written in the tragic style."[9] Higman suggests a reason:

> Historiography is founded on the notion that history-writing is a cultural activity firmly sewn into the fabric of modern society, and history writers, whether academic, public or amateur, are ineluctably drawn into that pattern and its deeper dynamic.[10]

In Trinidad, Carnival history has become a spin-off political industry which is used as an adjunct to tourism and nationalist politics.[11]

All this allows one to assert with some certainty that particular politics, ideologies, and personalities shape the writing and interpretation of history—that is, the selection and legitimization of facts and interpretations of the past—and consequently, social and academic discourse about the present. The orientation of Trinidadian (and West Indian) historians to the "heroizing" tendency in the present was illustrated by "Freedom Road," a series of lectures hosted by the University of the West Indies (UWI), St. Augustine, Trinidad, in commemoration of the two-hundredth anniversary of the abolition of the slave trade.

The first lecture on "The Meaning of Freedom" delivered by a UWI historian in April 2007 argued that the enslaved were really not slaves, and that they were free, and that it was their heroic resistance and not the Wilberforce lobby that resulted in the end of slavery. Though there were dissenting views, many of the remaining lectures, deemphasizing the "white" contribution to the point of erasure, and by extension the European component of West Indian history, followed in this vein. And the discursive thread of the first lecture was amplified and reproduced. This project was supported by the Trinidadian

Ministry of Culture and taken to schools and other educational and cultural institutions. Parallel statements were repeated in public by popular folk artists and by newspaper and radio commentators throughout the year.[12]

This is not to suggest that historical revisionism is objectionable *per se.* Much academic endeavor is justifiably directed to correcting historical narratives with the purpose of affecting the present. The term *histories from below* describes an accepted historiographic paradigm, and the French *Annales* School has provided the concept of *mentalité,* the examination of the "mental world" of particular groups during specific historical periods, which makes simplistic moral judgments, and conventional Rankean sources, problematic.[13] What is objectionable is when politically or emotionally unpalatable points of view are discarded or suppressed in favor of contemporary politics, with disastrous long-term effects.

These deleterious effects of a bowdlerized archive of knowledge and theory could include that it leaves scholars and social scientists unable to analyze or explain social dynamics and social problems, and derive solutions. This is evident in the widespread poverty, crime, and social decay in oil-rich Trinidad in 2010, especially in the context of its ambitions to achieve "First World status" by 2020 using its oil-wealth, efforts which are persistently stymied by its seemingly intractable and inexplicable social issues.[14]

Regionally, the lacunae in the academe's archive leave UWI's graduates and guardians inadequately prepared for confronting the real world, in and outside the region, and ultimately lead to a devaluation of the academe's, and the region's, cultural capital. And finally, wittingly and unwittingly, the new configuration of knowledge generates its own logic, and leads to what Benedict Anderson and Homi K. Bhabha both have addressed as the "invention" of traditions and nations which, in the West Indies, are bizarre chimeras of violence and poverty, whose discursive selves are detached from their materiality.[15]

Having laid out the initial connections between the underground and mainstream historical realities, and historical discourse, this chapter will attempt to do three things. First, it will examine and provide the theoretical framework for "underground history," or history which is deemed unpalatable by mainstream historians and other scholars. Second, it will examine the history of Trinidad and Tobago to show instances where there has been avoidance of the politically unpalatable facts, or of underground history, which has left gaps or distortions in the academic record. And third, the chapter examines the consequences of omitting underground history for contemporary understandings of the history and culture of Trinidad and Tobago and the rest of the Caribbean.

LOCATING THE UNDERGROUND

Underground history is not unknown or even new in historical study. Conventional historians like Eric Evans and Donald Thomas have already been cited, and many studies, both academic and popular, of the underworlds of Western societies exist. These include, for instance, Kellow Chesney's *The Victorian Underworld,* Andrew McCall's *The Medieval Underworld,* Fergus Linnane's *London's Underworld: Three Centuries of Crime and Vice,* Eric Scholsser's *Reefer Madness and Other Tales From the American Underground,* and James Henry's *The Blood Bankers: Tales from the Global Underground.*[16]

The underground may be described for the purposes of this chapter as a discursive and material space, where illicit and illegal commodities are traded and sought. It is a site of psychological and physiological excess: where appetites for substances, ideas, and practices (like narcotics, ideologies, and the use of the human body and mind in ways unacceptable to the dominant social-moral discourse) can be admitted and indulged. For example, the recreational use of cocaine, performance of homosexual acts, and the pervasion of alternative belief systems, like witchcraft, sadomasochism, or political anarchism. This intrinsic difference or divergence from the standards of mainstream society leads to a reconfiguration of values, practices, and the means of interface with the mainstream, which would allow both to coexist in the same physical space simultaneously.

It would be simplistic to equate the underground proposed here with the merely criminal, or with a specific subculture. It is more fruitful to think of the phenomenon as a "dark reflection" or the equivalent of the subconscious of the mainstream world, a necessary transgressive domain underlying a surface order, possessing many commodities similar to those in the mainstream material economy, but governed by different modes of interpretation, discourse, values, morality, and ontology. The desire for transgression appears to be an inbuilt part of the human psyche, since manifestations of the underground are equally potent at society's conservative centre and its outlaw fringe. This can be illustrated, in a general way, in American counterculture and British establishment culture (such as Freemasonry), from the nineteenth century to the present.

THE ROOTS OF THE AMERICAN UNDERGROUND

The nineteenth century in the United States provided a fertile ground for underground life and activities other than Freemasons. According to Theda

Skopcol and Lynn Oser, in a special issue of the journal *Social Science History* in 2004, formal secret societies and fraternal organizations analogous to the Freemasons abounded in Victorian America. But another, more interesting perspective of the roots of the American underground is provided by journalist John Leland in his book, *Hip: The History.*

Leland describes the posture known in American popular and counter culture as "hip." "Hip-ness," loosely translated, is an *avant gardist* appreciation of and familiarity with invisible but vital social forces, which sets those "inside" few with the ability to channel them (via creative ventures in music, art, and cultural innovation in speech, style, signification, and fashion) apart from the mainstream. The posture began with the institution of slavery, and the creative interplay of black and white populations, especially on plantations, where, despite America's size, because of the structure of the plantations, "the races lived together, unequally but intimately."[17] This necessitated a private knowledge among the enslaved, which was unavailable to their enslavers—hence "hip" was born. From this association came the existence of an alternative, surreptitious culture, which allowed the enslaved to conduct their private discourses. Much like in the Caribbean, the Africans developed their own vernacular, values, and cultural idiom, but also created a negotiated culture that formed a bridge to the mainstream.

The ontological interplay of enslaved and enslaver in the Caribbean has been described at length in Brathwaite's Creolization thesis.[18] But of additional value here is Leland's idea that the underworld's materiality and discursivity is in a state of continuous engagement with the mainstream world, in much the same way the Freudian superego endlessly battles the urges of the subconscious in the field of consciousness.

Leland describes critical moments in the meeting of these two cultures in an ongoing dialectical encounter as a "convergence," which reshapes society, and identifies six such convergent moments in American history.[19] He labels the ground where "hip" thrives as "a shadow culture," whose late nineteenth-century agents were writers and artists, such as Walt Whitman, Herman Melville, and Henry Thoreau, who "celebrate[d] the individual and non-conformist, advocating civil disobedience, savoring the homoerotic, and above all claiming the sensual power of the new." The characteristics of what Leland identifies as "the first convergence" were such that "the writers . . . sought to invent a literature and identity for a nation whose mandarins still preached the high culture of Europe. Outlawed in their sexual practices, tax habits or literary ideals, they defined civil disobedience, not just in politics, but in culture and lifestyle."[20]

BRITISH UNDERGROUND CULTURE

However, even those who constitute the heart of the social order appear to need to step outside of it, and in so doing, subvert it. The Victorian British and American criminal underworlds have already been described, but another manifestation of the psychological and physiological imperatives that generate an underground is materialized in the existence and practices of secret societies and fraternal organizations, in particular Freemasonry, which draws its memberships from among the higher, central echelons of society. This was particularly true of the nineteenth century in Europe. According to J.M. Roberts, Europe, between 1815 and 1914, was particularly rich ground for secret societies: "For about a century-and-a-half, large numbers of intelligent Europeans believed that much of what was happening in the world around them only happened because secret societies planned it so."[21]

Chief among these societies in the West in the nineteenth century was Freemasonry. As Eric Hobsbawm observes: "Freemasonry, in eighteenth-century Britain, was a network pervading the whole of society, and particularly the educated classes—the professional people, the civil servants and administrators. It also engendered *a general psychological and cultural climate, an atmosphere which suffused the mentality of the age* (my italics)."[22] Furthermore, Hobsbawm observes that the climate encouraged brotherhood among men of disparate classes, and general values of egalitarianism and progress, such that "Under the aegis of Grand Lodge, the entire caste system became less rigid, more flexible than anywhere on the continent. . . . Strictures against religious and political prejudice served to encourage . . . [a] kind of egalitarian spirit."[23]

This provides an article of proof that the underground shapes the mainstream in ongoing interaction. From the flux emerge challenges to orthodoxy and social transformation, as the 68-ers of Paris, the Hippies of Vietnam-era United States, and the Hosay revelers in nineteenth-century Trinidad did. It seems obvious, then, that denying the existence of the underground, and its agency, creates a negative lacunae in the academic archive, the existence and consequences of which will be examined nearer the end of this chapter.

HISTORICAL APORIAS: THE BLACK AND COLORED UNDERWORLDS OF NINETEENTH-CENTURY TRINIDAD

The consequences of bowdlerizing history to satisfy political agendas are most evident in a single, gaping hole in the orthodox conceptions of the intellectual and political development of the region. This is the absence in every major study of West Indian nationalism, the axiom that that nationalism was certainly contributed to by the European ideas of egalitarianism, rebellion, and fraternity transmitted through Freemasonry, which was pervasive in the Caribbean, and to which many, if not all, upper and middle class black and colored men belonged. No major study has yet been done of the phenomenon; neither has the phenomenon been even acknowledged as a shaper of political or social consciousness in the region.

In his landmark work, *The Caribbean: An Intellectual History,* Denis Benn proposes an intellectual trajectory of Caribbean thought which may be taken as West Indian orthodoxy. He begins with the planter historians like Edward Long and the Old Representative System of government, continues with Crown Colony government, through to independence nationalism, Marxism, and, finally, ethnic-nationalism. This schema culminates in the present with the ethnic vindication and inversion achieved.

Benn's schema is indebted to Gordon Lewis's seminal *Main Currents in Caribbean Thought* and complemented by Paget Henry's *Caliban's Reason* and O. Nigel Bolland's *The Birth of Caribbean Civilization.* It is further complemented by a later, much broader work by Silvio Torres-Salliant, *An Intellectual History of the Caribbean,* which encompasses the Hispanophone and Francophone Caribbeans. The studies of the development of nationalism in the Anglophone Caribbean have a single element in common: that is the central or seminal role they ascribe to John Jacob Thomas. Thomas was a nineteenth-century Trinidadian savant, who formulated a theory of linguistics from principles in his *Theory and Practice of Creole Grammar,* and was elected to the British Royal Philological Society in 1873.[24] Orthodoxy argues that Thomas was both a culmination and point of origin of Black Nationalist ideology and ambition.

Bridget Brereton's closely argued and well-researched article "John Jacob Thomas, An Estimate," lays out the orthodox academic case, citing Thomas's race consciousness, and his considerable scholarly achievement, noting with some bemusement his admiration of British culture and relatively mild assessments of white Trinidadian Creoles. Though Brereton acknowledges Thomas's reactionary ideas—for example, those concerning property qualifications for suffrage—in concluding, Brereton stops short of naming Thomas a proto-nationalist, but endorses C.L.R. James's assessment of Thomas as being a (superior) precursor to Marcus Garvey.[25]

Later writers would follow from this premise. Benn places Thomas at the beginning of an indigenous line which would culminate into the Über-ethnic nationalist, Eric Williams, and proceed to the present condition of ethnic nationalism. He characterizes Thomas's *Froudacity,* a response to the British historian J.A. Froude whose book, *The Bow of Ulysses,* disparaged the West Indian colonies and indigenous politicians, as "an episode in the ongoing political struggle for reform of the Crown Colony system."[26] Paget Henry, likewise, appropriates Thomas into the lineage of Afro-Caribbean intellectuals in his study, *Caliban's Reason*—the work outlines the Afrocentric foundations of Caribbean philosophy. And the Caliban metaphor, according to Torres-Salliant, is the ultimate "native topos" or "cultural synecdoche."[27]

None of these studies mentions or seems aware of the fact that Thomas was a Freemason. But when this fact emerges, its treatment is casual. The only book-length study of Thomas, Faith Smith's *Creole Recitations,* makes brief mention of Thomas being a Freemason in literally a few sentences, but spends all its resources on locating Thomas in a racial-nationalist matrix, where "commentators tested the extent to which *Negro* could be linked with *distinguished* or *respectable,* dislodged from *White.*"[28] This blindness to the subjectivity of someone like Thomas and transferring the subjective idea to Caliban is an excellent example of the ideological reframing of the black and colored historical narrative. Wilson Harris notes this in his essay, "History, Fable, and Myth in the Caribbean and Guianas," in examining the Thomas-Froude encounter. Harris contradicts C.L.R. James's assessment that Thomas had triumphed over Froude, labeling the exchange a "comedy of manners," and suggesting that James and his antecedents were psychologically incapable of confronting the sordidness of the Caribbean's history.[29]

Perhaps an unconscious manifestation of this unwillingness to acknowledge an unpleasant reality, is the choice of Caliban—the inarticulate, violent, primitive, a historical-political android, created by the political technology of nationalist historiography. Indeed, Torres-Salliant suggests this when he writes that: "We cannot epistemologically afford to deflate the harshness of the past, the grim images that stand out as we perform the unsavory act of remembering."[30]

The Caliban figure overwrites several personalities and types (including Thomas, who was diametrically opposed to the very notion of Caliban) to create an archetypal political subject, incorporating the attributes of enraged "radicals" who "struggled" against "white oppression," and eliding those who were comfortable within the discourse of empire as subjects of empire. And the trope of the Caribbean subject embodied in Caliban (which appears in the creative and critical work of George Lamming, Kamau Brathwaite, and Aime Cesaire) provides an excellent illustration of the power inversion without an epistemological shift: that is, rather than deserting the margin-centre paradigm, the characters have merely been switched.[31]

In this dispensation, Caliban is at the centre, and Prospero's contributions are being whittled away on the margins. This formulation merely makes the region an epiphenomenon of European reality, and not a *thing in itself,* capable of generating its own reflection and reflectivity. But to bring Caliban to the centre, epistemic violence must be enacted on the viable Eurocentric discourses of morality, duty, patriotism, and the values and idealism which must affect the *tabula rasa* or colonized subject to transform him or her into an agent of the inevitable new order. But this evasion of the harshness of the reality, manifest in the desire for the simplistic panacea of inversion, was, as Higman notes, always foremost in the minds of nationalist historiographers.

In fusing the lives and materiality of the people with the ideal of independence, Gordon Lewis prefaces his discussion of political nationalism with "cultural nationalism" in which, he opined, "the Caribbean nationalist ideology finds its most assertive expression." The vehicle of this expression was "the Creole urban intelligentsia . . . that developed from Havana to Port of Spain in that [nineteenth-century] period." Lewis also invokes the trope of "resistance" as an early component, and writes "the culture carriers as always were the despised lower classes."[32] As already discussed, this point of view has become the "official" one, and several studies have already been cited to show that the Carnival and "jamette" cultures in the nineteenth century are used as crucibles for national development, or starting points of nationalist trajectories.

The preceding briefly sketches the close connection between cultural, political, and ethnic nationalism. This makes it all the more bewildering that the major cartographers of West Indian intellectual and political traditions could be so utterly oblivious to a major, highly developed body of ideas such as Freemasonry, which was an acknowledged shaper of the better aspects of Victorian ideals and culture, by orthodox British historians like J.M. Roberts, Jasper Ridley, Eric Evans, and Eric Hobsbawm. In his history of the Freemasons, Ridley points out that the greatest reformist statesmen in the United States were Freemasons: Theodore Roosevelt, who crafted the New Deal, Chief Supreme Court Justice John Marshall (1805–35), who "did more than anyone to mold the constitution of the United States and to establish the Supreme Court as an upholder of the rights of American citizens," and Earl Warren, also a Chief Justice (1953–69), a key figure in establishing the Civil Rights of African-Americans.[33]

Given the high visibility of not only Freemasons, but the Masonic movement in the West Indies, it is highly unlikely that this enormous lacuna is accidental, since it is impossible to open any newspaper of nineteenth century Trinidad (at least) and not encounter multitudinous references to an active and pervasive Masonic movement, which, if the records of the Grand Lodges of England and Scotland are accurate, was liberally distributed through the region—from Jamaica to Guyana.

To return to the main thesis of this chapter: the obsession with ethnic nationalism has erased crucial historical evidence and connections—I propose that all the material and ideological deficiencies in West Indian historiography described above are manifest in the studies of Thomas's role and intellectual antecedents, given the one crucial omission in all studies of his life. He is presented as the proto-nationalist, based on one book, *Froudacity,* which was a response to another book. But the bulk of his writings, in the newspapers of the time, are ignored, *as is his being an active and high-ranking Freemason in Trinidad.* Thomas was inducted into the Lodge Eastern Star in Trinidad in 1871.[34] He was also listed in the *New Era* newspaper as an active member of the Royal Arch Chapter of the Scottish Craft in 1881.[35]

In his relationship with Freemasonry and its effect on his worldview, Thomas's life can be used as a synecdoche for the black and colored middle classes of the last third of the nineteenth century. Contemporary orthodox accounts, such as those listed above, agree that these men were intellectually gifted, politically astute, rebellious, at times rabidly anti-colonial, and made the first concrete steps to Trinidadian political autonomy. No account till now has mentioned that if not all, then a vast majority, were Freemasons, and what this could mean for the emergence of Trinidadian, and West Indian nationalism. Among these men were Michel Maxwell Philip, Edgar Maresse Smith, and H.S. Billouin, lawyers, newspaper publishers, and men of all colors from virtually every walk of middle class life.

FREEMASONRY IN NINETEENTH-CENTURY TRINIDAD

John Cowley's *Carnival, Canboulay, and Calypso* is the most authoritative account which feeds the popular conception of nineteenth-century Trinidad's cultural and social landscape, and nationalist trajectory generated by the masses and their "jamette" carnivals and culture. These were violent, rowdy, and patronized mainly by those whom Gordon Lewis describes as the "despised lower orders." Indeed, Cowley's work, along with, *inter alia,* Gordon Rohlehr's, Milla Riggio's, Errol Hill's, Gerard Aching's, Keith Nurse and Christine Ho's, form the discursive engine of Trinidadian (and West Indian) mainstream auto-definition: to place Carnival and its developmental trajectory as super-signifiers of the region and its social and cultural productive capacity.[36] The success of this agenda, assisted by the new global consumerist order, which has the Metropole as producer of technology and science, and

the Caribbean as producer of elementary, primitive (Caliban-esque) products, has been spectacularly successful, to the point of an aphasic posture to
notions of any other trajectory, more closely allied with Eurocentric ideas,
origins, and products, intrinsically involved in the formation and evolution of
the modern West Indies.

Despite all the evidence and rhetoric which paint the "jamette" world as the
"official" nineteenth-century underground, there was another underground
space in the nineteenth century where the black and colored middle classes
were able to gather, fraternize, and immerse themselves in an ethos which
would prove crucial to their many struggles for autonomy: the Masonic
Lodge. Indeed, the Masonic Lodge was only one of the many fraternal
societies that abounded in the nineteenth century which included the Forest-
ers, Mechanics, and numerous Friendly Societies, whose membership came
from the small, lower-middle class, and respectable poor black and colored
populations.[37]

Two types of lodges existed in Trinidad: those of English and Scottish
Constitution. The first and longest surviving Trinidadian Masonic Lodge, the
Lodge United Brothers (LUB), which came to Trinidad with the French planters in the late eighteenth century, is of the Scottish Constitution. The Scottish
lodges because of their more liberal outlook were, in the nineteenth century,
more willing to accept black and colored applicants, unlike the conservative
English lodges. This remained so for most of the nineteenth century.

As to what Freemasons believed and promulgated, this much is evident
in the earliest surviving work on Freemasonry in Trinidad, *The Sure Guide*,
written in 1819. It gives a brief history and outline of its aims, which display
a general accord to those of Victorian society outlined above:

> Many advantages are gained [from Masonry], the Chinese, Arab, Turk, and the
> savage will embrace a brother Briton, Frank or German, and will know that,
> beside the common ties of humanity, there is still a stronger obligation to in-
> duce him to kind and friendly offices. The Spirit of the fulminating priest will
> be tamed and a moral brother, though of a different persuasion, will engage his
> esteem. Thus, through the influences of Masonry, which is reconcilable to the
> best policy, all those disputes, which embitter life, and sours the temples of men
> are avoided—while the common good, the general design of the craft, is zeal-
> ously pursued.[38]

The book provided an introduction to the practice by outlining the prereq-
uisites for prospective inductees, chiefly good character and that they be recommended by members of the lodge. It identified the "points of fellowship"

as support for other masons, industriousness, keeping secrets, and prayers for the efforts of other brothers.

By the last third of the nineteenth century, masonry had become an accepted part of the social order in Trinidad. There were advertisements in the press for Masonic paraphernalia.[39] Newspapers like *Fair Play* and *New Era* were owned and edited by Freemasons, and along with others, these carried frequent advertisements and reports of Masonic events.[40] At least one governor became a Freemason in Trinidad: Sir Sanford Freeling, who was initiated into the Royal Prince of Wales Lodge in Port of Spain on November 16, 1881.[41] At least one other governor, Sir Napier Broome, came to Trinidad a practicing Mason.[42] And, as expected, many prominent Trinidadians of the period were Freemasons: Louis de Verteuil, Michel Maxwell Philip, Robert Guppy, Jules Espinet, Adolphe de Boissière, and Daniel Hart. Equally prevalent on the returns were the names of prominent families: Wainwright, Knaggs, Gordon, Knowles, St Hilaire, and Alcazar.[43]

Two reports of Masonic activity in the press in the 1890s convey a good deal about the craft in Trinidad and what it enjoined. The first event was a church service held in 1890, hosted by the Lodge United Brothers, but extended to Masons of many different lodges. They "marched to Trinity Cathedral" to be addressed by Anglican Bishop Hayes, and the Rev. R.H. Moor, both Freemasons and Masonic chaplains. The bishop, in his sermon, enjoined his flock to seek success in the conventional arts, but directed them to the more important "arts of unity and love, of benevolence and courtesy, and of wide-reaching philanthropy." Masons were also encouraged to look to the lodges of England, whose efforts were dedicated to public service ("the public weal") and to not confine their works and intentions to the "walls of their lodge."[44]

Evident here is the desire to impart the Victorian values of public service and self-restraint. A report, a few years later, reveals another dimension of the Masonic movement in Trinidad: the extent of its reach. In 1894, an article on the consecration of the Royal Prince of Wales Lodge of Port of Spain included in its list of attendees, Chief Justice Sir John Goldney, Governor Sir Napier Broome, and "members of the Legislative Council, a Colonial Secretary, Commandant of the Troops, the Bishop, Director of Public Works, Postmaster General," among many others. Goldney confessed it was the first time in his judicial career he had participated in a Masonic celebration in a colony in which he served.[45]

As to how the ideals of the movement affected the self- and nationalist perceptions of Creoles, some evidence can be found in an article that Thomas wrote about the "Nationality of Negroes" in the Trinidadian newspaper, *New Era*. Thomas warned his readers against insularity in formulating ideas of nation and self:

Greece borrowed letters and science from Phoenicia and Egypt; Rome, intellectual culture from Greece, and all the nations of civilized Europe are debtors to
Rome on similar grounds. That we should rebel against this law of international
borrowing would be a manifestation of self-sufficiency as unprecedented as it
would be fatal.[46]

The similarity of this enjoinment to that of *The Sure Guide* (quoted above) is
evident. In another article in *New Era,* Thomas revealed the insidious "com-
plexional prejudice" within the island's black community:

color prejudice is a ladder with almost numberless rungs. It is a system of social
segregation and retaliation. Favoritism, sycophancy, levity and a cravenness
too base to be characterized, have made its [*sic*] highest standpoint a tower of
strengths from which its influence on imitative persons, according to the degree
to which their blood is diluted, operates in a manner which some deplore, and
all can but too well appreciate.[47]

Neither is the role of Freemasonry in developing a revolutionary consciousness to be undervalued. Jasper Ridley reports that while popular lore might
have attributed an overblown role to Freemasonry in the American and French
Revolutions, there is no doubt that, particularly in the French Revolution, the
ideals and ideas of Freemasonry played a crucial part. Ridley suggests that the
spread of lodges throughout Europe in the latter half of the eighteenth century
was intimately connected to the revolutionary tenor of the period:

The more the enemies of the [French] Revolution denounced the Freemasons,
and held them responsible for the American and the French revolutions, the
more revolutionary the Freemasons became. If Masonic lodges were places
where revolutions were planned, that was where ardent young revolutionaries
wished to be.[48]

A century later, the Freemasons were entrenched in orthodoxy in England,
but in France (and Ireland) the Masonic creed was linked by detractors to
the ideals of democracy and liberalism, which at the time were at odds with
monarchism:

While British Freemasons rigidly adhered to their rule that Freemasonry must
not become involved in politics, the French Freemasons in the Grand Orient not
only took part in political activity but went so far as to become closely involved
with one political party, The Republican Party, which later became the Radical
Socialists.[49]

It can be reasonably asserted that this political component was not absent
in Trinidad. The first Trinidadian Reform Movement was represented by

Philip Rostant in the mid-1880s, and the second a few years later, from 1892 to 1895, which involved more people than it previously did, persons such as Edgar Maresse Smith, Henry Alcazar, C.P. David, and Vincent Brown, all of whom were instrumental in fomenting the Water Riots of 1903.[50] Key members of the Reform movement (and later, the Water Riots), particularly the more radical ones, were Freemasons: Randolph Rust, Maresse Smith, Robert Nanco.[51] The major study of the Water Riots, Alvin Magid's *Urban Nationalism*, published in 1988, does not acknowledge this fact.[52]

THE INDIANS IN TRINIDAD

If Afronationalist conceptions of Trinidadian history (mirroring regional narratives) are couched in tropes of resistance, rebellion, and violent challenge to the status quo, Indo-conceptions are the opposite. The major documents outlining the Indo-Trinidad historical narrative overwhelmingly present a "pioneer narrative" of pious, hard-working peasants, struggling in a hostile environment to (re)create a home. This narrative has been a largely reactive one, generated in response to populist conceptions of Black Nationalism and an Orientalist colonial conception of Indo-life and culture.

In introducing the first edition of the volume of essays, *From Calcutta to Caroni,* editor John La Guerre noted that "scholarly interest in the subject [of Indians in the Caribbean] has not matched its social and political significance."[53] The post-Black Power period saw a surge of research and interest in the question, and the pioneer narratives begin roughly with Gerad Tikasingh's PhD thesis, "The Establishment of the Indians 1870–1900."[54]

Many studies were done after World War II, such as Morton Klass's *East Indians in Trinidad,* Arthur and Juanita Niehoff's *East Indians in the West Indies,* Jane Rubin's *Culture, Politics and Race Relations,* and Yogendra Malik's *East Indians in Trinidad.*[55] However, these authors were non-Trinidadians; while they noted the nationalist dilemma faced by the Indo community, their engagement was disinterested, unsympathetic, and free from nostalgia. Tikasingh's study marked the emergence of a seminal Indo-perspective, steeped in the themes of piety, cultural retention, and pioneer tenacity.

Coincident with Tikasingh's thesis came the first academic convocation examining the Indian presence in the Caribbean, a conference at UWI, St. Augustine campus in Trinidad in 1975, the proceedings of which were published as *East Indians in the Caribbean: Colonialism and the Struggle for Identity.* In the introduction, writer V.S. Naipaul commented on the invisibility of Indo-Trinidadians, their lack of knowledge about the past, the need for Indians to not be entombed by ritual, and the necessity of a higher intellectual life. In brief, this was a silent, peripheral, and ignorant community, despite its numbers.[56]

Thus, as late as the 1970s, this was a largely "un-written" community and early works focused on establishing the "credentials" of Indo-Trinidadians as citizens and contributors to the nationalist effort and on responding to the discourse of nationalism which had been created by Afronationalist scholars, such as Eric Williams. The foci of these collections was archeologizing and archiving Indo rituals and retentions like the *panchayat,* and religious observances, primary data about Indian labor and entrepreneurialism, politics, and ethnic relations. Indeed, these themes persisted through the 1980s, 1990s, and the first decade of the twenty-first century in collections such as *India in the Caribbean, The Enigma of Ethnicity,* and *Across the Dark Waters, The Construction of an Indo-Caribbean Diaspora,* and two subsequent editions of *Calcutta to Caroni.*[57]

Bridget Brereton sums up this post-Independence Indo-narrative as one which required its subscribers to struggle, since

> despite the discrimination and oppression, despite the contempt of other Trinidadians who saw them as heathen coolies, Indo-Trinidadians continued to endure and rise in the socio-economic scale. Through hard work, discipline, frugality (at times to excess), strong family support, faith in their ancestral religions and a commitment to deferred gratification in the interest of the next generation, Indians achieved success in farming, business, education and the professions. And all this on their own, without benefit of handouts, government patronage or any favors.[58]

However, in the rush to discursively construct a suitably credentialed pioneer community, and to arm them for the post-independence culture wars, which saw a fierce competition for political power divided sharply along ethnic lines from 1956 to 1986, and less sharply post-1986, the narratives ignored the less noble, but no less important, underside of Indians and Indian life, which had persisted from the nineteenth century. According to Tikasingh, the last three decades of the nineteenth century saw the transformation of the Indian community from "an agglomeration of immigrant laborers" to "an identifiable community, putting down roots in the community."[59] In this community, the less palatable activities were attributable to the environment and circumstances not due to the choices made by the indentured people. Uxoricide, for example, was an indication of "the despair Indians felt within

a context of a shortage of females."[60] But Tikasingh does not examine the
other possibilities of the uneven sex-ratio: male homosexuality, polyandry,
and prostitution by Indian women.

Similarly, in examining Hinduism in Trinidad, Tikasingh "reads" it against
pre-existent and dominant Christianity. He observes a "Hindu revivalism in
Trinidad" in the late nineteenth century, and comments on the emergence of
Hindu "phunts"—Sewnarain, Oghur, Ramanand, and Kabeer—in Trinidad,
which he described as "reformist sects of the orthodox Hindu religion which
attempted to remove the obstacle of caste, emphasized the path of devotion to
salvation . . . and made Hinduism accessible to all Hindus." In this account,
animal sacrifice (Kali) pujas were a "distinct cult practice . . . in the 1860s to
mid-1870s," but by the late nineteenth century, "the absence of any reference
to such practices perhaps indicated their disappearance." He quotes from,
inter alia, two sources, a report done by a colonial official and newspaper
reports.[61] And, in concluding, Tikasingh premises his thesis of the establishment of Indians on three things: economic achievement, reconstitution of
social and religious institutions into Indian villages, and the formation of a
"group consciousness."[62]

This trend, of interpreting the Indian historical progression as an Indo-
"reconstitution of culture" and "retention of Indian traditional values" begun
by Tikasingh was continued by other Indo-scholars. These included (the
already-mentioned) *Calcutta to Caroni,* which went through three editions
between 1976 and 2005, Samaroo and Dabydeen's edited collections *India
in the Caribbean* and *Across the Dark Waters,* and Samaroo and Ann Marie
Bissessar's *The Construction of an Indo-Caribbean Diaspora,* in addition to
Kelvin Singh's *Race and Class Struggles in a Colonial State,* Tina Ramnarine's *Creating Their Own Space,* and Kris Rampersad's *Finding a Place:
Indo-Trinidadian Literature.*[63]

Sherry Ann Singh's PhD thesis, "The *Ramayana* Tradition and Socio-
Religious Change in Trinidad, 1917–1990," in which she argues that the
Hindu/Indo-Trinidadians followed an ontological and sociological developmental trajectory, the outlines of which were based upon the Hindus's
revered *Ramayana* tradition, was, in many ways, the culmination of the
epistemological movement. It essentially continued and chronologically
extended Tikasingh's thesis. Singh writes: "The various dimensions of the
Ramayana tradition encapsulated the form and innate values and attitudes
of the public to the most private aspects of Hindu life" and "its enduring
function as doctrine within the spheres of family and communal life and
internal politics . . . indicated the tradition's . . . indispensability to Trinidad
Hinduism."[64]

Though Singh's approach is sophisticated, taking account of change and acculturization, she yet places "tradition" or "pure" Hinduism in a binary opposition with inevitable local modifications.[65] Thus, the fundamental tropes of retention and continuity are not challenged. Neither is the fundamental assessment of the Indian/Hindu subject in Trinidad.

The single significant work which diverges from this epistemological trend is Steven Vertovec's *Hindu Trinidad,* published in 1992. Vertovec remarks that the assumption that the indentured laborers "'picked up in Trinidad 'where they left off' in India . . . was certainly not the case."[66]

Works such as Sherry-Ann Singh's have merit, but the issue taken with these studies here is that they did not deviate from the epistemological pattern laid down by Tikasingh's monolithic thesis, itself the product of a matrix of political, social, and ethnic factors at the time of its writing in the early 1970s, the peak of post-Independence Black Nationalism. What these accounts have done is to obscure critical aspects of Indo-existence, leading to incomplete understandings of the Indo-community, especially its religion, culture, and status signification (or caste).

THE INDIAN UNDERGROUND IN NINETEENTH-CENTURY TRINIDAD

During Trinidad's 2010 Carnival, a young Chutney singer named Ravi Bissambar (aka Ravi B), won the Carnival Chutney Monarch title with a song titled "Ah Drinker." This song made reference to his prowess as a rum drinker, and belonged to the category known as "rum songs." Other sub-genres included songs describing sexual relations between relatives, neighbors, and sex with animals. Ravi B's song predictably drew much criticism from the "respectable" sectors of Indo society, chiefly academics, professionals, and people with access to the media. The song's narrative was that the protagonist was an avid and unrepentant drinker, and pointed to a dimension of Indo society, that which did not accord with the "pioneer narrative"—a considerably more violent and raunchy version of Indo life than the religious, abstemious society that was created by the scholars. Indeed, this counter-narrative has always existed, but has apparently been ignored by other academics.

The newspapers of the nineteenth century, from roughly 1860 onwards, are rife with reports of Indians being prosecuted for brutal wife-murders, violent assaults, and their practice of suing each other liberally for trifles. The *Port of Spain Gazette* reported on the trial of Battoo for the murder of Churaman, which involved intrigues about buried money and using a cutlass to sever the victim's throat. Another bizarre report about a wake that was published in the same edition of the newspaper, showed another dimension of the hidden underbelly of Indo society in Trinidad. It was reported that: "The funeral festivities began with dinner at three o'clock . . . and ended with the whole of the happy mourners getting furiously drunk before eight o'clock that night, and having a general fight before the manager's house." These were not uncommon activities.[67]

Another Trinidadian newspaper in 1875, which reported a murder-suicide, gave a glimpse of the dark underside of Indian religious practice in the colony:

> An industrious and well-behaved coolie who had saved some means lately got intimate with another of his countrymen who practices what is known here under the name of obeahism [sic]. This villain appears to have acquired an immediate and powerful influence over the mind of the other, as was shown by his beginning to ornament his house with the heads of cocks and the feet of fowls and various bones, and from being a peaceable becoming a quarrelsome man. . . . [T]he well-behaved coolie was persuaded by the tempter that, to gain the higher degrees in his magic art he must shed human blood, cut his own throat, and that his preceptor would resuscitate him in Calcutta.[68]

The saga ended with the "well-behaved coolie" killing a man in the field, and then himself.

Similarly, the idea of an industrious, chaste population is contended in the primary data. Apart from the domestic and social violence, in 1890 the *Port of Spain Gazette* recorded the capture of "Macoon the Bandit" and his gang of robbers, who had terrorized a rural district. Macoon was equipped with "a gun, a revolver and a cutlass," and patterned himself after Robin Hood. According to the *Gazette,* "a characteristic story is related of his stopping a man with two cans of food, taking one for himself and telling the bearer to come back to the same place the next day for his empty can." After Macoon's wife was arrested,

> a manager in the district received a threatening letter from Macoon to the effect that his life would be taken in three days. . . . On one occasion he went up to a policeman looking for him and said: "You want 'am Macoon? Me see 'um just gone dat side' and while the blue-coated minion of the law was proceeding, he remarked to the bystanders that the Policeman was a fool."[69]

Additionally, there were stories of Indian illegal gambling houses, and Indian forgers, who forged passes and immigration certificates, and Indian opium smokers.[70]

The sex trade appears to have been another active region of the under-ground world. A visiting British official, D.W.D. Comins, observed in the early 1890s: "A good-looking young woman receives much admiration and many are no-doubt polyandrous, and some regular prostitutes which cannot be wondered at."[71] There were also reports of concubinage on estates, where shopkeepers, headmen, and overseers used their positions to make sex slaves of their female charges.[72]

But women also exploited their scarcity and deserted traditional roles: wives left abusive husbands, some of who resorted to uxoricide. Sarah Morton, wife of the Rev. John Morton, noted of the Indian women their "loose practices in respect of marriage." She illustrated this in an exchange with an Indian woman:

> I said to the East Indian woman, whom I knew to be the widow of a Brahman: "You have no relatives in Trinidad, I believe?"
>
> "No madame," she replied. "Only myself and my two children. When the last [immigrant] ship came in, I took a papa. I will stay with him as long as he treats me well."[73]

In addition to social practices and ontology, there was also the crucial issue of religion. Tikasingh reports that "the mid 1880s saw 'a marked spirit of revivalism' following the latest introduction of a reformist sect the Kabeer Phunt." He names four phunts (Seunarain, Ramanand, Oughur, and Kabeer) and remarks that they "made the Hindu religion accessible to all Hindus." He also mentions in an anodyne way, the issue of caste: that "there was a tendency for these sects to have high-caste men as their lead-ers." But "nevertheless their membership included lower-caste Indians and all went through 'a kind of baptism' and were invested with 'a fragment of Tulsi.'" He mentions the "Sadhu" movement as a generally positive development.[74]

Like the erasure of J.J. Thomas and the creation of Caliban by Black Nationalist historians, here is the clearest example of *ideological reframing* of historical material, which set the epistemological pattern. Tikasingh quotes in support of this religious revivalism, a series of articles in the *Port of Spain Gazette* in 1884. The parts of these articles he redacts reveal a slightly less anodyne state of affairs. The *Gazette's* interest had been piqued by a concern for the laboring population *qua* laborers, and a new "religious innovation" connected to Brahmanism, which had threatened the stability of the estates. The religious rite was described in the essay "Brahmanism and its Phases in Trinidad," in the same edition, as one of the fruits of a "religious revival-ism," which had gripped "particularly those not entitled to high caste rank," and which desire had been exploited by the higher castes. The essay also connected the emergence of peripatetic sadhus in Trinidad to this revivalist impulse.[75]

The Brahmins (continued the report) had devised a means of "capturing" even the lower castes, like the Sudras, who, "although they can never be raised to the exclusive castes, can yet be flattered by a kind of baptism in which they are told the mystic word and invested with a fragment of Tulsi." Thereafter, "the comfortable old Brahmin who has consecrated a goodly number of god-children . . . is set up for life and the mischief created on many estates by this baptism and the creation of Sadhus . . . is not easy to be conceived." The writer gives an example of the havoc on one estate where,

> nearly all the young men left their wives, fasted and nearly lost their wits. The driver had to be discharged but his evil influence continued. The system of baptism and extortion is not only the cause of disorganization on estate laborers, but in many villages, painted and seminude Brahmins have equally succeeded in their pernicious trade. They invariably thrive and their ignorant victims are not only well fleeced, but in too many instances it leads them into excesses of Gunga [*sic*] smoking and opium eating. . . . Another bad result of these religious freaks is that the coolies refuse meat and other kinds of nourishing food.[76]

From this brief passage, even if generous allowances are made for Orientalist misconstruance, a considerably different picture of the Hindu "revivalism" emerges: one of religious extortion, a Brahminical confidence scam, and the seduction of the Hindus into drug abuse, sexual deviance, and idleness. But there is more.

The revivalist sects Tikasingh identified were also noted in a report written by the visiting British official, D.W.D. Comins. A local informant informed Comins that while two of the sects were relatively harmless, at least one was not. This phunt, Oughur (Anghor or Aghori), Comins reported, was "unclean" and devoted to sensualism. According to Indian scholar B.D. Tripathi, writing about the Oughurs:

> They believe in human sacrifice . . . no food is prohibited for them and are ex-pected to eat even decomposed corpse[s]. Some of the sects mix their excreta with water and filter them through a piece of cloth and drink [it]. They believe such an act renders a man capable of great spiritual achievement. Aghoris eat human as well as animal flesh. They keep their initiation secret, and what is known is as follows: The guru blows a conch shell accompanied by loud music. He then mixes something in a human skull and pours it over the clean-shaven head of the neophyte. The candidate is then given some liquor and made to eat food collected from the lower castes, and finally asked to put on ochre colored clothes of Shaiva ascetics. During the rite, the guru whispers some mystic formula into the ear of the candidate. In some cases eating human flesh is part

of the initiation rite, after which a rosary of animal bones is placed around his neck.[77]

It seems reasonably clear here that the narrative of chaste, law-abiding Hindus is severely flawed, to say the least. Indeed, this desire to edit out the less than wholesome practices of the Hindus/Indians is clearly indicative of an urge of the section of the community still responding to the Victorian stereotype of the Indian as a heathen, hard-drinking, and woman-abusing peasant. However, the fact that Chutney music and culture, which celebrates sexual deviance, rum-drinking, and violence is the most successful, popular, and fastest growing mass entertainment genre of Indo-Trinidadian popular culture at home and internationally, demonstrates that these urges are far from defunct.

INVENTED COMMUNITIES: INDO- AND AFRO-TRINIDADIAN

The evidence has indicated that there have been considerable distortions and omissions, if not redactions of the historical record for reasons connected to nationalism, as defined in the contemporary Caribbean. The data have, in the main, come from Trinidad and Tobago, but the case of the Freemasons is applicable throughout the Caribbean, and the case of the Hindu/Indian underground is applicable to largely Guyana and Trinidad and Tobago.

The Trinidadian Hindu community (a metonym for the Indian community) remains still enrapt in its conception of itself as a "pioneer" one, steeped in religious values (which bear a striking resemblance to what the sociologist, Max Weber, identified as "Protestant" values).[78] Where there is change in the narrative, it is largely in response to the Black Nationalist narrative of rebellion and resistance. Indeed, there are now moves to reframe the 1884 Hosay Riots to an "act of resistance" by Indians/Hindus in response to repression by an evil colonial government, though the Hosay Riots derive their origin from a Muslim festival.[79]

Trinidad's Indians are divided into many communities based on religion, including Christians, Hindus, and Muslims, though Hindus are the majority. A main division among the latter is the Sanatanist (orthodox) and Samajist (reform) Hindus. There are popular cults such as the Sai Baba movement, the Yoga schools, and the Indian missions (for example, the Chinmaya Mission). And a few "outlaw" strains of Hinduism identified by Vertovec, also exist— Shakti-sects, Bhakti-sects, Vaisha, and Shaiva—devoted to Mother Worship, worship of Shiva, of Vishnu, and various subdivisions or "*sampradayas*." These include higher and lower gods, blood sacrifice, and animism. However,

Vertovec notes that a certain amount of homogenization occurred, which saw the Brahmins's beliefs and practices overwrite the others—not erasing them, but forcing them underground.[80]

Today, that schism persists, with an astonishing variety of informal Hindu practices, involving animal sacrifice, but with an orthodox organization, the Sanatan Dharma Maha Sabha, being widely recognized as the "voice" for Hindus. The leader of this organization, who is a regular columnist for a daily newspaper, wrote, *inter alia,* a long paean to Brahminism in 2009, in which he defended the tenets of the caste system, and responded to those who sought to "vilify the Brahmin community locally."[81] A later column enjoined Hindu/Indian womanhood to the virtuous Sita, heroine of the *Ramayana.* This construction generates a generic reaction in the populist and public spheres. The first is from the Afrocentric-ethnic nationalist ideologues, whose ideology is neo-Garveyite nationalism. One of the proponents of this ideology, Tony Martin, "reads" Indo-Trinidadian politics and consciousness within an epistemological framework of Black Nationalist Consciousness of Indo-Trinidadians, that "Indian racial consciousness . . . has tended to assume a more narrowly communal posture with a resultant focus on the African, more than on the European, as the primary adversary."[82]

It is clear that this narrowness and adversarial posture to Africans are the primary signifiers of Indos for Martin, and presumably his co-ideologues, since the argument begins setting out the case that Indian indentured laborers were brought to the West Indies to prevent the islands from becoming the property of the Africans. He covers the familiar ground laid out by Tikasingh, but uses the "group consciousness" and religiosity to confirm the Indians's separatist impulses, and their unflattering and racist perceptions of Africans.[83]

While Martin is refreshingly explicit in his opinion, these interpretations of conservatism, piety, and self-reliance as narrow-mindedness, exclusivism, and anti-Africanism, have tended to be surreptitiously embedded in mainstream (nationalist) discourse. Indeed, various scholars (Rohlehr, Yelvington, and van Koningsbruggen) have argued that Trinidadian Afro-nationalism relies on these interpretations for its continuance—in effect, "nationalism" is defined as Afro-derived culture. Anything that does not conform is "racist and unpatriotic."[84] Ramcharitar, in the (already-cited) essay "Tourist Nationalism in Trinidad and Tobago," argued that even the contemporary discourses of tourism are theatres where this opposition can be continuously enacted, with the purposes of maintaining the dominance of the Afro-national discourse, supported by academia and state cultural authorities, and the creation of nationalist imagery and symbolism.

In his biography of Edgar Maresse Smith, a radical Trinidadian lawyer and proto-nationalist of the late nineteenth century, Adam Smith notes his being a Freemason, but gives this fact a mere paragraph, concluding that "the Masonic movement helped to develop middle-class leadership, however to a lesser extent than the debating clubs. It did not provide political education."[85] Similarly, in *The Pursuit of Honor,* his biography of H.O.B. Wooding, a key figure in the Trinidadian independence politics, political scientist Selwyn Ryan devotes four pages to Wooding's Masonic ties. Though he quotes Wooding's son as saying, *"religion and masonry formed his mind* (my italics)," Ryan's reading of the Masonic movement in Trinidad is entirely racial: "Wooding embraced Free Masonry [*sic*] at a time when Masonic Lodges in Trinidad and Tobago reflected the ethnic stratification of the society more than they do now."[86]

Faith Smith's dismissal of J.J. Thomas's Masonic connections has already been noted, but her reasons for this provide another disturbing article of proof of the problematics of "nationalist" historiography. Smith writes, after speculating on Thomas's lodge affiliation, that: "The Lodge records, should they ever become public, will be an important means of *understanding how Thomas and other men imagined themselves as free citizens across social divisions* (my italics)."[87] Smith's research in unearthing the details of her thesis was formidable and considerably more than adequate. Yet, she apparently missed the consistent, lengthy, and numerous references to Freemasonry in the nineteenth-century Trinidad press, and the fact that many of the significant *dramatis personae* in her study were Freemasons, such as lawyer Edgar Maresse Smith, journalist Samuel Carter, and solicitor general Michel Maxwell Philip. Furthermore, the records of the Grand Lodges of England and Scotland are available upon request.[88] The lacuna therefore, in my opinion, bespeaks an ideological deficiency (which translates itself into a self-imposed limitation, in this case, unavailability of data) which shapes nationalist historiography.

Thus, when masonry is acknowledged, any notion of its ideals, ideas, and principles in forming a significant stratum of Trinidadian men, and their potency in forming a nationalistic ethos—or, indeed, *even what those ideas were*—are entirely absent. However, it can hardly be accidental that so many of the Trinidadians of all ethnicities who, like Wooding, have directly shaped the history of Trinidad and Tobago in the twentieth century, have also been Freemasons. These include F.E.M. Hosein and L.C. Hannays (Lodge Rosslyn); George Fitzpatrick and Adrian Cola Rienzi (Lodge Alexandra); Henry Hudson Phillips (Lodge Eastern Star); Anthony N. Sabga (LUB); Sir Isaac Hyatali (Lodge Arima); and Patrick Solomon (Lodge Caribbean Light). And these are merely the names available from sparse Grand Lodge records.

I would go further in postulating, however, that not just Masonic ideas, but *ideas* outside ethnic nationalism seem to be absent from the construction of the history of Afro-Trinidadians. Andrew Bundy, commenting on the post-colonial politics of the Caribbean, notes that, unlike the Hispanophone and Francophone and Dutch Caribbean, in the Anglophone Caribbean,

> literary artists have no recognized status in their community. It is the politicians—those educated to doctoral level in England, others writing notable studies of political history—who mobilize public opinion and command literacy. Constant inculcation by the public sphere . . . puts an imaginative frame around the individual.[89]

The reference to "politicians educated to the doctoral level in England" points unambiguously to Eric Williams, through whose agency Trinidad and Tobago derived its character, epistemic and otherwise, and its historiographic perspective. From Williams's *History of the People of Trinidad and Tobago,* the history of Trinidad reflected his personal "struggles" with colonialism, Europeans, and various stumbling blocks in his passage to success. In his superb essay, "History as Absurdity," Gordon Rohlehr makes the same point, that Williams's personality was imprinted on the infant nation, and its formation of self-conception and identity (its historiography) in an immediate way. From his advent as the long awaited messiah, to his (more concretely) stocking institutions with his disciples, and subverting them with his tyranny, Williams's will, his personality, and his machinations for permanent political power formed the culture and historiography of Trinidad. It was a culture that sought restitution from Europeans for his personal humiliations, but yet still steeped in a Fanonian yearning for whiteness, or the approval of those he claimed to despise. Rohlehr writes: "Like Swift, Williams found his ambition thwarted by the world toward which he aspired and his dignity undermined," which fed into a "daydream which the colonial has of humiliating Massa."[90]

In another virtuoso academic performance, "Apocalypso and the Soca Fires of 1990," Rohlehr details this apocalypse which began with the "hijacking" of the Black Power movement, and its transformation into a kind of "grassroots hucksterism" by Williams's People's National Movement, and substituting Carnival, and various forms of a tendentiously engineered "folk" culture, for the useful legacies of colonialism.[91]

The culmination of this epistemological violence is stated succinctly by Gerard Aching, in refining the philosophy in Earl Lovelace's seminal novel on Carnival and society in Trinidad, *The Dragon Can't Dance.* Commenting on the poverty, alienation, and general wretchedness of the characters, Aching proposes that these are virtues, mutually exclusive with Metropolitan ideas of progress:

Nonpossession, therefore, is a historical practice and ideology. The notion that Calvary Hill should give rise to a proud aristocracy of the poor asks the reader to fathom how this ideology generates *a humanism that runs counter to the country's particular post-independence initiatives to gain economic strength* (my italics).[92]

CONCLUSION: THE TRINIDAD FRANKENSTEIN IN 2010

In 2010, it is axiomatic that nations are invented entities, created by discourses, texts, and ideologies, as well as by geography, history, and politics. In the practices that generate all these discourses, the agendas and individual and group orientations of discourse-makers are crucial in ensuring which texts "speak" and which are suppressed.[93] In the Metropole, where media, academic and popular, are widely diffused, while there are dominant conceptions of history and nationalism, counter narratives are readily available, leading to a not always productive dialogic tension. The recent historic passage of health care reform in Barack Obama's United States, while taken for granted as an indispensable part of any advanced nation's social infrastructure, generated fierce opposition and threats of derailment at every turn from Republicans screaming "Socialism"—ostensibly a purely ideological argument.[94]

Thus, despite mistakes, some of them of gargantuan proportions, in metropolitan societies, there is the potent possibility of valuable dialectical transformation from the engagement of opposing ideas. As I opened this chapter arguing, this process seems to be entirely absent from Trinidadian and West Indian social discourses—where there is suppression and the use of institutional power to foment violent conflict instead of constructive engagement. The dominant post-independence nationalist construct, ethnic nationalism, seems to have no extensions into economic, political, or social theory, or practice. Indeed, all these necessary institutional processes remain externally impelled (by policy edicts and prescriptions from institutions like the International Monetary Fund, World Trade Organization, and various agencies of the United Nations). In all this, local gatekeepers again ignore evidence and argument of unique regional imperatives, which require innovation and creative reformulation of historical ideas—not their erasure and denial in the name of an absurd autonomy.[95] Hence, Caribbean nations move through time, but seem to materially (socially, economically, and intellectually) disintegrate the further they move from the order of colonialism into more and more ardent ethnic nationalisms.

As also proposed at the beginning of this chapter, the decay in the moral sense because of the suppression of the discussion of the darker aspects of the Caribbean's past—in brief, its capacity for evil, its often unwholesome sexual nature, its psychological distortions, its racial neurosis, its anti-humanist Plantation past—has led to a curious ontological posture. There is a *rhetorical morality* which is entirely disconnected from praxis. The practice of erasing, or re-writing the dark side of human existence, also alters the acknowledgement of their presence, and their agency, which allows them to grow unchecked. Thus, in the public discourse, there is a meta-ritual of propriety in the parliaments, the courts, and elections, and increasingly, education. But there is no corresponding materiality of this rhetoric. The societies remain, in effect, in states of unnatural, macabre moral infantilism. Because of the discursive transformation of violence and nihilism into socially acceptable or morally invisible, an ontological confusion has become entrenched, resulting in an absurd social theatre that Naipaul named and described in *The Mimic Men*.[96]

Derek Walcott, in his essays "What the Twilight Says" and "The Muse of History," also recognizes the urgency of this state of affairs, but it is Wilson Harris who captures the phenomenon most clearly, as an "illiteracy of the imagination." When social groups are socialized in what Harris calls "block functions" for the purposes of "stability" (or its later synonym, "development") the practice impoverishes the collective. Harris writes: "If we have societies which are locked into certain functions, which read the world in only one way, then a fanaticism grows out of that, terror grows out of that—a total refusal, a total difficulty to read the world in any other way, to make any kind of adjustment."[97]

There can be no better example of the reality of this than the Trinidad and Tobago of 2010. After an eight-year oil and gas bonanza, which saw hundreds of billions of dollars earned and spent from increased oil prices, pervasive rhetoric about development and attaining "First World Status," the nation's water and sewerage services have reached much less than half its population. Its hospitals are inefficient and brutal, and its people in the grip of an orgy of violent crime by which its academics, politicians, and institutions seem dumbstruck, and are unable to provide an explanation, much less a solution. There is no single reason for this, but to return to the beginning of this essay, diagnosis, analysis, and critical inquiry are entirely absent from the approaches.

These absences are significantly the result of an epistemological aporia, which comes from incomplete archives of knowledge and theory, resulting in infertile imaginaries, barren academes, and impotent institutions.

Notes

1. Eric J. Evans, *The Forging of the Modern State: Early Industrial Britain, 1783–1870* (London: Longman/Pearson, 1996), 323.

2. Donald Thomas, *The Victorian Underworld* (London: John Murray, 1998), 19.

3. See, for example, Margarite Fernandes Olmos and Lizabeth Paravisini-Gebert (eds.), *Creole Religions of the Caribbean: An Introduction from Vodou and Santeria to Obeah and Espiritismo* (New York: NYU Press, 2003), 131–54.

4. For a discussion on Creolization, see Verene Shepherd and Glen Richards (eds.), *Questioning Creole* (Kingston: Ian Randle Publishers, 2003).

5. This phenomenon is widely discussed in business and management literature. See, for example, William L. Gardner, "Impression Management in Organizations," *Journal of Management* vol. 14, no. 2 (1988): 321–38, and Paul Rosenfeld, *et al, Impression Management, Building and Enhancing Reputations at Work* (New Jersey: Thomson Learning, 1995). There is even a Wikipedia page on it.

6. Barry W. Higman, *Writing West Indian Histories* (London: MacMillan, 1999), 202–04.

7. Laënnec Hurbon, "Ideology," in *General History of the Caribbean, Volume VI, Methodology and Historiography of the Caribbean,* ed. Barry Higman (London: UNESCO/MacMillan Educational, 1999), 158–60.

8. Higman, *Writing West Indian,* 245.

9. William Green, "The Creolization of Caribbean History: The Emancipation Era and a Critique of Dialectical Analysis," in *Caribbean Freedom, Economy and Society from Emancipation to the Present,* eds. Verene Shepherd and Hilary Beckles (Kingston, Princeton and London: Ian Randle Publishers, Markus Weiner and James Curry, 1996), 31–32.

10. Higman, *Writing West Indian,* 148.

11. Raymond Ramcharitar, "Tourist Nationalism in Trinidad," in *New Perspectives on Caribbean Tourism,* eds. Marcella Daye, *et al* (New York: Routledge, 2008), 38–59.

12. One example is a show entitled "The Word," reviewed in the Trinidad *Sunday Express,* Section II, April 8, 2007.

13. Jim Sharpe, "History from Below," in *New Perspectives on Historical Writing,* ed. Peter Burke (London: Polity, 2001), 25–42.

14. The facts of Trinidad's paradoxical degeneration into crime have been documented in various regional and international media. A June 2010 report prepared under the auspices of the Council on Hemispheric Affairs (COHA) summarizes the situation. The report is available at http://www.coha.org/trinidad-and-tobago-the-big-guy-on-a-difficult-block/. Accessed June 6, 2010. See also Dorn Townsend, "No Other Life: Gangs, Guns and Governance in Trinidad," a working paper, published December 2009, by the Geneva-based Small Arms Survey. Report available at http://www.smallarmssurvey.org. Accessed June 6, 2010.

15. A good example of this divorce of materiality and discursive constructions is the treatment of homosexuality: the official position on homosexuality is that it virtually does not exist. On a "Women's Platform" convocation during Trinidad and Tobago's 2010 elections campaign on 20 May, then Culture and Gender Affairs Minister, Marlene MacDonald, confirmed that the (then) Government's gender policy would not "recognize" homosexuality by way of same-sex unions or decriminalizing same-sex relations between consenting adults. Yet, as Thomas Glave's, ed., *Our Caribbean* (Durham: Duke University Press, 2009) showed, homosexuality is a part of Caribbean life. Another excellent example is the posture to Obeah, and conventional religious practice—official proclamations declaim conventional Christian (or Hindu) worship, but the reality is that many worshippers avail themselves of Obeah and conventional religion simultaneously.

16. Kellow Chesney, *The Victorian Underworld* (London: Temple Smith, 1970); Andrew McCall, *The Medieval Underworld* (London: Sutton Publishing, 2004); Fergus Linnane, *London's Underworld: Three Centuries of Crime and Vice* (London: Robson Books, 2003); Eric Scholsser, *Reefer Madness and Other Tales From the American Underground* (London: Allen Lane, 2003); James Henry, *The Blood Bankers: Tales from the Global Underground* (New York: Four Walls Eight Windows, 2004).

17. John Leland, *Hip: The History* (New York: Harper Perennial, 2005), 20.

18. Edward Kamau Brathwaite, *The Development of Creole Society in Jamaica 1770–1820* (Kingston: Ian Randle Publishers, 2005 [1974]).

19. Leland, *Hip: The History,* 13.

20. Ibid., 41, 45.

21. J. M. Roberts, *The Mythology of the Secret Societies* (London: Secker and Warburg, 1972), 1–16.

22. Eric Hobsbawm, *The Age of Capital, 1854–1875* (London: Abacus, 2001), 286.

23. Ibid., 248.

24. O. Nigel Bolland, *The Birth of Caribbean Civilization* (Kingston: Ian Randle Publishers, 2004), 295.

25. Bridget Brereton, "John Jacob Thomas: An Estimate," *Journal of Caribbean History* vol. 9 (May 1977): 22–42.

26. Denis Benn, *The Caribbean, an Intellectual History* (Kingston: Ian Randle Publishers, 2004), 70.

27. Silvio Torres-Salliant, *An Intellectual History of the Caribbean* (New York: Palgrave Macmillan, 2006), 200.

28. Faith Smith, *Creole Recitations, John Jacob Thomas and Colonial Formation in the Late Nineteenth-Century Caribbean* (Charlottesville and London: University of Virginia Press, 2002). Thomas's Freemason ties are mentioned on pages x, 31 and 55.

29. Wilson Harris, "History, Fable and Myth in the Caribbean and Guianas," in *The Selected Essays of Wilson Harris,* ed. Andrew Bundy (London: Routledge, 1999), 152–56.

30. Torres-Salliant, *An Intellectual History,* 203.

31. See George Lamming, *The Pleasures of Exile* (London: Pluto, 2005), 118. See also Kamau Brathwaite, "Caliban's Guarden [*sic*]," *Wasafiri,* issue 16 (August 1992):

7–19, and Aime Cesaire, *A Tempest: Based on Shakespeare's the Tempest* (New York: Theatre Communications Group, 2002).

32. Gordon K. Lewis, *Main Currents in Caribbean Thought* (Baltimore: Johns Hopkins, 1983), 240–41.

33. Jasper Ridley, *The Freemasons* (London: Arcade, 1999), 274.

34. From membership lists provided by the Grand Lodge of Scotland.

35. "Provincial Grand Royal Arch Chapter," *New Era,* March 28, 1881. This account actually reproduces a lecture Thomas gives to the convocation of Freemasons.

36. Errol Hill, *Trinidad Carnival: Mandate for a National Theatre* (London: New Beacon, 1997); Gerard Aching, *Carnival and Popular Culture in the Caribbean: Masking and Power* (Minnesota: University of Minnesota Press, 2002); Keith Nurse and Christine Ho, *Caribbean Popular Culture and Globalization* (Kingston: Ian Randle Publishers, 2005).

37. Raymond Ramcharitar, "The Hidden History of Trinidad: Underground Culture in Trinidad, 1870–1970," PhD Dissertation (St Augustine, Trinidad: University of the West Indies, 2007), 142–45.

38. Seth Driggs, *The Freemason's Sure Guide or, Pocket Companion* (Port of Spain: The Author, 1819), 6.

39. *The Star of the West,* August 4, 1870.

40. Joseph Lewis owned *New Era,* and Henry Schuller Billouin owned *Fair Play.* Billouin published a booklet in 1900, the *Guide Book to Masonic and Friendly Secret Societies in Trinidad, BWI, For the Current Terms of the Year 1900* (Port of Spain: The Author, 1900). It appears the only surviving copy of this resides at the British Library.

41. Information on nineteenth-century membership returns for five lodges: Royal Philanthropic, Prince of Wales, Royal Trinity, Hervey and Royal Phoenix, supplied by the Grand Lodge of England.

42. "Royal Prince of Wales Lodge," *Port of Spain Gazette,* November 29, 1894. Broome is listed as a "Brother in attendance" in this report.

43. Grand Lodge of England returns.

44. "The Freemasons," *Port of Spain Gazette,* June 27, 1890.

45. "Royal Prince of Wales Lodge," *Port of Spain Gazette,* November 29, 1894.

46. "Nationality of Negroes," *New Era,* September 23, 1872.

47. *New Era,* September 14, 1874.

48. Ridley, *The Freemasons,* 137.

49. Ibid., 223.

50. Bridget Brereton, "The Reform Movement in Trinidad in the Later 19th. Century," unpublished paper delivered at the 1973 Association of Caribbean Historians Conference at the University of the West Indies, St Augustine.

51. Rust, Nanco and Maresse Smith are named as officers for the Rose Croix Chapter in the Trinidad Kilwinning Lodge by H.S. Billouin in his *Guide Book to Masonic and Friendly Secret Societies in Trinidad, BWI, For the Current Terms of the Year 1900.* As already indicated, Joseph Lewis was also listed as one of the officers. Because of the relatively limited store of archival data, and the lack of access to

Trinidadian records, it cannot be said with certainty that the others, like Emmanuel Lazare, Rostant, C. P. David, *et al,* were members, but it seems very unlikely that they would not have been.

52. Alvin Magid, *Urban Nationalism, A Study of Political Development in Trinidad* (Florida: University Presses of Florida, 1988).

53. John La Guerre, "Preface to the 1974 Edition," in *Calcutta to Caroni and the Indian Diaspora,* eds. John La Guerre and Ann Marie Bissessar (St. Augustine: School of Continuing Studies, 2005), xxii.

54. Gerad Tikasingh, "The Establishment of the Indians, 1870–1900," PhD Dissertation (St Augustine: University of the West Indies, 1973).

55. Morton Klass, *East Indians in Trinidad* (Illinois: Waveland Press, 1988 [1961]); Arthur and Juanita Niehoff, *East Indians in the West Indies* (Milwaukee: Milwaukee Public Museum, 1960); Jane Rubin, "Culture, Politics and Race Relations," *Social and Economic Studies* vol. 11, no. 4 (1962); and Yogendra Malik, *East Indians in Trinidad: A Study in Minority Politics* (Oxford: Oxford University Press, 1971).

56. V. S. Naipaul, "Introduction," in *East Indians in the Caribbean: Colonialism and the Struggle for Identity,* eds. Brinsley Samaroo and Bridget Brereton (New York: Kraus International Publications, 1982), 1–10.

57. Brinsley Samaroo and David Dabydeen (eds.), *India in the Caribbean* (London: Hansib, 1987); Ralph Premdas (ed.), *The Enigma of Ethnicity* (St. Augustine: School of Continuing Studies, 1993); Brinsley Samaroo and Anne Marie Bissessar (eds.), *The Construction of an Indo-Caribbean Diaspora* (St. Augustine: School of Continuing Studies, 2005); Brinsley Samaroo and David Dabydeen (eds.), *Across the Dark Waters: Ethnicity and Indian Identity in the Caribbean* (London: MacMillan, 1996); John LaGuerre (ed.), *From Calcutta to Caroni* (St Augustine: School of Continuing Studies, 2005).

58. Bridget Brereton, "Contesting the Past: Narratives of Trinidad and Tobago History," *New West Indian Guide* vol. 81, nos. 3 and 4 (2007): 169–96.

59. Tikasingh, "The Establishment of the Indians," 9.

60. Ibid., 275.

61. Ibid., 282–83.

62. Ibid., 360.

63. Kelvin Singh, *Race and Class Struggles in a Colonial State Trinidad: 1917–1945* (Calgary and Kingston: University of Calgary and University Press of the West Indies, 1994); Tina Ramnarine, *Creating Their Own Space: The Development of an Indian-Caribbean Musical Tradition* (Kingston: The Press, University of the West Indies, 2001); Kris Rampersad, *Finding a Place: IndoTrinidadian Literature* (Kingston: Ian Randle Publishers, 2002).

64. Sherry Ann Singh, "The *Ramayana* and Socio-Religious Change in Trinidad, 1917–1990," PhD Dissertation (St. Augustine: University of the West Indies, 2005), 331–34.

65. Ibid.

66. Steven Vertovec, *Hindu Trinidad: Religion, Ethnicity and Socio-Economic Change* (London: Macmillan, 1992), 87.

67. *Port of Spain Gazette,* September 10, 1867.

68. *Fair Play,* April 8, 1875. This appears to be one of the rare surviving reports of this kind. While reports are numerous of Afrocreole Obeah, there are only a few for Indian Obeah.

69. "Capture of the Desperado Macoon," *Port of Spain Gazette,* April 18, 1890.

70. "Opium Smoking, Does it Harm the Coolie?" *Port of Spain Gazette,* October 17, 1893; "Coolie Gambling House," *Port of Spain Gazette,* August 15, 1893; "Another Coolie Dodge," *Port of Spain Gazette,* October 27, 1892.

71. D. W. D. Comins, *Note on Emigration from India to Trinidad* (Calcutta: Bengal Secretariat Press, 1893), 36–37.

72. Walton Look Lai, *Indentured Labor and Caribbean Sugar: Chinese and Indian Migrants to the British West Indies, 1838–1918* (Baltimore: Johns Hopkins University Press, 2003), 143.

73. Sarah Morton, *John Morton of Trinidad: Journals, Letters, & Papers* (Toronto: Westminster, 1916), 342.

74. Tikasingh, "The Establishment of the Indians," 282–83.

75. "Immigration," *Port of Spain Gazette,* January 19, 1884.

76. "Brahmanism and its Phases in Trinidad," *Port of Spain Gazette,* January 19, 1884.

77. B. D. Tripathi, *Saddhus of India: The Sociological View* (Bombay: Popular Prakashan, 1978), 73–74.

78. Max Weber, *The Protestant Ethic and the Spirit of Capitalism,* trans. and eds. A.M. Henderson and Talcott Parsons (New York: The Free Press, 1964).

79. Kelvin Singh, *Bloodstained Tombs, The Muhurram Massacre of 1884* (London: MacMillan, 1988). In recent years in Trinidad, there have been marches commemorating this event.

80. Vertovec, *Hindu Trinidad,* 106–112. This confirms my own knowledge and research from visiting various Hindu temples and ceremonies in Trinidad between 1991 and 2010.

81. Sat Maharaj, Secretary of the Sanatan Dharma Maha Sabha, writing in the *Trinidad Guardian,* May 21, 2009, A18.

82. Tony Martin, "African and Indian Consciousness," in *General History of the Caribbean: Volume V: The Caribbean in the Twentieth Century,* ed. Bridget Brereton (London and Paris: UNESCO and Macmillan, 2004), 256–57.

83. Ibid., 258.

84. Kevin Yelvington, "Introduction," in *Trinidad Ethnicity,* ed. Kevin Yelvington (London: MacMillan, 1998), 13.

85. William Adam Smith, "Advocates for Change within the Imperium: Urban Colored and Black Upper Middle Class Reform Activists in Crown Colony Trinidad, 1880–1925," PhD Dissertation (St. Augustine: University of the West Indies, 2000), 42.

86. Selwyn Ryan, *The Pursuit of Honor: The Life and Times of H.O.B. Wooding* (St. Augustine: Institute of Social and Economic Research, 1990), 61.

87. Smith, "Advocates for Change within the Imperium," 33.

88. The author availed himself of both in London and Edinburgh in 2005 and 2008, after e-mail correspondence with the librarians.

89. Andrew Bundy, "Introduction," in *The Selected Essays of Wilson Harris,* 30.

90. Gordon Rohlehr, *My Strangled City and Other Essays* (Port of Spain: Longman, 1992), 24.

91. Gordon Rohlehr, *The Shape of that Hurt and Other Essays* (Port of Spain: Longman, 1992), 308.

92. Gerard Aching, *Carnival and Popular Culture in the Caribbean: Masking and Power* (Minneapolis: University of Minnesota Press, 2002), 53.

93. Homi K. Bhabha makes this point in his essay "Narrating the Nation." See Bhabha, *Nation and Narration* (London: Routledge, 1992).

94. This cry was echoed in virtually all media during and after the 2008 US Presidential Election. Raj Patel's *The Value of Nothing* is just one of the many books that note this fact. See Patel, *The Value of Nothing: How to Reshape Market Society and Redefine Democracy* (New York: Picador, 2009), 74.

95. The best example of this is Lloyd Best and Kari Levitt's formulation of the Plantation Economy model, as a replacement for classical Keynsian, Ricardian and Lewisian models of Caribbean economy which has been ignored by policymakers. See Best and Levitt, *The Theory of the Plantation Economy: A Historical and Institutional Approach to Caribbean Economic Development* (Kingston: University Press of the West Indies, 2009).

96. V. S. Naipaul, *The Mimic Men* (London: Penguin, 1967).

97. Wilson Harris, "Literacy and the Imagination," in *The Selected Essays of Wilson Harris,* 79.

Chapter 2

Slave Instruction by the Anglican Church and the Transformation of Slavery

D. A. Dunkley

INTRODUCTION

This chapter makes two related arguments. It examines the central role of the Anglican Church in the provision of instruction, which was gradually transformed into a system of education for the slaves in the British Caribbean colony of Jamaica. This occurred before the abolition of slavery in 1834, an important point since scholars, such as Shirley C. Gordon, M. K. Bacchus, and Howard Fergus, have sided with the view that no formal educational system existed in the Anglo-Caribbean before abolition in 1834.[1] The second point made in this chapter is that the slaves divulged a great deal of agency in their interactions with the system of instruction. Resistance shaped many aspects of slave life, as Michael Craton and other historians have shown, and this chapter shows that resistance, a form of agency, was evident in the ways that the slaves reacted to the instruction that they were given by the clergymen and curates of the Church of England.[2] The chapter also adopts the view that slaves exposed to any form of education were placed in a position of advantage, which proved useful in their resistance endeavors. Maurice St. Pierre offers a theoretical framework for this assessment. He notes that it is "usually those who are better educated" who will assume the leadership roles during revolts and other types of resistance.[3]

It is possible to flesh out some of this agency using the correspondences of the clergymen, curates, and the bishop of Jamaica during slavery. A large proportion of these documents—which are used in this analysis—were also generated by the curates employed by the evangelical organization known as the Church Missionary Society (CMS), which had a branch in Jamaica known as the Jamaica Auxiliary of the CMS (JCMS), and both of which had close ties to the Anglican Church. Slaves changed the material and pedagogical aspects of instruction, and these changes were recorded by the persons who taught them. These documents indeed provide us with plenty of access to slave agency, though this is one of the most challenging events to reconstruct, since these and most of the other documents about slavery and slave life originated with the people who controlled the slaves.

ORIGINS OF SLAVE INSTRUCTION

Early government involvement in the provision of instruction in Jamaica was an indication that a system was under consideration. Of course, during this early period there were significant challenges to overcome, most notably the objections raised by the planters and other slaveholders. The view which they held was that instruction, even if this was deeply religious in nature, threatened their ability to control the slaves. Masters rightly suspected that instruction had the potential to assist the slaves in their effort to obtain any form of freedom. However, these objections created only difficulties for instruction; they were not enough to permanently block the plans of the English crown, which supported slave instruction, for the government of Jamaica.

From the early years of the English conquest of the island, which occurred in 1655, the crown's interest in slave instruction was evident. Governors were told, for instance, to assist the Established Church in its effort to spread its "Doctrine and Discipline" among all of the inhabitants of the new colony of Jamaica. This encouragement would be accompanied by the decision to provide the clergymen with access to political offices in the colony. From the start of the eighteenth century, for example, it was noted that clergymen were to be appointed to the parish Vestries. These bodies administered the affairs of the parishes, and most importantly, they controlled the expenditures of tax revenues at the parish level. As members of the Vestries, it was stipulated that no meetings were to take place without the clergymen being present. The stipulation provided an assurance to the crown and its governors in the island that the clergymen would have a definitive influence over key expenditures, including any that was made for instructional purposes. At the time, instruction was provided by the church, and so, any monies spent on the churches also indirectly benefitted their outreach programs, such as instruction. Governor Phillip Howard, who was the governor of Jamaica in 1685, was given strict instructions by the crown to remove any obstacles that the clergy might face as the custodians of the church and its various roles in the community.[4]

Writers such as Edmund Hickeringill, an Anglican cleric who visited Jamaica around the time of its conquest, also wrote about the importance of instruction in his 1661 book, *Jamaica Viewed.* Hickeringill was of the opinion that instruction could help the English to establish their control over Jamaica. His focus was reserved for the remaining Amerindian population that was still on the island in the wake of the English conquest. The enslaved African population in Jamaica was still small, but in the coming years this population would increase as the Sugar Revolution became a reality. Hickeringill's views, nonetheless, indicated strong support for instruction from an early observer who had given considerable attention to the future of the colony under English rule. He did not share the perspective that the slave owners themselves would develop that instruction was "incompatible" with the domination of Jamaica or of those of its inhabitants who were non-white or non-British.[5] This view advocating incompatibility, especially as it related to slavery, would continue to exist alongside the opposite viewpoint that supported instruction as an aid rather than a hindrance to domination in any form, including domination under slavery.

More than a century after Hickeringill's book was published instruction was still receiving support from its advocates, who believed that extending popular education to Britain's slave colonies in the West Indies would invariably benefit the whites who controlled the colony. In 1818, for example, English educator John Rippingham extolled the virtues of instructing what he referred to as the "masses" in the colonies to further enhance the power of colonial masters.[6] R. C. Dallas, who became more popularly known for his two-volume *History of the Maroons* published in 1803, also later wrote in support of instructing the "lower classes" throughout the British Empire. Instruction, Dallas noted in a book published in 1815, reduced the "ignorance" and "deplorable" condition of the lower rungs of society, and, at the same time, generated their loyalty for the social order.[7] Dallas's point was exactly the same one that many clergymen had been vocalizing to counteract the objections of the slaveholders and to diminish their fears about slave instruction. The clergymen had received real proof that instruction could be done in such a way that it benefited the owners of slaves. This proof was provided by the Moravian missionaries who began arriving in Jamaica in 1754.

The Moravian success with slave instruction made two important points as far as the Anglican clergymen were concerned. Their arrival in Jamaica came in the aftermath of their tremendous success in the Danish West Indies, where their participation in slave instruction showed a significant shift in the "received practice and theory" of enslavement.[8] Planters in the Danish West Indies had embraced the view that instruction could pacify the slaves and could encourage them to work harder for their masters. The planters of Jamaica, who continued to raise objections to instruction, therefore exposed only that they were intransigent and unwilling to accept the truths which had been revealed by the developments that had taken place in other colonies. The second point concerned the fact that the Moravian missionaries who came to Jamaica had been invited to the island by a select group of Jamaican planters. These were members of the Moravian Church themselves, but who also owned considerable estates in the western parishes of St. Elizabeth and Westmoreland.[9] Because of their decision to allow the missionaries to instruct their slaves, these planters were spared the damage that was caused by the slave rebellion in 1760. One report from the missionaries stated that none of the slaves on the estates where they preached and taught their version of Christianity had joined those referred to by one pro-planter writer as the "disaffected" rebels.[10] Almost all the rest had answered the call of rebel leader Tacky to take up arms and fight for their freedom. The Moravians were an extremely important example for the cause of slave instruction because, as J.E. Hutton commented later in his 1872 *History of the Moravian Church,* the missionaries showed their complicity with the slaveholders by owning slaves themselves, and by the fact that they "never came forward as champions of liberty," "never pleaded for emancipation," and "never encouraged their converts to expect it."[11]

The invitation to the Moravian missionaries had also indicated that the Jamaican planters were now divided on the issue of slave instruction. And those who supported it were not part of a diminishing number, but one that was gradually increasing. Among these were the planters who allowed early Anglican clerics such as the Rev. William Manning access to their slaves. And Manning, when reporting on what he did with this access, stated that "I have first instructed them [the slaves] in the principles of Christianity." Manning, who was the bishop of London's commissary in Jamaica—the local manager of the clergy—was also in charge of organizing the clergymen so that they could mount a more effective campaign against the remaining intractable slave masters. Among his vital assets in early eighteenth-century Jamaica was the Rev. Lewis Boneval. Boneval was willing to risk a great deal to improve the state of instruction. Eventually, he was accused of teaching the slaves "not to obey their masters." In his response to the accusation, Boneval showed that he was committed to his duties and would not allow the planters to discourage him from proceeding with his work. He did not even deny teaching the slaves a measure of Christian independence. Instead, he admitted encouraging them to give "to God the things that are God's, & to Caesar the things that are Caesar's."[12]

Boneval's defiant attitude might have been an exception to the rule, but he was certainly not the only clergyman willing to publicly give support to slave instruction. Rev. John Venn, who was chaplain of the planter-dominated legislature known as the House of Assembly, used his close association with some of the most prominent slaveholders in the island to advocate for instruction. Venn was the author of a pamphlet which outlined the reasons why the planters should give their support to slave instruction while he was serving as the rector for the parish of St. Catherine, whose capital, Spanish Town, was the capital of the island. Venn had realized his advantageous position and this seems to have helped him to develop the courage to put down on paper his thoughts and instruction. The pamphlet, which was dated 1751, was sent to Lambeth Palace to be viewed by the bishop of London, head of the Church in the colonies.

Venn did not wish for just any kind of instruction. His was to be a superior one that would, in his point of view, benefit both slaves and masters. He was critical, for instance, of the approaches taken in the Spanish islands and identified Cuba where, he noted, the Catholic priests had converted the slaves without prior instruction. This had turned those enslaved people into "Christian only in Name." No such tragedy should be the outcome of any effort to convert slaves in British territories. Venn therefore insisted that instruction should be given in preparation for conversion to Christianity, as this was the only sure way that the slaves would "truly improve." By using carefully selected words such as "improve," Venn crafted an argument that was designed to change the perspective of even the planters who voiced the most extreme objections to instructing the slaves. What Venn appealed for was for the planters to focus on the outcome of instruction: his supposed "fact" that the slaves would become "better" slaves. Christianity, in Venn's final analysis, could aid slavery.[13]

Almost the same opinion was voiced by Rev. John Lindsay in his own unpublished manuscript, which he completed around 1788. Lindsay revolted against the absence of Christianity in the slave colonies in this virtual teaching manual for the later providers of instruction employed by the CMS. Lindsay's opinions were very similar to those of the Moravian, Baptist, and Methodist missionaries, who also supported instructing the slaves, though some of them for a very different reason. The presence of two distinct viewpoints, both of which encouraged instruction, was not an unfounded phenomenon in the Caribbean colonies of Britain. When planters came out later in support of Amelioration—improving slavery—the colony was also divided between those planters who advocated it, and those who opposed it, and both couched their perspectives in arguments to bolster or strengthen slavery. Similarly, the debate over instruction raged between people such as Rev. John Lindsay who feared that without it, slavery would die, and those who had the opposite view that with it, slavery stood a greater chancing of dying as well. As for

Lindsay, he said that there were clear "virtues" in Christian instruction which, in fact, provided the "vital flame" needed to "actuate the whole design" to protect slavery by improving the condition of the slaves. Lindsay was one of the clerics, who, like John Venn, agreed with the idea of Amelioration in principle, but also said that controlling it carefully was of great necessity. One of the mechanisms for instituting this control was to place instruction in the hands of actual teachers who had the requisite training. Lindsay called these "a sufficient Number of Gentlemen of Education from the Universities," who could help to "bring the Clergy into repute" if employed to work on behalf of the church as ordained clerics in their own right.[14]

A critical moment for change was fast approaching in Jamaica as the end of the eighteenth century drew nearer. And one of the problems that needed to be solved for instruction to take its place among the momentous changes was the credibility setbacks occurring from within the ecclesiastical establishment. Planters had always pointed to the fact that many clergymen conducted themselves worse than some of the slaveholders that they complained about. And clerics who observed their colleagues eagerly concurred. One account from a rector stated that "Drunkenness, Debauchery, and Profaneness" described far too many of his compatriots. Rev. Pilkington, rector of Portland parish, raised some of the same concerns. He noted that his colleagues had damaged the reputation of the church and all the clerics in the island. They had contributed to the moral decay of society, a place which had become known for its "Immorality and scandalous living."[15]

Critical to these observations was the evidence that they provided of the willingness of the clergy to engage in self-criticism. Among their numbers were clerics who willingly acknowledged that they had done as much damage to church projects like slave instruction as the slave masters who still objected to it. If instruction was to materialize right across the island and become the start of widespread education with religious teachings as its basis, then the clergy would have to undergo a process of cleansing and renewal. What in fact happened fell short of the changes some of the rectors wanted to see. Material incentives were provided alongside some of the tools that the clergy needed to perform their role as teachers. In 1724, for example, a shipment of books arrived at Kingston Harbor, accompanied by a Mr. Barrett, whose services had been procured with the expectation that he would work as a schoolmaster. The books which arrived on the ship with Barrett were said to have been imported for the "catechetical Instruction of the Youth & particularly of the Negro Children & others in the parish." Barrett was to teach the children of poor whites and those of enslaved people. No distinction was made between the two groups when the necessity of schooling was discussed. Barrett was put in charge of running a library in which the books that arrived with him were to be kept for use by his students and as reference material for the clerics and catechists to consult. The advice Barrett was given was this: "It is on the condition of you instructing the Negro Slaves & the better to enable you thereunto that the foregoing Library is bestowed upon you as well as the other Encouragement." During the same year, another shipment of books arrived which were to be set aside for those students who were "lately Converted." This implied that some amount of progress was expected in the performance and attainments of the pupils.[16]

As head of the colonial church, the bishop of London periodically requested reports on the state of initiatives connected to the church, such as instruction. One of these formal inquiries was made in 1723. The responses provided by the clergy gave important insights into the status of instruction in that year. Almost all of the rectors reported difficulties with the planters. No rector voiced any objection to instruction in principle. Those who doubted the enterprise would work raised these doubts on the basis of their assessment of the obstacles they faced as a result of the planters' denying them access to the slaves. Some planters were unwilling even to allow any of their slaves to attend church. Rev. Galpin, however, reported having gained access to a small number in Port Royal where he was the parish rector. These slaves, though small in number, gave the reverend hope that things would improve in time. In anticipation of improvement, Galpin initiated additional weekly services, which brought his total to three services each week. Another rector, the Rev. John Kelly in St. Elizabeth, stated that he had started preparing some of the slaves for conversion having gained limited access to a few. Similar activities were reported by Rev. John White in the parish of Vere, despite the fact that almost "none of the masters will admit any [slave] baptized."[17] The proposition that was subsequently made in 1728 to build "free schools for the slaves" was based on the cautious optimism revealed by the clergymen who had been teaching small numbers of slaves.[18]

SLAVE INSTRUCTION AND THE CHURCH MISSIONARY SOCIETY

Social reformers interested in promoting the ideas of the English Reformation of the sixteenth and early seventeenth centuries had been advocating widespread education under the auspices of the Anglican Church since the 1640s, in order to generate social cohesion and the loyalty of the masses. In

1647, Samuel Hartlib proposed "general schooling over the land" as one of the steps needed to institute "social control" and to make the general population "tractable and submissive."[19] Gloucester and other counties in England passed ordinances establishing some of the first basic teaching standards to regulate teaching in schools and which provided evidence that the ideas of Hartlib and other reformers, such as Samuel Harmer, had gained the attention of the authorities.[20] In the 1780s, Parliament took the decision to support "a sound Christian education," a move bolstered by the view that schools were to function mainly "as Civilizing influences," where students were "contained and their abilities channeled into skilled work and respectable behavior."[21] Schools were institutions of indoctrination whose primary responsibility was not to the students but to the state and its church. Schools which appeared during the latter half of the eighteenth century, as Kenneth Morgan observes, were brought into existence to "spread orderly behavior" and "social cohesion" through "rudimentary, educational instruction."[22]

What these developments in England meant for English colonies was not hard to see. Jamaica had its own official turning point in 1797, when its Assembly enacted legislation to improve the condition of the Anglican clergy, with the expectation that the rectors would lead the colony towards some of the same social change that was occurring in England. The legislation increased the annual salaries of the clerics from £200 to an average of £270, and a further encouragement was provided in the form of a compensation fund, similar to the one started in England and Ireland, which would benefit the wives and children of clergymen who passed away while working for the colonial church. This investment was expected to yield good returns, specifically that the clergy would "instruct in the Doctrines of the Christian Religion such Negroes as may be willing to be baptized on every Sunday."[23] By the time that the CMS arrived in Jamaica in the 1820s, the idea of widening the educational provisions in the colony to give the slaves access to at least religious instruction was well established and efforts in that direction were underway.

The CMS established a subsidiary in Jamaica, the Jamaica Auxiliary of the Church Missionary Society, which subsequently spent about £132 annually on school projects across the island until the 1834 abolition of slavery. The expenditure, which would increase beyond that average figure in some years, would eventually help to bankrupt the CMS and its local subsidiary after slavery was abolished. During the one-year period of 1830–31, for example, £400 was spent on schools in just one of Jamaica's parishes: Portland. Those large expenditures, which indicated a serious, though still fledgling instructional program, were due, in part, to the hiring of trained teachers. The preferred candidate had to be a graduate of the CMS's training institution in London, most of them white males between the ages of twenty and forty. Some of them came to the island as married men who brought their wives and children; most, however, were single. It seemed quite obvious that the ideal teacher was a single white male.[24]

The plan to hire teachers who would quickly integrate into the colony and get on with their teaching did not always work out as intended. One of the teachers who arrived in 1826, Henry Clarke Taylor, lodged complaints about his accommodation and the room he was given to teach in, soon after his arrival. Clarke had brought his wife with him to the island, which probably aggravated his eagerness to be adequately situated with agreeable housing and a school room that he saw as suitable. He seemed to have been led into believing that sufficient preparation had been made for his arrival. The realty he encountered, however, was far different. Although Taylor benefitted from an accommodating planter named James Wildman, an avid supporter of slave instruction, Taylor lodged his complaints about his circumstances to the JCMS. He also revolted against joining the local militia as a reservist. It became clear to Wildman that Taylor was unwilling to compromise and seemed not to have accepted that the provisions made for him to teach in the island were still undergoing development. In time, Wildman requested that Taylor be replaced with another teacher-catechist.[25]

Despite his early troubles, Taylor was an enthusiastic catechist. He had ordered a shipment of some sixty books which had been sent with him on the ship that took him and his wife to Jamaica. Those books, some of them Psalters, were subsequently loaned to students in Taylor's classes, with the stipulation that each of them "return it safe." Taylor invested a great deal of trust in his students. He had developed no doubt about his students' interest in his tutoring. He found encouragement in the students' willingness to learn, which in no small way compensated for the challenges that he had faced initially. One of the advantages that these teacher-catechists had was the assurance that they would receive the support of the JCMS. Not in all instances was this support possible or adequate, as was seen when Taylor was removed from Wildman's estate. However, the JCMS seemed keen to advertise that it would come of the defense of any catechist who had a legitimate concern or complaint. In 1830, for example, the catechist J.C. Sharpe, who taught children and adults at the Maroon village known as Accompong in St. Elizabeth, reported facing harassment from the English supervisor in the village, John Hylton. Sharpe's report was copied to the governor, who instructed his secretary, William Bullock, to settle the dispute by writing to Hylton. The supervisor was accordingly warned against interfering with the work of the catechist. Similar support was, in time, given to Taylor after he raised his objection to joining the militia. The newly installed bishop of Jamaica, Christopher Lip-scomb, ever the consummate diplomat, maneuvered to have Taylor exempted from militia duty. Privately, Lipscomb told Taylor to just get on with his work and the matter would die without fanfare. Publicly, Lipscomb said he supported the planters, realizing that he needed their support to continue the development of instruction in the island.[26]

A further word on Lipscomb is needed here. He was the first local bishop of Jamaica, appointed in 1824. Prior to this, the head of the Anglican Church in Jamaica and other British colonies in the region was the bishop of London. Having a bishop situated in the island aided the plan to develop instruction into a widespread educational system, one that catered to the majority of the population, which was enslaved. Lipscomb was no liberator of the slaves, as some accounts might suggest. He was more interested in counteracting the missionaries, whose influence over the slaves had been increasing since about 1820. His appointment was partly connected with the fear of the planters that the missionaries would continue to improve their standing in the slave community, and would, in due course, encourage the slaves to seek their emancipation. Lipscomb was to promote the planter ideology, but while doing so, he would also manage the development of instruction. Like the planters who supported him, Lipscomb underestimated the ability of the slaves to use instruction for their own benefit.

Lipscomb, like the catechists who came to work for the JCMS, can also be described as one of the "foot soldiers of imperialism."[27] They were all involved in promoting the state church of England. In this regard, they worked for the cause of Englishness in the colony. This was why it was so crucial that the catechists were persons with training in England. Gone were the days when imperialism rested on the shoulders of planters, many of whom were still suspicious about developments like instruction, many of whom still supported the old-fashioned view of slavery as an institution that was most effective if it was based on brutal domination. The new view, which advocated the use of indoctrination to accomplish domination, also had the added benefit of encouraging loyalty to the crown of England. Through the church and its servants, such as Lipscomb and the catechists, Englishness in the colony stood a better chance of surviving and growing.

Lipscomb, aware of his crucial role, seemed never to have missed an opportunity to advertise the changes that he had seen in the colony. He viewed these as improvements, noting on one occasion that "a very general wish to ameliorate the condition of the slaves," by offering "to instruct them in the Principles of the established Church . . . seems to pervade the great mass of Proprietors." He based this report on observations he had made while touring the island, but also on reports from the clergymen in the field. Rev. Burton in St. Thomas in the Vale, for example, had stated that: "On the part of the Proprietors & Attorneys I have always experienced a readiness & anxiety to afford their Slaves reasonable time & opportunity for religious Instruction by the established Clergy."[28] In 1831, there were reports of planters who had also assigned their bookkeepers to teaching duties. Some 300 slaves were receiving lessons from bookkeepers in that year, "young men," the report went on to state, who had been put "in charge of the negroes" while still working "under the" supervision of the "overseers." Other planters made hefty investments in school-building projects. One parish had received money from planters for a school that could hold as many as 500 students.[29]

Sociologist Orlando Patterson has a well-known thesis that describes slavery as "social death," and to support this view he uses absenteeism among the planters/slaveholders to show how callous slavery could become.[30] Absenteeism left attorneys and managers in charge of the estates in colonies like Jamaica, which meant that the persons left in charge of the slaves, were more likely to abuse them. As logical as this argument might seem, there were planters like Wildman, who was also an absentee, who visited his estates in Jamaica. And while visiting, as Matthew "Monk" Lewis himself also did, these otherwise absentee planters made investments in the development of instruction for the slaves. It was noted, for instance, that Wildman had put measures in place to "exempt" from "night-labor" and "all severe exertions of any kind," slaves who expressed an interest in attending school.[31] Planters such as Wildman were, of course, interested in protecting slavery, but they shared the view that indoctrination was a better way to maintain the institution. These absentees, like Lipscomb, the clergy, and catechists, were the new foot soldiers of imperialism.

We have digressed too far now. One last point needs to be made in this section about what the slaves were learning in the schools. It is clear that not all of them were exposed to only Bible Knowledge. It is hard to see how books such as *Ruff's Botanical History* or *Caesar's Commentaries* benefitted the teaching of Christianity.[32] What seems to be the more appropriate assessment is that instruction took on developments of its own. The fledgling system generated its own growth. It was not easy to control every aspect of instruction after it was started. Catechists and clergymen had their own views which crept into the instructional provisions and the teaching process, sometimes even without the knowledge of the JCMS or Bishop Lipscomb; sometimes without the awareness of the teachers themselves. This was possible especially since there were teachers like Joshua Wood, a thirty-eight year old trained teacher, who had been teaching before he was seconded to Jamaica.[33] Having teaching experience increased the likelihood of these teachers using their initiative to reconfigure the teaching that they did. There is no good reason to believe that teachers in the past were any less creative because of institutional pressures and limitations than they are in the present day. Teachers have always found creative ways to overcome the problem that they face.

THE SLAVES AND INSTRUCTION

One of the fears of the proslavery writer James Macqueen was that slave instruction would "bring about emancipation."[34] The view was not unfounded. Macqueen had lived in the West Indies and during that time had observed some of the changes introduced under the banner of Amelioration. He was also voicing sentiments which were shared by the planters, who themselves lived in close proximity to the slaves and could observe the developments taking place in the slave community from that vantage point. In fact, one of the complaints proslavery writers and planters had against the anti-slavery campaigners in England was the fact that many had never seen the colonies or slavery themselves. Macqueen had thus entitled his 1824 book *The West India Colonies; the Calumnies and Misrepresentations Circulated Against Them* to make the point that writers such as him had lived in the slave colonies, where they had received not just knowledge of slavery, but firsthand knowledge.

Of course, facts and interpretation could often differ. However, it was hard not to acknowledge that instruction had developed from its humble beginnings largely due to complaints of clergymen, who were eager to promote the Anglican Church. More and more it seemed that a system had evolved and was still developing. In 1828, there were reports that as many as 75,000 slaves were already receiving instruction under this rudimentary system dominated by the Anglican clergy and the catechists of the JCMS. This figure was expected to rise even further in the coming years. The church boldly announced that it would, in due course, have the entire slave population of the island exposed to some kind of schooling.[35]

The fear that instruction was paving the way for emancipation had another dimension to it. How the slaves had been responding to instruction was also responsible for the link that was made between instruction and emancipation both by proslavery writers and their slaveholding allies. The objections that some of them were still raising with regard to instruction were partly based on the responses of the slaves. The number of slaves with access to instruction, for instance, had been growing alongside the investments made by the planters. It was thus becoming increasingly clear to these planters that they were caught in the whirlwind of a change that they themselves had helped to foment. There were reports from Kingston that even mutual aid organizations started exclusively for whites, such as the Ladies Society of Kingston, had been donating money to the cause of slave instruction. One such report stated that 2,065 slaves in Kingston, along with another 234 in other parts of the island, were receiving instruction that was funded by money from the Ladies Society.[36] Instruction was helping to change the relationship between other entities in the society. It was breaking down the barriers between opposing ecclesiastical bodies. Back in 1823, the British Foreign and Bible Society, an Anglican affiliate, had sent "a supply of New Testaments" to Moravian missionaries in the island. The latter described the donation as "truly acceptable" and "so seasonable a gift." They, too, had been experiencing, since about 1820, a turnaround, which had increased their need for reading materials in their slave schools. Increasing numbers of slaves were gravitating towards schools operated by other missionary societies too, namely the Baptists and Methodists.[37]

After observing both the investment of the planters and the church, and the agreeable responses of the slaves, Bishop Lipscomb commented in 1828 that a real system had indeed developed at that point. Naturally, Lipscomb credited its development to "the proprietors and teachers." However, he also spoke with delight about the slaves, and commented on what he called the "quiet and civilized manners" that they seemed to have eagerly received from their teachers. Lipscomb indeed felt that the slaves should receive some of the praise for the system that was present. He knew that even if some of these slaves had been forced to attend the schools initially, the fact that they remained in school signaled their interest.[38]

Catechists such as Ebenezer Collins provided Lipscomb with the reports that he used to formulate his views about instruction. Collins had reported that "many" of the slaves in his parish, some of them "not yet ten years old," were attending his school regularly. A good proportion had acquired the ability to "read well," and could "follow the church prayers on the Sunday with a great deal of propriety." The ability to read was, of course, an outcome of their willingness to learn. Collins was encouraged by this reaction and started to plan for the future. He said that it was only a matter of time before the "generality," who knew "nothing about what is said to them," would nonetheless acquire the ability to read and comprehend whatever was relayed to then.[39]

Expectations were high among the teachers of the slaves. Those who were experiencing difficulties, such as Taylor, looked to the slaves for inspiration. In this indirect way, the slaves had started to influence their teachers, even those, who, like Taylor, had referred to some of their students as "rather dull" or "indifferent," or, as Taylor also said, he had one girl who was "almost an idiot." Despite having these strong views, Taylor said that as a group, the slaves in his school had demonstrated to him that they had the "capacity to learn as any other race of people." In his own racial view of things, Taylor credited his enslaved students with encouraging him to carry on his teaching. He even developed instructions for new teachers, advising that they should be cautious because the slaves were artful and cunning. Never, he advised, "stoop down" to their level. But at the same time, Taylor was conscious of the fact that this warning might not be practical in every classroom. He knew as a fact that no teaching took place without the slaves' approval of the teacher. So, in his next piece of advice, Taylor warned his new colleagues to try their best "not to be upon a level with them [the slaves]," but to "raise them up to your standard" even if it was necessary to begin one's teaching by stooping.[40]

The systems used to deliver lessons varied between Dr. Andrew Bell's and Mr. Joseph Lancaster's. Reports were received telling of the successes of these systems in other parts of the British Empire, such as India. However, slaves in the Caribbean presented a new challenge. Lancaster's insistence on classroom discipline might work with only some slaves. Other catechists therefore applied Bell's approach, which advised "*perfect instruction*" or the "not passing over any lesson, or any part of a lesson, till it be well and thoroughly learned."[41] Teaching by rote or repetition was applied to overcome the difficulties involved in teaching the slaves. It was not simply a matter of what was known in terms of pedagogy. Within the limitations of what was known, teachers had to apply, as best they could, a pedagogy that gave them some assurance that they could convince the slaves to learn from them.

Bell's system was probably used more widely in the Caribbean context because it relied on participation from students and interaction with the teachers. Spelling lessons, for instance, were delivered by "first pronouncing the words after the teacher, and then proceeding to spell the words slowly and deliberately." A similar approach was applied to the teaching of computation: "the several students set down the respective numbers from the lips of each other" while "listening to their reasons for these." This was seen as more effective than the "solitary" approach, wherein the student learned on his or her own through practice, which "frequently fails to teach."[42]

When Lipscomb toured the schools in Jamaica in 1825, he received reports advising of "the great uncertainty & capriciousness of the Negro character," which made it "difficult to make sure of their attendance even where great pains have been taken." Lipscomb realized from these reports that slave agency was at play in the delivery of instruction. The same sort of thing was visible in the churches, where, as Lipscomb added himself, "whenever a

Preacher is popular they [the slaves] dress out their children & themselves." This was "a sure sign that they are in good humor." After considering the matter, Lipscomb decided to warn that the best approach for dealing with the slaves was to abandon "severity and harshness," which had "never yet gained one Convert." The slaves, Lipscomb added by way of justification, observed "every particularity of manner & gesture," and the most successful clergymen, for instance, were those who had given in to the slaves' "great predilection for a powerful valorous service."[43]

Rev. Mann's experiences in Kingston confirmed what Lipscomb was advertising. In 1824, Rev. Mann stated that he had observed the presence of slaves in his church who lived in other parishes. Some of them "come from various parts of the country," Mann stated, and based on what he had seen, "not one third of the number of Slaves mentioned to have been Baptized in Kingston belong to Kingston." Rev. Mann was almost sure that this had something to do with the 907 slave baptisms he had performed up to that point, and the 124 slave marriages.[44] These were things the slaves wanted, and they would travel almost any distance and take almost any risk to acquire them. Those pastors who were still reluctant to perform slave marriages were not as popular as Rev. Mann. Slaves who gravitated to his church did so because they perceived him as flexible and progressive.

These decisions that the slaves were making were not isolated from other aspects of their lives. They were part of a whole host of agency-related activities that had been building up in the slave community for some time. Lipscomb reported on, with some amount of objection, the dynamic of Sunday marketing, which had survived among the slaves in spite of objections raised by the ecclesiastical community. This was one of the things on which most preachers could agree. Missionaries also registered their dissatisfaction with the slaves engaging in commercial activities on the Sabbath. But nothing could stop it. The government had to move the market in downtown Kingston from Princess Street to Solas on West Street just to make it less visible on a Sunday.[45] There is no need here to go into further discussion about Sunday marketing, since ample research exists on this form of agency or resistance by the slaves. Scholars such as Sidney Mintz, Douglas Hall, Hilary Beckles, and Roderick A. McDonald have done good work on the phenomenon. Neville Hall's research has also shown the presence of independent economic activities within the enslaved communities of the Danish West Indies—on the islands of St. Thomas, St. Croix, and St. John.[46]

Many slaves who engaged in silent forms of resistance such as Sunday marketing and school attendance did so to raise themselves and their relatives to a higher position in the slave community. Proslavery writer Bernard Senior encountered one of these slaves named William in St. Elizabeth,

Jamaica, and reported on their brief exchange in his 1823 book, *Jamaica, As It Was, As It is, and As It May Be.* Senior was struck by William's capacity for self-improvement, stating that the view shared by other slaves and some whites was that William was of "excellent character." William was known for his wide-range of vocations: he was a barber, shoemaker, horse dealer, and fiddler. He made money from buying livestock from other slaves at fair prices and had used some of this money to build himself a house. It had separate rooms, a sideboard in the dining room, a Grecian lamp hanging in the hallway, and other furnishings. William even expressed fear of losing his acquisitions because of unrest started by other slaves, which might disrupt the relationships that slaves such as him had developed with other enslaved persons and with whites.[47]

Subtle or silent resistance in the classrooms had helped to shape the state of instruction, a fact recorded during the decade of the 1820s. Writing in 1826, the catechist, Thomas Jones, alluded to having encountered this subtle demonstration of slave agency in the classroom. Jones indicated that the slaves made sure that their teachers earned their confidence before any teaching could proceed. Jones said that he had to "first endeavor to gain their Attention, then their Affection, and lastly their confidence." Only after delivering those assurances could Jones announce that he had "taught them." He was able to conduct lessons "every morning from seven o'clock to nine—from ten to twelve and in the afternoon from one to two, and from two to five." Clearly these students were children, who had perhaps learned some of their agency from their parents. Jones had added that he was also able to teach adult slaves separately "from Seven in the Evening from the first of April [1826]." In time, as word spread that he was a flexible and accommodating teacher, the size of his classes grew. He had fifty-four students under instruction at the time of writing this report, and was in a position to register that "there are forty-three in monosyllables," in addition to "one young woman who had begun to read in the New Testament." Jones also appealed for more investment in instruction having figured out how to appease the slaves who attended school. It was with delight that he reported collecting "upwards of ten pounds towards an intended Organ" for the church, a donation which the slaves used to show their gratitude and willingness to work with the teacher. According to Jones, they had begun to "express themselves as very thankful in having amongst them a Teacher of Religion."[48]

Not all teachers of religion had the same experience as Jones. Slaves in the parish of Westmoreland rejected some of the missionaries who tried to become their teachers. This response was felt to be the wisest when reacting to any missionary who had earned the unfortunate title of *"Parson-Negro."* This term, which the slaves themselves used, was intended to describe the disrespect that some of these missionaries faced, especially from the planters, many of whom viewed the missionaries as a threat to the social order. It did not matter to some slaves that these missionaries were perceived as their supporters and on that basis were ignored or treated contemptuously by reactionary planters. What concerned these slaves the most was that "even the Overseer never goes to hear those people, or admit them to his table—that they were never sent for as Clergymen to bury or baptize white people."[49] The fact of the matter was that pastors who were popular among the planters were also in a better position to help the slaves help themselves. These pastors were therefore the most likely ones to receive widespread approval from the slaves.

It is true that missionaries in Jamaica were the victims of widespread disapproval from the planters. Legislation was enacted in the late eighteenth and early nineteenth centuries to ban missionaries from preaching without licenses issued by the planter-dominated Vestries in the parishes. Of course, the Anglican clergymen, who were members of the Vestries, supported the suppression of the missionaries. Only the Moravian missionaries seemed to have been spared this treatment, and more than likely this was because they were invited to the island by planters. Consequently, they attracted only a limited number of other slaves until the situation changed in the 1820s. A growing number of slaves began to enter the various missionary churches and schools. This improvement was recorded by both Baptist and Methodist missionaries, but it came after a larger number of slaves had already received baptism from the Anglican clergymen.

One of the ways in which the Anglican Church established its popularity among the slaves was through its control over instruction. Most of the clergymen provided some form of instruction. Almost every school in the island had some kind of relationship with the established church. And as the links between schooling and the church developed, the latter and its clergy attracted more slaves. It seems the church had successfully convinced a growing number of planters to give their support to instruction, which also aided the development of schooling in the island. This was proof to the slaves that the church had enough power to help them in their own self-improvement. Planters in the parish of St. Thomas in the East had put aside £6,000 for school construction in the 1820s. Also during that period, an industrial school was started in Spanish Town with funding from planters. A master was hired from England, someone with training and experience, having before that worked for the National School Society in England. He was given a strict mandate: "catechize the Slave population three days a week." Back in St. Thomas in the East, planters formed the "Society for the Conversion and Religious Instruction and Education of the Negro Slaves." In 1826, this organization had 2,219 slaves in its total of thirty-eight schools spread across Morant Bay, the Plantain Garden River valley, the Blue Mountain valley, Bath, and Manchioneal.[50]

CONCLUSION

It is clear to this writer that more research into the instruction offered to slaves in Jamaica and the Wider Caribbean is needed. This research will help to unearth more detail about the role played by the Anglican Church, information that can be used to better compare the role of the church with that of the missionaries. One of the assumptions in Caribbean history seems to be that the Protestant missionaries played a more substantial role in the movement towards the abolition of slavery and later emancipation or full freedom. However, the Anglican Church was the first ecclesiastical body to establish a foothold in the colonies and was able to improve its standing among a sufficiently large number of whites and slaves before the missionaries could do the same. Right up to the year before the 1834 abolition, missionary churches and meeting houses were being ransacked and burned by planters, and this was done with the support of Anglican clerics themselves. One of these clerics, Rev. George Wilson Bridges, is the subject of the next chapters 4 and 5 in this volume. The persecution of the missionaries was partly motivated by the fear that they might erode the influential position of the Anglican Church. The popularity of the church was not in doubt, and it was a popularity that people from within and outside of the church were willing to fight to maintain.

Instruction did not begin with the 1834 abolition and the Negro Education Grant that came with it. Neither did a real system of education start at that point. Efforts to construct a system were being pursued during slavery, and during the 1820s that system began to materialize in more obvious ways. The objective of providing the slaves with instruction was to indoctrinate these slaves using religious doctrines and principles; the same objective remained a crucial part of the educational offerings after abolition. The churches were still in charge of most of the endeavor during the post-abolition period, and, gradually, secular influences were introduced. The Mico Charity played an important role in the secularization of British West Indian education through its institution in Jamaica for the training of teachers to work in both denominational and non-denominational schools.

Another significant development which had started during slavery had to do with how the slaves reacted to instruction. There is enough evidence that slave agency shaped much of the classroom interaction. Many slaves seemed to have viewed instruction as something that was beneficial to them, provided that they could influence how they were being taught. A marked power struggle unfolded inside classrooms where slaves were instructed to obey their master and abide by church teachings. Where the slaves received no indication that they had the power to influence their teachers, almost no teaching could take place. The clergy and catechists themselves divulged some of the ways in which they had to struggle with the slaves to get them to accept their tutoring. The ultimate objective of the slaves might not have been in all cases to use instruction to somehow achieve their freedom gradually. Some of them no doubt gained satisfaction from knowing that they had resisted yet another attempt to dominate their lives.

Notes

1. See the works by Shirley C. Gordon, *A Century of West Indian Education* (London: Longman, Green and Co., 1963), 18; "The Negro Education Grant 1835–1845: Its Application in Jamaica," *British Journal of Educational Studies* 6, no. 2 (1958): 141, 146; and "Schools of the Free," in *Before and After 1865: Education, Politics and Regionalism in the Caribbean,* eds. Brian Moore and Swithin Wilmot (Kingston: Ian Randle Publishers, 1998), 3, 5. Also see M.K. Bacchus, *Utilization, Misuse and Development of Human Resources in the Early West Indian Colonies from 1492 to 1845* (Ontario: Wilfred Laurier University Press, 1990), 220, 223, and Howard A. Fergus, *A History of Education in the British Leeward Islands, 1838–1945* (Kingston: The University of the West Indies Press, 2003), 10.

2. Michael Craton, "Forms of Resistance to Slavery," in *General History of the Caribbean, Vol. III: The Slave Societies of the Caribbean,* ed. Franklin W. Knight (London and Basingstoke: UNESCO/Macmillan, 1997), 222. For the frequency and importance of slave revolts in Jamaica, also see Richard B. Sheridan, "The Jamaican Slave Insurrection Scare of 1776 and the American Revolution," *The Journal of Negro History* vol. 61, no. 3 (July 1976): 290, 291.

3. Maurice St. Pierre, *Anatomy of Resistance: Anti-Colonialism in Guyana, 1823–1966* (London and Basingstoke: Macmillan, 1999), 16.

4. Instructions for our Trusty and well beloved Sir Phillip Howard, November 25, 1685, 97, Fulham Papers, Lambeth Palace Library, London (hereinafter referred to as FP) XVII. Also see Instruction to Thomas Windsor, March 21, 1661/62, 93, and Instructions for our Trusty & well beloved, 1681, 95, FP XVII.

5. See Edmund Hickeringill, *Jamaica Viewed,* 3rd. ed. (London: B. Bragg, 1705 [1661]). For a modern rehearsal of the point that slavery and slave instruction were "incompatible," see this work by the historian Carl Campbell: *Colony & Nation: A Short History of Education in Trinidad & Tobago, 1834–1986* (Kingston: Ian Randle Publishers, 1992), 10.

6. John Rippingham, *Mr. Rippingham's Tracts upon Education in General, including a Statement of the Principles and Modes of Education in England and Scot-*

land: with Especial Consideration upon the Present State of Education in Jamaica (Kingston: Printed by George Worrall Struper, 1818), 4.

7. Robert Charles Dallas, *The New Conspiracy Against the Jesuits Detected and Briefly Exposed* (London: Printed for James Ridgeway, 1815), 249.

8. N. A. T. Hall, "Education for Slaves in the Danish Virgin Islands, 1732–1846," in *Education in the Caribbean, Historical Perspectives,* ed. Ruby Hope King (Kingston: Faculty of Education, University of the West Indies, 1987), 2, 16.

9. For an account of the arrival of Moravian missionaries in Jamaica, see J.H. Buchner, *The Moravians in Jamaica. History of the Mission of the United Brethren's Church to the Negroes in the Island of Jamaica, from the Year 1754 to 1854* (London: Longman, Brown, & Co., 1854), 21–24.

10. Bridges, *The Annals of Jamaica,* Vol. 2 (London: Frank Cass, 1968 [1828]), 98.

11. Joseph E. Hutton, *A History of the Moravian Church* (Grand Rapids: Christian Classics Ethereal Library, 2000 [1872]), 128.

12. William Reading to Henry Maule, February 15, 1723, 159, FP XVII; Rev. Lewis Boneval, Jamaica, to the Bishop of London, December 24, 1739, 1, FP XVIII.

13. John Venn, Jamaica, to the Bishop of London, June 15, 1751, 48, 52, FP XVIII.

14. John Lindsay, *A Few Conjectural Considerations upon the Creation of the Human Race. Occasioned by the Present British Quixotical Rage of Setting the Slaves from Africa at Liberty. By an Inhabitant of Jamaica. The Reverend Doctor Lindsay Rector of St. Katherine's in that Island. St. Jago de la Vega. July 23, 1788,* Unpublished manuscript (London: British Library, 1788), 227, 229.

15. William Pilkington, Kingston, Jamaica, to the Bishop of London, July 23, 1769, 61, FP XVIII.

16. Catalogue of Books and Instructions Sent with Mr. Barrett, Jamaica, 1724, 175–80, FP XVII.

17. Queries to be Answered by every Minister, April 20, 1723, 215, 220, 234, FP XVII.

18. Marquis Duquesne's Remarks on the Difficulties Attending the Conversion of the Negros, May 15, 1728, 254, FP XVII.

19. Samuel Hartlib, *Considerations Tending to the Happy Accomplishment of England's Reformation* (London: Publisher unknown, 1647), 21–22.

20. Samuel Harmar, *Vox Populi, or Glostersheres Desire* (London: Printed for Thomas Bates, 1642), sig. A4.

21. C. H. Firth and R. S. Rait, eds., *Acts and Ordinances of the Interregnum, 1642–1660, Vol. 1* (London: Published by His Majesty's Stationary Office, 1911), 431.

22. Kenneth Morgan, *The Birth of Industrial Britain: Social Change, 1750–1850* (Harlow: Pearson Education, 2004), 48, 51.

23. An Act for the Better Establishment of the Clergy of this Island, December 23, 1797, 95–96, FPXVIII; Robert Sewell, Agent for Jamaica, to the Duke of Portland, April 12, 1798, 100, FP XVIII.

24. A Statement of the Jamaica Auxiliary Church Missionary Society's Fund for 1831, Church Missionary Society Manuscripts, University of Birmingham Library (hereinafter referred to with CW) /07D/5.

25. Henry Clarke Taylor, Salt Savannah, Vere, to Rev. Edward Bickersteth, London, February 26, 1826, CW/083/2; Henry Clarke Taylor to the Secretaries, Church Missionary Society, London, May 28, 1827, CW/083/15; Henry Clarke Taylor to the Secretaries of the Church Missionary Society, November 1, 1826 and February 9, 1827, CW/083/13.

26. William Bullock, King's House, to John Hylton, July 21, 1830, CW/03A/11; Jamaica Auxiliary Church Missionary Society Proceedings, July 26, 1830, CW/03A/12; Rev. John Stainsby, St. John's, to William Bullock, On the Subject of Our Catechists Doing Militia Duty, Letter to the Governor's Secretary, August 19, 1830, CW/03A/13; Bishop Christopher to Henry C. Taylor, Liguanea, Jamaica, July 8, 1826, CW/083/25.

27. Trevor Burnard uses this phrase, "foot soldier of imperialism," to described the implications of the brutality that overseer/planter Thomas Thistlewood meted out to slaves under his control. See Trevor Burnard, *Mastery, Tyranny, and Desire: Thomas Thistlewood and His Slaves in the Anglo-Jamaican World* (Chapel Hill: University of North Carolina Press, 2004), 7.

28. Bishop Christopher Lipscomb to Lord Bathurst, March 12, 1825, 16, Colonial Office Papers, National Archives, Kew (hereinafter referred to as CO) 137/267; Extracts of a Letter from Rev. W.G. Burton, Rector of St. Thomas in the Vale, to the Bishop of Jamaica, August 8, 1825, 51, CO 137/267.

29. Letter from the Bishop of Jamaica to Lord Viscount Goderich, 29 August 1831, House of Commons Parliamentary Papers (hereinafter referred to as HCPP) 1831–32 (481); A Few Simple Facts for the Friends of the Negro, 1828, CW/012/5/1.

30. See H. Orlando Patterson, *The Sociology of Slavery: An Analysis of the Origins, Development and Structure of Negro Slave Society in Jamaica* (Rutherford and Teaneck: Fairleigh Dickinson University Press, 1975). Also see Patterson, *Slavery and Social Death: A Comparative Study* (Cambridge and London: Harvard University Press, 1982).

31. Letter from the Bishop of Jamaica to Lord Viscount Goderich, August 29, 1831 and May 24, 1832, 4, HCPP 1831–32 (481). For information on absentee planter James Wildman, see Mary Turner, "Planters Profits and Slave Rewards: Amelioration Reconsidered," in *West Indies Accounts: Essays on the History of the British Caribbean and the Atlantic Economy in Honor of Richard Sheridan*, eds. Richard B. Sheridan and Roderick A. McDonald (Kingston: The Press, University of the West Indies, 1996), 244–47.

32. Return No. VI. Books Belonging to the Church Missionary Society at its Station in Papine, Jamaica; for the Year Ending December 31, 1824, CW/08D/4.

33. Church Missionary Society, *Register of Missionaries (Clerical, Lay and Female), and Native Clergy from 1804 to 1904, in Two Parts. Part One* (London: Published for Private Circulation, 1896), 26, 21.

34. James Macqueen, *The West India Colonies; the Calumnies and Misrepresentations Circulated Against Them by the Edinburgh Review, Mr. Clarkson, Mr Cropper, etc.* (London: Baldwin, Cradock, and Joy, 1824), xi.

35. A Few Simple Facts for the Friends of the Negro, 1828, CW/012/5/1.

36. Ibid.

37. *Periodical Accounts Relating to the Missions of the Church of the United Brethren, Established among the Heathens,* Vol. X (London: W.M. McDowell, for the Brethren's Society for the Furtherance of the Gospel among the Heathen, 1823), 424.

38. Letter from the Bishop of Jamaica to Lord Viscount Goderich, August 29, 1831, HCPP 1831–32 (481).

39. Ebenezer Collins to the Secretaries, Church Missionary Society, London, June 13, 1828, CW/025/2.

40. Henry Clarke Taylor to the Secretaries, Church Missionary Society, London, December 20, 1827, CW/083/18; Henry Clarke Taylor, Salt Savannah, Vere, to the Secretaries, Church Missionary Society, London, June 7, 1826, CW/083/9; Henry Clarke Taylor to the Secretaries, October 11, 1826, CW/083/12.

41. Joseph Lancaster, "Report of Joseph Lancaster's Progress from the Year 1798 with the Report of the Finance Committee for the Year 1810, to which is Prefixed an Address of the Committee Promoting the Royal Lancasterian System for the Education of the Poor," in *Tracts on Education, 1776–1880,* by Joseph Lancaster (London: Printed at the Royal Free School Press, 1811), v, iv; Rev. N.J. Hollingsworth, *An Address to the Public, in Recommendation of the Madras System of Education, as Invented and Practiced By the Rev. Dr. Bell, F.A.S.S. F.R.S. ED. With a Comparison between His Schools and those of Mr. Joseph Lancaster* (London: Printed by Law and Gilbert, 1812), iv, v, x.

42. Hollingsworth, *An Address to the Public,* ix.

43. Bishop Christopher to Bathurst, March 12, 1825, 16, CO 137/267.

44. Rev. J. Mann, Rector of Kingston, to Bishop Christopher, April 25, 1825, 27, CO 137/267.

45. *The Public Advertiser,* June 24 1825, CO 137/267; Joseph Barnes, Mayor of Kingston, and Rev. J. Mann, Rector of Kingston, to Bishop Christopher, June 17, 1825, 47, CO 137/267.

46. For information on Sunday marketing during slavery, see Sidney Mintz, "Slave Life on Caribbean Plantations," in *Slave Cultures and the Culture of Slavery,* ed. Stephan Palmié (Knoxville: The University of Tennessee Press, 1995); Sidney Mintz and Douglas Hall, "The Origins of the Jamaican Internal Marketing System," in *Caribben Slavery in the Atlantic World: A Student Reader,* eds. Verene Shepherd and Hilary McD. Beckles (Kingston, Oxford and Pinceton: Ian Randle Publishers, James Curry Publishers and Marcus Wiener Publishers, 2000); Roderick A. McDonald, *The Economy and Material Culture of Slaves: Goods and Chattels on the Sugar Plantations of Jamaica and Louisiana* (Baton Rouge: Louisiana State University Press, 1993); Hilary McD. Beckles, "An Economic Life of their Own: Slaves as Community Producers and Distributors in Barbados," in *Caribben Slavery in the Atlantic World,*

op cit; and N. A. T. Hall, "Slaves' Use of their 'Free' Time in the Danish Virgin Islands in the Later Eighteenth and Early Nineteenth Century," in *Caribben Slavery in the Atlantic World,* op cit.

47. Bernard Senior, *Jamaica, As It Was, As It Is, and As It May Be* (New York: Negro Universities Press, 1969 [1823]), 40.

48. Extract from the Report of Thomas Jones of the Church Missionary Society, transmitted to the Bishop of Jamaica, June 9, 1826, 107, CO 137/267.

49. Rev. Stanford, Westmoreland, Jamaica, to the Bishop of London, July 22, 1788, 67–68, FP XVIII.

50. Bishop Christopher to Lord Bathurst, September 16, 1825, 50, Bishop Christopher to Lord Bathurst, November 9, 1826, 127, and Memorial of the Magistrates and Vestry of St. Thomas in the East, Jamaica, to the Right Honorable Earl Bathurst, 1826, 129, CO 137/267.

Chapter 3

Education for the Future

Shaking off the Shackles of Colonial Times

Benita P. Thompson, S. Joel Warrican, and
Coreen J. Leacock

INTRODUCTION

To discuss education in the Caribbean without reference to the influence
of colonialism is to deny the pervasive and co-dependent relationship of
the colonizer and the colonized. But to further discuss education within the
context of colonialism, a working definition is needed to bring clarity to this
discourse. Colonialism within the context of this discussion refers to the
imposition of economic and political relationships within a society by another
country. In this case, the imposers were the British and the society on which
they imposed was located in the Caribbean.

One of the features of colonialism is the need of the colonizers to appear
to have the best interests of the colonized at heart, and this is very well illustrated in the field of education. Indeed, the British colonizers of the Caribbean
may be likened to Paulo Freire's oppressors, whose paternalistic approach
to education is designed to silence the masses, and who used schooling in
their attempt to rationalize the irrational and to gain acceptance for structures
which are oppressive.[1] This no doubt is what Norrel London meant when
he asserts that the major focus of colonial education was to "teach students
those values, attitudes and beliefs which were to make them hard working
and responsible hewers of wood and drawers of water."[2] In this chapter, we
examine the legacy of colonialism on the educational system in the Caribbean
region, and explore the impact of that legacy on modern-day practices in the
field.

THE PERVASIVE INFLUENCE OF THE PAST

It is difficult to deny that in the past, the method and content of education in the English-speaking Caribbean perpetuated British values and

consciousness.[3] This point of view is further substantiated by London, who suggests that "formal education in most of the West Indies originated and found expression within the general framework of British colonialism."[4] Colonial ideology imposed itself not only on the subject matter taught, but also on the administrative procedures and management practices in British West Indian schools. In fact, Shirley C. Gordon further notes that "there was an absence of an indigenous incentive for the development of popular education in the British West Indies."[5]

Gordon's description of secondary education illustrates the colonial influence on post-emancipation West Indian education. Gordon reports that the content of secondary education was not in keeping with the needs and interests of the West Indian society, explaining that whereas the society needed to be trained in areas such as science and technology, with particular focus on agriculture, emphasis was placed on the classics and the arts; subjects unnecessary for the development of the British colonies during the post-emancipation period, but that reflected what was valued by the colonizers.[6]

After emancipation, the British government assigned the Anglican Church to a key role: the creation of a new society. Evidence indicates that education in the British West Indies was largely fashioned after religious and imperial systems, with little if any input from the local governments. Historical evidence further indicates that competing Protestant denominations—Anglicans, Baptists, Moravians, Wesleyans, Presbyterians, and Jesuits—managed a vast system of elementary and secondary schools in the region. New churches and schools were then built with British tax revenues and the network of parishes was expanded.[7] Norbert Ortmayr asserts that after emancipation, there was need for a new system of control; hence the church and the school system were replacements for the whip of the overseer.[8] On the surface, the notion of providing education for the disenfranchised members of the West Indian population appeared to be laudable. But evidence suggests that the focus of the education policy in the West Indies was geared to keeping the black population on the lowest rung of the employment and social ladder, while being subservient to their white colonial masters. In essence, the education system promoted docility, subservience, deference, and reverence for all things British.[9]

We believe that this bias in education that favored the Colonial power projected itself into the twentieth century and even right into the post-independence setting. As a result, the countries of the English-speaking Caribbean are still struggling to shed the shackles of colonialism. In the next section, we discuss some of the education relics of the colonial past of the region and explore the impact of these remnants on current practices in the field.

THE SHACKLES OF COLONIALISM

As mentioned earlier, evidence suggests that the aim of education was to maintain a docile population, and we believe that for a large proportion of the former slaves and their descendants, this was the case. However, some came to the realization that education could contribute to improvement in people's personal situations and there were efforts to make more education available to more people. Thus, what started out as the colonizer's means of control and benign oppression came to be seen as having possibilities for the emancipatory transformation of those who received it, and despite the colonial association, significant strides were made in education since emancipation. Education was, and is still seen by many as the gateway to upward social mobility, and as such, a premium has always been placed on its acquisition. The value of education continues to be so high that in the Caribbean, the trend is for governments to allocate a significant proportion of revenue to education in comparison to other sectors.[10]

There is no doubt that the English-speaking Caribbean has witnessed many significant developments in education. For example, there has been the establishment of the University of the West Indies, numerous national colleges and other institutions of higher learning; the setting up of the Caribbean Examinations Council; provisions for early childhood and adult education; and most importantly, the achievement of universal primary and secondary education in most of the Caribbean countries. However, despite the considerable accomplishments over the years, a number of deficiencies still exist in the education systems throughout the region. The debate surrounding education centers on whether the substantial investment made in the education sector is commensurate with educational returns. Such debates are fuelled by the seemingly low performance of many of our students. The 2007 World Bank report on school and work in the Eastern Caribbean made the following observations with regards to relatively low student performance in that sub-region:

> Despite having received up to 11 years of formal education, school leavers often have no diploma or marketable skills. . . . Some struggle with daily use of basic skills, such as reading, writing and arithmetic, as indicated by the results of Common Entrance Exams (CEE) at the primary school level and secondary school Caribbean Examination Council (CXC) exams in English and mathematics.[11]

Various theories have been suggested to explain the performance of students who pass through our education system. Some point to social and economic factors; others blame changes in values and morals; still others implicate twentieth-century phenomena such as the Internet and other developments in electronic technology. While we are not disputing the possible contribution of these factors, in this paper we have chosen to focus on the remnants of the colonial past as explanations for the perceived less-than-desirable returns for the significant investments in education. Again, we acknowledge that there may be many more conditions left over from our colonial past that influence current education practices, but the ones we want to present are (i) the common entrance examination, (ii) the hierarchical structure of the secondary school system, (iii) streaming, and (iv) the selection, recruitment, and professional development of teachers.

THE COMMON ENTRANCE EXAMINATION (CEE)

The CEE is a predominant and controversial feature of the education systems of the Caribbean. It is often hailed as the fairest way of transferring children from primary level education to the secondary level. Despite the fact that there have been numerous calls for its abolition, it either remains firmly entrenched in some countries or has been disguised and re-introduced under another name in others. How did this examination come to be such an integral, immovable part of the Caribbean education systems? We offer one response: it is a relic of our colonial past.

The CEE in the English-speaking Caribbean is a derivative of the Eleven-Plus examination that was used in the British school system. It is a high stakes examination taken by students at about age eleven to facilitate their movement from primary to secondary school. The examination was used in England to determine the type of education children would receive after they completed primary education. Essentially, what the examination did was to exclude those who were deemed unsuccessful from the prestigious grammar schools that would then prepare them for university entry. Around 1944, the examinations started to be used to assign students to one of three types of schools that existed in England: Grammar, Technical, and Modern. Now it seems that the original idea was that these types of schools would all be equally prestigious, with each focusing on a specific curriculum. However, as we will see later in this chapter, this intention did not quite come into being, and so the schools were hierarchical in order, with the grammar schools being at the top. Hence, the Eleven-plus examination was the tool used to determine the educational fate of children at eleven years old. All indications are that this method of selecting students for the various schools was not without its difficulties. Of the Eleven-plus examination, Harold Dent wrote:

It has to be recorded that since 1945, the "Eleven-plus," as it is universally known, has been the cause of more anxiety, frustration and disappointment than any other feature in the English educational system: in fact, it would hardly be an exaggeration to say than all the other features combined.[12]

Apart from the anxiety associated with the Eleven-plus examination, there were other criticisms that were levelled at it in England. For example, not only was it said that the examination created an educational elite, it was also suggested that the margins of error were wide enough to allow the misallocation of a considerable number of children.[13] The fact is that in England at that time, the Eleven-plus examination was an intelligence test that was largely associated with the work of a then prominent British educational psychologist, Cyril Burt.

Who was Cyril Burt and why did he advocate a measure such as the Eleven-plus examination? Burt was born on March 3, 1883, in Stratford-upon-Avon (the birthplace of William Shakespeare). Burt was educated primarily at Oxford University, gaining a degree in philosophy and a teacher's diploma there in 1907 and 1908, respectively. He studied psychology in Germany and also at Oxford. Burt later taught psychology at the University of Liverpool, University of Cambridge, and University College of London. Between 1913 and 1932, he was the chief psychologist with the London County Council, where he was responsible for psychological research and applied psychology for the London school system. In 1946, he became the first psychologist to be knighted in Britain. Burt was the author of numerous articles, some written under pseudonyms. He is credited for important work in the development of statistical methods of data analysis, notably factor analysis; this in association with his work in intelligence testing. He was particularly known for his work with twins. Burt studied twins raised separately to establish the theory of hereditary intelligence. About five years after his death in October 1971, this work was scrutinized and Burt was accused of fraud. It was alleged that he fabricated the data used in his studies of twins.[14] Ironically, his work also became the basis on which others went on to "prove" the intellectual inferiority of black people.

This Eleven-plus examination, or the intelligence test reputed in England to cause anxiety, promote elitism, and misallocate students, was apparently bequeathed to the colonies in the West Indies as the best means of allocating students to secondary schools. Throughout the region, it was variably known as the Eleven-plus, the Common Entrance Examination, and also as the Screening Test. (Many of us, before we got the name right, thought that our teachers, parents, and older siblings were saying "screaming test." This notion was backed up by the fact that there was often much screaming associated with the examination: children screaming with glee when they passed, and parents screaming in anger and disappointment when their children did not pass.) Lest we appear to be saying that the examination was of no value at all, let us now take a look at its contribution to the education landscape in the region from the middle of the twentieth century.

The origin of the CEE in the Caribbean dates back to the 1950s and, as mentioned earlier, was considered a fairer, more scientific method of selection for entry into secondary schools. But why was there a need for selection in the first place? The fact is that in that era, there were limited places in schools for students to pursue secondary education. The countries of the Caribbean all had grammar-type schools, fashioned after those in England. Prior to the inception of the CEE, only students whose parents could afford to pay school fees and those who were fortunate enough to be granted a scholarship were the primary beneficiaries of secondary education. Referring to the desire for secondary education and the lack of financial resources to fulfill this desire, Gordon provided the following account from the Marriott-Mayhew Report of 1933:

> The facts and figures that we have given suggest that the proportion of the population which can afford to pay for secondary education is small. We had plentiful evidence, however, of a strong desire for secondary education and believe that it is mainly insufficient means which keeps the enrolment at its present figure.[15]

The situation was that many students, who it was believed had the ability to pursue education at the secondary level, were unable to do so because of lack of money and opportunity. This system of accessing secondary education was deemed undesirable and the CEE was introduced so that "all students irrespective of economic status, class, creed, or religion, within the limits of ability, would have equal chances of holding a place in a high school."[16]

Dawn Gunter cites Jamaican educator Alfred Sangster, who, in 1982, described the impact of the CEE in Jamaica and noted that, "in the first year of the CEE, the number of free places awarded, some 1,900, represented the first major attempt to broaden the base of secondary education based on ability rather than on ability to pay."[17] While the proponents of the CEE usually refer to its advantage in terms of impartiality, Gunter posits that social class still played a part in the selection process, and explains that at that time, 60 percent of the secondary school population was from the upper and traditional middle classes.

If the purpose of the CEE was to select students for the limited places in the secondary school in the early part of the twentieth century, then the implication is that the CEE was not meant to be a permanent feature of the education system. It is reasonable to expect that as more places became available to the point where all students completing primary education could be offered a place, then the need for selection would be gone; the examination would have served its purpose and could be gracefully retired. However, this is not the case.

In the latter half of the twentieth century, into the start of the twenty-first, the countries in the Caribbean have all but a few achieved universal secondary education, with enough places in secondary schools for all students completing primary education. However, the CEE or some variant of it remains. The persistent and prevailing argument for its continued existence rests with its advantage of being the most impartial method of selection. The question that should be asked though is, why do we need to select if there are places in secondary schools for all students? To us, the answer seems to be that this shackle of our colonial past is a relic with which we seem unwilling to part. It holds our education system firmly in its grasp.

One possible reason for the seeming unwillingness of countries in the region to abandon the CEE could be the reluctance to relinquish the status that is given to certain schools. The fact is that based on the results of the examination, students are assigned to secondary schools, and the most prestigious schools tend to take in the students who perform best on the examination. What makes these schools so prestigious? Again, the answer lies with a relic of the colonial past of the region: the grammar school system and the hierarchical structure of secondary schools that its existence created.

THE HIERARCHICAL STRUCTURE OF SECONDARY SCHOOLS

As with the CEE, the grammar school culture that is very much entrenched in the education system in the English-speaking Caribbean was imported from Britain during the colonial period. Grammar schools were a part of the British education system from as far back as the seventh century AD. A foray into the history of education in Britain reveals that these schools were originally connected to religious groups such as the monasteries and churches. According to Dent, one of their most important purposes at that time was to ensure that Christian scholars of the era were well versed in the Latin language: this being the language of religion, law, and government throughout Christendom, and, indeed, for anyone who was contemplating a career serving the church or the state.[18] This apparently lofty purpose of the early grammar school even back then gave these schools some prestige. In fact, Dent stated: "It is therefore not surprising that from the start the grammar school enjoyed a higher status, and was staffed by better paid teachers, than the Song school."[19]

With the appearance of Oxford and Cambridge universities in the twelfth and thirteenth centuries respectively, grammar schools became the institutions for preparing students for university entry. These schools delivered a classical curriculum, including subjects such as rhetoric, classical history, geography, and mythology, along with religious knowledge.[20] Indications are that these schools remained committed to this classical curriculum down into the eighteenth century, with little or no interest shown in science, despite advances made in that area. Of note is that in these early days, girls were not admitted to grammar schools and there was no equivalent place of learning for them.

Though the grammar schools suffered some setbacks down through the centuries, they and the type of education they provided managed to survive in England. Even though other types of schools existed, grammar school education was prized. By the start of the twentieth century, the prestige of the grammar school was still widely recognized in England. In the early 1900s, the tripartite system of secondary education was in existence in England. Under this system, there were three distinct types of schools that offered post-primary education: "the recognized Secondary schools (which were all grammar schools), the group of quasi-vocational schools known generically as Junior Technical schools, and the various kinds of Senior Elementary schools."[21] By the early 1940s, these schools had become Grammar, Technical, and Secondary Modern schools, respectively. The grammar schools continued to offer a highly academic curriculum, with their students generally going on to write General Certificate in Education Ordinary and Advanced level examinations, and moving on to university education. These schools produced the highly intellectual members of the community. Technical schools were designed to meet the needs of those students whose minds, it was assumed, predisposed them for industrial and commercial fields. Of such a student, the Norwood Report explains that his:

> interests and abilities lie markedly in the field of applied science or applied art. . . . He often has an uncanny insight into the intricacies of mechanism whereas the subtleties of language construction are too delicate for him. To justify itself to his mind, knowledge must be capable of immediate application, and the knowledge and its application which most appeal to him are concerned with the control of material things. He may have unusual or moderate intelligence: where intelligence is not great, a feeling of purpose and relevance may enable him to make the most of it.[22]

Thus, these students were seen as having some ability, but not of the kind that would benefit from the grammar school type of education. They were educated for work in areas such as mechanical work, agriculture, and craft.

The third type of school in the tripartite was the Secondary Modern. According to Dent, these schools did not focus on the traditional school curriculum, but were free to develop programs based on the interests of the students.[23] The students at these schools were not subjected to the pressure of external examinations. Of the student who Norwood felt could benefit from this type of school, he wrote:

> The pupil in this group deals more easily with concrete things than with ideas. He may have much ability, but it will be in the realm of facts . . . he finds little attraction in the past or in the slow disentanglement of causes or movements. His mind must turn its knowledge or its curiosity to immediate test; and his test is essentially practical. He may see clearly along one line of study or interest and outstrip his generally abler fellows in that line; but he often fails to relate his knowledge or skill to other branches of activity. Because he is interested only in the moment he may be incapable of a long series of connected steps . . . abstractions mean little to him. Thus it follows that he must have immediate returns for his effort, and for the same reason his career is often in his mind. His horizon is near and within a limited area his movement is generally slow [*sic*], though it may be surprisingly rapid in seizing a particular point or in taking up a special line. Again, he may or may not be good with his hands or sensitive to Music or Art. . . . Within this group fall pupils whose mental make-up does not show at an early stage pronounced leanings in a way comparable with the other groups which we indicated.[24]

Behind this erudite language is the notion that these schools were intended for students who were seen as having less mental ability than those served by the two other types of schools: those destined for the lower level positions in society.

When one considers the nature of the tripartite system of secondary education, it is easy to see how, in a country where academic education is valued, a hierarchical system could exist. Indeed, at the time in England, grammar schools looked down on the Technical and Secondary Modern schools, and Technical schools did the same to Secondary Modern schools. What is also noteworthy is that one of the purposes of the Eleven-plus examination discussed above was to assign students to one of these three types of schools, based on their performance. And, like the Eleven-plus examination, the hierarchical nature of schools was passed on by the British colonizers of the Caribbean region to the countries that they colonized.

How did this organization of schools become part of education systems of the region? To what extent has this legacy, this relic from the past, shackled the education systems throughout the English-speaking Caribbean? What impact is it currently having on the countries that fiercely cling to it? We will now discuss these issues.

The notion of a public education system came to the West Indian colonies in the 1830s, and was generally championed by religious organizations with missionary agendas.[25] By the mid to late nineteenth century, three avenues to education were available in the British West Indies: wealthy planters who could afford to, sent their sons abroad, usually to England but also to North America, to be educated; exclusive schools were established for local whites who lacked the resources to seek education abroad or whose parents did not want their sons making the perilous journey back to England; and schools were also established for the academically able of the "intermediate group of non-Whites."[26] For those educated in the colonies, the local schools were patterned after the grammar schools in England. These schools, many of which were associated with religious denominations, could be found in all of the British colonies in the region. As in England, students at these schools pursued a classical education, and, again as in England, this continued down into the twentieth century. As was mentioned earlier, in the mid twentieth century, when there were not enough school places for all children completing primary level education, only the "brightest" selected by the CEE attended the prestigious grammar schools. These students were often the envy of the others not fortunate enough to pass that examination.

By the 1930s, the need for increased access to secondary education led to the proposal of Modern Secondary schools in some of the countries. These schools would provide a non-classical curriculum, a curriculum that would meet the local needs of the countries. However, as was the case in England, the idea of such schools was viewed with suspicion. Indeed, referring to the resistance to the proposal, the Moyne Commission reported: "These proposals of the 1932 Commission aroused a good deal of local opposition, on the mistaken ground that they were designed to lower the standard of education for the people."[27] Why might this sentiment exist? It is possible that this was the case because to the West Indian population, secondary education was synonymous with the British-bred, classical education that was offered in the grammar-type schools. Thus, even with the advent of other types of schools in the region, the grammar-type school reigned supreme. What impact is this relic from the past having on the education system in the region? Let us see.

As was mentioned earlier, prior to the CEE, only students who could afford to pay or who were fortunate enough to obtain a scholarship attended the grammar-type schools. These schools had status not only because of their British heritage, but also because they were accessible only to those with social standing (the economically well off) or to those who were intelligent enough to gain the scholarships. With the advent of the CEE, the grammar-type schools maintained their prestige, being the schools that took in the top performers on that examination. All other schools and the students who attended them were believed to be inferior. This perception persisted down to the present time, when in most of the Caribbean countries there is universal secondary education. With universal secondary education, each country provides a national curriculum that is followed in all schools. Hence, the notion of a Classical education has been removed. Yet, the grammar-type schools are still favored. The reasons for this generally lie in the British heritage of these schools and the fact that they are allotted the students who score highest on the CEE. But in the face of universal secondary education, where each student leaving primary school can be offered a place at the secondary level, why do we still remain shackled to a system that selects students for certain schools in a manner that maintains a hierarchical order, where students are either elevated or put down based on the secondary school they attend? We believe that this may be linked to a sociological phenomenon advanced by Ralph Turner.

Turner presents an interesting perspective on schooling and education, rooted in a functionalist philosophy. In his paper titled "Sponsored and Contest Mobility and the School System," published in 1960, Turner discusses education as a gateway to upward mobility.[28] According to Turner, "within a formally open class system that provides for mass education the organizing folk norm which defines the accepted mode of upward mobility is a crucial factor in shaping the school system, and may be even more crucial than the extent of upward mobility."[29] In other words, the school system of a country is influenced by that country's beliefs about how people move up the social ladder. Turner presents two different ways in which this may be done. These he terms *contest mobility* and *sponsored mobility*. His explanation of this phenomenon provides a lens through which we can explore the hierarchical school system in the Caribbean region. In his explanation of contest mobility, Turner writes:

> Contest mobility is a system in which elite status is the prize in an open contest and is taken by the aspirants' own efforts. While the contest is governed by some rules of fair play, the contestants have wide latitude in the strategies they may employ. Since the prize of successful upward mobility is not in the hands of an established elite to give out, the latter cannot determine who shall attain it and who shall not.[30]

Turner uses the education system in the United States as an example of contest mobility at work. He likens this system to a sporting event in which all the contestants have equal opportunity to claim one of the few, highly regarded prizes, and whether the prize is attained or not depends solely on the initiative and effort of the contestant. The idea is that upward mobility is a fair race in which all runners are on equal footing. Turner's concept of fairness though may be called into question since, at the time this work was published, schools in the United States were segregated along racial lines. Even today, when one considers the well-publicized condition of inner city schools, fairness in the US system is questionable.

Explaining the concept of sponsored mobility, Turner writes:

> Under sponsored mobility elite recruits are chosen by the established elite or their agents, and elite status is given on the basis of some criterion of supposed merit and cannot be taken by any amount of effort or strategy. Upward mobility is like entry into a private club where each candidate must be sponsored by one or more of the members. Ultimately the members grant or deny upward mobility on the basis of whether they judge the candidate to have those qualities they wish to see in fellow members.[31]

This system, Turner suggests, is the one to which the British system adheres. He states that this approach to upward mobility rejects the notion of contest and instead "favors a controlled selection process." Speaking of this process, Turner writes:

> [T]he elite or their agents, deemed to be best qualified to judge merit, choose individuals for elite status who have the appropriate qualities. Individuals do not win or seize elite status; mobility is rather a process of sponsored induction into the elite.[32]

How is this reflected in the education system? Evidently, the Eleven-plus or CEE is used to identify those with appropriate qualities for elite status, namely those deemed of high intelligence, and these ones are exposed to not only an exclusive education that supposedly renders them academically superior to other students, but also the attitudes and interests that would help them to assume membership of this elite set. This is the type of education generally associated with the grammar schools, and, as Turner points out, this type of education prepares students for higher education, to be part of the middle class and to assume the higher-status occupations. What Turner's explanation back then implies is that under the British system, the school one attended served as a gateway to an elite position with good possibilities for bettering one's social and economic standing. Apparently, these possibilities are still sought after in the Caribbean countries formerly colonized by Britain.

How then is the hierarchical organization of schools inherited from colonial days affecting education systems in the English-speaking Caribbean? It has created a situation in which, though there is universal secondary education, a selection examination continues to be used to ensure that certain schools (those with grammar school traditions) are allotted the "best" students. This state of affairs contributes to a situation in which each year, an average of 20 percent of students leaving primary schools enter prestigious secondary schools, while the other 80 percent are sent to schools that do not carry the same currency in the society. What is even more damning is the fate of those students who are assigned to the schools at the bottom of the hierarchy. Students entering these schools often develop a sense of malaise and apathy towards school and education, and in some cases to society in general. We believe that this is far too high a proportion of young people to alienate because of adherence to relics that keep education firmly shackled to the past.

The act of separating students based on perceptions of their ability is even more deeply rooted in the education system than often meets the eye. This is evident in a practice common to many primary and secondary schools in the Caribbean: streaming. Let us examine this practice and its effects on the education systems in the region.

STREAMING

Streaming, the practice of segregating students into groups defined by ability levels, was present in England in post-colonial times.[33] In Britain, not only were schools organized in a hierarchical manner, but many schools further organized their students in classes based on their perceived ability. John Lawton and Harold Silver reported some of the practices and views related to streaming in schools in England. They indicated that some schools either organized internal examinations for new students, or used the results of the external examinations (most likely the Eleven-plus examination) to classify their incoming students. According to them, the practice of streaming in England was criticized from as early as the 1950s. In some cases, "setting" was also practiced. Here, students were grouped for the various subjects that they were studying according to ability. Streaming and setting apparently survived in Britain down into the twenty-first century.[34]

No doubt in the early and mid-twentieth century, the idea of instructing students in homogeneous groups seemed logical. However, back then, as is still the case today, there were many arguments against it. For example, Adam Gamoran writes:

> There are two main problems associated with setting and streaming. First, when educators divide students by achievement levels, they also tend to segregate them by race, ethnicity, and social class. Because of inequality in the wider

society, test scores tend to be stratified along these dimensions, so classes restricted to high-achieving students tend to have a higher number of majority-race and privileged social class students relative to their proportion in the overall student population of the school. Correspondingly, minority and disadvantaged students tend to be overrepresented in low-level classes. . . . The second problem with streaming and setting is that the achievement levels of students in different classes—unequal to begin with—become even more and more unequal over time. These growing inequalities do not merely reflect students' different starting points, they also relate to students' different experiences in high- and low-level classes.[35]

Apparently, these criticisms of streaming were relevant in early twentieth-century Britain and equally so today. And, as in Britain, this relic from colonial days can still be found in school systems in the English-speaking Caribbean. Let us consider the role of streaming in the education systems in the Caribbean.

First we want to establish that, despite outward moves to eliminate streaming in schools in the region, the practice still persists. Whether systemic or practised by individual schools, in some countries students sit in classes with their "own kind" with destructive results. The extent to which streaming is entrenched in the education systems in the region can be illustrated by the fact that even in cases where streaming is not practised on the school level, teachers have the tendency to group students in their classes according to ability. For example, Benita Thompson found that students in the lower streamed schools and/or classes were more likely to engage in disruptive behaviors than those in the high streams.[36] Joel Warrican also reports the deleterious effects of streaming on the self-esteem of students in a Caribbean secondary school.[37] Further is the heart-rending comment of the five-year-old who was overheard announcing that she was in the "duncy" class at school.[38] Also telling is the classroom in which the teacher had two groups: one in front of the chalkboard, benefiting from instruction, such as it was, and a second group behind the board because, in the words of the teacher, "they cannot read."[39] These outcomes of streaming are serious enough for parents to do whatever they can to ensure that their offspring do not find themselves in the undesirable low stream.

Consequently, what is noticeable is that the majority of students in the lower streams in the schools are from the lower socioeconomic bracket. This is not surprising when one considers what is often required for students to be placed in the high stream. It is not uncommon for parents to seek extra tuition for their children, but, of course, this calls for financial resources, and it is less likely for parents of students in the low socioeconomic bracket to have such funds readily available. Because of this "lessons" phenomenon, students from the lower socioeconomic group, when they find themselves in the low streams, have little chance of breaking out. The notion of a lessons phenomenon draws attention to another undesirable development related to streaming: classroom teachers who supplement their income by teaching extra lessons after school using school facilities. There are increasing cases of teachers offering to provide extra lessons after school for a fee. While we are not against teachers supplementing their income, nor are we suggesting that there is no need to provide extra tuition for those who may need it, sometimes the manner in which it is done can only be described as extortion. For example, in some cases, teachers have made participation in fee-paying after school classes compulsory by refusing to re-teach during regular school time any content that was covered in these out-of-school-time sessions. It is almost as if some teachers unscrupulously take advantage of parents' and their children's fear of ending up in a school or stream that would diminish their status in society.

Thus, as with the other relics that shackle the education systems in the region, streaming has had and continues to have adverse effects on the Caribbean. Like the other practices discussed above, streaming promotes conditions such as inequality and elitism in the Caribbean societies. In communities as small as those in the region, such divisions serve no useful purpose.

One final relic from the past that continues to affect the education systems in the region relates to the manner in which teachers are recruited and selected. The process used to recruit, select, and develop teachers that is practised today is to a large extent, influenced by the colonial past of the region. Let us consider how some of these practices evolved in Britain and in the colonies in the Caribbean.

SELECTION, RECRUITMENT, AND PROFESSIONAL DEVELOPMENT OF TEACHERS

As was mentioned earlier, as far back as medieval times, education in Britain was associated with religious organizations. Consequently, those recruited as teachers were also associated with those organizations. Dent points out that:

> for close on a thousand years, from the coming of Augustine to the Reformation, the Church controlled absolutely, and was almost exclusively the provider of, all organized education. . . . Every teacher had to be licensed by the bishop, who also . . . appointed all Grammar and Song school headmasters. With but rare exceptions all teachers were clerks in the orders of the Church.[40]

Thus, in the early history of education in Britain, teachers were male and connected to the church. Indications are though, that by the fifteenth century, laymen were recruited to teach in not only secular schools, but also in schools affiliated with the church. In 1554, when schools and universities were made agents of the Catholic Church, the reigning monarch ordered that school-masters be scrutinized for suitability, resulting in their being examined and approved by the bishop before they were allowed to teach.[41]

Despite this, down into the 1600s, there were several complaints levelled at those appointed to teach in schools. Some were accused of great cruelty, beating their charges so severely that parents were forced to withdraw their sons from their care. Others were considered idle and incompetent. However, Lawton and Silver point out that it was apparently very difficult to have such men removed from their posts. Perhaps one of the reasons for such difficulty was the fact that recruiting and retaining teachers was problematic. Lawton and Silver indicate that whereas some teachers were dedicated to the profes-sion, "others saw it as a temporary employment until some more gainful appointment . . . came their way. Often a master divided his attention between teaching and a cure or preachership, to the school's detriment."[42] Perhaps identifying the crux of the matter, Lawton and Silver continue:

> The financial rewards in some schools were so meagre that capable men were hard to find and keep, and here the master might be a young man straight from university, perhaps without a degree, not old enough for a deacon's order or a curacy.[43]

The constant shortage of competent teachers continued into the 1700s and 1800s. This shortage, along with the costs involved in making educa-tional provisions, contributed to the emergence of the monitorial and later the pupil-teacher systems. Of the emergence of the monitorial system, Dent wrote that it was recognized that "elementary education could be provided at an extremely cheap rate, and involve the employment of very few teach-ers, if the simple expedient were adopted of using older pupils to teach the younger."[44] Lawton and Silver give a very graphic depiction of this monitorial system. According to them, the monitors, also called teachers and assistants, may be as young as ten or eleven years old, and could have a group of ten to twenty students under their supervision. Speaking of their duties, Lawton and Silver wrote:

> The monitor drilled his group in work in which he has been previously drilled by the master. General monitors supervised the overall work in the different subjects as well as in general discipline. The role of the monitor was to teach the units of work, to recommend pupils for promotion and to keep order.[45]

How were these teachers prepared for this role? Lawton and Silver tell us: "In a well-organized school a monitor might be given tuition out of hours by the master . . . in other schools he might receive perfunctory instruction."[46]

Apparently, this system was more prevalent at schools that served the poor in the community. It is perhaps the absence of trained, competent teachers that contributed to the dismal depiction of these schools. For example, Lawton and Silver indicate that in some schools, the monitorial system operated on a scheme of reward and punishment: the rewards being meagre while the punishment was severe.[47] Referring to the latter, they wrote:

> Punishments for swearing, lying, quarrelling, talking, coming to school dirty or late, playing truant, telling tales, being disobedient or absent from church included confinement to a closet, suspension in a basket, the pillory, being hand-cuffed behind, being washed publicly, wearing a fool's cap and expulsion.[48]

The cruelty and indignity of such treatment was compared with that of boys from more affluent backgrounds: "While the upper-class boy in the public school had to be content with flogging as a punishment, the boy from a poor family had a wider range of punishments—though in these schools in this period rarely corporal punishment."[49]

One gets the impression that even the teachers might have been subjected to this treatment since they were, in effect, still students. Despite the apparent shortcomings of the monitorial system and the schools in which it was implemented primarily, there is evidence that in the 1830s and 1840s some grammar schools also adopted it. Lawton and Silver suggest that this system may have survived because of "the lack of or inadequate training for teachers, a high proportion of whom became teachers only after having tried other occupations."[50] They pointed out that where teachers were relatively well paid, they were able to attract a better supply of teachers.

Of note is that late into the 1840s, the process of recruiting teachers through the monitorial system was still dominant in England. This system was replaced by the pupil-teacher system in 1846. According to Dent, under the pupil-teacher system, children over thirteen years were identified and apprenticed under the head teachers for a period of five years. These students would teach during the school day, and receive instruction themselves outside of school hours. During the period of apprenticeship, pupil-teachers wrote annual examinations. They were also paid a salary. The head teachers also received payment for supervising and teaching these apprentices. On successfully completing their apprenticeship, pupil-teachers were certified to write a further examination in order to qualify to enter a teachers' college or to take up a post as an Uncertified Teacher in an Elementary school.[51]

No doubt this brief walk through the history of teacher recruitment and preparation may strike a chord among those who have been following developments in education in the English-speaking Caribbean. Many of the practices highlighted here have been so deeply rooted in the education systems in the region that though their harmful effects are recognized, there appears to be a fear or perhaps an unwillingness to consider alternatives. What are the manifestations of these shackles and what impact have they been having?

As was the case in England, schools in the English-speaking Caribbean have a history of association with religious organizations and of selecting teachers based on this association.[52] In addition, in these countries, there was also the difficulty of finding and recruiting suitable candidates for the profession. Referring to this phenomenon in Jamaica and highlighting a cause, Millicent Whyte wrote: "It was unlikely too, that the local teaching force would attract suitable recruits when their European counterparts were paid twice their salary."[53] As was the case in England, the shortage of suitable recruits along with the high cost of providing education contributed to the adoption of the pupil-teacher system across the region. Writing about this system in the Leeward Islands, Howard Fergus pointed out that these individuals were seen as a source of "very cheap labor."[54] The pupil-teacher system in the British West Indian colonies mirrored closely that existing in England at the same time. According to Fergus, these teachers, also called "apprenticed monitors," were unpaid, untrained senior pupils who were given extra tuition to equip them to teach junior pupils and some of them went on to become professional teachers.[55] They were usually recruited between the ages of fourteen and seventeen years, after having completed standard seven examinations or its equivalent. These pupil-teachers, apprenticed for three years, progressing through a series of annual examinations, and having successfully completed these examinations, studied for an additional three years in order to become an uncertified teacher. A further three years of studying was required before the pupil-teacher could qualify as a certified teacher.[56] Fergus wrote:

> The pupil-teacher system was ideal for maintaining a grossly under-financed program of elementary schooling, but stopped narrowly short of being exploitative child labor. Judged by its purposes it was highly successful and the teacher-apprentices obtained in the process an element of secondary education that they would not have otherwise received.[57]

Thus, though he acknowledged that the system had some merit, Fergus also pointed to its potentially abusive nature. Of note is that though Fergus was writing about the Leeward Islands, he might well have been referring to any of the countries with a British colonial past, since this system was in place in all of them.[58] Indeed, the pupil-teacher system remained part of the education system of some of the English-speaking Caribbean countries right down into the 1980s.

What has this legacy left in our schools? We believe that some of the most undesirable practices that are presenting themselves today are linked to these relics from the past. One example, perhaps a remnant of the monitorial system, is the notion that children must be dealt with harshly in order for them to learn. While the days of humiliating and frightening students by suspending them in baskets or locking them in dark spaces may be gone, the same results are often obtained by some current classroom practices. For example, perhaps believing that they can shame students into doing better, some teachers deal insensitively with their charges, calling them names, banishing them to back seats, beating them, and excluding them from some activities for frivolous reasons. We believe that such unnecessarily harsh treatment only serves to alienate groups of students. Interestingly, it is often with nostalgia that adults who themselves experienced some of this harsh treatment speak of their school days. Many of them recount, almost fondly, tales of canings received for inconsequential misbehavior. Unfortunately, some who have had these experiences are now themselves teachers and see nothing wrong with using these same methods on their own students.

Another relic of the past that is having an impact on education systems of the region is the quality of individuals who are recruited. Today, as in the past, the weak remuneration associated with the teaching profession continues to make it difficult to attract and retain people who are dedicated to the profession. Today, school doors still revolve constantly with individuals who use teaching as a stop gap while they await opportunities to pursue more prestigious or lucrative careers. Because they have no intention of remaining in the profession, these individuals tend not to seek training and merely teach as they were taught. Perhaps worse than those who are merely using the profession to make enough money to pursue their real careers are those who enter the profession because they can find nothing else to do. Because of the scarcity of suitable individuals, there is usually room for such ones to enter teaching. Like the pupil-teachers of the past, these ones often lack the knowledge and training to be effective in the classroom. It is not uncommon for students who have just completed secondary education to return to the classroom as teachers the next academic year. But unlike the pupil-teachers of the past, there is often no program of supervision and apprenticeship. What is even more worrying is that some of these teachers are sent to primary schools because there is the perception that anybody can teach this program and not the secondary one. In some cases, these teachers remain in the classroom for years before they are trained. By the time they do access training, they have already perfected practices that are less than effective for teaching and learning. The current methods of recruiting, selecting, and preparing teachers for the classroom show definite signs of being influenced by the legacy left by the British colonizers.

The question is, can anything be done to loosen these shackles that keep the education systems of the region firmly locked in the past? We believe that it can, but we are not naïve enough to believe that it will be easy. What we are suggesting is a battle against ideas that are not only ingrained in the education system, but also in the psyche of the people of the region. We are aware that there are some in the community and in high places who, like the wise men in Harold Benjamin's Saber-Tooth Curriculum, see these ideas as eternal verities that must be maintained.[59] The fact is that the Caribbean cannot deny or ignore its colonial past, nor the influence it has had on the education systems in the region, but there is no reason to allow that past to continue to keep education in these countries manacled to practices that might have served their purpose but are now obsolete. Leaders and thinkers in the region must be brave and shake off the shackles that are detrimental to the development of education in the region. We shall now go on to make some suggestions that these leaders may find useful for this activity.

EDUCATION FOR THE FUTURE

Perhaps one of the greatest challenges for those who regulate education in the English-speaking Caribbean is the abandonment of the CEE as a placement tool. The notion of students being assessed as they transfer from primary to secondary school is not without merit. Indeed, the results of such an assessment can provide useful information for their new schools. What is problematic is the use of the examination results to assign students to schools in a manner that maintains the inequitable hierarchical structure. Used in this manner, the CEE only serves to divide the society by promoting an elite few at the expense of the self-worth of many.

Abandoning the selection test can alleviate this situation, and relieve students (and their parents!) of the anxiety often suffered as the examination date approaches. A further advantage of abandoning the examination as a placement tool is that the practice of teaching towards the test could be dropped. Because of the high-stakes nature of the CEE, it is not uncommon for teachers to focus on the areas that are examined, while reducing the amount of time spent on areas not examined, but that are vital to the rounded development of the students. The emphasis is on drill and practice in preparation for the examination, and opportunities for developing skills such as enquiry and investigation are diminished. Removal of the CEE as a selection examination, especially now that universal secondary education is a reality in most of the Caribbean countries, would be a meaningful step towards breaking free from these shackles of the colonial past. Does that mean that there would be no scope for students with exceptional potential to be identified and their talents developed? No, it means that all schools would have the capability to help all students who pass through their doors to attain their maximum potential. As it currently exists, the CEE only identifies academic potential. Its removal could force the education system to find means to identify and nurture students with other talents.

One of the greatest concerns of parents in the region is for their children to be assigned to a "good" school. "Good" often means former grammar school with some prestige. This is linked to the hierarchical arrangement of the schools across the region. Indeed, one of the reasons that the system survives is that many of the policymakers are themselves products of these prestigious schools and are reluctant to see this prestige lessened. We believe, however, that the prestige that many of these schools have comes because of their history and their culture brought from the past. While we have no quarrel with a school having prestige, we believe that this should not come by virtue of its being allotted the best students. Rather, any prestige that a school develops today should be based on the knowledge that, no matter what the quality of the students it receives, the school is able to help them to maximize their potential.

Currently, many of the prestigious schools hold on to esteem earned in the past. In many cases, even when they are allotted the students judged to be best, based on the results of the CEE or its equivalent, their ability to add value to these students' academic profile appears inadequate and parents often must pay for private tuition for their children, first when they are in primary school so that they would pass for a good school, and later when they are in secondary school so that they can receive needed assistance with their academics. What is ironic is that at the secondary level, the teachers to whom their children go for these extra classes are often those who are employed at the less prestigious schools. Would these parents transfer their offspring to one of these less prestigious schools to access this kind of tuition for free? Not likely! They prefer the prestige of the former grammar schools. Perhaps this is because of the social ethos of these schools. It appears that the social network that opens up to students attending these schools makes paying for extra tuition worthwhile. What we are saying is that we believe that the reputation of many of the prestigious schools in the region was built in the past, and that currently little is being done to add to that reputation. Modern-day students appear to be no longer as entranced by all the tradition as former students, perhaps because those traditions seem alien to their reality. We believe that this may be the opportune time to begin new traditions: not just for former grammar schools, but for all schools. These traditions could be related to equality of schools, equity of provisions for all students, and the acceptance and celebration of excellence in all areas of endeavor, rather than just academics. Breaking this particular shackle will call for courage and selflessness, since, as was said before, several of the policymakers are part of the "old boys" (we are fearful of saying "old girls" as this may conjure up a picture entirely different from what we intend!) social network of the grammar school culture.

The whole notion of having students attend the secondary school assigned to their address would be pointless if this next shackle is not broken: streaming in schools. As was mentioned earlier, this practice sees students being segregated according to ability. This shackle must be broken at two levels: the policy level and the classroom level. Once the hierarchy of schools is broken, a policy against streaming within schools and classes must be introduced, and closely monitored. However, such a policy would be ineffective if teachers are not trained to meet the needs of mixed ability classes. Thus, the training programs being offered in the various teacher-training institutions across the region would have to reflect this. This would call for some commitment from the authorities as it would require not only programs for new teachers, but also opportunities for those already practising to be re-trained and supported as they work at acquiring the new skills. The fact is that teachers have grown accustomed to working with homogeneous groups of students and most of them are comfortable doing so. Asking them to step out of their comfort zone without training and support will make it more likely that the new ideas would be poorly implemented, or worse, not implemented at all.

The last shackle that we discussed related to selection, recruitment, and preparation of teachers. Current practices are derived from a system that permitted the hiring of untrained and sometimes under-qualified individuals to teach. We saw that historically this was linked to the poor remuneration of teachers. We recommend that this be the first step to break this inefficient way of staffing schools. Salaries for teachers must be on par with those of other professionals with similar levels of training. This would attract more suitable individuals. We also recommend obtaining a level of commitment from those desirous of entering the profession by asking them to access training before entering the classroom. This should replace the revolving door to the profession with a turnstile, permitting entry to only those who are genuinely interested in making a career of it. Another step that should be taken involves establishing minimum qualifications for entering the profession and only recruiting individuals who meet this minimum requirement. This measure, along with better remuneration, would contribute to the recruitment of some of those highly qualified individuals who go off to pursue other career options.

These are all viable alternatives that can be explored in order to bring freshness to education in the region.

CONCLUSION

That the countries in the Caribbean region were colonized by Europeans is a historical fact. Indeed, several of them were colonies of Britain and many of the institutional practices that are in existence today reflect the influence of these visitors. The field of education did not escape this influence. As colonizers do, Britain introduced policies and practices that perhaps served a purpose at the time (of course, being the colonizers, it would have been Britain's purpose). The fact that these policies and practices have continued to exist for hundreds of years is an indication of the strength of the hold that the colonizers had on the region: not just a physical hold, but apparently also a psychological one. This hold is so strong that even after declaring themselves independent, countries maintain and seek justification to perpetuate practices that are no longer relevant and that are detrimental to the people of the region.

But, perhaps what we are seeing in the region is the classic catch-22 situation. In order to break the shackles of colonialism, we need visionaries, people who can think creatively and who are innovators. But the systems under which the people of the region are educated are deep-rooted in the past, a past in which education was not designed to promote such qualities despite the lip service they are given. Does that mean there is no hope? Not necessarily. Deep down, the leaders of the region know what must be done. What is needed to get things going is courage: courage and commitment to doing what is right, even if initially it may not be popular. Yes, we cannot ignore the past and what it contributed to the development of the region. But we do not have to pay such homage to it that we cannot abandon things that no longer work. Those charged with taking education forward in the region must let go of the nostalgia and do what is best for future generations. Only then can the shackles of the colonial past be broken and a new legacy be built.

Notes

1. See Paulo Freire, *Education for Critical Consciousness* (New York: Crossroad Publishing, 1974).

2. N. A. London, "Policy and Practice in Education in the British West Indies During the late Colonial Period," *History of Education* 24, no. 1 (1995): 99.

3. Shirley C. Gordon, *A Century of West Indian Education: A Source Book* (London: Longman, 1963), 3.

4. London, "Policy and practice in education," 94.

5. Gordon, *A Century of West Indian Education,* 2.

6. Ibid.

7. Ibid.

8. Norbert Ortmayr, "Church, Marriage and Legitimacy in the British West Indies (Nineteenth and Twentieth Centuries)," *History of the Family,* 2, no. 2 (1997): 142.

9. London, "Policy and practice in education," 91.

10. USAID Economic and Social Database (2007), http://qesdb.usaid.gov/lac/index.html, Accessed April 28, 2008. Education Expenditure as a percentage of Government Expenditure for some Caribbean Countries are shown below:

Country	2003	2004	2005
Barbados	17.3	16.7	16.4
Belize	18.1	-	-
Br. Virgin Islands	-	17.8	12.4
Grenada	12.9	-	-
Guyana	-	12	14.5
Jamaica	9.5	-	8.8
St. Kitss & Nevis	12.7	-	-
St. Lucia	-	15.6	16.9
St. Vincent & the Grenadines	-	20.5	16.1

11. World Bank, "School and Work: Does The Eastern Caribbean Education System Adequately Prepare Youth For The Global Economy? SKILL CHALLENGES IN THE CARIBBEAN: Phase I Report (2007)": 3, http://siteresources.worldbank.org/INTOECS/Resources/OECSReportSchoolandWork Nov5.pdf., Accessed on June 2, 2010.

12. H. C. Dent, *The Educational System of England and Wales* (London: University of Oxford Press, 1963), 104.

13. Ibid.; John Lawton and Harold Silver, *A Social History of Education in England* (London: Methuen and Co., 1973), 424.

14. "Cyril Burt," *New World Encyclopaedia,* April 3, 2008, 18: 46 UTC, http://www.newworldencyclopedia.org/entry/Cyril_Burt?oldid=685294, Accessed on July 10, 2010.

15. Gordon, *A Century of West Indian Education,* 270.

16. Dawn E. Gunther, "Performance on the Common Entrance Examination of all aged schools in Jamaica," MA Thesis, University of the West Indies, Mona, 1984, 36.

17. Ibid.

18. Dent, *The Educational System,* 10.

19. Ibid., 10.

20. Lawton and Silver, *A Social History of Education,* 117.

21. Dent, *The Educational System,* 102.

22. "Norwood Report," *Curriculum and Examinations in Secondary Schools Report of the Committee of the Secondary School Examinations Council appointed by the President of the Board of Education in 1941* (London: HMSO, 1943), 3.

23. Dent, *The Educational System,* 117.

24. "Norwood Report," 3.

25. Gordon, *A Century of West Indian Education,* 1.

26. "Education," http://www.mongabay.com/reference/country_studies/caribbean—islands/HISTORY.html, Accessed on May 29, 2010.

27. Gordon, *A Century of West Indian Education,* 271–72.

28. Ralph H. Turner, "Sponsored and Contest Mobility and the School System," *American Sociological Review,* 25, no. 6 (1960): 855–67.

29. Ibid., 856.

30. Ibid.

31. Ibid.

32. Ibid., 857.

33. Alan C. Kerckhoff, "Effects of Ability Grouping in British Secondary Schools," *American Sociological Review* 51, no. 6 (1986): 842.

34. Lawton and Silver, *A Social History of Education,* 441–42.

35. Adam Gamoran, "Standards, Inequality and Ability Grouping in Schools," *Briefings* no. 25 (September 2002): 3, 4.

36. Benita E. Thompson, "An Investigation into Certain Psychosocial Variables and Classroom Disruptive Behaviors among Barbadian Secondary Schools," PhD Dissertation, University of the West Indies, Cave Hill, Barbados, 2007, 188.

37. S. Joel Warrican, *Hard Words: The Challenge of Reading and Writing for Caribbean Students and Their Teachers* (Kingston: Ian Randle Publishers, 2005), 92–105.

38. This comment was overheard by one of the authors.

39. One of the authors observed this classroom while visiting a primary school in the Caribbean.

40. Dent, *The Educational System,* 13–14.

41. Lawton and Silver, *A Social History of Education,* 99–100.

42. Ibid., 119.

43. Ibid.

44. Dent, *The Educational System,* 18.

45. Lawton and Silver, *A Social History of Education,* 242.

46. Ibid.

47. Ibid.

48. Ibid., 243.

49. Ibid.

50. Ibid., 246.

51. H.C. Dent, *The Training of Teachers in England and Wales, 1800–1975* (London: Hodder and Stoughton, 1977), 17–21.

52. Gordon, *A Century of West Indian Education,* 5, 9–13.

53. Millicent Whyte, *A Short History of Education in Jamaica* (London: Hodder and Stoughton, 1977), 26. Also see Gordon, *A Century of West Indian Education,* 198.

54. Howard A. Fergus, *A History of Education in the British Leeward Islands, 1838–1945* (Kingston: University of the West Indies Press, 2003), 97.

55. Ibid.

56. Ibid., 98.

57. Ibid.

58. See Whyte, *A Short History of Education,* 59; Carl Campbell, *Colony and Nation: A Short History of Education in Trinidad and Tobago* (Kingston: Ian Randle Publishers, 1992), 37; and Gordon, *A Century of West Indian Education,* 192, 203–04, 208–10.

59. Harold Benjamin, "The Saber-Tooth Curriculum," in *The Curriculum: Context, Design and Development,* ed. R. Hooper (Milton Keynes: Oliver and Boyd, Edinburgh/Open University Press, 1971). 7–15.

Chapter 4

The Life of
Rev. George Wilson Bridges

The Jamaican Experience

D. A. Dunkley

INTRODUCTION

Rev. George Wilson Bridges was not a nice person, and there might be questions raised as to why the present writer would select such an objectionable character for historical inquiry. The fact is that Bridges played an important role in the maintenance of slavery in Jamaica and other British colonies in the Caribbean. In a number of ways, Bridges also contributed to the demolition of enslavement. As an Anglican clergyman in Jamaica, Bridges was in a position of tremendous influence and power. He could manipulate planters and planter-politicians; he enjoyed the favors of one of Jamaica's longest serving governors; he was part of an organization that was responsible for some of the most violent reactions against abolitionism; his participation in this organization also served as a reminder of the pervasive destructiveness of slavery, an impression that helped to hasten the demise of enslavement in the British colonies.

Bridges was an avid writer, who made contributions to the recorded history of his time and of the island of Jamaica. Later, he became a photographer and interacted with important figures in the development of photography in the nineteenth century. To not investigate Bridges is to miss a good opportunity to gain new insights into history of the nineteenth century, both from the perspective of the Caribbean and the wider Atlantic World. This chapter provides a detailed assessment of the time that Bridges spent in Jamaica. The chapter which follows can be seen as part of this account. It examines the post-Jamaica period of the life of Rev. Bridges, with special emphasis on the rector's newfound passion for photography, as it evolved in the nineteenth century.

THE SOCIAL CONTRACT

Rev. Bridges arrived in Jamaica about 1815 or 1816, as a newly minted clergyman of the Anglican Church. Jamaica had been undergoing important changes since the latter part of the nineteenth century. Most notable among these was the effort being made to Ameliorate the condition of the slaves. The Consolidated Slave Act passed by the legislature of the island, its House of Assembly, in 1784 had addressed important issues such as the provision of regular food supplies, clothing, and medical attention for the slaves.[1] Masters who had unused land on their estates were also advised that they should grant the slaves plots on which to grow their own provisions, which would substitute for providing them with regular food supplies. In 1797, the Assembly passed another act which stipulated that only slaves twenty-five years and older should be imported into the island. This act was proposed by four of the most prominent planters in the island—Simon Taylor, Henry Shirley, George Murray, and Lewis Cuthbert—whose argument was that the act was to encourage planters to purchase slaves who were young and presumably robust enough to withstand slavery.[2]

The actions taken in 1784 and 1797 can be viewed as admissions from within the slaveholding establishment in Jamaica that the conditions of enslavement were not good and slaveholders could and should try to improve these conditions. Part of these efforts to recover slavery from further deterioration focused on how the slaves could improve the conditions themselves. Slaveholders were thus encouraged to provide the slaves with the means to grow their own food. They were also to receive better medical attention, which would aid them in their self-improvement; and only slaves seen as old enough to survive the institution were to be imported into the island. None of this is to suggest that the slaveholders were interested in helping the slaves to achieve any kind of independence or freedom. Ameliorating slavery was motivated by the desire to maintain and prolong the institution, rather than to end it. The measures were adopted partly in response to the campaign to abolish the slave trade, which had been growing in England since 1780, and which would achieve its objective in 1807 when the British Slave Trade was officially abolished. Abolition itself stimulated additional legislation to protect the institution of slavery. In 1816, around the same time that Rev. Bridges made his appearance in Jamaica, the Assembly revamped the Slave Act. The stipulations were delivered in stronger language and the penalties were severer. Higher fines were imposed on masters who failed to regularly supply the slaves with the means for their maintenance and protection.[3]

Slave Registration, adopted in the following year, was another measure that aided in the maintenance of slavery. It gave the government of Jamaica and colonial authorities in England a mechanism through which to monitor abuses by the masters that had the potential to damage the slave system. Registration was renewed at three-year intervals and provided data on slave births and deaths, and the conditions under which those births and deaths had taken place. Less than desirable conditions would, in theory, stimulate sanctions against slave masters.[4] These measures did not stop the abuses faced by the slaves, but the attention that was being placed on these incidents made it harder for slaveholders to commit them without reprisal. When the slave named Cuffee, for instance, was murdered by his owner, Thomas Ludford, in 1817, news of the incident quickly reached the governor of Jamaica, the Duke of Manchester. Manchester responded by calling the murder "one of singular atrocity," and issued an order for Ludford's apprehension and trial. Ludford, who was living in the parish of Clarendon, fled the island to escape the sanctions.[5]

Similar developments were recorded in other colonies of Britain in the Caribbean; Jamaica was not alone in the attempts to Ameliorate slavery to protect the institution. In 1811, for example, the sadistic slave master, Arthur William Hodge, was hanged for murdering several of his slaves on his plantation in the British Virgin Islands.[6] In 1824, all British Caribbean colonies adopted additional measures designed to further Ameliorate slavery, measures which this time had originated in England, and which put all of the colonies in practically the same position with regards to the effort to improve and preserve slavery.

Rev. Bridges joined that section of the Jamaican slaveholding elite that supported the measures to prolong the life of slavery. He would later comment, however, that in light of the changes that he had seen, Jamaica would become "one of the first colonies from which Slavery will be finally eradicated."[7] Like the elite that he supported, Bridges was of the view that the colonial inhabitants, meaning the whites in Jamaica, should be allowed the chance to control the pace at which emancipation would evolve in the island. Interference from any quarter, whether from the Colonial Office in London or from the antislavery campaigners, would only increase the anxieties of the slaveholders which, in the end, would encourage them to return to old practices out of the fear of losing control of the island because of an emancipation that had materialized too quickly. Bridges did not, it is true, propose any specific date when Jamaica or other colonies would be ready for freedom. His main concern was always to protect the social order, and if this meant delaying emancipation for an indefinite period, he was willing to support that decision.

He reacted almost violently to British abolitionists William Wilberforce and Thomas Clarkson in his later publications, arguing that their demands for immediate emancipation had ignored the developments which had taken place as a result of Amelioration. Bridges accused Wilberforce and Clarkson of reaching "inaccurate and premature" conclusions based on "false" information about slavery and Amelioration process.[8] These statements indeed confirmed, as Elsa Goveia has noted, that Bridges became "a most determined advocate of the planter government." Less certain, however, is Goveia's other suggestion that Bridges was also an unrestricted supporter of "the system of Negro enslavement in the West Indies."[9] What is clearer is that Bridges gave his support to slavery in so far as he felt that the institution was beneficial to society. He knew that at some point slavery would become counterproductive and emancipation would have to be instituted as its replacement. Becoming one of the actual residents of the colony was instrumental in the shaping of these views, which appeared in Bridges' most important publication, the two-volume work entitled *The Annals of Jamaica.* This work, published in 1828, suggested even in its title that Jamaica should be viewed using its gradual development over the course of time. Later French historians, referring to themselves as the *Annales School,* adopted a similar approach to history as a continuum rather than as a set of sudden or abrupt changes. The continuum is evident despite the fact that change is "perpetual."[10] To understand history, one has to examine how the forces of continuity help to bring about change over the course of many years. For Bridges, the continuum approach was both a practical historical method and a more accurate way to present historical data about Jamaica.

Bridges had been developing this view from before he arrived in Jamaica. He was born in Essex, southeast of England, in 1788. Over time, his father had become a landowner and had acquired interests in the "considerable commerce in corn, malt and coals" in the southeast.[11] Bridges was raised with a great deal of appreciation for the fortunate circumstances that the society had gradually afforded his family. His parents were able to enroll Bridges into a traditional English grammar school. Later, he was sent to Oxford University to study divinity and history alongside the progeny of the traditional British elite. While at Oxford, Bridges developed a greater attachment to the social order and a growing interest in and respect for the past. He was particularly intrigued by the larger questions relating to the processes that had caused the formation, evolution, and development of societies, especially his own society of England. Bridges would go on to join the established Church of England after having earned his bachelor's degree in divinity and history at Oxford. It was while he was at Oxford that Bridges also wrote his first known book, *Alpine Sketches,* published in 1814. This book offered a preview of some of his early conservatism and prejudices.

Bridges wrote *Alpine Sketches* during the summer of 1814 while on a tour of Europe. He wrote about having started his tour in Germany, which he slightly regretted, stating that it "seemed a bad omen at the outset of my tour."[12] He would go on to provide further proof that he had developed a hierarchy that he had arranged for European societies. Germany was not at the top of this hierarchy, neither was France. Bridges recorded his disappointment in France because of the degeneration into extremism which had followed in the wake of its 1789 revolution. Here, Bridges was referring specifically to Napoleon Bonaparte, whom he viewed as a usurper who had assumed the reins of power in France to signal the climax of an age of extremity. Bonaparte's rise was in this sense not an accident; it was the result of historical processes occurring over several years, starting from the outbreak of the bloody revolution. That revolution itself was preceded by monarchical abuses, which had alienated the French people from their monarch. Some of these views slowly revealed that Bridges was influenced by the ideas of the Enlightenment philosopher Jean Jacques Rousseau, himself a Genevan observer of European history and contemporary affairs.

Bridges recounted with a great deal of regret the destruction caused by Napoleon's army in Antwerp, Belgium. With this, his dislike for and distrust of Napoleon became more concrete. Napoleon's army had ransacked and pillaged one of Belgium's citadels of traditionalism in Antwerp, one of its churches. According to Bridges, Napoleon's army had taken "all the paintings out of the church, except a few minor ones, destroyed the monuments, and actually put the embellishments up for public sale."[13] Bridges was also critical of the people he encountered in Leonen, Holland. They had not been touched by Napoleon's forces, but Bridges nevertheless found reasons to depict these people in a derogatory and derisive manner. He commented that they had a "mode of reckoning distance," for example, that was "most barbarous." They had clung to "old poppish legends" or practices of the Catholic Church despite the enlightened disapprovals revealed by the more progressive churches, such as the Anglican Church. Bridges was occasionally willing to abandon his firm admiration for tradition to defend the creations of his own society. He disapproved of some of the practices of Catholicism which, over time, had been shown to be backward by other churches, namely the Church of England. While in La Valais, Switzerland, Bridges dealt a similarly serious and condemnatory blow to the lifestyle chosen by the people living there. They had resisted progress and the price they paid for this was poverty. Sadder was the fact, according to Bridges, that these "poor" people had chosen to remain at a stage where they desired practically "nothing." Their "rusticity of manner, and ignorance of luxury" were clear signs of their self-imposed limitations on "their desires as well as their wants."[14]

Great changes had been taking place not just in Europe but elsewhere across the world. For a youngster such as Bridges, who had been developing a strong conservative view of society, the changes had appeared all too suddenly and seemed to suggest that destruction was on the horizon. Mention has already been made of how distrustful and skeptical Bridges was of the

French Revolution. Similar revolutions had occurred in North America in 1776 and in the former French colony of San Domingue in the Caribbean in 1791. Both had also, along with the French Revolution, impacted greatly on British society, a fact that was known by Bridges, especially after he began his time at Oxford where he started to read widely. The effects that these revolutions had on Britain were not hard to see. Britain had been dragged into a war, for example, with revolutionary France in 1793, for reasons related to Britain's "security and trade."[15] Before that, Britain had lost a large proportion of its empire in North America, which subsequently formed itself into the new republic known as the United States of America. British forces had been ordered to attack San Domingue after the slaves in that country had taken control of it from France and had abolished slavery across the entire former colony. Slaveholders in nearby British Jamaica began to express the fear that the abolition of slavery in San Domingue would spread to their island. In time, Jamaica too would be under a government of ex-slaves. One of the books that Bridges would later write, after joining the Jamaican elite, expressed this same fear, which had appeared in the island from before his arrival there. The title of this book, *Dreams of Dulocracy,* published in 1824, meant "a government of slaves." However, the ideas that Bridges expressed in this book had been fashioned before he relocated to Jamaica, having read about the revolutions in France and elsewhere, having seen some of the effects that these sudden changes had on Britain and continental Europe, and having included in the wide reading that he did as part of his intellectual development, Rousseau's increasingly famous 1762 book, *The Social Contract.*

Rousseau's influence on Bridges needs to be mentioned briefly because of the way that Bridges chose to interpret the ideas of this Enlightenment thinker. Bridges used Rousseau's ideas to confirm his own preconceptions about government and its role in society, and about social harmony and the advisable pace of social change. He was attracted to Rousseau because of statements advising that governments should operate "with the execution of the laws and with the maintenance of liberty both civil and political," and also that governments "in order to be effective, should be relatively stronger in proportion as the people are more numerous." In other words, with "everything being balanced . . . there should be equality between the product or the power of the government . . . and the product or the power of the citizens."[16] Of course, Bridges was thinking only of the citizens who were already free; slaves did not factor into good governance, unless there were changes in the will of free people resulting in the development of the view that slavery should be overturned. When this happened, it was the duty of the government to institute the needed changes, but at the same time ensure that whatever alterations were instituted, these corresponded with the will of the citizens who were free from before. In short, slave societies should change only if the people in charge of them had decided that changes were necessary.

These ideas are important to show that not all British subjects exported to the colonized Caribbean came there empty-headed and there developed their ideas about social hierarchy, which then determined their views about important institutions such as slavery.[17] Bridges was undoubtedly influenced by Jamaica, but he came to the island with well-developed convictions of his own. One of these ideas that would help to fashion his interpretation of Jamaican slave society, was expressed in the story that Bridges told about the Alpine town of Frutigen in his book *Alpine Sketches.* In Frutigen, Bridges wrote that he had discovered a somewhat unique place in Europe that was "worthy of being" the "residence" of no less a figure than the man who was most instrumental in his intellectual development: Rousseau. The people of Frutigen seemed to Bridges to have accomplished that delicate balance between good governance and good citizenship. Their town was small and isolated, which were probably among the reasons why the people there were able to develop such a harmonious relationship with their rulers. This harmony was evidenced by the high value that the people placed on self-sacrifice. They were ready to do whatever it took to protect their town and fellow citizens. One of their famous folktales revealed the willingness to make these sacrifices in the tragic story of two young lovers, Rolland and Hildergarde. During a battle with an enemy, Rolland had mistakenly killed Hildergarde's father, and upon realizing that he might never again recover the love that Hildergarde had for him, and that Hildergarde might never return to happiness knowing that her father's killer was still living, Rolland made the ultimate sacrifice of taking his own life.[18] Bridges appealed for a similar readiness to sacrifice from the enslaved people in Jamaica. For Bridges, the greater good in Jamaica's case was the harmonious continuation of society, until such time that change could evolve without causing severe disruption.

Bridges rose quickly into the upper echelons of Jamaican society because of his views on the social order and social change. He was able to swiftly reap the rewards of the social hierarchy that he supported. He developed a good friendship with Governor Manchester, who had been advocating Amelioration of slavery, which accorded with the views of Bridges. Manchester chose Bridges to be the first Anglican clergyman for the parish that was formed in 1814 named in honor of the governor himself. The appointment as the rector of the parish of Manchester proved to be tremendously beneficial to Bridges. Within a few years, as he later recounted, Bridges had made enough money to consider himself a confirmed member of the island's elite. He added that he had arrived in Jamaica with practically nothing. His mother had given him a loan of £20, money that Bridges was able to repay within a short space of time, and continued afterwards to send gifts to his mother in England on a regular basis.[19] By 1823, when Bridges was already transferred to the parish of St. Ann, he was earning £1,118 per year.[20] His annual salary at that time was £420 and the remainder of his earnings came from the services that he performed as rector: christenings, baptisms, weddings, and funerals. Bridges was one of the clergymen who accepted payment from slaves in return for performing their baptisms. He saw baptism in the established church as a crucial part of Amelioration. As the rector of Manchester, he had performed 12,000 slave baptisms, and was anticipating doing another 5,000 before he was transferred to St. Ann.[21]

Bridges chose Jamaica because, like many other Englishmen, he saw the island as a place where opportunities to improve one's social status and economic circumstances abounded. His experiences after joining the Jamaican white community would, in fact, validate this view. However, Bridges also possessed qualifications that people in positions of power, such as Governor Manchester, looked upon as potentially useful. Although Bridges himself had developed a knack for self-promotion, he became one of Manchester's assets. Bridges would go on the include Manchester's tenure as governor in his major work, *The Annals of Jamaica*. He wrote about Manchester's time as governor as a period in which the "adherence to established rules and precedents" was established. This partly explained why Manchester served for one of the longest—if not the longest—periods of any governor, from 1808 to 1827. Also during that time, Bridges noted, Manchester was able to transform the courts so that they could more judiciously disseminate justice. It was Manchester who increased the number of judges in the Grand Court to four, a measure designed, according to Bridges, "to secure the rights of individuals and the credit of the colony." Manchester abolished the Court of Errors to give Jamaicans access to the King's Council as their highest court of appeal, which in Manchester's view was more likely to judge local cases with greater impartiality. Of course, Manchester was heavily criticized for these decisions by the Jamaican planters, but the criticism had not succeeded in stopping the governor from instituting many of the changes that he had seen as necessary. Bridges even suggested that much of the effort to Ameliorate slavery, much of its successes, were due to the work done by Governor Manchester.[22]

Bridges arrived in Jamaica with the ability to use other people to his advantage. He befriended Governor Manchester fully aware that this kind of alliance was a good investment in his future in the colony. Bridges had been doing the same thing since his time at Oxford. He wrote in *Alpine Sketches* that he had obtained accommodation in Paris, while on his tour of Europe, from a family that was connected to the French Court. The arrangement was made through a friend that Bridges had at Oxford, a fellow student named

T. Elde Darby, who was mentioned in *Alpine Sketches*. Capitalizing on another acquaintance, Bridges made a calculated decision to dedicate book to Rev. Joseph Jefferson, archdeacon of Colchester, someone who could help Bridges to secure his ordination in the Anglican Church and obtain a valuable benefice in England or elsewhere. Bridges was fully aware of the marketability of his Oxford connection, and he therefore made sure that he stated on the title page of *Alpine Sketches* that the book was written by "a member of the University of Oxford."[23]

When Bridges was called upon by the Freemasons in St. Ann in 1827, to address them at one of their meetings in the parish, the reverend took that invitation as an opportunity to also promote himself by stating his interest in the welfare of the colony. Bridges advised the Freemasons that they were the leaders of Jamaica and that they should "step forward" and take their rightful place "as the saviors of our country." He went on to stress that the Freemasons were among the "happy few" in the colony, who could save Jamaica from divisive and destructive forces such as the missionaries or "dissenters."[24] Bridges was frequently critical of the missionaries, whom he referred to with the derogatory term of *dissenters*. He condemned the various groups of missionaries which had been arriving in the island since the eighteenth century, but usually Bridges reserved his most caustic remarks for the Baptists and Methodists. He saw these groups as threats to the social order, and mainly because of their interference with the institution of slavery. Bridges had already warned about the dangers from other outside forces, such as the abolitionists in England, in his earlier work entitled *Dreams of Dulocracy*. This book advised all of the free people in the colony, but principally the slave owners, that a government of the slaves would be established in Jamaica if external forces were allowed to influence the slaves into pursuing freedom on their own.[25] Protecting the society was always the centerpiece of Bridges' ideas, but he was also aware of the fact that showing an interest in maintaining the status quo was a form of self-promotion.

BRIDGES AND SLAVE AGENCY

You might have noticed the absence of the term *proslavery writer* from the assessments made of Bridges up to this point. This is the identification that on the surface would seem to be the most appropriate for Rev. George Bridges. However, upon close consideration of his background before he came to be a resident of Jamaica, and also upon examination of his subsequent interest in climbing up the social ladder of the colony, the categorization of Bridges as a proslavery writer becomes less certain. The interest that

Bridges showed in maintaining the status quo would naturally mean that he would become an advocate of prolonging the most pervasive institution in the colony: the institution of slavery. To what extent then can we say that Bridges was truly interested in slavery? We know for certain that he advocated preserving slavery for an unspecified number of years, but we also know that his motivation for doing so was to protect the social order from which he benefited personally.

How much does any of this really matter? Is it not just semantics that Bridges was a crusader for the status quo and by virtue of that a proslavery advocate? Isn't the end result or the fact that Bridges supported slavery the most important thing? However, historical accuracy demands revisiting old designations that become questionable when more light has been shed on the subjects under scrutiny.

What really makes Bridges a complicated subject to assess was the fact that he was not merely a writer. He acted out some of what he suggested in his publications. One of his fears, as already stated, was that a government of slaves would take control of the colony. This was one of the reasons why even after the 1834 Abolition Act, Bridges proposed the implementation of Crown Colony government in Jamaica. He saw this as the only form of government that could save the colony from diverting into black rule. Of course, Bridges avoided using this kind of strong, racial language when making his suggestion, which is again part of the reason it is hard to designate Bridges as a proslavery advocate. His advice was that: "There can be little doubt . . . that if the Governor of Jamaica were assisted by an enlarged council . . . and left to the more unrestrained exercise of his own judgment, and of the King's prerogative, his government would rather be one of ease and utility."[26] And before Bridges wrote this, he had also complained in *The Annals of Jamaica* that whites in Jamaica had abandoned Christianity which had encouraged the slaves not to obey them. Referring to what he called the "continued depression" of the slaves, Bridges lodged complaints against the whites whose abandonment of Christian teachings had helped to create this state of affairs. He stated that the "character" of the slaves had been adversely affected by facts such as these: "Empty churches, the unhallowed burial of the dead in the fields and gardens, the criminal delay of baptism . . . the discouragement of marriage, and the profanation of the Sabbath . . . models which the slaves can hardly be expected to improve."[27] Missionaries made these same observations and for once, Bridges would have accepted their support. James M. Phillippo, the Baptist missionary, recounted in his 1843 book that "unblushing licentiousness" was rampant in Jamaica "from the Governor downwards through all the intermediary ranks of society," and to make matters worse, much of this was carried on "in the broad light of day."[28] Historian Trevor Burnard has confirmed that for the seventeenth and eighteenth centuries at least, not many white marriages took place in Jamaica.[29] Many planters, however, kept a mistress, an observation that Maria Nugent, wife of the then governor, made in the early nineteenth century.[30]

The actions Bridges took helped to change the course of Jamaica's history. He reacted, in the first instance, against the slaves, directing his retribution towards an enslaved woman named Kitty Hilton, who belonged to the church and was assigned to the rector's household in St. Ann. Hilton accused Bridges of brutality in 1828. According to Hilton, Rev. Bridges had given orders for her to be severely whipped and thrown in a lockup without medical attention. Hilton escaped and walked for the entire night with the open wounds on her body to seek justice from the magistrates and the Council of Protection in St. Ann. These Councils had been set up to hear the protestations of slaves who had reasons to complain about their masters. The only known sanction imposed on Bridges was that he was removed as a justice of the peace for St. Ann. He was allowed to remain as a clergyman.[31]

This incident was certainly not an isolated one. A number of slaves had been lodging formal complaints about the treatment that they received from their masters. This was a sign of slave agency to those slaveholders who were directly affected. It also signaled that the slaves had been capitalizing on the improvements made under Amelioration. Slaves now had the chance to be heard in court, and could testify in court cases involving not only the people who owned or possessed them, but other whites and free people of color in the society as well. In 1822, Bess Meighan, an enslaved woman, reported to the slave court that her "possessor," Clarissa Paslow, had given orders for her (Meighan) to be "severely and cruelly beat." Afterwards, added Meighan, she was "confined in irons during the night" in accordance with Paslow's wishes. Paslow was called before the slave court to respond to the accusations. She told the court that Meighan was insolent and had disobeyed her orders.[32] Six years after this case was heard, Rev. Bridges was called upon to appear before the Council of Protection in St. Ann to answer to the accusations brought against him by Kitty Hilton, a slave in his household. Embarrassed by the summons, the reverned decided he would ignore the Council.

A visible sign of the agency of the slaves was manumission. Between 1808 and 1830, there were 10,793 slave manumissions in Jamaica. The periods when the largest number of manumissions took place coincided with significant events that had changed the conditions of enslavement. There were 1,819 manumissions between 1808 and 1810 after the Abolition of the Slave Trade, passed in 1807 but which took effect in 1808. Between 1811 and 1813, the number of manumissions fell to 490. As previously stated, following the Slave Act of 1816, Severer penalties were imposed on slave masters. Harsher fines, were now facing those masters who did not provide their slaves with regular or adequate food supplies (or land as a substitute), clothing, and medical attention, along with allowing the slaves to become members of the Anglican Church through instruction, conversion, and baptism. After the 1816 Slave Act, manumission increased again from 1,302 during the period 1814-16 to 1,998 during 1817-19. The Slave Registration Act, ratified in 1817 and adding to Amelioration of slavery, also coincided with the increase in manumission. Slaves were granted a measure of protection and empowerment by Registration, the latter of which manifested in their manumission.[33]

The view that manumission materialized in two ways is an insufficient interpretation of what the records state. This view can be found in the work of B.W. Higman, who states that "slaves released by manumission differed according to whether they purchased their freedom or were manumitted by a benefactor."[34] In all cases, the slaves were the ones ultimately responsible for their release from slavery through manumission. Manumissions demonstrated slave agency even when these resulted from bequests made in the wills of masters for their slaves to be freed following their deaths. There was always, even in these instances, a price that the slaves had to pay in order to be freed. Often, this price was a prolonged period of servitude until "the death of a devisee."[35] A number of manumissions were also paid for by the slaves in question, who used their own savings in the transactions. They negotiated mutually acceptable prices with their owners or possessors. These prices could be as low as £50 or as high as £140 for each slave that was manumitted. The price of manumission was a good source of income for not just slave masters, but also the colonial government of Jamaica. In this sense, the slaves who paid for their manumissions surrendered payments to two groups in the society to obtain their freedom. Between 1808 and 1822, government earnings from manumission amounted to £15,261. Slaveholders earned a total of £246,874 during the same period. The total earnings surrendered to both groups amounted to £262,135.[36] The price tag on manumission was quite significant. Also significant was the noticeable increases in the monies surrendered during those periods following the critical changes in the conditions of enslavement. Naturally, the earnings from manumission would increase at those moments since a larger number of slaves applied for their freedom at those times, and a larger number were required to make the other payments in the form of additional periods of sacrifice in order to obtain their release from slavery.

Slave revolts were a consistent feature of Jamaican slave society. Revolts were a sign of the discontentment of the slaves and their willingness to risk their lives in the pursuit of freedom. Revolts signaled agency, and following each revolt, slaveholders resorted to a range of reactionary measures to suppress the slaves with the hope of preventing future demonstrations of their agency. Bridges wrote about slave revolts in *The Annals of Jamaica*. He viewed these revolts as an important part of Jamaica's history. They were clear indications of the agency of the slaves, stimulated by discontentment due either to the fact that the slaves had been granted too much freedom, or too little. The process of Amelioration that was introducing this freedom, according to Bridges, was an important but delicate business. This was why, argued Bridges, it was necessary to allow only capable slaveholders to influence the process and pace of Ameliorating slavery. Bridges wrote that: "Mankind is ever prone to embrace a splendid error rather than a sober truth," therefore, the measures needed were those that were "well calculated to affect the senses, and to make a deep impression on the minds of the ignorant multitude." Bridges blamed "the dangerous influx of barbarous Africans" before the Abolition of the Slave Trade for the revolts which occurred in Jamaica during that period. It was the enslaved Africans newly imported into the country, he added, who had "overpowered those indulgencies" that "masters were anxious to confer."[37] Beyond the prejudicial views which were unleashed in these remarks, the trepidation that revolts aroused in Bridges was just as visible.

It was within the context of this fear that Bridges delivered his account of Tacky's Revolt in 1760. He recounted the underhanded measures that the slaves had resorted to in preparation for the unrest, stating that they found it "necessary to observe the strictest secrecy in their midnight consultations." This was such a tumultuous and widespread revolt, he added, that Martial Law was declared and the Maroons were approached to assist the Militia with the suppression of the rebels. Extreme measures were adopted in its aftermath, showing further the extent of the damage caused by this slave revolt. It had forced the slaveholding elite to resort to every extremity that the law provided to avoid future revolts from occurring. Bridges mentioned that slaves requiring leave from the plantations had to obtain tickets from managers or overseers. The slaves could no longer play drums or blow horns; these were seen as attempts to sound alarms. They were banned from gaming and drinking. Manumitted slaves had to wear a blue cross on their right shoulder to distinguish them from slaves. No slave was allowed to travel on a Sunday, except for the purpose of selling fresh milk and fish. All taverns and shops that sold to slaves were to be closed on Sundays as well.[38]

Although Bridges supported these measures and saw them as necessary, he expressed his disappointment with their necessity. He highlighted the fact that these measures were imposed because of what the slaves had done. They stood as a testimony to the power that the slaves had. This power had made the measures both "imperfect and precarious" because of the fact that they "seldom inspire virtue," and "can never be expected to restrain vice." Other problems were created by these very same measures. One by one, each of them was "disregarded by its objects, distrusted by its framers, and made the subject of bitter reproach by its enemies."[39] In effect, the slaves by virtue of the agency that they had demonstrated in the recent revolt led by Tacky, had forced the slave masters to divulge further evidence of their own relative powerlessness over the slaves. This powerlessness was made even clearer by the disgruntlements expressed by the same architects of the measures which were adopted to supposedly prevent acts of violent resistance by the slaves in the future. Slaveholders had also, because of the same measures, exposed themselves to more serious criticism from anyone who had a grouse with slavery. The slave revolt had helped to transform the slaveholders "from being considered ornaments of empire . . . almost overnight" into being considered as "pariahs," to borrow Trevor Burnard's statement made while observing other causes of the transformation of masters into "pariahs."[40] It was an important turnaround because it would aid the campaigns against the slave trade and slavery later in the eighteenth century and afterwards.

One of the points that Elsa Goveia makes about Bridges is that he distorted the history of Jamaica. This is surely another view that needs to be reconsidered.[41] Bridges, while writing in support of the slaveholders, inadvertently revealed a great deal about the condition of the slaves. The views expressed by Bridges were those which the slaveholders also held, views that revealed some of their deepest fears concerning enslavement, some of their failures when dealing with the slaves, and some of the difficulties that they were encountering while trying to retain control over a slave population whose determination to obtain freedom was not a figment of anyone's imagination. Freedom by any means necessary was becoming increasingly visible, and Bridges, observing events unfolding in Jamaica, found ample proof that this was true. He was not engaged in distortion at all; he did not conjure up a "host of imaginary enemies."[42] He was recording Jamaica's history from the slaveholders' perspective, but was also including the slaves in this recording of events. In a number of ways, he showed that the slaves were makers of Jamaica's history before the abolition of slavery just as the slaveholders were.

When the 1831 slave rebellion erupted, Bridges had acquired a sufficiently important status in the society to embark on a campaign whose objective, in his view, was to protect the society that had given him such an ample, and intellectually productive life. That rebellion occurred at a time when Bridges was very much a confirmed member of the Jamaican elite. He had already delivered an address to the powerful Freemasons in St. Ann. He had, in that same year, disregarded a summons to appear before the Council of Protection in St. Ann, and the only known repercussion was the loss of his appointment as a justice of the peace in the parish. Bridges was still a member of the powerful Anglican clergy. Early in 1832, he joined the organization known as the Colonial Church Union (CCU) as one of its founding members, and through that organization, Bridges was implicated in attacks against Baptist and Methodist missionaries and their chapels and meeting houses in St. Ann.[43]

The CCU did not confine its activities to the parish of St. Ann. There were branches of the organization in several parishes. Attacks on Baptist missionary William Knibb were recorded in Falmouth in the parish of Trelawny in 1832. According to one report, "Mr. Knibb, one of the missionaries, paid a visit to Falmouth early in March. For three successive nights his lodging was stoned, and he was cautioned by two respectable gentlemen against venturing out in the evening, as a party had clubbed together to tar and feather him." Recounting similar events in St. Ann, the report also stated that, "On Friday night, February 10th, at about 10 o'clock, a number of men rushed into the chapel at St. Ann's Bay, and violently destroyed the windows with part of the pews and benches . . . and on the following Tuesday, in the forenoon, the whole buildings, comprising the chapel and residence, were pulled down and the materials stolen." The missionaries identified "The Colonial Church Union" in their reports on the attacks, and added that "the predominant object" of the organization was "to procure the expulsion of all the Missionaries from the island."[44] The missionaries estimated that the damage caused by the attacks on their establishments had amounted to £20,000.[45] This figure was reduced to £12,750 by an independent inquiry that was commissioned by the British monarchy, after receiving news of the attacks from the Jamaican government. The Jamaican authorities considered the matter as quite a serious one, which also warranted the attention of British parliamentarians, as well as the crown. The only disagreement was the amount of compensation that was to be paid to the missionary societies. No other attempt was made to downplay the attacks in which the CCU had been implicated.[46]

A local newspaper in Jamaica established that Bridges was linked to the CCU and the activities that its members had undertaken. He was described in this newspaper as "the Rev. 'Trooper'" of the organization, and dissatisfaction was expressed in light of the fact that Bridges was one of the "servants of the Most High God."[47] These were very serious allegations since Bridges had an association with the Church of England as one of the clergymen in Jamaica. Considering this along with the recently ended slave rebellion, officials in London became even more concerned about the abolition of slavery. The Jamaica rebellion was quite costly. An estimated £161,570 was spent on suppressing it. The lives lost increased that cost quite tremendously. Even planters could not deny that the rebellion had significantly damaged their labor supply. About 200 slaves were killed during the rebellion, and another 500 were executed in its aftermath.[48] Without a doubt, the role that Bridges played after this rebellion placed him on the wrong side of history. His involvement with the CCU implicated him in the events which were unfolding just prior to the decision in London to abolish the institution of slavery. The CCU itself was formed in January 1832 and was ended by Royal Proclamation in January 1833. Its supporters decried its downfall after just one year, and were convinced that the CCU was brought to an end by the forces of change, whose influence had reached both the government of Jamaica and the authorities in Britain. The proslavery newspaper in Jamaica, *The Kingston Chronicle and City Advertiser,* announced that it was indeed "the clamorous complaints of the Sectarian Party," which had "forced upon the Government" the proclamation from the royals that brought the existence of the CCU to a close.[49]

FINAL WORDS ON ABOLITION AND ITS AFTERMATH

Bridges addressed the issue of abolition in a letter published in 1835. It remains the last known publication in which he mentioned slavery, along with its abolition. He entitled this extensive letter *Emancipation Unmask'd,* which gave an indication that he was not one of the supporters of the decision to end slavery in 1834. Bridges was still adamant that slavery should have remained and still did not specify any timeframe for ending it. He described abolition as "a rash experiment" and a "great national error," and went further to predict that it would cause the ruin of the British colonies in the Caribbean.[50] Before the problems he highlighted would fully unfold, Bridges suggested the adoption of measures to protect the plantations and the social order of the colonies. It was clear from what he said in his letter that he believed that the former slaveholders were not ready for the abolition of slavery. This further positioned them as the opponents of the former slaves, who, of course, wanted nothing short of unfettered freedom. Bridges was, in fact, describing a dialectical relationship between the former slaveholders and former slaves. According to the reverend, it was this relationship that would shape colonial life in the coming years. As it turned out, he was right.

In *Emancipation Unmask'd,* Bridges had therefore suggested measures which, in his view, the former slaveholders would be well advised to use if they were to successfully counteract the ex-slaves. Now known as apprentices in Jamaica and in most of the other colonies, the ex-slaves were determined to end every last vestige of enslavement. This meant working for wages that they felt were fair, paying household rents which were just, and receiving equal treatment in all other aspects of life involving interactions with the people and institutions once responsible for their enslavement. The endeavor of the ex-slaves to accomplish these objectives were adequately recorded by observers from Britain and America, who visited the colonies during what was known as the period of Apprenticeship.[51] It was this system of Apprenticeship, under which the ex-slaves classified as apprentices, which was the source of many of their problems with making the transition from slavery to complete emancipation. Apprenticeship regulations imposed on the former slaves an additional period of partial enslavement, in which they were required to work for their former slaveholders for forty-five hours per week without compensation. Only the very young enslaved children, those below five years of age, were granted full freedom in 1834. All the others had to wait until Apprenticeship was deemed a failure and abandoned in 1838.

For George Bridges, writing as early as 1835, Apprenticeship was a shortsighted plan for other reasons. It gave the apprentices the promise of freedom, which empowered them even more than they were empowered before. Apprenticeship, according to Bridges, was not "slavery disguised," as one Baptist missionary would describe it, but "half slavery," since it gave former masters only a portion of the power that they once had over the now former slaves.[52] Considering the position that the former slaveholders were in, Bridges thus proposed that they should employ the services of immigrant laborers from Europe, whose presence in Jamaica would weaken the position of the ex-slaves and their ability to use work stoppages or the refusal to work to sabotage plantation production. Bridges also suggested that the plantation owners, in particular, should gradually move towards the mechanization of production to reduce their reliance on laborers, who could be the source of a great deal of trouble for the planters. A third suggestion was Crown Colony government, which would have the power to better control the labor force.[53] Every one of these suggestions was implemented in some form in Jamaica in due course.

I am not suggesting that Bridges was able to predict future events in Jamaica. At least one of his suggestions was already unfolding when he was writing *Emancipation Unmask'd*. A recently published study by Verene Shepherd has reminded us of the presence of a short-lived experiment with white immigrant laborers in Jamaica in 1835.[54] The proposals that Bridges made provided (rather than predicted) an early indication of how the former slaveholders, especially the planters, viewed emancipation. These views established, as Shepherd has suggested in her study, the primary role that contestation would continue to play in Jamaica as the former slaves and former masters competed for control of the colonial landscape. Bridges' proposals also showed the peculiar interest of the former slaveholders in combining modern and pre-modern ideas, which was visible in their effort to maintain the plantation economy using many of the same practices that they had used during slavery. This singular endeavor which reeks of both intransigence and evolution can help modern-day historians to develop further their descriptions and analyses of the period. Important also was the fact that Bridges highlighted in his propositions the discordance between metropolitan views of the colonies and those of the British people who were colonial residents. This is a dispute that had gained strength with the rise of abolitionism in Britain and would continue, as Bridges indicated, to sharpen distinctions between Britons in Britain and Britons abroad. In many respects, as some of the recent literature has been showing, the measurements used to define Britishness in Britain in fact, predicated on oppositional features identified in colonies such as Jamaica.[55]

CONCLUSION

George Bridges had arrived in Jamaica with his wife, Elizabeth Raby, nee Brooks. She left him in 1834 to return to England, and took with her their first-born child, who was named George after his father. The departure of his wife had a serious, adverse effect on Bridges. He wrote about it with noticeable regret in his unpublished account of his life that he completed in 1862. In addition, he lost his three daughters, who were still quite young, in 1837 from a tragic boating accident in Kingston Harbor on New Year's Day. Recounting their accidental deaths, Bridges said that the loss of his daughters had "utterly crushed" him. It was in that same year, having lost so much in his personal life, that he decided to leave Jamaica and never return. He took his other son, William, with him on a tour of "*the backwoods*" of Canada, where Bridges said that he developed his interest in photography.[56] When he left Jamaica, he did this for personal reasons, but we cannot discount the fact that he had also suffered another crushing defeat when slavery was abolished in 1834.

The same man who had written so much about slavery, decided to never again write about the issue after the publication of his extensive 1835 letter. This indicates to this writer that Bridges was far less interested in slavery than designating him as a proslavery writer would suggest. His interest in the social order that slavery had helped to establish and maintain was greater. Early influence from the work of Rousseau had helped to shape the views Bridges later expressed in his publications about Jamaican society while he was a resident of the island. He acknowledged his defeat when abolition was enacted. Embittered by the Abolition Act, Bridges decided to outline measures that he thought could help to salvage what was left of the social order. Always central to his views was that the slaves and then ex-slaves had tremendous power and had demonstrated this in their revolts and other acts of resistance. There is little reason to dispute that Bridges was conservative, and that his conservatism manifested in reprehensible and insensitive acts of violence against at least one slave (based on what is currently known), and support for the persecution suffered by missionaries, who were viewed by Bridges as the facilitators of the social unrest caused by the enslaved. However, Bridges is interesting for the same reasons he can be hated and disregarded. His views were shared by others and he did not act alone. He represents the time in which he lived and the people he considered his compatriots and equals. Subjecting him to further study is therefore a matter worth exploring.

Notes

1. Robert E. Luster, *The Amerlioration of the Slaves in the British Empire, 1790–1833* (New York: Peter Lang, 1995), 4.

2. Copy of Letter from Simon Taylor, Henry Shirley, George Murray, and Lewis Cuthbert, Esquires, to the Earl of Balcarres; Dated December 12, 1797; and Transmitted in His Lordship's Letter to the Duke of Portland, of December 1797, 3–5, House of Lords Record Office (herinafter referred to as HLRO) HL/PO/JO/10/8/115.

3. An Act for the Subsistence, clothing, and the better regulation and government of slaves; for enlarging the powers of the council of protection; for preventing the improper trnasfer of Slaves, and for other purposes.—December 19, 1816, 52–74, House of Commons Parliamentary Papers, hereinafter referred to as HCPP) 1818 (433).

4. For information on slave registration, see B.W. Higman, *Slave Population and Economy in Jamaica, 1807–1834* (Kingston: The Press University of the West Indies, 1995).

5. Copy of a Letter from His Grace, the Duke of Manchester to Earl Bathurst; with Two Enclosures. King's House, Jamaica, June 21, 1817, 259, and Copy of a Letter from the Earl Bathurst to His Grace the Duke of Manchester. Downing Street, August 11, 1817, 267, HCPP 1818 (433).

6. See John Andrew, *The Hanging of Arthur Hodge: A Caribbean Anti-Slavery Milestone* (Bloomington: Xlibris Corp., 2000).

7. G. W. Bridges, *Dreams of Dulocracy* (London: Whitmore, 1824), 42.

8. G. W. Bridges, *A Voice from Jamaica; in Reply to William Wilberforce, Esq. M.P.* (London: Longman, Hurst, Rees, Orme, Brown, and Green, 1823), 9.

9. Elsa V. Goveia, *A Study on the Historiography of the British West Indies to the End of the Nineteenth Century* (Mexico: Instituto Panamericano de Geografia e Historia, 1956), 102, 106.

10. Marc Bloch, a member of the French *Annales School,* was one of the proponents of viewing history as a continuum. See Bloch, *The Historian's Craft* (Manchester: Manchester University Press, 1992). See especially the chapter "Historical
Time" in which Bloch states on page 24 that in history, "time is, in essence, a continuum. It is also perpetual change."

11. Estate and Family Records, 26 December 1811, Essex Record Office or ERO,
D/DC 36/15 and D/DC 36/13, 14.

12. G.W. Bridges, *Alpine Sketches* (London: Printed for Longman, Hurst, Rees,
Orme, and Brown, 1814), 3.

13. Ibid., 26.

14. Ibid., 10–11, 14, 45, 139, 140.

15. Frank O'Gorman, *The Long Eighteenth Century: British Political and Social
History, 1688–1832* (London: Hodder Education, 1997), 233, 234.

16. Jean Jacques Rousseau, *The Social Contract, or Principles of Political Right,*
trans. H. J. Tozer (Hertfordshire: Wordsworth Editions limited, 1998), 58, 59.

17. The argument that slave society in the Caribbean helped to shape the views of
British settlers upon their arrival in the colonies can be found in Trevor Burnard, *Mas-
tery, Tyranny, and Desire: Thomas Thistlewood and His Slaves in the Anglo-Jamaican
World* (Chapel Hill: University of North Carolina Press, 2004)

18. Bridges, *Alpine Sketches,* 152, 201–04.

19. G. W. Bridges, *Outlines and Notes of Twenty-Nine Years* (London: Published
Privately, 1862), 28.

20. Ibid.; G. W. Bridges, *The Statistical History of the Parish of Manchester; in
the Island of Jamaica* (Jamaica: Wakefield Press, 1824), 13.

21. Bridges, *The Statistical History,* 15.

22. G. W. Bridges, *The Annals of Jamaica, Vol. 2* (London: Frank Cass and Company Limited, 1968 [1828]), 303, 304.

23. Bridges, *Alpine Sketches,* vi and the title page.

24. G. W. Bridges, *A Sermon Delivered in the Parish of St. Ann, Jamaica, before
the Worshipful Masters, the Officers, and Brethren of the Seville Lodge of Free and
Accepted Masons, on the 4th November 1827* (Falmouth, Jamaica: Printed for the
Seville Lodge by Alex. Homes, 1827), 10, 13, 19.

25. See Bridges, *Dreams of Dulocracy.*

26. G. W. Bridges, *Emancipation Unmask'd in A Letter to the Right Honourable
The Earl of Aberdeen, Secretary of State for the Colonies* (London: Edward Churton,
1835), 27.

27. Bridges, *The Annals of Jamaica,* 4.

28. James Murcell Phillippo, *Jamaica, Its Past and Present State* (London: John
Snow, 1843), 124–25.

29. See Trevor Burnard, "A Failed Settler Society: Marriage and Demographic
Failure in Early Jamaica," *Journal of Social History* vol. 28, no. 1 (Autumn 1994):
63–82.

30. Philip Wright (ed.), *Lady Nugent's Journal of Her Residence in Jamaica from
1801–1805* (Kingston: The University of the West Indies Press, 2002), 29.

31. No. 1. Copy of a Dispatch from Sir George Murray to the Earl of Belmore, Downing-Street, October 23, 1829. Enclosures 2., 3, 4, and No. 10. Copy of a Despatch from Viscount Goderich to the Earl of Belmore, Downing-Street, February 19, 1831, 11, 12, 13, HCPP 1830–1831 (231).

32. Appendix, No. 7. Proceedings of the Board of Commissioners of Indian Claims, with the Correspondence and Documents Appertaining to the Same. Honduras. Jamaica, 1820–1823, 69, HCPP 1823 (457).

33. (No. 3)—a Return of All Manumissions Effected by Purchase, Bequest or Otherwise, since January 1, 1808, 8–129, HCPP 1823 (347); Return of All Manumissions Granted in Jamaica between 1817 and 1830, 15 August 1832, *Lords Journals Vol. LXIV,* 463, HLRO HL/PO/JO/10/8/988.

34. B. W. Higman, *Slave Population and Economy in Jamaica, 1807–1934* (Kingston: The Press University of the West Indies, 1995), 178.

35. (No. 3)—a Return of All Manumissions Effected by Purchase, Bequest or Otherwise, 119.

36. Ibid., 8–129.

37. Bridges, *The Annals of Jamaica,* 5–6, 63, 64.

38. Ibid., 91, 92–93, 100.

39. Ibid., 100.

40. Trevor Burnard, "Powerless Masters: The Curious Decline of Jamaican Sugar Planters in the Foundation Period of British Abolitionism," The Elsa Goveia Memorial Lecture 2010, Department of History and Archeology, University of the West Indies, Mona, March 2010, 1.

41. Goveia, *A Study on the Historiography of the British West Indies,* 106. Describing Bridges, Goveia states that: "Few lunatics can have been more fully convinced that all the rest of the world was mad than was this strangely wild clergyman, when he conjured up his host of imaginary enemies."

42. Ibid.

43. *St. Jago de la Vega Gazette,* February 11–18, 1832, 4. Copies of this newspaper can be found at the National Library of Jamaica, Kingston.

44. Baptist missionaries, Jamaica. Return to an address of the Honorable the House of Commons, dated 25th July 1832;—for, memorial and statement of the Baptist missionaries in Jamaica; dated April 19, 1833, 3, 4, 5, HCPP 1833 (540).

45. Ibid., 5.

46. Estimate of the sum required to enable His Majesty to make a grant to the Baptist Missionary Society, and to the Wesleyan Missionary Society, on account of expenses incurred in the erection of certain chapels destroyed in the island of Jamaica, July 10, 1834, 451, HCPP 1834 (476).

47. *The Watchman and the Jamaica Free Press,* March 28, 1832, 8. Copies of this newspaper can be found at the National Library of Jamaica, Kingston.

48. H. Orlando Patterson, *The Sociology of Slavery: An Analysis of the Origins, Development and Structure of Negro Slave Society in Jamaica* (Rutherford, Madison, and Teaneck: Fairleigh Dickinson University Press, 1975), 273. See also Richard Hart, *Slaves Who Abolished Slavery Volume 2: Blacks in Rebellion* (Kingston:

Institute for Social and Economic Research, University of the West Indies, 1985), 323.

49. *The Kingston Chronicle and City Advertiser,* 21 January 1833, Page unknown. Copies of this newspaper can be found at the National Library of Jamaica, Kingston.

50. Bridges, *Emancipation Unmask'd,* 3.

51. See, for example, these two books: Joseph Sturge and Thomas, *The West Indies in 1837* (New York: Cosimo, Inc, 2007 [1837]), and James A. Thome and J. Horace Kimball, *Emancipation in the West Indies: A Six Months' Tour in Antigua, Barbadoes, and Jamaica, in the year 1837* (New York: The American Anti-Slavery Society, 1838).

52. Phillippo, *Jamaica, Its Past and Present State,* 171.

53. Bridges, *Emancipation Unmask'd,* 3, 10, 20, 21, 27.

54. Verene A. Shepherd, *Livestock, Sugar and Slavery: Contested Terrain in Colonial Jamaica* (Kingston: Ian Randle Publishers, 2009), 193.

55. See, for example, Srividhya Swaminathan, "Developing the West Indian Pro-slavery Position after the Somerset Decision," *Slavery and Abolition,* vol. 24, no. 3 (December 2003): 40–60. See page 40.

56. G. W. Bridges, *Outlines and Notes,* 10–12; John Hannavy, ed., *Encyclopaedia of Nineteenth-Century Photography, Vol. 1: A-I* (London: CRC Press, 2008), 211–12.

Chapter 5

"Faithful Delineations"

Rev. George Wilson Bridges and Photography

Russell Lord

INTRODUCTION

Photography was put to many uses in the nineteenth century. It so quickly seeped into various discourses (scientific, artistic, industrial, social, political, religious, etc.) that photography's identity was highly contested from the moment of its origins, if not even before that. Standard texts re-cast photography's history as a series of technical advances or discrete aesthetic movements, but these texts often ignore the broader role that photography has played in the development of human thought over the past two hundred years.

The following chapter aims to describe just one example of how photography was inherently involved in such developments from the very beginning. It does so by discussing the life of one early photographer, Rev. George Wilson Bridges, and his attempts to invoke photography in the search for Biblical truths. Although Bridges was one of the most prolific photographers of the mid-nineteenth century, and was personally connected to one of photography's inventors, William Henry Fox Talbot, he has received very little attention; this is the first major essay to discuss Bridges' life in photography.

Bridges' photographic practice is emblematic of a widespread nineteenth-century interest in the empirical study of Christian Scripture, and as such, his story engages with major debates about religious truths, and the truth of photography, and raises important questions about the imperatives behind these kinds of empirical inquiry. This essay will examine Bridges' use of photography in relation to this movement that we might call Christian Positivism.

"UNADORNED TRUTH"

In 1852, a sixty-four-year-old George Bridges wrote to the inventor of photography, William Henry Fox Talbot, "Long have I been anxious to pay my
respects to you, & lay at the feet of my kind Preceptor . . . the fruit of my
seven years wanderings." Talbot had been instrumental in helping Bridges
learn the photography process, and Bridges was eager to show Talbot some of
the 1,700 photographs that he had produced on his seven-year journey around
the shores of the Mediterranean Sea. Now, safely back in England, Bridges
was attempting to publish these photographs. He enclosed some samples—
actual photographs with descriptive letterpress text—and continued in his letter: "I am employing them as you see: provoked thereto by some friends who
set a higher value upon unadorned Truth, than does the vulgar world."[1]

After an eventful and controversial life as a cleric in Jamaica and Canada,[2]
the Rev. George W. Bridges devoted most of his remaining years to photography, becoming one of the most prolific, early British photographers (see
Illustration 5.1). Although his publication was a failure—originally issued
in parts, very few copies exist today and none are complete—Bridges ultimately found a way to connect the two halves of his life within it, combining
his Oxford theological training with the "unadorned Truth" of photography.
In the final part, which was published under the title *Palestine As It Is, In a
Series of Photographic Views Illustrating the Bible,* Bridges attempted to use
photography to prove the authenticity of Holy Land sites in Christian Scripture, conscripting photography as an ally in the search for Biblical truths.
His search was part of a larger phenomenon in the middle of the nineteenth
century in which Christian scholars and theologians tried to reconcile their
passionately held beliefs in the truth of Scripture with accurate empirical
study. Bridges' photography career, therefore, engages directly with the major
debates of his time (science vs. religion), and poses serious questions about
the moral and social imperatives behind the early uses of photography.

In 1839, William Henry Fox Talbot and Louis-Jacques-Mandé Daguerre
introduced photography to the world.[3] Their inventions were immediately
aligned with accuracy, and were considered, by critics and the public alike,
unique ways to create unmediated records of one's first hand observations.
Talbot referred to the first process he invented as "the art of Photogenic
drawing, or the process by which natural objects may be made to delineate
themselves without the aid of the artist's pencil."[4] Since photography seemed
to be a mechanical process, in which objects drew themselves without any
human intervention, it quickly came to be seen as a more truthful medium
than traditional practices like drawing or painting. George Bridges, perhaps
playfully referring to Talbot's Victorian description, described this peculiar

Illustration 5.1: Bridges in Egypt. Detail from *The Photographer before his Tent on the Site of the Pyramid of Khafre (Chephren),* salt print from calotype negative, 1851, 6 1/2 x 8 ½ inches (the whole print). Metropolitan Museum of Art, New York. While Bridges probably set this picture up, there is a pencil note on the mount stating "Julian took this."

quality as the "faithful delineations" of photography.[5] With this poetic term, Bridges cleverly unified the dual meanings of "faithful" (an accurate copy, or a belief in the unknowable) in the singular concept of photography. It was the perfect turn of phrase since Bridges would ultimately attempt to use the "faithful delineations" of photography to legitimize his own theological beliefs and historical narratives.

Bridges' first encounter with photography came sometime in 1844 or 1845, when he saw the first fascicle of Talbot's *The Pencil of Nature,* the first published book to include actual photographs, at the home of Thomas Attwood. Bridges returned to England in 1842 from Canada and his son, William, began school in Maisemore, where Attwood lived. Coincidentally, one of William's classmates was Talbot's nephew, Val (William Henry Edgcumbe, later 4th. Earl Mt. Edgcumbe), through whom Bridges was put in touch with the Talbot family. Having been much impressed with *The Pencil of Nature,* Bridges called upon Talbot at his home, Lacock Abbey, in December of 1845. Talbot was in London, but Bridges very quickly endeared himself to Talbot's mother, Lady Elisabeth Feilding, and Talbot's wife, Constance, regaling them with tales of his travels and playing to their preconceived notions of the Canadian frontier. Constance wrote to Talbot, "We all like Mr. B. very much—he has a great deal to say & has traveled in a great many different parts of the world. He lived seven years in the backwoods of Canada & still holds a hut there of his own building which he lets to a Lady, on payment by her of one Wolf's skin per annum."[6] After a week-long stay at Lacock, Lady Elisabeth informed Talbot of Bridges' departure "in a Cloke formed of Buffalo skin which he used to sleep on in Canada."[7] Talbot responded "It is seldom one hears of so chequered a lot as that of Mr. Bridges. It is the romance of real life."[8]

Bridges was interested in taking up photography, so with a firm footing in Talbot's family circle, he began to correspond with Talbot, asking him for recommendations as to where to get prepared paper. The photographic process that Bridges would ultimately use was what Talbot called the calotype process (after the Greek "kalos" for beautiful and "typos," image), which produced a paper negative, from which multiple positive prints could be made (see Illustration 5.2). Despite the fact that Talbot was notoriously cantankerous about the use of his process (to the point that lawsuits were brought against those that impinged upon his patent), Bridges had so ingratiated himself, that Talbot had "no objection to Nicole's teaching him the art, if he will promise us in return some good Syrian views, especially Jerusalem."[9] Nicole was Nicolaas Henneman, Talbot's valet and photographic assistant. Although it appears that Henneman never did teach Bridges the photography process, he would be helpful for Bridges in the future, often making prints from Bridges' negatives when the reverend failed to master the printing process.

At the end of January 1846, Bridges departed from Portsmouth on the HMS *Superb* for Paris, and from there he proceeded to Malta. He sent Talbot

Illustration 5.2: Rev. George W. Bridges, *Temple of Wingless Victory, Lately Restored,* calotype negative, 1848, 16.7 x 20.6 cm. Metropolitan Museum of Art, New York.

the address of a merchant on Malta through whom he could be reached. While in Paris, though, Bridges picked up his first camera, writing to Talbot that he was "building an instrument here by Chevalier in some measure an improvement on the one he made for Mr. Calvert." The Rev. Calvert Richard Jones was a Welsh painter and close friend of Talbot's cousin, Christopher Rice Mansel Talbot.[10] By the end of March, Bridges was on Malta with Calvert Jones and "Kit" Talbot (as he was known) sharing with them the photographic paper that Talbot and Henneman had sent. Since he had not yet learned the calotype process, Bridges felt that the coveted paper would be better put to use by Jones.[11]

At the end of April, Bridges reported his first "success in the . . . attempts at Talbotype" (as some of Talbot's supporters called the calotype process), producing negatives of foliage and vegetation on the island. It appears that during their time together, Bridges received training in the calotype process from Jones, but even after a couple of months of work, the process was no sure thing. Having given most of the prepared paper to Jones, who, along with Kit Talbot, had departed by this time, Bridges was forced to prepare his own. Choosing amongst sheets of paper at hand, Bridges only succeeded "tolerably well" once out of every ten or twelve attempts, but even these few possessed spots that Bridges found "fatal to the positive copies."[12] As a result, Bridges made repeated pleas to Talbot (and even one to Lady Feilding) to replenish his supply of prepared paper.[13] In 1844, Talbot supported Henneman in opening a commercial photographic printing establishment in Reading, England, so it was therefore through Henneman, that Bridges obtained much of the paper that he used.[14]

Henneman's assistance was indispensable also in the production of prints from Bridges' negatives, a process that proved all but impossible for the traveling Bridges. After trying to produce positives or "copies," he wrote to Talbot, "I fail altogether," and implored the inventor for further instructions. Even after several months of back and forth on the topic, Bridges still struggles, writing that he is "quite in despair—utterly discouraged by my failures in trying to copy some of the [negatives], & much inclined to give up all attempts in an art which stops short of utility just at the very point when one thinks to have attained it.—I shall be very glad to send the negative to your people to save the trouble of copying myself in any quantity— but still I should like to be <u>able</u> to do it myself upon occasion—otherwise the art is little available, or creditable to the distant traveler."[15] Throughout his travels, Bridges found it more convenient to produce two similar negatives of each subject, and send one to Henneman in England, who would produce the requested number of prints for Bridges and send them on to his contact in Malta.

Over the next seven years, Bridges traveled throughout the Mediterranean region, producing over 1,700 paper negatives in Palestine, Constantinople, Egypt, Athens, Algeria, Italy, and Sicily. He also produced several images on Malta, and exhibited some prints in a local bookseller's shop.[16] By far his most entertaining anecdote concerns his efforts to photograph the volcanic Mt. Etna on nearby Sicily, where Bridges would spend the summer months of 1846 and 1847 to escape "the insufferable heats & glare of a Malta summer." Bridges was friendly with the Abbot of the Benedictine Convent of St. Nicolo at Catania, "the last habitation in ascending Etna," and the Abbot lent him his rooms at the convent since the monks lived there only in the winter.[17] During his stay in 1846, Bridges dared to climb to the bottom of the volcanic crater. He had just positioned his camera and removed the lens cap when "at the moment an explosion took place—I ran off & came back when it had passed, 3 ½ [minutes] had elapsed—& [the negative] stood depicted." Bridges made a second exposure "caught between the explosions," which showed "the mouth of that tremendous abyss."[18]

Although Bridges repeatedly mentioned his plans to travel throughout the Mediterranean region, his correspondence with Talbot drops off at the end of the summer of 1847 while he is still living between Sicily and Malta. In one rare letter from Athens, dated November 1848, Bridges revealed that he has "for the last few months . . . been hovering in this part of the world," following his son's Naval ship, the *Volage*. Bridges explained that he had a severe attack of cholera but had still managed to collect a portfolio of "more than 200 Grecian views & marbles."[19]

Bridges' next letter to Talbot came four years later, in October of 1852, shortly after he had returned to England.[20] Bridges quickly set about deciding what to do with his by now massive collection of negatives and prints, ultimately deciding to issue the actual prints in a serial publication: *Selections from Seventeen-Hundred Genuine Photographs: (Views—Portraits—Statuary—Antiquities.) Taken Around the Shores of the Mediterranean Between the Years 1846—52. With, or Without, Notes, Historical, and Descriptive.* This incredibly cumbersome (but still ambiguous) title seems to have intentionally left room for the series to develop as Bridges saw fit, or as the available prints and other resources dictated. Even the shape and schedule for its issue was left deliberately vague, with each part "to be issued occasionally, in numbers, or in sheets."[21] Interested parties were directed to subscribe through Daniel Alder, a stationer, print seller, and toy dealer in Cheltenham. Perhaps because a potential subscriber could not predict what they would receive from Bridges' aimless description, the project was largely a failure. Copies that exist are partial and inconsistently so.

It may be that Bridges recognized the need for a stronger focus by the end of the 1850s, for he issued part five of his project with a separate, and more specific, title. *Palestine As It Is: In a Series of Photographic Views, Illustrating the Bible* consisted of twenty-one photographs of places of significance in Biblical history, and was probably completed by 1859—significantly, the same year that Charles Darwin published his *Origin of Species*.[22] The remnants of these publications and the letters to Talbot comprise the bulk of extant information on Bridges' photographic practice. But even in the absence of any illuminating archive, there are still several assumptions that we can make about Bridges' intentions with photography and these intentions raise important questions about the use of photography during its earliest years.

THE USES OF PHOTOGRAPHY

To begin with, Bridges embodies a typical figure in photography's early years in England: an essentially unemployed man with a significant amount of time to spend on the photographic process. Bridges had been heavily compensated for his position in Jamaica, but that money disappeared quickly, and when he finally encountered photography, he probably saw it as a potential source of financial gain. Although Bridges and Talbot were from different social classes

(Bridges had come from a fairly wealthy family, but their fortune had been largely the result of industrial development, and Talbot was a member of the landed gentry), Bridges was a bit of a social climber and he used his position as a clergyman, and his interest in the photography process to open the necessary doors for his introduction to the Talbot family.[23]

While in Malta, Bridges must have benefited from the immense wealth of Christopher "Kit" Talbot, whose fortune, bolstered by investments in transportation and metal works, was so great that he was referred to as "the wealthiest commoner of his time."[24] Kit was by far wealthier than Bridges had ever been, and he, his wife Charlotte, and Calvert Jones were traveling around the Mediterranean on his private yacht, "The Galatea." When Charlotte became sick and died rather suddenly on Malta, Bridges, who certainly had experience with tragedy (his three daughters had drowned in a boating accident in Jamaica, prompting his move to the Canadian frontier), expressed his "hope that my feeble aid may have somewhat relieved the agonized mind of the poor sufferer."[25] Calvert Jones confirmed Bridges' compassion, writing to Henry Talbot that Bridges "proved a most kind and good man (especially in endeavoring to afford comfort to your poor cousin)."[26] From these exchanges, it appears that Bridges had been so welcomed into the fold, that even if his personal wealth was dwindling, he had the support of a powerful group of acquaintances directly connected to Talbot. This support was necessary for the costly practice of photography; as Bridges explained to Talbot, "It is certainly an aristocratic art—rather expensive I find it in itself."[27]

Money was one thing, time another. Despite Bridges' diligent efforts and practice, it took him a couple of months before he could report something resembling success in producing negatives, and it would take almost a full year before Bridges could make prints from those negatives himself. Fortunately, Bridges had plenty of time to devote to perfecting the process, since, aside from following his son's progress in the Navy, he had nothing else to do. As he shadowed his son around the Mediterranean region, Bridges probably began to think of his photographic practice as a kind of employment, but despite this, Bridges repeatedly characterizes his situation as an aimless pursuit, referring to himself as a "poor idle wanderer." Even his final project, the *Selections from Seventeen-Hundred Genuine Photographs,* would be published under the epithet "A Wayworn Wanderer." These rhetorical conceits, however, were probably necessary to conceal Bridges' base financial motives from his genteel benefactors and his potential audience.

Nevertheless, in describing his photographic practice as a recreational or purposeless activity, Bridges also seems to be establishing himself as a genteel photographic artist. Indeed, several scholars have attempted to establish paper negative photography as *the* artistic form of the various nineteenth-century photographic processes, pointing to its massing of light and shadow, and overall softness of effect, as evidence for its interpretation as an aesthetic endeavor.[28] Bridges' rhetoric about photography would seem to confirm these hypotheses. Throughout his letters to Talbot, he frequently refers to the calotype process as an art. Bridges gushes "I am deep in Talbotype . . . interested-anxious to make use of the art," and implores Talbot to send him news of "anything new in the photographic art."[29] Elsewhere, Bridges comments that "people here & everywhere, are in exticies [*sic*] with the product of your wonderful art."[30]

This kind of language is not uncommon amongst early photographers, so it is no surprise that their work has found its way into the narratives of art history. It is important to note, however, that the word *art* in the mid-nineteenth century was widely applied to any craft done well; it did not necessarily denote pretensions to fine art or claims to purely aesthetic conditions. Still, even photographers whose projects possessed strict documentary or empirical objectives have had trouble wresting free from the confines of an art historical framework. August Salzmann, for example, also photographed in Jerusalem in the 1850s with the intention of validating the archeological theories of his friend Louis F. de Saulcy through photography. "Photographs," Salzmann declared, "are not reports, but rather conclusive brute facts."[31] Nevertheless, Salzmann's closely cropped and often radically flat photographs have been admired by historians more for their abstract graphic design than for the extent to which they do or do not confirm de Saulcy's assertions. Eugenia Parry Janis and André Jammes summed up this interpretation: "The expressiveness of these documents is unquestionably the result of the photographer's own invention."[32] Salzmann, however, admitted that a mysterious assistant named Durheim produced fifty of the images, and these fifty today remain indistinguishable from those made by Salzmann himself. In other words, even when everything about Salzmann's photographic project (its collaborative nature, its singularly mundane objective) seems to reject the persistent frame of art history, the beauty of the images themselves insists upon their inclusion within it.

Bridges who, unlike Salzmann, signed his negatives (a gesture that could be both a nod to artistic tradition in keeping with his efforts at gentlemanly comportment and a means of preventing piracy) and continually insisted that his photographic hobby was a leisurely or purely creative endeavor, runs the risk of being discounted as a failed photographic artist, but the direction that his final project takes suggests that much more is at stake. In *Palestine As It Is*, Bridges introduces photography as a source of indisputable truth and then projects this truth onto Biblical subjects. Bridges thus takes his place within the nineteenth-century movement to legitimize Biblical history through experiential study, a movement that developed as a faith-based counterpoint to the age of industrialism and scientific enquiry.

For example, in 1838, just a year before Talbot introduced photography to the world, Edward Robinson, the chair in Biblical literature at the Union Theological Seminary in New York City, traveled through Palestine. Robinson's childhood in New England had been saturated with the study and recitation of scripture, as befitted a region founded upon puritanical principles. Robinson explained that "from his earliest years the names of Sinai, Jerusalem, Bethlehem, the Promised Land, become associated with the earliest recollections and holiest feelings." Robinson's voyage to Palestine presented an opportunity to reconcile these recollections and feelings with first-hand experience. Robinson wrote: "I had long meditated the preparation of a work on Biblical Geography; and wished to satisfy myself by personal observation as to many points on which I could find no information in the books of travelers. This indeed grew to be the main object of our journey."[33] His resulting publication, *Biblical Researches in Palestine,* was one of the first critical investigations of Biblical sites. Robinson's book represents the beginning of a phenomenon that Kathleen Stewart Howe refers to as "geopiety," the attempt to "illustrate the close connection between geography and the Bible."[34]

For visitors who, like Robinson, fondly recalled their Scripture lessons from childhood, the Holy Land offered a transcendent experience. One French visitor, upon arriving in Jerusalem, declared, "I truly shivered in the presence of the famous city. This time, there was in my feelings a mixture of those great emotions that every serious and good-willed person feels at such a view, especially thinking of the extraordinary influence that this point on earth had on the destiny of mankind for the last nineteen centuries."[35] For the faithful, conditioned by the words of Scripture, the mere sight of the physical land gave way to visceral, emotional responses, stirred by the reflection that "God himself spoke on these banks"[36] or the thoughts that they were walking in the "footsteps of our Lord and his Apostles."[37]

Photography gave those interested in demonstrating this connection a new weapon. Historically, depictions of this physical land had been drawn by competent draftsmen, but despite the fact that drawings had sufficed before the invention of photography, they were greeted with suspicion immediately thereafter.[38] One French publisher explained that, thanks to photography, "places will no longer be reproduced from drawings that are always more or less modified by the taste and imagination of the painter."[39] Reverend Albert Augustus Isaacs spoke even more severely: "We well know how often *the pencil* is proved to be treacherous and deceptive; while on the other hand the *fac simile* of the scene must be given by the aid of the *photograph.*"[40]

And so photography became *de rigueur* for any project attempting to prove something. It did not take long, however, before the use of photography as evidence became a kind of trope, with photographs being used to prove things that they could not possibly prove. It was as if the mere mention of the word "photography" on one's title page ensured that the contents held a legitimate claim to truth, even if the contents concerned debates of the highest order. The Reverend Alexander Keith's immensely popular book *Evidence of the Truth of the Christian Religion Derived from the Literal Fulfillment of Prophecy Particularly as Illustrated by the History of the Jews and the Discoveries of Modern Travelers* contained prints made after daguerreotypes (unique photographic images on silver-coated copper plates), that were presented "to the unbeliever as the positive evidence of Christianity" and to "convince the unprejudiced inquirer or the rational and sincere believer, that it is impossible that his faith be false."[41] The desire to produce "positive evidence of Christianity" represents a phenomenon that, in a reversal of Reverend Keith's syntax, we might term *Christian Positivism*, and it is a phenomenon in which Rev. George Wilson Bridges plays a part.

THE *CHRISTIAN POSITIVISM* OF REV. BRIDGES

On the introductory page to each part of his *Selections from Seventeen-Hundred Genuine Photographs,* Bridges makes plain his faith in photographic truth: "Whoever doubts the truth of these views, doubts the truth of Heaven's own blessed light itself! For them: 'No hireling Artist plants his paltry desk / To make degraded Nature picturesque.' They are delineated by no earthly pencil."[42] Bridges, the consummate clergyman, cleverly links photography with a traditional religious metaphor in which light *is* truth. As Bridges sees it, God created the Heavens, the Heavens emanate truth as light, which is then faithfully recorded on photographic paper. In this narrative, the medium of photography is the messenger, with its "faithful delineations" tracing the shapes and forms of Heavenly truth.

Of course, the question still remains: just exactly what "truth" is being conveyed in Bridges' images? A closer look at a few particular photographs demonstrates that the photographs fail to prove the points or answer the questions that Bridges raises in his own text. For example, much of the text that accompanies his images concerns the authenticity of a particular place of Biblical significance. In the text for "Arch of 'Ecce Homo,'" (Illustration 5.3), Plate 14 in Bridges' *Palestine As It Is,* he argues that the location seen in the photograph is in fact the site of the presentation of Christ to the public from Biblical legend: "If it could be realized as an undoubted fact that this gateway was the scene of the incident, and exhibition, to which its name refers, what an overwhelming thought for the beholder." As support for his argument, Bridges points to the remains of very ancient structures nearby and suggests that this place must, at the very least, have been preserved "in the general overthrow of all around either for some especial purpose of utility, or by some venerable motive arising from a popular tradition." Since Bridges cannot imagine the utility, he presumes that it must be out of respect for tradition that these ancient stones, which are "precisely similar to those still seen in the most ancient foundations of the old Temple walls, [and] in the enclosure of the Machpelah Cave" have survived until Bridges' lifetime. In the burgeoning, mid-nineteenth-century field of archaeology, this imprecise examination may have passed for a convincing argument, but even if it did, the reader would not have been able to visually judge its merits from Bridges' photographs. For example, there are no close-up images of the stones that Bridges describes for the reader to consider. Instead, the photograph of the Arch presents only a broad, sweeping, recessive view of the walls; while Bridges' photograph of the Cave of Machpelah (Illustration 5.4), Plate 63, is even less detailed and taken from a distance that prevents even a diligent observer from discerning stone patterns. In both of these cases, the photographs prove nothing but the fact that these particular views were present, in front of Bridges' camera, in the early 1850s.

It is also worth noting that, because the publication was a failure, we also lack contemporary accounts of the persuasive power of Bridges' "faithful delineations." Unlike other photographic works of the time, which often were lauded for their accuracy, or truth, the voice of public reception remains mute with regard to Bridges' work. Perhaps Bridges' project failed in part because it lacked a specific objective, such as that of Salzmann's project, and thus its success depended upon the strength of the views themselves. To say nothing of Bridges' style (many of his pictures, and especially his negatives, are quite beautiful examples of early photography), many Westerners found pictures of Palestine uninteresting when compared with the grander views of Rome, Athens, and Egypt. Maxime du Camp, who traveled with Gustave Flaubert through Egypt and Palestine, produced several hundred photographs throughout his journey, but only six in Jerusalem, as he found it "absolutely uninteresting."[43]

Complete disinterest, however, was one of the most innocuous responses for a traveler's encounter with Jerusalem and the rest of Palestine. The dirtiness of Palestine was something that almost all nineteenth-century visitors discussed in their writings. "There is certainly no city in the world that he will sooner wish to leave than Jerusalem," wrote W.H. Bartlett. "Nothing can be more void of interest than her gloomy, half-ruinous streets and poverty

Illustration 5.3: Rev. George W. Bridges, *Arch of "Ecce Homo,"* salt print from calotype negative, c.1850. Canadian Centre for Architecture, Montreal.

Illustration 5.4: Rev. George W. Bridges, *Cave of Machpelah,* salt print from calotype negative, c.1850. Canadian Centre for Architecture, Montreal.

stricken bazaars."[44] Mark Twain wrote, "Even the olive and the cactus, those fast friends of a worthless soil, had almost deserted the country. No landscape exists that is more tiresome to the eye than that which bounds the approaches to Jerusalem."[45] Flaubert was the most vicious: "All around it stinks to death . . . Jerusalem is a charnel-house surrounded by walls. Everything rots in it- the dead dogs in the streets, the religions in the churches."[46]

These critical observations might at first seem incongruous with the ecstatic declarations professed by the pious travelers at the sight of the Holy Land, but both the good and the bad may in fact be driven by the same urgent desires. For example, Bridges both delighted in the passion inspired by Christianity's birthplace, but bristled at its ruinous state, which he believed to be the result of imprudent or ignorant caretakers. At the entrance to the Church of the Holy Sepulchre, Bridges laments that, "the venerable door-ways, built of precious marbles, and carved in elaborate devices, eight hundred years ago, open but upon Moslem arrogance, and Christian falsehood."[47] The Church itself had been "so often mutilated, burnt, defaced, destroyed, and still only partially restored—while its Christian character is . . . desecrated by Moslem spite shewn in the erection of a minaret close to the ancient bell-tower."[48] Throughout Bridges' *Palestine As It Is* comments such as these abound, revealing a not so subtle subtext in which Bridges emphasizes the disorder and decay of the Holy Land to highlight the need for its rescue. It is as if Bridges' photographs of crumbling structures and rubble-strewn streets were intended as a call-to-arms for pious, Western believers. Seen in this context, the title *Palestine As It Is* is both a statement of fact and an elegy: it laments the glory of the past by drawing attention to the neglectful present.[49]

Taken together, the negative and positive observations made by Western visitors were intended to support the same narrative: hiding beneath the wreckage was a place of profound inspiration that was desperately in need of aid. It was common amongst Western writing to lay blame on Middle Eastern-ers' "lack of civility." These criticisms could range from slight to very serious. Talbot published a short essay explaining that Bridges had "recently returned from a long journey in Egypt, Syria, and other parts of the Levant, and . . . has written to me respecting the difficulties he had to contend with in those scarcely civilized regions."[50] The difficulties that Talbot referred to no doubt ranged from Bridges' lack of access to adequate photographic chemistry and supplies to contending with onlookers curious about the photographic pro-cess. But Bridges may also have communicated his lack of respect for many Muslim practices to Talbot. Throughout his publications, Bridges objects strongly to the Muslim influence in Palestine, interpreting several buildings as "Moslem insults" to pre-existing Christian structures.[51]

CONCLUSION

Rev. Bridges' criticism of Muslim influence may not have been as grandiose as that of François-René de Chateaubriand, who believed that the Crusades had been necessary to rid the world of "a cult that was civilizations enemy."[52] But it was certainly still damaging, especially embedded within a project that proclaimed its validity using the indisputable "truth" of photography. It may be clear today that photography does not guarantee truth (indeed, one could write a complete history of photography's shortcomings in this arena), but the mid-nineteenth-century public bought this concept indiscriminately.

While the writing of the history of photography still largely depends upon art historical narratives of style, great images, and individual accomplishments, Bridges' story demonstrates that photography was put to many different uses, even in its earliest years, and that its images often held significance far beyond their aesthetic merits. Photography's peculiar characteristics made it a particularly useful tool for the empiricist projects of the nineteenth century. As we continue to explore the arguments behind these projects, we would do well to critically examine just what kind of truth is being drawn by photography's "faithful delineations."

Notes

I would like to thank the following people for their assistance with the research for this project: Larry J. Schaaf; Louise Désy, Renata Guttman, and Colin MacWhirter at the Canadian Centre for Architecture; Stuart Malcolm at the National Library of Scotland; and Hans P. Kraus, Jennifer Parkinson, and Meredith Friedman at Hans P. Kraus, Jr., Inc. I would also like to thank Douglas Nickel and Roberto Ferrari for their advice on the direction of this essay. Finally, I am grateful to my colleagues at the Metropolitan Museum of Art: Malcolm Daniel, Jeff Rosenheim, Mia Fineman, and Jacob Lewis for letting me discuss various aspects of this topic with them throughout the writing process.

1. George Bridges, 4 Raymond Terrace Cheltenham, to William Henry Fox Talbot, October 26, 1852. British Library, Fox Talbot Collection, London (hereafter referred to as FTC). Transcripts of the letters between Bridges and the Talbot family are accessible online at The Correspondence of William Henry Fox Talbot Project, http://foxtalbot.dmu.ac.uk/ While most of the originals are held in the British Library, London, some of the letters are still in private hands. These have been noted in the following notes.

2. For the story of Bridges' life before photography, see D.A. Dunkley's chapter in this volume.

3. Talbot invented a paper-based photography process, while Daguerre's process produced an image on a highly polished sheet of copper, coated with silver. See Janet

E. Buerger, *French Daguerreotypes* (Chicago: University of Chicago Press, 1989), and Larry J. Schaaf, *The Photographic Art of William Henry Fox Talbot* (Princeton: Princeton University Press, 2000). Talbot and Daguerre were only two of several people who claimed to have practiced some form of photography before its 1839 introduction. Pierre Harmant offers a list of twenty-four such claimants: See Pierre Harmant, "Anno Lucis 1839: 1st. part," *Camera,* no. 5 (May 1977): 39, and "Anno Lucis 1839: 3rd. part," *Camera,* no. 10 (October 1977): 40.

4. William Henry Fox Talbot, *Some account of the art of Photogenic drawing, or the process by which natural objects may be made to delineate themselves without the aid of the artist's pencil* (London: R. and J.E. Taylor, 1839).

5. Rev. G. W. Bridges, *Palestine As It Is: In a Series of Photographic Views, Illustrating the Bible* (London: J. Hogarth, 1858–59?), text for plate XIV.

6. Constance Talbot, Lacock Abbey, to William Henry Fox Talbot, December 10, 1845, FTC.

7. Elisabeth Theresa Feilding, Lacock Abbey, to William Henry Fox Talbot, December 17, 1845, FTC.

8. William Henry Fox Talbot, London, to Elisabeth Theresa Feilding, Lacock Abbey, December 19, 1845, FTC.

9. William Henry Fox Talbot, London, to Elisabeth Theresa Feilding, December 13, 1845, FTC.

10. George Bridges, Paris, to William Henry Fox Talbot, February 2, 1846, FTC.

11. George Bridges, Malta, to William Henry Fox Talbot, March 30, 1846, FTC.

12. George Bridges, Malta, to William Henry Fox Talbot, Lacock Abbey, April 27, 1846, FTC.

13. George Bridges, Malta, to Elisabeth Theresa Feilding, May 17, 1846, Private Collection.

14. Although Talbot supported him in certain respects, the Reading photographic and printing studio was Henneman's operation and he oversaw it from the beginning of 1844 to 1846 when he moved to London. See Larry J. Schaaf, *H. Fox Talbot's The Pencil of Nature, Anniversary Facsimile, Introductory Volume* (New York: Hans P. Kraus, Jr. Inc., 1989).

15. George Bridges, Malta, to William Henry Fox Talbot, October 25, 1846, FTC.

16. "I regret to see that of the copies which Cowderoy [the land agent at Reading] sent to Muir here for sale, those which are exposed to the light, hung up in rooms, are fading fast." George Bridges, Malta, to William Henry Fox Talbot, May 1, 1847, FTC.

17. George Bridges, Convent of St. Nicolo, Etna, to William Henry Fox Talbot, August 25, 1846, FTC.

18. George Bridges, Malta, to William Henry Fox Talbot, October 25, 1846, FTC. This letter includes a list of negatives that Bridges sent to Talbot and the two of Etna are listed as numbers 66 and 67.

19. George Bridges, Athens, to William Henry Fox Talbot, November 20, 1848, FTC.

20. George Bridges, 4 Raymond Terrace Cheltenham, to William Henry Fox Talbot, October 26, 1852, FTC.

21. Rev. G. W. Bridges, "A Wayworn Wanderer," in *Selections from Seventeen-Hundred Genuine Photographs: (Views—Portraits—Statuary—Antiquities.) Taken Around the Shores of the Mediterranean Between the Years 1846–52. With, or Without, Notes, Historical, and Descriptive* (Cheltenham: no date), title page.

22. This last part may also exist only in partial form, but of the three known copies, two have twenty-one plates and the third has nineteen. All three are in the same order. The two larger copies are in the Canadian Centre for Architecture, Montreal (PH1980: 901: 01- PH1980:901:21) and the National Library of Scotland, Edinburgh (Phot.med.43) and the third recently sold at auction (Gros & Delettrez, Paris, June 23, 2011, lot 160) Rev. George W. Bridges, *Palestine As It Is: In a Series of Photographic Views, Illustrating the Bible.* (London: J. Hogarth [1858-9?]). It is also possible that Bridges was inspired to produce a volume devoted to Palestinian images based upon the success of Francis Frith's photographic work: Douglas R. Nickel, *Francis Frith in Egypt and Palestine: A Victorian Photographer Abroad* (Princeton: Princeton University Press, 2004). Darwin's empiricism represented the kind of scientific thought that motivated many theological scholars to justify religious belief with rational arguments. For information on Darwin's effect on visual culture and empirical study, see Diana Donald, *Endless Forms: Charles Darwin, Natural Science, and the Visual Arts* (New Haven: Yale University Press, 2009).

23. See Dunkley's chapter in this volume.

24. John Vivian Hughes, *The wealthiest commoner: C.R.M. Talbot, M.P., F.R.S. (1803–1890)* (Aberavon, Port Talbot, W. Glam.: [the author] 1977).f

25. George Bridges, Malta, to William Henry Fox Talbot, March 30, 1846, FTC. This letter was written just one week after Charlotte's death on March 23.

26. Calvert Richard Jones, Naples, to William Henry Fox Talbot, April 29, 1846, FTC.

27. George Bridges, Malta, to William Henry Fox Talbot, February 2, 1847, FTC.

28. See for example, Andre Jammes and Eugenia Parry Janis, *The Art of French Calotype* (Princeton: Princeton University Press, 1983), and Roger Taylor, *Impressed by Light: British Photographs from Paper Negatives, 1840–1860* (New York: Metropolitan Museum of Art, 2007).

29. George Bridges, Malta, to Elisabeth Theresa Feilding, May 17, 1846, Private Collection.

30. George Bridges, Convent of St. Nicolo, Etna, to William Henry Fox Talbot, August 25, 1846, FTC.

31. Auguste Salzmann, *Jérusalem. Etudes et reproductions photographiques de la Ville Sainte depuis l'epoque judaïque jusqu'a nos jours.* 2 vols. (Paris: Gide et Baudry, 1856), 3. Salzmann was, in effect, rescued from canonical art history by Abigail Solomon-Godeau, "A Photographer in Jerusalem, 1855: Auguste Salzmann and His Times," in *Photography at the Dock: Essays on Photographic History, Institutions, and Practices* (Minneapolis: University of Minnesota Press, 1991), 150–68.

32. Jammes and Janis, *Art of the French Calotype*, 247.

33. Edward Robinson, *Biblical Researches in Palestine and the Adjacent Regions* (London: John Murray, 1856), 31. The first supplement was published in 1842.

34. Kathleen Stewart Howe, *Revealing the Holy Land: The Photographic Exploration of Palestine* (Santa Barbara, CA: Santa Barbara Museum of Art, 1997), 28.

35. Anonymous, *Le Tour du Monde* (Paris, 1862), vol. 5, 227. Quoted in Nissan N. Perez, *Picturing Jerusalem: James Graham and Mendel Diness, Photographers* (Jerusalem: The Israel Museum, 2007), 10.

36. Chateaubriand, *Itinéraire de Paris à Jérusalem,* 1881, quoted in Perez, *Picturing Jerusalem,* 10.

37. This is actually the title of one traveler's book: W.H. Bartlett, *Footsteps of Our Lord and His Apostles in Syria, Greece, and Italy: A Succession of Visits to the Scenes of New Testament Narrative* (London: Arthur Hall, Virtue and Co., 1851).

38. The contrived, picturesque views of Palestine by David Roberts do seem to have little in common with Bridges' stark photographs, but neither is necessarily accurate. Early photographs, by virtue of their lengthy exposure times, often eradicated any trace of human presence. The empty landscapes could seem all the more ripe for settling by Westerners as a result. A more thorough comparison of Roberts' and Bridges' images would be instructive. David Roberts, *The Holy Land. Syria, Idumea, Arabia, Egypt and Nubia. From drawings made on the spot* (London: F.G. Moon, 1842).

39. Noel-Marie-Paymal Lerebours, *Excursions daguerriennes: vues et monuments les plus remarquables du globe* (Paris: Lerebours et secretan, 1841–42), preface.

40. Rev. Albert Augustus Isaacs, *The Dead Sea: or Notes and Observations Made During a Journey to Palestine in 1856–7* (London: Hatchard and Son, 1857), 4. Isaacs' emphasis.

41. Alexander Keith, D.D., *Evidence of the Truth of the Christian Religion, Derived from the Literal Fulfillment of Prophecy; Particularly as Illustrated by the History of the Jews, and by the Discoveries of Recent Travelers* (Edinburgh: William Whyte and Co., 1848), xii.

42. Bridges, *Selections from Seventeen-Hundred Genuine Photographs,* half-title page.

43. Quoted in Perez, *Picturing Jerusalem,* 11.

44. W. H. Bartlett, *Walks about the City and Environs of Jerusalem* (London, 1843), 133.

45. Mark Twain, *The Innocents Abroad, or the New Pilgrims' Progress* (Connecticut: American Publishing Co., 1869), 555.

46. Gustave Flaubert, *Oeuvres completes* Vol. 2 (Paris: Société Les Belles Lettres, 1948), 197–98.

47. Bridges, *Palestine As It Is,* text to plate III.

48. Bridges, *Palestine As It Is,* text to plate II.

49. This Western view of Middle Easterners as negligent is an "Orientalist" trope, and its negative impact has been discussed within art historical discourse: see Linda Nochlin, "Imaginary Orient," in *Politics of Vision: Essays on Nineteenth-Century Art and Society* (Oxford: Icon Editions, 1989), 33–59; and Mary Anne Stevens, *The*

Orientalists: Delacroix to Matisse: European Painters in North Africa and the Near East (London: Royal Academy of Arts, 1984).

50. William Henry Fox Talbot, "The Traveler's Camera," *The Literary Gazette and Journal of belles letters, science and art* n. 1871, (27 November 1852): 876.

51. For example, Bridges, *Palestine As It Is,* text to plates XII and XIII.

52. According to Chateaubriand, the Crusades were "not only about the deliverance of the Holy Sepulchre, but more about knowing which would win on the earth, a cult that was civilization's enemy [Islam], systematically favorable to ignorance, to despotism, to slavery, or a cult that had caused to reawaken in modern people the genius of a sage antiquity and had abolished base servitude?" Chateaubriand, *Oeuvres,* as famously quoted in Edward W. Said, *Orientalism* (New York: Vintage Books, 1979), 172.

Chapter 6

Vectors of Venereal Diseases

The Perceived Threat of Prostitutes to Military Efficiency in Jamaica during World Wars I and II

Dalea Bean

INTRODUCTION

The history of sex in the Caribbean context has been intertwined with the control of one race/people by another. The power that European colonizers exalted over colonized peoples was not only one for monetary gain and political status, but also for rights to sexual access to those considered to be subordinate. Thomas Thistlewood's journal entries, for instance, are replete with references to the largely non-consensual sexual access he had to his enslaved women.[1] As Verene Shepherd has argued, male plantation administrators, such as Thistlewood, used their position as owners or managers of the subaltern to render colonized women sex objects over whom they could exercise power.[2] Sexual power and colonization in the Caribbean went hand in hand; and "sexploitation" of indigenous, African enslaved and Indian indentured women was part and parcel of the imperial project. This is made clear by Hilary Beckles, who convincingly argues that "the slave-owners right to extract a wide range of non-pecuniary socio-sexual benefits from slaves" led to "a legitimate stream of returns on capital, and [was] an important part of the meaning of colonial mastery."[3] Though the type of relationship under study was not exploitative in nature, which typified the relationship under slavery, the legacy of the "right" of the white male to the body of the subaltern woman is evident in the discourses of prostitution during war time after slavery.

As various authors show, the exploitation of women under slavery emerged from an "exoticization" of the cultural "other."[4] Kamala Kempadoo, in particular, argues that this exoticization has continued to dictate sexual relations in the Caribbean after slavery.[5] This "exotic" label given to the women of colonized peoples was an attempt on the part of colonizers to understand what was considered strange and to legitimize these women as sexual fantasies. As G. S. Rousseau and Roy Porter argued, "labeling the anthropological other as exotic legitimated treating the peoples of the 'third world' as fit to be despised and destroyed . . . while constituting them as projections for western fantasies."[6] This type of mindset was part of the reason why prostitution in the West Indies was so well-supported by white soldiers. "Colored" women were seen by soldiers in transit as attractive representations of uninhibited sensuality. This was a prime breeding ground for sexual liaisons between soldiers and local women of an ephemeral nature.

These short-lived relationships were not uncommon even before the end of slavery. As Beckles shows, urban centers during slavery catered in part to maritime activity by providing sexual favors, and as a result prostitution was as much in demand as any other social institution in the Caribbean.[7] Though prostitution of this nature was illegal in Jamaica, Beckles suggests that there was no vehement enforcement of the laws. This signaled the acceptance of prostitution as a natural part of military life. Inns, taverns, and lodging houses that catered to visitors, were primarily owned by women in twentieth-century Jamaica and had historical roots in the early nineteenth century. These houses and taverns were situated in areas such as Falmouth, Montego Bay, and Kingston, close to docks where they catered mainly to sailors. Legislators from the nineteenth to the mid-twentieth centuries surmised that these houses often doubled as discrete brothels. Indeed, if Paulette Kerr's analysis is correct, though brothels were never overt operations and it is not clear whether the majority of lodging houses and taverns were brothels, it is apparent that sexual services in exchange for money were practiced to varying degrees in these establishments. As Kerr has argued,

> it would be remarkable if for example, sailors and seamen after months at sea visited inns and taverns without expectations of sexual intercourse. And it would be foolish to believe that these lodging housekeepers did not capitalize on the gains which could be accrued to them by offering sexual favors at a price.[8]

This proved to be an advantageous arrangement for brothel owners, women who engaged in prostitution at various levels, and military patrons. Usually motivated by economic pressure, the first two accrued monetary benefits, while the third gained short-term companionship and an outlet for sexual fantasies.

The social evils that resulted from prostitution, as perceived by legislators and self-proclaimed upholders of the moral code in the society, were seen as the result of fallen womanhood, rather than a shared condition with women and willing patrons of their services. Definitions of prostitution signify how closely related it was to femininity and not to masculinity. An overarching definition was that prostitution entailed a woman offering her body commonly for lewdness for payment in return, particularly when foreigners were involved, in which case local women bore the brunt of the blame for the illegitimacy and the spread of venereal diseases (VDs).[9] These ideas which predominated in early twentieth-century Jamaica, appears to fit into the universal tendency to accept the need for military personnel to have regular sexual outlets (of a heterosexual nature), while condemning the women who provided such services.

SEX AND WAR: THE INEXTRICABLE LINK

The argument that sex and war are inextricably linked has been one of the primary catalysts for the acceptance of the right of military personnel's access to sex as frequently as possible. Sigmund Freud argued that the connection between acts of violence and eroticism was evident in the tendency of a society in wartime to throw off the repressions which civilization imposed in the human sex drive.[10] While societies at war might not totally abandon the moral codes that control sexuality in the Freudian sense, the methods of sexual repression were admittedly diluted. This *war aphrodisiac*, as John Costello terms it, is usually associated with men in combat. Costello explains that the urgency and thrill of war, as well as the realization that both military and civilian life could be cut tragically short in war, eroded moral restraints.[11] Others, such as George Hicks, argue that the military community of men was often obsessed with sex, particularly when they were confined to a regimented situation, and deprived of normal emotional outlets.[12] Also, as Ronald Ham posits, "war always tends to increase sexual activity because of the general heightening of nervous tensions and because the beauties of the fleshpots made a wonderful contrast to the horrors and absurdities of war."[13]

Caribbean bases were not usually the scenes of open warfare, but the "war aphrodisiac" accompanied the military personnel stationed there, as well as transient sailors. Jamaica made up for its lack of battle scenes with its exotic women, tropical climate, and the cultural and physical distance of the troops from their homes. Indeed, as Harry Benjamin and R.E.L Masters argue, military camps and bases, as well as ports, were the prime targets of brothels, taverns, and prostitutes the world over. As Benjamin and Masters point out:

> The men stationed there [at camps, bases, etc.] are frequently . . . off from their normal sources of sex gratification: wives and girlfriends. Moreover, there are

likely to be many young males, away from home for the first time, the incidence
of whose sex contacts rises sharply in the sudden absence of parental supervision. Particularly in war time, men live "as if there is no tomorrow" and squan-
der their money as they never would do at home.[14]

Typified by virility, over-exuberant manhood, heavy drinking, and consistent use of profanity, the soldier was expected to assert his masculinity as an
extension of his wartime duties. As Costello explains:

Soldiers in a world of ritualized masculinity both consciously and subcon-
sciously came to regard their weapons as extensions of their virility. . . . Military
discipline also produced, as a byproduct of its emphasis on obedience and masculinity, profane language and rebelliousness in off duty pursuits.[15]

Sex was seen as crucial to the military performance of combatants; without
it, they would *surely* perform their duties half-heartedly and ineffectively. The
ideology of armies is evidenced by this 1943 excerpt from a United States
infantry journal:

The Army does not officially condone profanity; unofficially, it knows it can do
little to stop it. The society of soldiers is not polite. It is a society of men, frequently unwashed, who have been dedicated to the rugged task of killing other
men, and whose training has emphasized that a certain reversion to the primitive
is not undesirable.[16]

So concerned were armies with the sexual satisfaction of their soldiers that
many made provisions for official military brothels. The French, for instance,
experimented with *maisons tolerées* or military brothels during World War I.
However, the Japanese were probably the most notorious in this regard, with
a system of providing "comfort women" for their troops.[17]

Concomitant with the tendency of armies to condone, if not encourage sexual license among its men, was the disapproval of the women who provided
these services. Women were punished for engaging in prostitution, while
men were not. In fact, there was a tendency to deliberately withhold punishment from troops who contracted VDs. For instance, the National Council of
Public Morals in Britain felt that, "as regards venereal diseases men must not
be threatened with additional punishment, which would cause them to hide
the disease until it is seriously advanced."[18] At best, men were encouraged to
use prophylactics and told which areas of cities were known for harboring
infected prostitutes.

Laws, such as the Defense of the Realm Act (DORA) and the Contagious
Disease Acts (CDAs) in Britain (the latter of which were instituted in the colonies, including Jamaica in 1864, 1866, and 1869), were instituted to regulate

the spread of venereal diseases and their chief vectors, "loose women." Under the CDAs, women had to endure mandatory medical inspection, and if found to be infected with a disease, these women could be detained for up to three months. Also, as Cynthia Enloe informs us, Cantonment Acts permitted colonial police to conduct compulsory genital exams on women around bases, to allow British soldiers to have sexual relations with local women, and without fear of contracting venereal diseases.[19] These gender specific penal codes made no mention of detaining or testing male customers. The CDAs were repealed in 1886, but they resurfaced during World War I in the form of the DORA. Number 40d of this act, for instance, mandated the incarceration of women for medical examination, and was blatantly in favor of the troops. It stated that, "no woman who is suffering from VD shall have sexual intercourse with any member of the HM forces, or solicit or invite any member to have sexual intercourse with her."[20]

The 40d was eventually repealed due to pressure from feminist groups. It was felt that these women were attacked not for their own good, but to protect men from infections while the women were in no way protected from the infections from those men. The CDAs, in particular, came under scathing attacks from the Social Purity Organization in England, headed by Josephine Butler. Butler and others vehemently argued that the laws violated the rights of women, that they allowed police absolute power over women, and that they punished the sex who were the victims of vice, and left unpunished the sex who were the main causes.[21] In sum, Butler and her supporters "inveighed against the terrible injustice of the double standard of morality which justified men's sexual exploitation of women, while women were supposed to be 'pure' and were punished if they 'fell.'"[22]

The tone of these legal enactments was partially due to prevailing Victorian stereotypes of the various manifestations of sexual behavior in men and women. These stereotypes accepted that men were lecherous. As Ruth Rose informs us, "Victorians described the male sex drive as strong, passionate and potentially destructive."[23] The burden was placed on women to keep this sexual interest in males at bay, and also considered overt female sexuality as corrupt. As Kempadoo reports,

> Women's bodies and female sexuality represented all the negative aspects of sex. . . . Women were seen as possessing powers which could arouse forbidden desires. She was portrayed as temptress, the source of distraction, corruption and potential rebellion.[24]

This view garnered support from early twentieth-century medical practitioners, who theorized that women who had the venereal diseases syphilis and gonorrhea, showed no symptoms of their infection. This led to the myth that all women were vectors of the disease, who potentially carried these inherently without being infected from an external source. As Brandt explains, "the asymptomatic nature of the disease in women even led to the idea that virtually all women carried gonorrhea without damage and could transmit [it] to their partners . . . she was contagious without having been contagioned. The woman was considered dangerous *ipso facto.*"[25] Suppressing prostitution was therefore seen as the major way to curb the spread of diseases. Brandt further informs us that:

> Physicians and social reformers associated VD, almost exclusively, with the vast population of prostitutes. They agreed that when a man left the moral path the road usually led to the prostitute, who they argued was the most prolific source of venereal infections . . . man could only get a VD from [a] "fallen woman."[26]

While Michel Foucault stresses that the confinement of sexuality in the Victorian era was a whole-scale repression, it is now widely accepted that unlike women, men's sexuality was seen as natural.[27] While these ideals never fully took root in Jamaica, Victorian ideals of womanhood did influence stereotypes of women in Jamaica. As Joan French and Honor Ford-Smith argue, "women were the repositories of chasteness, virtue and purity and a superior civilizing force, while men were creatures of unlimited sexual appetite and the source of vice which had to be controlled."[28] A woman's worth was defined by her sexual reputation. This was particularly evident during the war years, when men and women were often separated, and women were cautioned to be faithful to their men, while for men, the reverse was hardly ever mentioned. As an Air Force member asked a Jamaican columnist:

> I want to ask you to impress upon the girls we left behind us the importance of keeping up the morale of the boys at the front by being loyal to them . . . why can't these wives and sweethearts whom the boys of the army and navy are risking their lives for, realize that it is just as important for them to be loyal to their men as it is for men on the fighting line to be loyal to Uncle Sam?[29]

The columnist, Dorothy Dix, agreed that the onus was on women to be faithful to men who were risking their lives to secure the safety and freedom of their women. Again, there was no mention that men were to act similarly. Dix said,

> certainly when a man is risking his life to protect his country it doesn't seem much of a sacrifice for a woman to give up a few dates for him . . . going to battle where your letter with this bad news made him welcome the bullet that pierced his heart . . . no matter what you do after the war is over, be loyal to the boys while it is going on.[30]

In an environment where these ideas were prevalent, it is not hard to understand why prostitutes were viewed as unnatural women. They were seen as deliberately abandoning good character by being overtly sexual, and were therefore dangerous social deviants who threatened not only the purity of society, but also endangered women's status in society in general. Amy Bailey, writing in 1940, saw the status of all women in Jamaica as depreciating due to illegitimacy and the immoral behavior of a few members of the female population.[31] Prostitution was not normally seen as an entrepreneurial enterprise, as Amy Paul has theorized, but as an immoral craving for excitement and vanity on the part of a dangerous type of woman.[32]

WORLD WAR I AND THE INTERWAR YEARS

In Jamaica, the amateur prostitute was far more prevalent than any militarily established brothel. This amateur prostitute was defined as a "woman who is prepared for reward to engage in acts of lewdness with all and sundry or with anyone who may hire her for that purpose."[33] These women were seen by local and international policymakers as the greatest threat to military efficiency. While professional prostitutes were undoubtedly linked to the spread of VDs, amateurs suggested a freedom from disease because their sex work was sporadic.[34] This, it was felt, gave the soldiers a false sense of security to interact with these women. While brothels and known professional prostitutes were, in theory, easier to control and regulate, the average young woman who only occasionally roamed the streets looking for a "good time" for a minimal fee was elusive. As a physician in the United States wrote:

> The old time prostitute in a house or formal prostitute on the street is sinking into second place. The new type is the young girl in her late teens, and early twenties who is determined to have one fling or better . . . the carrier and disseminator of venereal disease today is just one of us so to speak.[35]

It was felt that sailors were particularly fond of these women, who were often servant girls, market women, and banana carriers at docks. As Mr. Winston Thomas said in an interview, "girls made themselves available for the sailors . . . and entertained them, when the ships leave off the port . . . those girls could come along and buy you a beer."[36] This "exceedingly dangerous class of woman" walked the streets looking for clients like "professional prostitutes," and they were hard to identify.[37] As the director of Medical Services surmised: "VD in Kingston is not so much a question of the professional prostitute (housed or street walker) as of the amateur or semi-professional. . . . VD appears to me to be spread primarily by the domestic servants, half starved dressmakers and under paid clerks."[38] The Moyne Commission also gave credence to this idea by arguing that women who acted as prostitutes, did so for economic reasons, and could be found at the docks at night, while carrying on regular work in the daytime.[39]

In addition, the prevalence of venereal diseases in Jamaica was linked to race as much as it was linked to class. As Kempadoo informs us, Europeans tried to place emphasis on the "'inherent' promiscuous, immoral and unclean character of working-class women and non-white peoples who did not, or refused to, adhere to European bourgeois family norms and ideals."[40] In subscribing to these views, men such as the medical officer of the country felt that the lower class women of African descent were prime sources of VD. In his mind, the small number of decent female companions in Jamaica, and the ever decreasing moral code of the "female descendant of the slave days," made Jamaica a haven for VDs.[41]

Apart from independent street walkers, the sale of sex to military personnel in Jamaica largely occurred in informal houses, which doubled as legitimate licensed hotels, taverns, and inns, and were almost impossible to regulate. As E. A. Glen Campbell informed Governor Denham, "the half has not yet [been] told of these places, some under the guise of Hotels, Board and Lodgings and others with no sign at all, only a collector at the gate who receives the fares and delivers the keys."[42] It was concluded that two major types of brothels existed: that of tenement yards with girls of all ages, who freely engaged in prostitution; and houses run by older women (following in the tradition of nineteenth-century lodging houses), who employed young girls from 12–16 years old as prostitutes.

However, of equal importance to legislators was the temperance bar, which was prevalent in towns in Jamaica. These bars were not allowed to sell spirits but sold beer and other liquors. This enabled them to have Trade Licenses, which did not allow police entry, rather than Spirit Licenses, which made provision for police entry at any time. Under Section 56 of the Spirit License, persons were not allowed to make their taverns, inns, or hotels the habitual resort of reputed prostitutes, whether they were there to solicit customers or not. Somewhat contradictory, the law did not prevent the owner from allowing any such person to remain to purchase food and drink.[43] As a result, these women would still frequent the establishments and, according to officials, wreaked havoc on unsuspecting troops. These places were seen as breeding grounds for illicit behavior, because they served alcohol, because they were under no police control, and because they could remain open all night. It was therefore suggested by various committees that temperance bars be forced to take out Spirit Licenses, and come under the purview of police patrol.

Authorities were able to identify a list of fifty-three common houses, where alleged loose women, living in Kingston, were visited by sailors. These were mainly on Luke Lane, Matthew's Lane, Water Lane, Princess Street, Orange Street, and West Street, among others.[44] United States marines and British soldiers were also spotted at the "Kit Cat" Bar, "Double B Bar," and "Queensbury" Bar in Kingston. These temperance bars were allegedly run by prostitutes who catered to soldiers and sailors.[45]

At times, officials sought to control temperance bars and brothels because they affected civilians. In particular, it was reported that school children were being lured to brothels, and that they were situated near to churches. In addition, there were complaints that brothels and temperance bars were invariably accompanied by loud noises, which disturbed residential areas and hotels, such as Myrtle Bank.[46] However, the overarching concern was to safeguard the troops from becoming infected with VDs. Governor William Manning, who served from 1913–1918, in a letter to Lewis Harcourt, Secretary of State for the colonies, was grieved to inform Harcourt that a "serious state of affairs exists in Kingston which is resulting in a great deal of diseases being introduced into His Majesty's ships which visit the port of Kingston."[47] Manning suggested that heavily infected areas should be put out of bounds by the military authorities. In one case, it was alleged by the inspector general that one particular woman was the source of all the cases of VD on the *H.M.D. Dragon* in 1934. In response to the allegation, the ship's authorities put the "Breezy Cottage," where the woman worked, out of bounds to their men.[48] No mention was made of the individual responsibility that men had for their health, or the fact that they had control over their sexual activity.

Military personnel were not attacked for their behavior by Jamaican authorities because they were seen as following "the very necessary call of nature."[49] As Howe has aptly argued, "sailors, volunteers and members of the military forces being male, were not held responsible for their actions. It was as if they had a right to engage in prostitution without risk."[50] To reduce this risk, however, legislators in Jamaica lobbied for tighter restrictions on these dangerous women. Protecting the troops from diseased women and infection preoccupied the minds of military and political authorities.[51] They tried to strike a delicate balance between protecting the troops from VDs and using measures that would not severely limit their sexual freedom. A law passed in 1918 (Law 6 of 1918) made the concealment of a VD a criminal offence, with penalties of fines and imprisonment.[52] Another bill introduced in 1923 (Law 37 of 1923), made provisions for the medical examination of persons convicted of prostitution. It also provided for the detention of these persons in a public hospital, if found to be infected with a venereal disease. If they were not infected, they would then face a fine or imprisonment for up to three months for the offence of soliciting.[53] However, this bill was criticized as being a diluted version of the CDAs, which had done nothing to stem the tide of amateur prostitutes, who were seen as more dangerous than "professional" prostitutes. The bill was abandoned in 1925.[54]

Though the tendency was to look to legislation to solve the problems brought on by prostitution, there were instances of criticism that men could not be controlled by acts of parliament. Prominent female speakers of the time were of the view that both men and women had equal responsibility for the spread of VDs. Mrs. Briscoe, an astute organizer during World War I, argued that the theory that men could sow their "wild oats" without responsibility was illogical. In her words: "If sex-sin is wrong in the women it is obviously equally wrong in the men. If sex restraint and purity is possible to the women it is surely possible to the men who boast of stronger will power."[55] Briscoe was one of the most vocal advocates for the abolition of the double standard that was subtly infiltrating the society. It should not be misconstrued that Briscoe was supportive of prostitution. In fact, she gained equal notoriety for condemning the profession of "fallen women." However, Briscoe's point of departure from the general public was that men who supported prostitution were as much to be blamed as the women who were prostitutes. According to Briscoe:

> Any woman who greets her fallen sister with a stare icy enough to freeze a sin, and meets her seducer with a genial smile is a traitor to the best interested of her sex. Freeze the woman if you like, but freeze the men equally. They are co-partners in a common act and together they should be acquitted or condemned.[56]

Despite the fact that this line of thinking may have actually impacted positively on the types of laws that were instituted in Jamaica, it was often rejected. Committees appointed to investigate the issue of VDs in Jamaica even went as far as to request the use of the laws and measures of Malta, Hong Kong, Singapore, Uganda, and Japan to control its prostitution.[57] A consensus among the relevant authorities indicated that legislation targeting women was the best remedy for various aspects of the problem. The authorities also felt that existing laws were vague and too weak to adequately address the pressing issue. For instance, the Vagrancy Act of 1902 stated that a common prostitute found wandering in a public place, and behaving in a riotous or indecent manner, would be liable to imprisonment not exceeding two months, with or without hard labor.[58] The wording of this act was repeatedly cited by medical officers and military heads as vague and hinged on far too many conditions for a prostitute to be taken off the streets. More importantly, the act did not make prostitution a crime. In addition, laws passed from as early as 1864, gave the police the power to suppress brothels and arrest their proprietors, who faced fines of up to $200 and imprisonment for up to three months. However, the police could not enter brothels without warrants, which in turn had to be accompanied by sworn declarations that such establishments were, in fact, operating as brothels.[59] There were obvious difficulties to get any man to say that he visited such an establishment for the purpose of sex, and it was therefore very difficult to get a warrant giving right of entry to suspected brothels. It was also suggested that a system of compulsory examination of women should be instituted to rid the island of those "rotten with disease and capable of infecting every male she may meet."[60] It was also indicated that fines for soliciting should be raised from 40 shillings because women could easily afford this paltry sum, and then resume their activities on the same day as their arrest.

As a result of legislative measures, during the early years of World War I, women were increasingly arrested for vagrancy, soliciting, prostitution, disorderly conduct, and loitering. A return from the Detective's Office showed that, from September 1914 to March 1915, 267 women were arrested for the above offences, while 162 were convicted.[61] Ether Madison and Annie Thompson, for instance, were arrested in 1916 for soliciting soldiers. Madison was sent to jail for fourteen days, and Thompson was sentenced to serve two months with hard labor.[62] However, not many women were brought in to face these charges, and the perception was that the legislation up to the 1920s was insufficient to deal with the scourge of loose women, who were possibly riddled with VDs. As E. L. Hunt has argued: "Under the existing laws, nothing can be done by way of isolating or closing the 'known houses.'"[63]

In an attempt to curb the spread of VDs, it was suggested that only older soldiers should be sent to Jamaica, as the younger soldier, released from home control, was incapable of resisting the temptation of the tropical climate, the relatively low price of rum, and the availability of prostitutes. Younger soldiers were reported as "falling prey" to women who lined the roads, from the bars to the camp, in an attempt to woo inebriated soldiers. It was estimated that thirty-eight per cent of the VD cases in 1933 were caused by the women who frequented South Camp Road.[64] Even with harsher measures, however, the rate of infection remained unaffected, and during the first year of World War II, senior medical officers in the Jamaica Command reported that more than 220 military personnel were admitted to hospital after contracting VDs.[65] The *H.M.A.S. Melbourne,* harbored in Kingston for five days during January 1915, reported four cases of syphilis, twenty-five cases of gonorrhea, and twelve cases of cancroids. In three visits between January and February 1915, the crew of 436 men had fifty-three confirmed cases of VDs reported aboard the ship.[66] These figures were almost the same during the interwar years. In 1919, for example, the cruiser *Cumberland,* which spent two months on the shores of Jamaica, reported that of the 650 men aboard the vessel, 420 had contracted VDs.[67] Between 1924 and 1934, the average yearly number of British soldiers admitted with VDs stood at 132 per 1,000 troops, or one in every eight men. Some twenty-two percent of the Northumberland Fusiliers had contracted VDs during the same period.[68]

Jamaica had earned the reputation as one of the worse stations for the military because of the reported cases of VDs. The infection rate among the general population was no better. In fact, the situation was deemed alarming. The Blue Books of Jamaica report that from 1914–1915 Jamaica had a reported 176 cases of syphilis at the primary stage, and in 1918–1919, the number increased to 139 reported cases. Gonorrhea had also increased from 368 reported cases in 1915–1916 to 590 reported cases in 1918–1919. There were several deaths from these diseases as well.[69] Compared to other countries, Jamaica undoubtedly faced a major problem with the spread of VDs during the early twentieth century. As Hyam has estimated, the figures for 1921–1926 show that the incidence of VDs in the army at home (in Britain) was 40 per 1,000, while in Egypt it was 103 per 1,000, in South China 169, in the Mediterranean and the West Indies generally, 156, and at the China Station it was 304.[70] Mrs. Rolfe estimated that while Jamaica had 363 reported cases of VD among its British troops during the interwar years (1930–1943), England had only sixteen reported cases.[71] Therefore, while other countries undoubtedly suffered from the presence of VDs, the number of cases reported in Jamaica outnumbered those in many of these countries. According to reports in *The Gleaner,* ships refused to call at Jamaican ports because of the fear of the prevalence of VDs. One editorial noted that:

> It seems clear that only two or three of the smaller units of the British fleet visiting the West Indian waters will be permitted to call in Jamaica and the stay with even those will be made as brief as is consistent with courtesy and with established practice of "showing the flag" at stations and colonies of strategic or historical importance.[72]

One cannot rule out the fact that soldiers were infected by the female prostitutes with whom they had sexual encounters. However, it was never contemplated that the women also contracted VDs from their clients in the military. In fact, the superintendent medical officer surmised that the problem was not the inability of the soldiers to refrain from loose sexual relations, but was almost surely the proliferation of prostitution and the large number of brothels in Kingston. As he noted:

It is absurd to hope to effect any great improvement in a few months by attempting to influence the morality of the persons concerned. The pressing question is how to reduce the rates at which Jamaica is becoming a center for the dissemination of disease among sailors, consequently reducing their efficiency during the war.[73]

Regulatory measures targeting prostitutes were put in place to protect the troops in particular. Army officials decided to treat the prostitutes as major threats to the efficiency of the soldiers. They argued that enlisted men should be at the peak of physical health. Protecting these men who were "of use to the king and empire" was a top priority. As Glenford Howe has explained, "while the army believed that sexual activity was vital to a soldier's happiness . . . it simultaneously regarded women and especially prostitutes as a source of pollution and a threat to morale and military efficiency."[74] In some cases, VDs were seen as greater threats to the war effort than the causalities caused by combat. The view that one "sick" woman could cause more deaths than 100 German cannons was heard more than once.[75] It was even suggested that Germany might have embarked on a campaign to use diseased prostitutes to cripple the Allied Forces fighting in Lisbon. Reports later showed that the Allies lost 1.5 million troops from VDs during World War I.[76]

VDs undoubtedly had long-term effects, which debilitated the infected and could render them inefficient. Infected persons had sores, rashes, and suffered hair loss, while in the long term, if untreated, the damage was worse, and some of the diseases were fatal. Syphilis could cause cardiovascular problems, loss of muscular coordination, partial paralysis, insanity, and organ failure. Gonorrhea was another serious malady that could result in arthritis, meningitis, and inflammation of the tissue surrounding the heart.[77] Soldiers faced a higher risk of cross infection because of their living situation, and since the army was against long-term hospitalization, the risk to non-infected persons in the army was always present. Syphilitics needed up to two years of confinement from healthy people and regular treatment before they were considered as cured, and during this time, they were to receive no fewer than fifty injections.[78]

Since women were seen as the sources of VDs, the perception was that they could cripple the military's efficiency. Claims made in Britain stated that the young women who had infected the soldiers had adversely affected the war effort.[79] But the problem did not stop there. British authorities were concerned about the spread of diseases at home (in Britain) that had been contracted in Jamaica. Men in the early stages of the diseases could unwittingly transmit it to their wives and girlfriends, and worse, to their unborn children. Prince Albert Morrow's "Social Disease and Marriage," published in 1904, chronicled the potential dangers of VDs to women and children. As Morrow explained, these maladies could become hereditary diseases, which were fatal to offspring. Children who survived infections at birth, faced a lifetime of suffering from congenital afflictions, such as syphilis. Among the problems these children developed, were severe mental retardation, meningitis, and blindness.[80] Prostitutes, the source of all of this, represented a threat to succeeding generations in not just colonies such as Jamaica, but in Britain itself. Howe explained that "the army felt it had a moral and patriotic responsibility to protect the soldiers so that they could return home healthy, and reduce the risk of their families and communities being 'innocently' infected."[81]

Though the focus was on regulatory campaigns, geared towards strengthening the laws against bars and women, there were a few attempts to treat infected civilians as well as military personnel during World War I and the interwar years. For instance, a women's VD clinic was set up in East Kingston in October 1935, under the direction of Dr. K. Leigh Evans, a government bacteriologist. Free examinations were conducted at the clinic, and treatments administered. Another VD clinic was established in Montego Bay in 1937, and a Dr. Clarke was put in charge. Tracts, pamphlets, and other educational materials were provided to persons thought to be at risk for infection. Lieutenant Colonel Anderson of the Jamaica Command became an advocate for providing military personnel with contraceptives.[82] During the interwar years, the public was also involved in suggesting measures to curb the spread of VDs. A number of these appeared in local newspapers, suggestions for mobile VD clinics, and bizarre ones such as the public flogging of women. As one person suggested:

> Flog the girls caught with tamarind rods in public. This might sound drastic but an evil of this sort which is spreading like measles and is undoubtedly playing havoc with thousands of men deserves a drastic remedy . . . after two or three of these public birchings you wouldn't get many of these Scarlet girls willing to risk the indignity.[83]

Suggestions of this nature showed the hatred for prostitutes and the perception that they had caused damage to the wholesomeness of men in the island. Fortunately, these suggestions were never taken seriously. But the Social Purity Association, formed August 31, 1916, offered more than just suggestions. Concerned with the poor state of sexual health in Jamaica, the Association examined the laws and showed how these could be improved. It embarked on an education campaign to educate the public about the issues. Immorality and the harmful effects of VDs were among those issues addressed.[84] The government also took the opportunity to appoint commissions to investigate the problems associated with the spread of VDs in the island. One committee was headed by Mrs. Neville Rolfe, secretary-general of the British Hygiene Council. Rolfe visited Jamaica in May 1936, with the aim of reporting to Governor Edward Denham (1934–1938) and the Legislative Council her study and findings. In the report, Rolfe stated that she believed that brothels were the focal point of infections, and that it was impossible to solve the problem of VDs if brothels existed. Rolfe, too, was of the opinion that infected women (rather than infected men) were a great danger to the community. In her estimate, ninety percent of professional prostitutes were infected, and she suggested, among other things, that a health officer should be selected and put in charge of a Venereal Disease Scheme. Dr. Ferreira filled the role in 1937.

In the report submitted by Rolfe, she suggested that clinics for men and women should be maintained in Kingston, Montego Bay, Spanish Town, and Port Antonio. Rolfe noted that this was necessary to curb the spread of VDs among the local population, and to allow Jamaica to fulfill its obligations under the Brussels Agreement.[85] A clinic for men was needed at the dock areas, and special counseling sessions were needed for women and children. The use of "quack" remedies had to be curtailed with urgently needed legislation. A proposal for £6,165 to be approved for the 1937–1938 period to equip VD clinics all over the island was submitted in response to Rolfe's suggestions.[86] The Venereal Disease Act of 1937 addressed the use of "quack" remedies by stipulating that only duly registered medical practitioners should treat persons with VDs. Anyone found administering treatments without proper approval, faced a fine of up to $20 and imprisonment for up to three months. After the first offense, the fine increased to $50, and the maximum term of imprisonment was changed from three to six months.[87]

There was a feeling that women should play key roles in the fight against VDs. Rolfe, in a lecture, suggested training female police to care for women and children.[88] The Moyne Commission recommended additional female doctors to work in gynecological clinics where the patients were also females.[89] Rolfe and the Commission advocated for the use of printed and audio-visual materials to educate the population about VDs. The Jamaica Social Purity Association took up the challenge and began using printed material to spread the required information. The Women's Social Service Association sponsored public lectures in another bid to educate the people about VDs. Influential citizens joined the list of persons who supported education as a way to curb the threats, and R. Youngman of the Port Welfare Committee was one of these persons. Youngman suggested that a vigorous campaign should be carried out to alert both men and women not just about the dangers of the diseases, but also the ease with which each could be contracted.[90]

WORLD WAR II

Despite these measures, the World War II era saw many of the trends during World War I and the interwar years continuing. Women again had to bear the brunt of the blame for the growing number of VD cases among the troops. The prevention of VDs involved simultaneously policing the prostitutes and protecting the military. One of the supporters of this approach was a committee known as the Port Welfare Authority, which was formed to protect the health of seafarers, in accordance with the Brussels Agreement. Many other bodies were represented on this committee, namely the Harbor Master, the Medical Department, the Police, the Jamaica Women's League, the Victoria League, and the Kingston and St. Andrew Corporation. The feeling among these other organizations was that regulatory campaigns against women and VDs should be started as a war-time measure to safeguard the efficiency of the military. The committee itself supported strengthening several existing laws to deal with VDs, prostitution, and to restrict the sale of alcohol. Similar to the campaign used during the First World War, it was felt that many people contracted VDs because of intoxication. As one naval commander argued, "there is always the difficulty that a naval rating, after partaking of cheap liquor, is not in complete possession of his senses and falls as easy victim to the allurements of a woman." The commander suggested that in the interest of naval ratings, those premises that sold alcohol should close at 6 pm to deter the men from being out late and consuming large amounts of alcohol during that time.[91]

Again, very few people supported the view that military personnel could not control themselves, and therefore needed the government to pass laws to help them to manage their urges. Many of the suggestions focused again on the so-called "dangerous" women. With respect to prostitution, the suggestion was that any person (meaning women) seen soliciting, or loitering with the intent of soliciting, in any public place, should be arrested without a warrant. A law should be passed making it mandatory for persons with VDs to notify the authorities. It was also suggested that stipendiary magistrates should try cases involving women who were prostitutes, and seen as sources of VDs. Other magistrates tended to be too lenient.[92]

For the most part, these recommendations failed to curb the spread of VDs. The problem was due not just to the women, but also to the men who always found ways to reach the women for sex. These men saw sex and alcohol as normal parts of military life, and were willing to risk a great deal to gain access to both. It was felt by some that if places for recreation were available, the troops would make use of these as alternative to brothels, but, in reality, this was not true. Nothing kept the men away from those establishments. Entertainment centers were provided, including the "Silver Slipper Plaza" in Cross Roads, which was a dance hall. The YMCA and playing fields were also built. In addition, the Victoria League and a woman named Mrs. Hawkes agreed to entertain naval ratings with trips and expeditions paid for by the League. This same organization started a Canteen Committee, whose aim was to make a home away from home for American sailors. Mrs. Hugh Watson, wife of the United States consul general in Jamaica, headed the Committee, along with the wives of military personnel.[93] Women's clubs, with women from the United States and Canada, were organized to provide entertainment to the troops, who were away from their countries. Two such clubs were the United Service Organization and the Maple Leaf Club.[94]

A report from a Dr. Ferreira showed that the schemes were not successful. Enlisted men continued to flock to the brothels and temperance bars. What each of the well-meaning committees failed to consider was that troops engaged in sex for entertainment, not because they had nothing to do. The mentality was illustrated in the novel *Small Island,* in which the character Gilbert Joseph, a Jamaican member of the RAF, explained how disgruntled men in the army were when they were told that they could not socialize with American women, because of the risk of contracting diseases. Joseph said that: "With our stomachs full, our thoughts had all returned to women. . . . No one knew how long we would be immured on this camp without seeing a curvaceous bosom, a rounded hip, a shapely leg."[95]

With no fear for their health and safety, it is evident that men in the army were mainly concerned with recreation involving food, drink, and the companionship of women. This trend that began during World War I continued during World War II, as the high rates of infection showed. Reports indicated that men from H.M. ships *Orion, Ajax,* and *York* contracted diseases quite rapidly in Jamaica. *Ajax* had eighteen known cases during a four-week stay, while *York* had a reported five cases during a seven-day visit. Without a doubt, *Orion* had the most alarming number of cases with a reported fifteen during a visit that had lasted for just two days.[96]

Even with the high rates of infection signaling that men were not refraining from random sexual liaisons, the authorities refused to place sanctions on the naval ratings. The commander-in-chief noted that "Kingston may have to be used as a base in war time. The psychological state of the liberty men, after many days at sea in war routine is likely to result in indulgence with wine and women."[97] Reports from members of the Port Welfare Committee upheld the double standard of allowing men to behave appallingly and blaming the women when things turned out badly. As Dr. Ferreira noted, "The control of the prostitute is best enforced by legal enactments, and efficient police action. The control of the sailor, including his prophylaxis is a matter for the Navy. It is up to the navy to regulate shore-leave and enforce prophylaxis."[98] Attempts to bring action against women started with including their names on dispatches from medical officers and naval commanders for penal action. Ten such women found in different bars were listed as possible carriers of VDs in 1940 by C.T. Hyatt, surgeon commander of a British ship. The majority of these women were black Jamaicans. At least two, however, were described as "tall, thin, well made English women."[99]

The commander, Hyatt, admitted that little could be done to change the oversexed nature of the women. Proper education could render some assistance, but the brunt of the effort had to be the suppression of street prostitution. Like others before him, Hyatt insisted that to cut VD figures, "the only practical solution is for prostitution to be . . . properly controlled with regular medical inspections." So, rather than impressing on the men the need to abstain from sex with the women, Hyatt proposed allowing them to engage in sex, but to ensure that the women were disease-free. Ships also refused to call at Jamaica because of the fear of VDs, and an admiral in the British fleet labeled Kingston the worst port he knew, even lower than Port Said, Egypt, and plainly stated that he would not permit the fleet to stop at Kingston.[100] This was embarrassing for the colony, to say the least. Jamaica had remained loyal to Britain during peacetime and during war. Officials in the island were distressed by the situation.

During World War II, many secret meetings were held with leading figures from the Canadian, Jamaican, English, and American military. In one of these meeting in 1941, for instance, the recurring issue of the danger caused by women was discussed. Inspectors Drake and O'Connor of the Jamaica Constabulary offered their assurances that the local police would arrest women engaged in prostitution. At the meeting, it was agreed that the men who went to prostitutes should be lectured to and given prophylactics. Treatment at the barracks for military personnel should be readily available, just in case the worst should happen.[101] Legislators joined the assault against prostitutes by pointing out that, though prostitution was seen as a social evil, under the law it was not illegal. As a result, Law 51 of 1941 was passed to amend the Offenses Against the Person Act. The amendment gave the police wider powers to deal with the problem of prostitution, especially in the brothels. The police vowed to launch a campaign to suppress prostitution in the country.[102]

Sergeant Major T. M. Cole targeted brothel owners in a campaign started in 1942. Two of these owners, Ione Biggs and Joycelin Johnson, were apprehended and ordered to pay fines amounting to £70 for their operation of the brothel known as "Hotel Bims" on John's Lane, Kingston. The case made headlines, and was a landmark case in the court system. It was the first time in a decade that such a case had been taken before a judge in Jamaica.[103] The hopes of reformers were renewed and for the first time in a long while, they saw that it was possible to close the doors of all the brothels in the city and end the scourge of VDs in the process.

Brothels were not easy to discover. They were disguised as lodgings and hotels, as indicated earlier in this chapter. Many were established on the waterfront where they offered other services to the crews of naval vessels. These establishments increased during World War II. A. Ritchie, a staff captain in the Jamaica Command, expressed his concern for "the alarming rise in the Incidence of Venereal Disease amongst military personnel" as a result of the increase. Ritchie added that he was worried "whether the Government can take any steps to abate these sources of evil and also whether roadside accosting can be dealt with by the Police as a civil offence."[104] Some of the brothels were established beside churches and elementary schools, and reports estimated that there were a total of sixty-two such establishments during World War II. These operated as hotels and lodgings, making it hard for them to be identified as brothels.[105]

One change that occurred during the World War II era was the growing realization that men were responsible for at least a part of their actions. In a letter to the governor, written by Edgar B. Hallett, secretary of the Jamaica Social Purity Association, the problem that the men themselves had to overcome was addressed. Hallett wrote that, "an opinion was freely expressed at the Meeting of the Association that any legislation should not be directed against the women only but that something should be done to hold diseased men responsible for spreading infection."[106] Sanitation Officer Glen Campbell also noted in a speech, that men should be held accountable for spreading VDs. According to Campbell, "I am aware that a woman is a more prolific source of infection, but when a man infects a healthy woman, he is responsible for every case resulting there from." Campbell added that any man who had built lodgings or rooms for the sole purpose of hiring "them out" for "promiscuous sexual offenses . . . is a moral leper and his foul den gives greater facility for the spread of venereal disease than the homes of one hundred prostitutes."[107]

CONCLUSION

It is undeniable that some women in Jamaica capitalized on the willingness of military personnel to spend money for sexual favors and businesses
thrived off the sale of sex and liquor when military personnel disembarked in
Jamaica. It is also true that the act of prostitution, without the use of prophylactics, could have led to the spread of infection, which would in turn have
deleterious effects on the health and efficiency of these men. However, the
fact that prostitution and VDs were synonymous with women was the major
hindrance to a successful campaign against the spread of infection. The focus
of legislators and military authorities was on lessening temptations, protecting soldiers from themselves, and blaming women, alcohol, and natural calls
of nature for the spread of VDs. Most of the attention was diverted away
from the problems involved in the sexual relations on the part of both sexes,
to figuring out how to get women off the streets.

While the control of prostitution in its entirety could have curbed the
spread of diseases, the error most administrations, including those in Jamaica,
made was to ignore men as part and parcel of the sex trade. The twin obstacles
of hypocrisy and false modesty that hampered the campaign needed to be
cremated in order for real progress to be made.[108] As physician Prince Albert
Morrow aptly explained:

> The fatal effect of every sanitary scheme to control VD has been that the mas-
> culine spreader of contagion has been entirely ignored as mythical or practically
> nonexistent; the woman has been regarded not only as the chief offender against
> morality, but the responsible cause of disease, all repressive measures to stamp
> out the disease of vice have been directed against the women alone. . . . VD
> seeks no man it must be sought in order to be acquired.[109]

Very rarely did this idea emerge from the Jamaican media or the relevant
authorities. As a result, regulations were not overwhelmingly successful in
curbing the spread of VDs, not so much because prostitutes were allowed
to practice their trade, but because even when these women were detained,
fined, or controlled through other means, troops would always seek out an
avenue to feed their need for sex. The policies may have borne more fruit had
they mandated the troops to take responsibility for their own actions. As a
"young bachelor," writing to the *Jamaica Times,* aptly noted:

> don't tell me about the prostitutes as our excuse for being vile. They would clear
> the scene if we did not encourage them, how is it that they keep from some of
> us? Can't you see then that we are not without fault? Surely no merchant would
> stock a line of goods for which he would never secure sale, be the goods ever
> so excellent.[110]

Notes

1. Thomas Thistlewood was a manager and enslaver who lived in Jamaica from 1750–1786. His journals have been published by Douglas Hall in the book, *In Miserable Slavery: Thomas Thistlewood in Jamaica, 1750–1786* (London: Macmillan, 1989).

2. Verene Shepherd, *I Want to Disturb My Neighbor: Lectures On Slavery, Emancipation & Post-Colonial Jamaica* (Kingston: Ian Randle Publishers, 2009), 31.

3. Hilary Beckles, "Property Rights in Pleasure: The Marketing of Enslaved Women's Sexuality," in *Caribbean Slavery in the Atlantic World: A Student Reader,* eds. Verene Shepherd and Hilary Beckles (Kingston: Ian Randle Publishers, 2000), 692. In other works, Beckles, Kempadoo, Bush, and others have also argued that though prostitution was a basis for domination over women during slavery, it was also manipulated by the women (particularly mulatto or colored women) who sometimes made strategic use of their exoticization to improve their status and that of their children. See Hilary Beckles, *Natural Rebels: A Social History of Enslaved Black Women in Barbados* (New Brunswick: Rutgers University Press, 1989); Kamala Kempadoo, "Continuities and Change: Five Centuries of Prostitution in the Caribbean," in *Sun, Sex and Gold: Tourism and Sex Work in the Caribbean,* ed. Kamala Kempadoo (Lanham: Rowman and Littlefield Publishers, 1999); and Barbara Bush, *Slave Women in Caribbean Society, 1650–1838* (Kingston: Heinemann Caribbean, 1990).

4. See, for instance, Fernando Henriques, *Prostitution and Society: Europe and the New World Vol. 2: Europe and the New World* (London: Maggibbon and Kee, 1963); Bush, *Slave Women in Caribbean Society;* Shepherd, *I Want to Disturb My Neighbor;* Beckles, "Property Rights in Pleasure"; Kamala Kempadoo, "Theorizing Sexual Relations in the Caribbean: Prostitution and the Problem of the 'Exotic,'" in *Confronting Power, Theorizing Gender: Interdisciplinary Perspectives in the Caribbean,* ed. Eudine Barriteau (Kingston: University of the West Indies Press, 2003).

5. Kempadoo, "Theorizing Sexual Relations," 160.

6. G. S. Rousseau and Roy Porter (eds.), *Exoticism in the Enlightenment* (Manchester: Manchester University Press, 1990). Quoted in Kempadoo, "Theorizing Sexual Relations," 161.

7. Beckles, "Property Rights in Pleasure," 694.

8. Paulette Kerr, "Victims or Strategists? Female Lodging-house Keepers in Jamaica," in *Engendering History: Caribbean Women in Historical Perspective,* eds. Verene Shepherd, Bridget Brereton, and Barbara Bailey (Kingston: Ian Randle Publishers, 1995). A similar analysis has also been done by Marietta Morrissey, who concludes that in the nineteenth century, the domestics in the British Caribbean tended to double as occasional prostitutes. See Morrissey, *Slave Women in the New World: Gender Stratification in the Caribbean* (Lawrence: University Press of Kansas, 1989).

9. Joanna Phoenix, *Making Sense of Prostitution* (New York: St. Martin's Press and Palgrave, 1999), 24.

10. Sigmund Freud, *Reflections on War and Death* (1917), quoted in John Costello, *Love, Sex, and War: Changing Values, 1939–45* (London: Collins, 1985), 10.

11. Costello, *Love, Sex, and War,* 17.

12. George Hicks, *The Comfort Women* (St. Leonards: Allen & Unwin, 1995), 3.

13. Ronald Hyam, *Empire and Sexuality: The British Experience* (Manchester and New York: Manchester University Press, 1992), 151.

14. Harry Benjamin and R. E. L. Masters, *Prostitution and Morality: A Definitive Report on the Prostitute in Contemporary Society and an Analysis of the Cases and Effects of the Suppression of Prostitution* (New York: The Julian Press, 1964), 132.

15. Costello, *Love, Sex, and War,* 120–21.

16. Quoted in Costello, *Love, Sex, and War,* 115.

17. The name, however, belies the reality of the task for Chinese, Japanese, and Korean females involved in an official system that gave Japanese forces the power to rape them. It has been estimated that as many as 140,000 "comfort women" serviced about thirty men a day after being abducted (many at a very young age) and were sold into a lifetime of sexual slavery. George Hicks traces the development of the comfort system and tells the painful stories of women who, miraculously, survived years of torture as sex slaves. These stories can be found in Hicks' book, *The Comfort Women.*

18. *The Gleaner,* March 7, 1917, 16.

19. Cynthia Enloe, *Bananas, Beaches, Bases: Making Feminist Sense of International Politics* (London: Pandora, 1989), 82.

20. Lucy Bland, "In the Name of Protection: the Policing of Women in the First World War," in *Women-In-Law: Explorations in Law, Family and Sexuality,* eds. Julia Brophy and Carol Smart (London: Routledge and Keegan Paul, 1985), 32.

21. Judith Walkowitz, *Prostitution and Victorian Society: Women, Class, and the State* (Cambridge and New York: Cambridge University Press, 1980), 3.

22. Sheila Jefferys, "Women and Sexuality," in *Women's History: Britain 1850–1945,* ed. June Purvis (New York: St Martin's Press, 1995), 195.

23. See Ruth Rose, *The Lost Sisterhood: Prostitution in America, 1900–1918* (Maryland: Johns Hopkins University Press, 1982).

24. Kempadoo, "Exotic Colonies." Op cit.

25. Allan Brant, *No Magic Bullet: A Social History of Venereal Disease in the US Since 1880* (New York: Oxford University Press, 1985), 10. Brant highlights the views of a French physician in this passage. However, as Dr. Rhashelia Crawford informed me personally, this myth may have been predominant because the female reproductive system, being largely concealed, may not have been as obviously diseased as the male. In men, early symptoms of syphilis and gonorrhea become visible and uncomfortable soon after infection. Women have early symptoms which, if left untreated, usually disappear within a few days, though they are still infected with the disease.

26. Brant, *No Magic Bullet,* 31.

27. For a full discussion on the repression of sex in the Victorian era and its relationship with the issue of power, see Michel Foucault, *History of Sexuality* (New York: Vintage Books, 1990).

28. Joan French and Honor Ford-Smith, *Women and Organization in Jamaica 1900–1949* (The Hague: Institute of Social Studies, 1985), 169.

29. *Jamaica Times,* October 1943, 4.

30. Ibid.

31. Though not blaming women solely for the economic problems which drove some to prostitution, Amy Bailey argued that, "We are not taken seriously by most anyone, and for the most part we accept it complacently . . . our illegitimacy problem is a sad reflection on our social and economic system. Womanhood in Jamaica is held cheap because of those very reasons." See "Our Women, Their Status," *Public Opinion,* December 28, 1940, 14.

32. In the Caribbean, works such as Amy Paul Raquel's, "'It isn't love, it's business': Prostitution as Entrepreneurship and the Implications for Barbados," PhD Dissertation (Los Angeles: University of California, Los Angeles, 1997), and Joan Ross-Frankson's, "The Economic Crisis and Prostitution in Jamaica: A Preliminary Study," Paper for Presentation at Symposium: Issues Concerning Women, 1987, have examined female prostitutes mainly as business people.

33. Phoenix, *Making Sense of Prostitution,* 24.

34. This idea appeared in *The Gleaner,* July 30, 1917, 11.

35. Dr. John H. Stokes wrote this in an American medical journal. See Costello, *Love, Sex, and War,* 290.

36. *The Gleaner,* March 23, 2000, Section D, 15.

37. Venereal Disease, Colonial Secretary's Office Correspondences: Jamaica Archives (hereafter referred to as CSO) 1B/5/76/ 3 #219.

38. Director of Medical Services report, February 9, 1938. Venereal Disease in Jamaica, Representations of the Port Welfare Committee, 1937–1941, CSO 1B/5/77 #2 1937.

39. As a result of widespread upheavals in the British West Indian colonies in the 1930s, the British government appointed the West Indian Royal Commission on August 5, 1938 to investigate the social and economic conditions in the various territories, and to make recommendations for improvements where necessary. The Commission was led by Lord Moyne, and became known as the Moyne Commission. See "West India Royal Commission, 1938–1939, Report and Recommendations," London: His Majesty's Stationary Office, 1940. For information on prostitution, see page 239.

40. Kempadoo, "Continuities and Change," 10.

41. Letter from the superintendent medical officer to the colonial secretary, March 27, 1936, Venereal Disease in Jamaica, CSO 1B/5/79 #258 1934. The tendency to link sexual reputations to race was also prevalent in the regulatory campaigns in Puerto Rico, and has been closely examined by Eileen J. Suárez-Findlay, in her work *Imposing Decency: The Politics of Sexuality and Race in Puerto Rico, 1870–1920* (London and Durham: Duke University Press 1999).

42. (Brothels Control Of) Letter from E.A. Glen Campbell, Office Chief, Sanitary Officer, to Edward Denham, January 1, 1938, CSO 1B/5/77 #95.

43. "Spirit License Act," *Laws of Jamaica,* February 1, 1928.

44. List from the Detective's Office, Kingston, March 20, 1915, Venereal Disease, CSO 1B/5/76/3 #219.

45. File, CSO 1B/5/77 95.

46. For more information, see Night Noises, Kingston, CSO 1B/5/77 #293 1934.

47. Letter from Governor Manning to Lewis Harcourt, May 15, 1915, Colonial Office Records: Public Record Office (now The National Archives, United Kingdom), Kew (hereafter referred to as CO) 137/709.

48. Letter from Inspector General to the Colonial Secretary, March 14, 1934, Venereal Disease in Jamaica, CSO 1B/5/79 1934 #258.

49. Venereal Disease, CSO 1B/5/76/ 3 #219.

50. Howe, *Race, War, and Nationalism,* 145.

51. This is in not unique to Jamaica. For a comparison of legal issues and prostitution in the wider Caribbean, see Suárez-Findlay, *Imposing Decency,* and for work on Puerto Rico, see Jose Flores Ramos, "Virgins, Whores and Martyrs: Prostitution in the Colony, 1898–1919," in *Puerto Rican Women's History: New Perspectives,* eds. Félix V. Matos Rodríguez and Linda C. Delgado (New York: M. E. Sharpe, 1998). For work on Trinidad, see Vishnoo Franklin Gopaul-Maharajh, "The Social Effects of the American Presence in Trinidad during the Second World War, 1939–1945," MA Thesis (St. Augustine: University of the West Indies, 1984), and for the Netherland Antilles, see Kempadoo, "Exotic Colonies."

52. This was passed at the local level, but was rejected by the Colonial Office, which had adopted a tendency to veto laws in the colonies that were deemed as harsher than those in Britain. For an overview of prostitution in England and attitudes towards it, see Fernando Henriques, *Prostitution and Society: Europe and the New World Vol. 2: Europe and the New World* (London: Maggibbon and Kee, 1963), and June Purvis, ed., *Women's History: Britain 1850–1945* (New York: St. Martin's Press, 1995).

53. Venereal Disease—declared to be a modifiable and infective disease, incidence of disease among sailors and the military: reports on the prevalence of syphilis, CSO 1B/5/76/3 #219.

54. Brothels Control Of (Regarding Law 51 of 1941), Report in CSO 1B/5/77 #95 1936.

55. Two part lecture by Mrs. Briscoe, carried in the *The Western Echo,* June 1, 1918, page unknown.

56. *The Western Echo,* June 1, 1918, page unknown.

57. CO 137/709.

58. "Vagrancy Act," *Laws of Jamaica,* May 23, 1902.

59. "Offences against the person act 1864, section 66 and 68, Suppression of Brothels," *Laws of Jamaica* 1864.

60. Venereal Disease, CSO 1B/5/76/3 #219.

61. Ibid. Most women were arrested for disorderly conduct.

62. *The Gleaner,* August 2, 1916, 14.

63. Venereal Disease, Letter from E.L. Hunt, February 2, 1922, CSO 1B/5/76/3 #219.

64. Venereal Disease, CSO 1B/5/76/3 #219.

65. Venereal Disease, Letter from the Senior Medical Officer, Jamaica Command, to the Headquarters Military Command, February 3, 1916, CSO 1B/5/76/3 #219.

66. Venereal Disease, CSO 1B/5/76/3 #219.

67. *The Gleaner,* August 24, 1934, 12.

68. Venereal Disease in Jamaica, CSO 1B/5/79 #258 1934.

69. *Blue Books of Jamaica,* EE 21; Prostitutes were not thought to be the major causes of these cases. Prostitutes at the waterfront were mainly patronized by troops. As Mrs. Rolfe argued in the "Social Hygiene Report on Jamaica," prostitution was not largely supported by the residents. The Commission saw commercial prostitution as a luxury that was beyond the reach of many working class civilians. See the "West India Royal Commission, 1938–1939, Report and Recommendations."

70. Hyam, *Empire and Sexuality,* 89.

71. Venereal Disease and Social Hygiene Report on Jamaica, CSO 1B/5/76/3 #219.

72. "Why they Won't," *The Gleaner,* January 17, 1934, 12.

73. Dispatches, July 7, 1915, CO 137/712.

74. Howe, *Race, War, and Nationalism,* 145.

75. Excerpt from *La Democracia* in Puerto Rico, quoted in Ramos, "Virgins, Whores, and Martyrs," 60.

76. Costello, *Love, Sex, and War,* 289.

77. See Brant, *No Magic Bullet,* particularly pages 10–15 for the effects of these diseases on the human body.

78. In Jamaica, syphilis was treated over long periods with irrigation and regular doses of salvarsan, mercury, sulfarsenol, amarsan, or mapharsen. Anti-gonorrheal medications included proseptasine, uliron, and urinary antiseptics, and albucid and later penicillin. See Venereal Disease Clinic report on results of treatment 1937–1939, 1B/5/77 1937 #209, and *The Gleaner,* August 4, 1942, 10.

79. *The Gleaner,* July 24, 1916, 8.

80. Brant, *No Magic Bullet,* 14.

81. Howe, *Race, War, and Nationalism,* 145. Congenital syphilis was also a cause for concern in Jamaica. A large number of the cases of syphilis between 1907 and 1914 were inherited. While there were forty-nine cases of primary syphilis, forty-three of secondary infection, there were fifty-eight reported cases of inherited syphilis, which lead to twenty-nine deaths. In 1936, another twenty-one children in public hospitals were diagnosed with syphilitic stigmata, while one other had gonorrhea. See Venereal Disease and Social Hygiene Report on Jamaica, CSO 1B/5/76/3 #219.

82. Venereal Disease in Jamaica, 1B/5/79 #258 1934.

83. James Herbert, "Do you agree with this?" *The Gleaner,* February 12, 1938, 25.

84. See *Hand Book of Jamaica* (HBJ) 1939, 564.

85. Under this international agreement, governments undertake to provide facilities for the free diagnosis, treatment, and hospital accommodation of the seafarers of all nations visiting their ports who are suffering from venereal diseases. Until 1936,

Jamaica was in breach of some of the provisions of this agreement, and a Port Welfare Committee was set up to address the discrepancies. See Venereal Disease and Social Hygiene Report on Jamaica, CSO 1B/5/76/3 #219.

86. Message from The Governor to The Legislative Council, November 23, 1936. Establishment of VD Clinic Kingston. Printed Message from Governor Denham on hygiene, 1937, CSO 1B/5/77 #84 1937.

87. "Venereal Disease Act," *Laws of Jamaica,* July 18, 1937.

88. *The Gleaner,* May 23, 1936, 7. This issue of female policing has been examined by Lucy Bland in "In the Name of Protection."

89. "West India Royal Commission, 1938–1939," 170–71.

90. Venereal Disease in Jamaica Representation of the Port Welfare Committee, 1937–1941, CSO 1B/5/77 # 2 1937.

91. Venereal Disease in Jamaica, Representations of the Port Welfare Committee, 1937–1941. Memorandum from Inspector W.A. Orret, CSO 1B/5/77 #2 1937.

92. Venereal Disease in Jamaica, Representations of the Port Welfare Committee, 1937–1941. Port Welfare Committee Memorandum, CSO 1B/5/77 #2 1937.

93. For information on the activities of the Victoria League, see *The Gleaner,* April 20, 1940, 10, and *The Gleaner,* September 27, 1941, 12.

94. For more information on these service clubs, see *The Victory Book: A Patriotic Publication (the entire profits of which will be dedicated to the imperial war effort),* editress Mrs. Robert Watts (Kingston: Gleaner Company Limited, 1941 and 1945).

95. Andrea Levy, *Small Island* (London: Headline Book Publishing, 2004), 128.

96. Venereal Disease in Jamaica Representations of the Port Welfare Committee, 1937–1941. Dispatch from the Commander in Chief, America and West Indies Station. To the secretary of admiralty, January 3, 1939, CSO 1B/5/77/1937 #2.

97. Venereal Disease in Jamaica Representations of the Port Welfare Committee, 1937–1941. Dispatch from the Commander in Chief, America and West Indies Station to the secretary of admiralty, January 3, 1939, CSO 1B/5/77 #2 1937.

98. Venereal Disease in Jamaica Representations of the Port Welfare Committee, 1937–1941. Letter from Dr. Ferreira, Medical Officer in charge of VD Clinics to Director of Medical Services, CSO 1B/5/77 #2 1937.

99. Venereal Disease in Jamaica Representations of the Port Welfare Committee, 1937–1941. Letter from C. T. Hyatt to the Medical Officer of Health, Jamaica, April 10, 1940, CSO 1B/5/77 #2 1937.

100. *The Gleaner,* August 4, 1942, 10. Port Said in Egypt is geographically isolated and sits on a low, sandy ground, west of the Suez Canal and east of Lake Manzila. The port was known for its high rates of VD.

101. Brothels Control Of (Regarding Law 51 of 1941). Minutes of a Conference on measures to combat VD among troops, December 8, 1941, CSO 1B/5/77 #95 1936.

102. Brothels Control Of (Regarding Law 51 of 1941). Letter from J.D. Lucie Smith to the Secretary of the All Jamaica Youth Movement, T. H. Beecher, September 17, 1941, CSO 1B/5/77 1936 #95.

103. *The Gleaner,* January 22, 1942, 5.

104. From the Staff Captain, Jamaica Command to Colonial Secretary, October 1, 1941, CSO 1B/5/77 95.

105. Brothels Control Of (Regarding Law 51 of 1941). Letter from the All Jamaica Youth Movement Institution to the Colonial Secretary, September 6, 1941, and letter from the BITU, March 26, 1947, CSO 1B/5/77 #95 1936.

106. Brothels Control Of (Regarding Law 51 of 1941). Letter to the Governor from Edgar B. Hallett, Hon. Secretary, February 4, 1938, Jamaica Social Purity Association, CSO 1B/5/77 #95.

107. Brothels Control Of (Regarding Law 51 of 1941). *Gleaner* Clipping, Thursday, January 20, 1938, 8, CSO 1B/5/77 #95.

108. *The Gleaner,* January 20, 1938.

109. Quoted in Brant, *No Magic Bullet,* 37.

110. *Jamaica Times,* May 25, 1918, 11.

PART II

CULTURE

Chapter 7

The Manioc and the Made-in-France

Reconsidering Creolization and Commodity Fetishism in Caribbean Literature and Theory

Michael Niblett

INTRODUCTION

"Neither Europeans, nor Africans, nor Asians, we proclaim ourselves Creoles."[1] This, of course, is the now famous and widely quoted opening line from *Éloge de la Créolité* by the Martiniquans Jean Bernabé, Patrick Chamoiseau, and Raphaël Confiant. The manifesto, published in 1989, sought to establish "creoleness" as the prism through which to understand French Caribbean identity. With its accent on the interaction and imbrications of fragmented and diverse cultural legacies, the manifesto quickly became a favorite within the field of Postcolonial Studies. The latter, particularly in the 1990s, was dominated by a poststructuralist-inflected thinking, which tended to manifest itself in a disavowal of all forms of nationalism, hostility towards totalities, and a celebration of liminality, migrancy, and border-crossing.[2] Equally important was the theoretical paradigm of "hybridity," which frequently served as a kind of master trope for analyses of this sort. In its rush to assimilate créolité to such frameworks, however, postcolonialist-poststructuralist perspectives often obscured important differences of emphasis in the Créolistes' work. There was also a tendency to overstate the novelty of the manifesto's ideas (admittedly something the Créolistes themselves were guilty of) as part of a more general desire to trumpet the epistemic rupture concepts of hybridity supposedly represented in relation to what were construed as earlier, fixed, or monolithic notions of identity.[3]

The result was that a large body of earlier work on creolization, produced by writers and thinkers from across the Caribbean, was either neglected or distorted by being read back through the optic of hybridity. It took a Caribbean specialist, Richard D. E. Burton, to point out that even the terms of the

Créolistes' opening declaration were not new. They echoed the writings of the earlier Martiniquan intellectual René Ménil, whose 1964 article "Problèmes d'une culture antillaise" had argued for a West Indian specificity by declaring French Caribbean culture to be

> neither African, nor Chinese, nor Indian, nor even French, but ultimately West Indian. Our culture is West Indian since, in the course of history, it has brought together and combined in an original syncretism all these elements derived from the four corners of the earth, without being any one of those elements in particular.[4]

In general, the treatment of the Créolistes' work can be seen as fitting at least in part into the pattern identified by Silvio Torres-Saillant, who has remarked that: "Postcolonialists resignify paradigms that the Caribbean had long developed, repackaging anew and exporting them back to the dependent scholarly economy of the Caribbean. Thus an endemic formulation such as creolization turns into the more costly imported commodity known as hybridity."[5]

In this chapter, I want to begin by considering Patrick Chamoiseau's 1988 novel *Solibo Magnifique*. This is a work that has often been viewed in Postcolonial Studies in relation to the hybridity paradigm, especially with regards to its portrayal of the relationship between the French and Creole languages in Martinique. Here, however, I wish to approach it primarily in terms of how it registers and interrogates the impact on cultural practice of the socioeconomic changes that have occurred on the island since its integration as an overseas department of France in 1946. I want then to use that as a way into thinking about the idea of creolization, as well as about related but nevertheless distinct concepts such as transculturation, exploring how they have been ill-served by their appropriation under the aegis of hybridity. Finally, I will return to the novel to assess the kinds of political projects it elaborates, or that its aesthetics, at least, can be seen to intimate.

SOLIBO MAGNIFIQUE

Solibo recounts the police investigation into the death of the titular storyteller, who has been "snickt by the word" (that is, he chokes on the sounds caught in his throat during a storytelling performance).[6] Through this investigation and its effect on Solibo's final audience, the novel documents the fallout from Martinique's colonial past and departmentalized present. It portrays a clash and coexistence of realities from radically different moments in history, the result of the imperial imposition of capitalist modes and structures upon the island. The ensuing disjunction between competing understandings of space and time is neatly staged during Chief Inspector Pilon's investigation into what he believes is Solibo's murder. Take this scene, for instance, in which Pilon interrogates the witness, Bête-Longue:

> Monsieur Bête-Longue, what is your age, profession, and permanent address?
> –Huh?
> –The Inspector asks you what hurricane you were born after, what you do for the béké, and what side of town you sleep at night? Bouaffesse specifies.
> –I was born right before Admiral Robert, I fish with Kokomerlo on Rive Droite, and I stay at Texaco, by the fountain (pp. 95–96).

To classify his suspect, Pilon employs the language of state bureaucracy and the principles of social construction upon which it is predicated. As a member of the elite, Pilon has internalized a perceptual schema adjusted to norms and models originating in the metropole. Bête-Longue's initial incomprehension and eventual response indicate his rather different grasp of reality, one grounded in his practical experience of the landscape. Yet, it is Pilon's abstract framework that counts as legitimate, tied, as it is, to the ruling political dispensation. The power of the law here is inextricable from its ability to inscribe people within categories sanctioned by a state structurally integrated into a foreign system of government.

Now, the departmentalization of Martinique, as of Guadeloupe and French Guiana, had been broadly welcomed initially as a step on the road to decolonization. It quickly became apparent, however, that the consequences were, in fact, to be greater dependency and simultaneous over- and under-development. As Richard D. E. Burton notes, French manufactured goods flooded into the departments, "displacing locally made goods and undermining the very real degree of economic self-sufficiency that had obtained under the former dispensation." "Scarcely 25 years after departmentalization," continues Burton, "French West Indians were confronted by the effective erosion of the traditional economic base (agriculture, fishing, craft industries) and its replacement by a top-heavy service economy dependent on imported goods, themselves purchased by transfers of public and private funds from France."[7] *Solibo* captures the destabilizing effect had on the community by the disintegration of the occupations and crafts that once provided a mediating link to the environment. As the witnesses to Solibo's death contemplate how the island has changed—

> Richard Coeurillon and Zaboca spoke of a time of harvests and smokestack factories, at that time one man handled a machine, the other a scythe, that was time, but now if the fields are deserted and the factory whistles no longer give

rhythm to the day, now that your hands no longer know how to lash a rope, braid, nail, cut anything, where does time happen, Inspekder? Some say it's France, that there, there is time (p. 98).

—it becomes clear that if the modern service economy has emancipated people from laboring in fields and factories, it has also divorced them from any sense of control over reality: time itself is suffered; it is only meaningful elsewhere. In such circumstances the whole community could descend into the kind of madness and obsolescence Chamoiseau depicted as the fate of the odd-job men of the Fort-de-France market in his earlier novel *Chronique des sept misères.*[8]

In this respect, *Solibo* develops a concern that dominated many Francophone Caribbean novels in the 1970s, when recognition of the "cultural impoverishment" wrought by departmentalization resulted, as Beverly Ormerod notes, in a series of protagonists "whose personal alienation [was] suggestive of national confusion and distress regarding cultural identity."[9] Characters like the titular anti-hero of Vincent Placoly's *La vie et la mort de Marcel Gonstran,* found themselves locked in a world of madness and sterility, the history of their fractured communities as exhausted as the despoiled landscape. Such themes perhaps found fullest expression in Édouard Glissant's seminal 1975 novel, *Malemort.* Here, the obscuration of the community's history reduces people to a zombified or schizophrenic state, with the inability to articulate cultural memory manifested in a corporeal tension: "the jerking of the body," as the novel puts it, "suddenly arched in the impossibility of saying anything."[10]

As regards *Solibo,* it is clear that here, too, cultural representation is being arrested—indeed, strangulated. The very grounds of expression are being lost with the erosion of the material base: increasingly, it is no longer simply a disjunction between realities that is at stake, but the wholesale obliteration of one of them. As occupations and crafts disappear with the transformation of the Martiniquan economy under departmentalization, so too does the social history they kept in view. Discussing the character Congo, who makes manioc graters, the narrator expands on the relationship between certain foods, their methods of preparation, and the particular historical eras they evoke. During the "manioc epoch," Congo was able to make a living bartering his graters. However, the "Made-in-France stuff undid the manioc, putting it out of our way and even our memory. Now, wheat flour was needed for bread. Eating well meant eating steak and french fries" (p. 142). Congo continues to make graters, but his "anachronistic silhouette" has become a "hopeless symbol of those epochs when we had been different and from which now everyone turned away" (p. 142). The waning of Congo's craft thus signals the waning of historical memory. Replacing the manioc are those imported foodstuffs that, pre-packaged and sold in supermarkets, no longer bear the traces of the material practice required to produce them, or of the social relations determining their distribution.

If such is the fate of artisan crafts, then it should be no surprise that Solibo's occupation as a storyteller is similarly on the verge of extinction. In his well-known ruminations on storytelling, Walter Benjamin observes that this practice is itself "an artisan form of communication." "It does not aim to convey the pure essence of the thing, like information or a report," he argues. "It sinks the thing into the life of the storyteller, in order to bring it out of him again. Thus traces of the storyteller cling to the story the way the handprints of the potter cling to the clay vessel."[11] The fact that in Martinique, Solibo has "seen the tales die," testifies not just to the loss of stories and memories, but to "the suffering pulse of a world coming to an end" (pp. 156, 159). Solibo's death is inevitable in this sense, since he exists as a storyteller only in his connection to that world. Indeed, his stiffened corpse is emblematic of the reification and cadaverization of society as a whole, as it confronts what Glissant once called the "cultural genocide" of assimilation.[12] Tellingly, under the ruling political and socioeconomic dispensation, the only way put forward to preserve the history Solibo and his tales embody is to turn it into a commodity; yet, to do so only hastens its demise.

Solibo is well aware of this. He seeks to "inscribe his words in our ordinary life," but sees that besides "a few out-of-the-way places . . . the space for this folklore was dwindling. Organizers of the cultural festival had often solicited him for storytelling bits, but Solibo, dreading these kinds of conservation measures where you left life's theatre to stand within an artificial frame, had given mysterious excuses" (p. 156). The danger with such displays is that they abstract the storytelling performance from its social context. It becomes severed from lived experience, and is gradually made over into a commercial spectacle. A process that Richard Price has termed the "postcarding of the past" occurs whereby embedded historical and social meanings are leeched out of the cultural object or act, reducing it to an ornamental husk fit only to be marketed to tourists.[13] Moreover, the way in which storytelling becomes confined to officially sanctioned folkloric festivals suggests the public sphere is being eroded with the saturation of the civic domain by the commodity form. In *Solibo,* what was an open, publicly accessible, communicative practice that engaged with contemporary society—Solibo's final performance, for instance, took place on the Savannah in the middle of Fort-de-France—is being fenced off as picturesque heritage. (It is significant in this regard that the location of Solibo's final performance is ultimately cordoned off by the police, colonized by the state.)

Glissant has written extensively on the pernicious influence of such "folklorization." He is particularly concerned with the way that in Martinique, it is inextricably bound up with the status of the Creole language, the latter obviously being central to subaltern cultural practices, not least storytelling. "[A] national language is the one in which a people produces," he argues.[14] In order to articulate the community, structuring effectively its relationship to a reality ordered symbolically by this same representation, a language must be bound to the practices and institutions through which space-time structuration is effected and the rapport to the environment mediated. The difficulty for Creole is that both the system of production in which it was forged (the plantation), as well as the crafts to which it was later connected, have disappeared. Replacing them is an imposed system of exchange (between French goods and Martiniquan services). And "with the standardization of business . . . with the importation of all natural and manufactured products . . . Creole in fact, in the logic of this system, no longer has a *raison d'être*. . . . A language *in which* one no longer makes anything (so to speak) is a threatened language. A folkloric language."[15] The dangers of folklorization are acute for a mode of expression that has not been "structured" in relation to a system of production, and so lacks the dialectical connection to the world which would enable it to provide a reflection on the history that has shaped it. These concerns can be extended to cultural practice in general. For Glissant, the "folkloric background represented, reflected on, given a cultural thrust, is raised to the level of consciousness, shapes it, and—strengthened by the very action of reinforcing consciousness—criticizes itself as a consciousness in its new 'form' as 'culture.'"[16] In Martinique, however, the community has been denied the resources to reinforce its cultural articulation and initiate a self-reflexive critique, while the elite, who might have taken charge of guiding the move from folklore to consciousness, are "precisely that part of the social body whose function here is to be both alienated and alienating."[17]

The inability to re-establish a connection between cultural forms and material reality reinforces the ossification of the former, thereby neutralizing their potential to interrogate the received contours of the social world. It was for this reason that, as Fanon observed, when new kinds of engaged arts and practices emerged during the Algerian liberation struggle, it was the colonialists who rushed "to the help of the traditions of the indigenous society" in order to ensure they remained locked in a devitalizing aspic.[18] Thus, similarly in Martinique, writes Glissant, the "first official who comes along will defend indigenous cultural manifestations, and their 'enchanting' quality." He concludes: "Folkloric displays are therefore never part of a program of self-expression, which is what paralyses them."[19]

COLONIALISM, CAPITALISM,
AND COMMODITY FETISHISM

Such reification needs to be understood also within the wider context of the generalization of commodity production under capitalism. Indeed, it is the fetishism of the commodity that is centrally important to that attenuation of a sense of history we have observed. For Marx, of course, commodity fetishism arose from the peculiar social character of labor under capitalism, whereby the "labor of private individuals manifests itself as an element of the total labor of society only through the relations which the act of exchange establishes between the products, and, through their mediation, between the producers." The result is that to the producers, "the social relations between their private labors appear as what they are, i.e. they do not appear as direct social relations between persons in their work, but rather as material [*dinglich*] relations between persons and social relations between things."[20] Hence does the commodity now confront the producer as an alien object, with the labor stored within it concealed from view and the social relations between individuals that determine its production eclipsed. What we see in *Solibo,* then, is the way this effacement of social relations, and the nullification of an individual's sensuous connection to a thing, can extend right across the social world, entailing the commodification of the past and the traversing of subjectivities by the logic of capital (the trajectory, of course, of any number of societies under the social imperialism of late capitalism). Thus, there emerges what begins to feel like a perpetual present as antecedents are obscured and the possibility of alternative futures forgotten.[21]

In the *Economic and Philosophic Manuscripts of 1844,* the young Marx theorized the connection between the commodity form, the body, and the senses. Not only, he argued, does capitalism entail the producer's estrangement from his or her body (in the sense that human labor is invested in an object that then returns as an alien commodity), but also private property leads to the nullification of the senses, of those "*human* relations to the world—seeing, hearing, smelling, tasting, feeling, thinking, being aware, sensing, wanting, acting, loving."[22] "In place of *all* these physical and mental senses," writes Marx, "there has therefore come the sheer estrangement of *all* these senses—[by] the sense of *having.*"[23] Crucially, the senses have a history: they are conditioned by the object before them. Under the aegis of commodity production, when the thing they relate themselves to is a nonsocial object (insofar as its social character is occulted) the senses become lost in the object; they are themselves objectified. Thus the eye, for example, will become a *human* eye only when "its *object* has become a social, *human* object."[24]

This kind of reification or dulling of the senses is evident in *Solibo*. For the poor, it is bound up with the reduction of their lives to mere survival and that distance from reality which opens up as their trades become obsolete and local produce is replaced by imported French merchandise. For example, whereas Sidonise, the sherbet-maker, used to grasp the world via her practice, "today the sherbet was made elsewhere, she bought it in plastic boxes and put it in her sherbet maker for style, [and] since then she glided over the hours and everything else" (p. 98). For the elite, this distance is already embedded in their structural dislocation from the Martiniquan milieu, symbolized by the senior police officers' inability even to understand the existence of Solibo and his craft. Pilon, for instance, on hearing from one witness how the storyteller's speech is inextricable from his other sensory faculties—"[it's] the sound from his throat, but it's also his sweat, the rolling of his eyes, his belly, the gestures he draws with his hands, his smell"—can only grumble that "this doesn't make any sense!" (p. 99). Tellingly, his approach to investigating Solibo's death is to draw a geometrical plan designed to unlock the mystery. Yet by reducing every event and person into an abstract point on the diagram, he succeeds only in obscuring the significance of the storyteller's being "snickt by the word." Pilon's methodology, moreover, owes much to the French detective novels he enjoys, emphasizing the over-determined quality of alienation in the colonial context: weighing on the characters is not only the reification of a sensorium confronted by an equally reified object-world, but also the imported character of that object-world.

Taken together, the above examples highlight the way the effects of late capitalism often resemble more insidious versions of those felt under colonialism. "In the pit of colonial domination," writes E. San Juan, Jr., "the native's senses, no longer effective powers of worldly intervention, are mystified and estranged until she/he is finally deprived of any awareness of identity as producer, as the motive force of history."[25] This could just as well serve as a description of that nullification of sensory plenitude we have seen achieved through commercialization and folklorization. Indeed, the way these obscure the historical processes that structure the social world, preventing the latter from being grasped as something that can be acted upon, suggests the continuation (again albeit in more surreptitious guise) of what Amilcar Cabral described as the "essential characteristic of imperialist domination": the "negation of the historical process of the dominated people."[26]

For Glissant, in fact, Martinique represents something like the extreme edge of this negation: its trajectory from colony to department has meant social relations on the island have continued to be structured directly by external forces, while the internal class struggle, which should have served as the driver of an autonomously determined history, has been distorted and eclipsed. "When, in a society, the relations of production and exchange (which 'determine' class relations) are *dominated* by an outside factor," writes Glissant, "class relations in turn are obscured, becoming artificial *in terms of the social connection,* that is, the given society becomes incapable of finding in itself the 'motive' of its development."[27] The short-circuiting, thus, of class relations that conform to norms not of the Martiniquan milieu bestows upon the island a "non-history," the persistence of this disjunction between social forms and a social dynamic making it the "only extreme (or successful?) colonization in modern history" ["la seule colonisation extrême (ou réussie?) de l'histoire moderne"].[28] In addition, since the distortions in relations of production and class cannot be elucidated politically (precisely because of these same alienating distortions) the society lives this "non-history" at a latent level, manifesting it only through what Glissant calls "routine verbal delirium."

There is not space here to analyze the latter in detail, except to say that of the four types of delirium Glissant identifies, three only confirm the general alienation. They seek to reconcile the gap between lived experience and an imposed history by consolidating the latter, repressing its alienating effects. Such behavior is evident in a number of characters in *Solibo,* including Pilon. What interests me, though, is the fourth type of delirium, that of dramatization, which is said to externalize the "torment of history," its sufferers acting out the conflicts and disjunctions lived by the community, their extra-ordinary "madness," paradoxically the only way to make visible the everyday madness of colonial society.[29]

It is Solibo who most clearly exhibits the delirium of dramatization. With the disintegration of the material basis of his craft and the saturation of society with French modes and structures, the storyteller is to be found speaking "to the only one who could understand him, and we saw him go by with his lips beating out a silence, talking to himself. There were two of him, but out of tune with each other: abruptly stopping too many times while walking, arms flying in the air too many times, too much hesitation choosing the path at the crossroads" (p. 157). Solibo's madness—his being out of phase with the social world following its metropolitan-driven modernization—is played out on the street. His schizophrenic behavior, which theatrically manifests the tensions within himself, as well as the phenomenon of split identities, is not just seen by the public; more importantly, it is recognized as mad. It is this visibility that helps bring to consciousness the trauma experienced by society as a whole. Through his words and dramatic silences, Solibo forces the community to reflect on its precarious position and to grasp that another history is, or at least was, in existence—in contradistinction to the perpetual present established by the commodification of social relations under the current dispensation. In this way, the hold of those abnormal norms that produce the delirious status quo might be weakened, allowing the community to look beyond the consolidation of alienated identities, towards the only action that could extricate it from such behavior: the economic and political transformation of society.

However, if Solibo begins the process of raising consciousness, neither he nor the novel *directly* articulate what new social and representational forms might emerge with any such transformation. Solibo's delirious communication must itself be re-structured if it is to provide a coherent vision of a revitalized society. Yet, it seems that his constitutive connection to a vanishing artisan world means the storyteller can only go so far in this respect. He dramatizes the disintegration of collective representation with the decline of his own and other cultural practices; but the forging of a new mode of articulation that could both draw upon these older practices and engage with contemporary conditions is something he leaves up to a younger generation. Indeed, the necessity but also the difficulty of fulfilling this task is staged in the narrative through the interaction between Solibo and the character of the writer "Patrick Chamoiseau," who is positioned as the successor to the oral storyteller. The appearance of the author in the text could be viewed as a literary form of dramatizing delirium that acts out publicly, as it were, the novelist's attempts to continue Solibo's craft in the form of the novel.

THE PIRATING OF CREOLIZATION

It is here that I want to pause and address the issue of creolization more generally. Chamoiseau's literary production, with its incorporation of the oral tradition and its admixture of French and Creole, is certainly understandable as a form of "creolized" writing. In fact, Michael Dash has suggested that *Solibo* is "a better manifesto for the *créolité* movement than the polemical *Éloge de la Créolité*."[30] Now, as indicated earlier, both Chamoiseau's fiction and his theoretical work have frequently been subsumed under the rubric of hybridity by postcolonialist-poststructuralist theory. Indeed, hybridity has become a kind of catch-all for such related yet nevertheless specific concepts like creolization, *mestizaje,* and transculturation. Crucially, the conflation of these terms in hybridization discourse—terms that had been invested with specific socio-political valences in certain concrete contexts—is achieved by emptying them precisely of that socio-political content to leave them as little more than monikers for cultural dispositions.

In the Caribbean, where much of the intellectual work on, and practical application of, these concepts was first carried out, different states or movements or thinkers employed them at different times for different ends, from reactionary attempts to mask class or racial domination, to progressive programs aimed at bringing about radical social change. As this implies, a term like *creolization* was not merely a descriptive catchphrase. It was a way of understanding social relations, its meaning and role thus something to be fought over by competing interests with opposed views on how to organize society. Contrary to how it is often seen today, therefore, creolization (or transculturation or *mestizaje*) is not inherently emancipatory; it has the potential to become so, but only when linked—as it was in certain formulations in the Caribbean—to a critique of the existing social order, and an historically grounded political project aimed at the transformation of state institutions, class relations, and the existing conditions of existence. Mimi Sheller accurately summarizes what is at stake here when she observes that,

> [e]arlier generations of Caribbean intellectuals invented theoretical terms such as *transculturation* (Ortiz), *creolization* (Brathwaite), and *transversality* (Glissant) to craft powerful tools for intellectual critique of Western colonialism and imperialism, tools appropriate to a specific context and grounded in Caribbean realities.[31]

However, she continues,

> [t]he explosive, politically engaged, and conflictual mode of conceptualizing creolization in the nationalist period of the 1970s has been met with a later usage, from a different (metropolitan) location, in which creolization refers to *any* encounter and mixing of dislocated cultures. This dislocation has enabled non-Caribbean metropolitan theorists to pirate the terminology of creolization for their own projects of de-centring and global mobility.[32]

Lost in this pirating are the political meanings and subaltern agency associated with those earlier conceptualizations, which were bound up with a broader insistence on struggling for the realization of the social demands of the poor and the powerless.

Before having a closer look at the theoretical coinages cited by Sheller, it is worth taking, as a point of comparison, an influential formulation of Caribbean-ness from the 1990s, one that accords well with Sheller's account of the general thrust of later projects of de-centring and "global" mobility. This is Antonio Benítez-Rojo's *The Repeating Island: The Caribbean and the Postmodern Perspective*. Of course, this study is not written by a "non-Caribbean" theorist; and it remains very much concerned with the historical, geographical, social, and cultural specificities of the region. Nevertheless, in conceptualizing the Caribbean as "a meta-archipelago" that has "neither a boundary nor a center," and thus "flows outward past the limits of its own sea," to anywhere from Bombay and the Gambia to Canton and Bristol, Benítez-Rojo's arguments do chime somewhat problematically with those de-historicizing appropriations of the region as an abstract sign of hybridity.[33] He argues that the, as he sees it, polyrhythmic, fractal, and chaotic quality of Caribbean cultural practice embodies the possibility of social transformation through an ability to sublimate violence. He writes: "Within this chaos of differences and repetitions, of combinations and permutations, there are regular dynamics that co-exist, and which, once broached within an aesthetic experience, lead the performer to re-create a world without violence."[34]

Missing in this formulation is a consideration of the material contestation of the dominant order that would have to take place if the desire to "re-create" the world is to become the progressive project it is clearly meant to be. In a move that corresponds to Homi K. Bhabha's privileging of the agonistic over the antagonistic, social conflict is here evacuated, so that those polyrhythmic cultural practices now appear inherently emancipatory. Even then, the lack of attention to social determinants raises the further problem as to where such emancipatory potential could be grounded. Benítez-Rojo's arguments begin from an analysis of the socioeconomic organization of the Caribbean under the plantation system, which he views as central to the creolization process on account of its role in the violent bringing together of cultures. But in moving to talk about the transformative potential of the resulting creolized cultural practices, he offers no comparable consideration of the social formations that might materialize this potential: creolization or the polyrhythmic interaction of cultures is reduced to an "aesthetic experience."[35]

This, I want to argue, sits awkwardly with some of those earlier theories of Caribbean cultural dynamics. Fernando Ortiz's concept of transculturation is instructive here, not least because Benítez-Rojo devotes a chapter to Ortiz in *The Repeating Island,* in which he seeks to align the latter's work with the critical thrust of his own. He argues that Ortiz's *Cuban Counterpoint: Tobacco and Sugar* ultimately suggests "that Caribbeanness should not be looked for in tobacco or in sugar, but rather in the counterpoint of the myth of the Peoples of the Sea and the theorem of the West."[36] I find this reading problematic for a number of reasons. First, Benítez-Rojo displaces Ortiz's emphasis on the materialities of tobacco and sugar. His own counterpoint of the "West" and the "Peoples of the Sea"—the latter defined as those societies that are born from "marine" cultural flows and "undeveloped in the epistemological, theoretical, technological, industrial, imperialist, etc. senses"—ultimately fetishises both.[37] Each is assigned their own respective kinds of knowledge and reduced to, in the case of the "Peoples of the Sea," a geographically non-specific and socially undifferentiated cultural grouping, and, in the case of the "West," an equally undifferentiated quasi-geographical unit. Although Benítez-Rojo speaks of the historic connections between the "West" and the "undeveloped" world, his culturalist emphases obscure the unequal power relations and systemic imbrications of these sites that produce them as "developed" and "undeveloped." Combined with that elision of their internal social differentiation, what we are left with is transculturation as the interaction of cultural substances as they "flow" around the globe.

Now, it seems to me that Ortiz's ideas are better served in Fernando Coronil's analysis of *Cuban Counterpoint,* which Coronil reads as enabling the demystification of the same kinds of reified categories that Benítez-Rojo seems to re-establish with his talk of the "West" and the "Peoples of the Sea." "By examining how cultures shape each other contrapuntally," contends Coronil, "Ortiz shows the extent to which their fixed and separate boundaries are the artifice of unequal power relations. A contrapuntal perspective may permit us to see how the Three Worlds schema is underwritten by fetishized geohistorical categories which conceal their genesis in inequality and domination."[38] In contrast to Benítez-Rojo's de-emphasizing of social reproduction and his accent on the mingling of substantialized cultural flows, transculturation in Ortiz's work is better understood precisely as a social process and as inseparable from indigenization in a particular environment.

Speaking of the different social groups and cultures that arrived in Cuba, Ortiz describes how each was torn from their "native moorings" and had to face the "problem of disadjustment and readjustment, of deculturation and acculturation."[39] But he locates these transculturations *within* the production of social reality: they cannot be divorced from the related disadjustment and readjustment of socioeconomic structures and techniques of production, which in turn reorganize social relations and determine the framework—the relations of power and modalities of domination and resistance—in which cultural practices are reproduced and refashioned. On the influx of peoples from across the Atlantic, whose diverse origins he carefully differentiates rather than subsuming under the sign of the "West," he notes that "Some of the white men brought with them a feudal economy," while others "were urged on by mercantile and even industrial capitalism":

And so various types of economy came in, confused with each other and in a state of transition, to set themselves up over other types, different and intermingled too, but primitive and impossible of adaptation to the needs of the white men at that close of the Middle Ages. The mere fact of having crossed the sea had changed their outlook. . . . And all of them, warriors, friars, merchants, peasants, came in search of adventure, severing their links with an old society to graft themselves on another, new in climate, in people, in food, customs, and hazards.[40]

Signal in this description of the transculturation process is the way it invokes the "transmigration" not of cultural substances, but of socioeconomic structures and multiple class fractions, all of which are readapted and transformed within the new environment.[41] Turning next to the arrival of enslaved Africans, Ortiz is again careful to differentiate between the diverse cultures and levels of economic development of these peoples. Again, too, he describes their experiences not simply in terms of a "mingling" of cultures, but in relation to their position within the plantation system and the particular organization of labor, land, and property it instantiated. Thus, it is in the context of the totality of these readjustments and the related production of new social relations that, as practices are refunctioned and re-assembled, culture is re-made.

The perspective on cultural interaction Ortiz's work opens up for us, then, is one that retains an emphasis on culture as practice and on the materialities of the social world. The disassembly, intermixture, and reassembly of cultural forms are not independent of—or in themselves determining of—social reality, but folded into its very production. This helps us to understand the apparent contradiction Coronil highlights in *Cuban Counterpoint,* between Ortiz's declaration that tobacco and sugar are "the two most important figures in the history of Cuba" and his claim that the "real history of Cuba is the history of its intermeshed transculturations."[42] In fact, as Coronil points out, this contradiction is precisely one in appearance only, for in Ortiz's thinking those transculturations are inseparable from the relations of production which organize Cuban reality: they are a part of the interactions and conflicts between human factors that determine, and are determined by, the socioeconomic structures that produce the commodities of tobacco and sugar, these commodities subsequently appearing as independent entities and the social organization that determined their production as inevitable. For Coronil, Ortiz's personification of tobacco and sugar helps reveal precisely how the appearance of commodities as "agents in their own right . . . conceals their origins in conflictual relations of production and confirms a commonsense perception of these relations as natural and necessary."[43] By treating tobacco and sugar not as things but as social actors, Coronil suggests, Ortiz "in effect brings them back to the social world which creates them, resocializes them as it were, and in so doing illuminates the society that has given rise to them."[44] Hence, tobacco and sugar *are* the "two most important figures in the history of Cuba," but only insofar as these commodities contain and conceal the social relations and collective labor that enabled their production.

On this reading, it becomes possible to understand transculturation as more than just a description of a process, but as an optic on commodity fetishism that can be used to unmask the human agency and structural determinants this fetishism occults. Once related to the whole network of human relations that organize reality, transculturation becomes a way to map the social totality, restoring a sense of historicity to social formations that otherwise appear immutable. As Coronil puts it, transculturation "breathes life into reified categories, bringing into the open concealed exchanges among peoples and releasing histories buried within fixed identities."[45] Rather than stopping at the point at which it identifies the heterogeneous forces at work in society—as many of those later theories of hybridity do—transculturation moves to enable a totalizing perspective. By so doing—and without being in itself inherently emancipatory—it highlights the possibility of reorganizing a hegemonic social order, grasped now as the product of specific social relations.

Various other Caribbean theories of cultural interaction, while they need to be differentiated from transculturation, nevertheless share with it certain features that not only distinguish them from those later, problematic appropriations of ideas like creolization, but also enable one to establish an alternative genealogy for such theories that should revise how they are understood more generally. As in Ortiz's work, these formulations display an emphasis on the materialities of the social world, on conflictual relations of production and on a de-reifying totalizing perspective. For example, meditating on cultural identity and Indian labor, George Lamming argues that "the concept of labor and the relations experienced in the process of labor is the foundation of all culture, and this is crucial to what I mean by the Indian presence as a creative Caribbean reality":

> For it is through work that men and women make nature a part of their history. The way we see, the way we hear, our nurtured sense of touch and smell, the whole complex of feelings which we call sensibility, is influenced by the particular features of the landscape which has been humanized by our work; there can be no history of Trinidad and Guyana that is not also a history of the humanization of those landscapes by Indian and other forces of labor.[46]

A process of creolization is implied here (indeed, Lamming later makes use both of that term and transculturation), but it is understood in the context of indigenization through the reproduction of the social world and a material (bodily) interaction with the environment. On this view, then, it is not a case of Indian cultural legacies flowing into the Caribbean melting pot, but of the imbrication of the Indian community in a Caribbean social reality as part of its contribution to the very act of materially reproducing that reality.

Similarly, when Walter Rodney refers to creolization in his discussion of the relationship between those of African and Indian descent in late nineteenth-century Guyana, he does so in relation to their "work environment and their responses to capital at the point of production."[47] Moreover, he locates any progressive potential creolization might contain firmly within the context of a wider social struggle: its significance lies in the possibility of its helping to bring people together to strengthen a class-based alliance geared towards restructuring socioeconomic relations.[48]

In fact, creolization would increasingly be used in the Anglophone Caribbean as a way to articulate a class-based critique of the bourgeois nationalisms of the 1960s and 1970s. This theorization of creolization was actually used against other claims to creole-ness, which had been deployed to cement class domination (further giving the lie to celebrations of creolization as necessarily progressive). In Jamaica, for instance, lighter-skinned middle class people of mixed African and European descent had sought to idealize such a mixture as a means to facilitate national integration; yet, by doing so, they set themselves up—as the group that most closely reflected this mix racially —as the "natural" representatives of the nation over and above lower- and middle-class blacks.[49] In his 1971 study, *The Development of Creole Society in Jamaica,* Kamau Brathwaite attacked this idealization of creole-ness as inspired by colonialist conceptions of society:

> The educated middle class, most finished product of unfinished creolization; influential, possessed of a shadow power; rootless (eschewing the folk) or Euro-orientated with a local gloss; Creo- or Afro-Saxons. For them society is "plural" in so far as it appears to remain divided into its old colonial alignments. They are "West Indian" in that they are (or can be) critical of the colonial power. But they are dependent upon it.[50]

Brathwaite was writing in the context of increasing popular disillusionment with post-independence realities, in particular the failures of elites to push through anything more than constitutional reform. Amongst a broad section of "the working class, the radical or revolutionary intelligentsia, and the very volatile urban youth," there developed a renewed sense of cultural nationalism, and a desire for wide-ranging social change.[51] Brathwaite's alternative view of creole-ness to that upheld by the middle class accords with these sentiments, its foundation being the traditions and practices of what he calls the "folk." Having discussed the development of creole society in eighteenth- and nineteenth-century Jamaica, he muses on whether "the process of creolization will be resumed in such a way that the 'little' tradition of the (ex-)slaves will be able to . . . provide a basis for creative reconstruction."[52] Here, again, creolization is more than just the mixing of cultures. Instead, it is grasped as a differentiated process, one particular strand of which is fastened on to and conceived in terms of conflictual class relations, whence it becomes associated with the possibility of political reconstruction—of the reorganization of the state and the renewal of national consciousness in line with those "folk" traditions and the alter/native social consciousness they embody.

CREOLIZATION IN SOLIBO MAGNIFIQUE

There are a number of other elaborations of creolization I could cite here which fit with these general themes, Glissant's being perhaps the most obvious example.[53] But I want now to come back and ask what this slightly different, less culturalist take on creolization might imply with regards to *Solibo?* First, it is worth returning to Chamoiseau's joint theorization of créolité in *Éloge de la Créolité*. Here, the issue of how one realizes the emancipatory potential the Créolistes attach to creolized identities is somewhat problematic. As Shalini Puri observes, they offer little in the way of a program for "social, political, and economic regeneration," which would be required to ground the cultural politics they articulate.[54] In this sense, they replicate some of the shortcomings evident in much poststructuralist-postcolonialist hybridity theory; hence, it is no surprise that the latter has found the Créolistes' work so amenable to its way of thinking. Nevertheless, the Créolistes do retain something like that totalizing perspective I have suggested is integral to the kinds of politically engaged modes of conceptualizing creolization outlined above. "Créolité," they maintain, "is 'the world diffracted but recomposed,' a maelstrom of signifiers in a single signified: a Totality."[55]

Similar to the way Coronil reads Ortiz's concept of transculturation, I think that such an emphasis reflects the search for some way of mapping the social totality as necessary to being able to grasp its determining historical and human relations—and the optic provided by creolization is one means of doing so. In this regard, the storyteller's madness in *Solibo* can be understood as an unconscious and delirious attempt to manifest the totality of distorted, externally warped power relations that produce the kinds of problems—the split identities, the delirium, and so forth—that afflict the community. As I have already indicated, however, although he manifests these problems, Solibo is incapable of articulating them coherently; and neither he nor the novel *directly* projects an image of a transformed social world in which they could be resolved. Part of the reason, I would suggest, is that if creolization (like transculturation) can be deployed to help unmask commodity fetishism, the problem here is that the colonization and commodification of island life has reached such a point—recall Glissant's description of it as the "only extreme (or successful?) colonization in modern history"—that it is now near impossible to penetrate the reified crust of the social world.[56] With the complete displacement of production from the island, its transformation into what Glissant has called a "consumer colony," the saturation of the life-world with those Made-in-France products, and the disappearance of local economic bases—with all of this it has become extremely difficult to open up a perspective on, in Coronil's words, the "concealed exchanges" and "histories buried within fixed identities" due to their precipitous erosion and the baleful "postcarding" of the residue.[57]

Nevertheless, while the novel does not offer a straightforward answer to these problems, that is, while it does not invoke explicitly the possible grounds of a new social order, I think implicitly, in its creolized content, it does provide a kind of utopian figuration of something which presupposes that order and thus signals a way out of the impasse. It registers the faint, shimmering outlines of a world that has not yet emerged, but which could come into being. Crucial in this regard are all those histories the novel does uncover, histories that are bound up with creolized practices that provide a sensuous connection to the landscape and reality—the storytelling and the different kinds of food-making, and so forth. Obviously, these are shown to be disintegrating, and just to hymn their qualities does not respond to the social situation. Indeed, it raises the danger that one may end up simply wallowing in nostalgia for the past.[58] But, I think this is not what Chamoiseau is doing here, and that, moreover, his evocation of vanished or declining customs is assuredly not meant to suggest that this past can be resuscitated as it was and re-established as the norm in place of the alienated present. Rather, he evokes what is, in a sense, a deliberately mythified past, one designed to provide a kind of utopian repository in order to help think and, crucially, feel a way out of the blockages of the present. The evocation of those creolized practices is the evocation of the sensory plenitude they are associated with, a sensory plenitude that suggests the necessity for re-establishing a connection to the land, and presupposes the transcendence of a reified life-world and the commodity fetishism integral to it.

To clarify this point, I want to turn briefly to Chamoiseau's later novel, *Biblique des derniers gestes,* published in 2002. Here, the importance of a sensuous attachment to the landscape and its inextricability from the political struggle for greater independence is highlighted when the protagonist, Balthazar, rails against those who eat imported fast-food. Describing how his ability to survive as a resistance fighter has been, in part, due to his understanding of the environment, he declares: "I am not like you French-fry eaters, who no longer understand the secret sense of the world!"[59] Balthazar's remark underlines the wider political significance of the addiction to imported products. The inculcated preference for these ready-made foreign foodstuffs exacerbates economic dependency, alienating people from the local landscape and obscuring the knowledge which would allow for a productive connection to it. Without that attachment to the land, there will be neither a consumer demand for, nor an ability to produce, local goods. As Glissant has stressed, the "trend toward the international standardization of consumption will not be reversed unless we make drastic changes in the diverse sensibilities of communities by putting forward the prospect—or at least the possibility—of this revived aesthetic connection with the earth."[60]

CONCLUSION

Overcoming the nullification of the senses caused by their estrangement via reification and commodity fetishism—breaking with those Made-in-France goods in other words—is thus a key factor in even beginning to see a way through to establishing a liberated society. It is the importance of the emancipation of the senses that *Solibo* gestures to, indirectly, through its evocation of crafts and artisan practices. But the return to those practices is not in itself the end point in Chamoiseau's thinking. Rather, they are used to show the importance of re-establishing a sensory connection to the Martiniquan landscape, and of revivifying an anaesthetized sensorium. As such, they indirectly suggest the changed socioeconomic order that would be needed to properly fulfill this. Thus, the optic of creolization in this context is not just a means of identifying patterns of cultural interaction or hybridity. Its importance lies in its relationship to the forms of labor through which the world is produced and reproduced. Bound up with the network of social relations, material processes and human agencies involved in these forms, creolization has the potential to map this network and thereby excavate its contours from beneath the opaque aspic of reification. That is to say, creolization might be deployed to unpack a reified object world by providing, in its representation of cultural connections and entanglements, a kind of symbolic grid or key through which to read off the lines of material force and social contestation that comprise the obscured foundations of the dominant order. In this way, it might become possible to grasp the totality of the latter, and so point the way towards its systematic structural transformation through new modes of praxis.

Notes

1. Jean Bernabé, Patrick Chamoiseau, and Raphaël Confiant, *Éloge de la créolité* (Paris: Gallimard, 1993 [1989]), 13. "Ni Européens, ni Africains, ni Asiatiques, nous nous proclamons Créoles."

2. On this point, see Neil Lazarus, "The Politics of Postcolonial Modernism," *The European Legacy* 27, no. 6 (2002): 771–82.

3. On the Créolistes' tendency to overstate the novelty of the manifesto's ideas, see Richard Price and Sally Price, "Shadowboxing in the Mangrove," *Cultural Anthropology,* 12, no. 1 (1997): 6–10.

4. Quoted in Richard D.E. Burton, "The Idea of Difference in Contemporary French West Indian Thought: Négritude, Antillanité, Créolité," in *French and West Indian,* eds. Richard D. E. Burton and Fred Reno (London: Macmillan, 1995), 146.

5. Silvio Torres-Saillant, *An Intellectual History of the Caribbean* (New York: Palgrave and Macmillan, 2006), 44.

6. Patrick Chamoiseau, *Solibo Magnificent,* trans. Rose-Myriam Réjouis and Val Vinokurov (London: Granta Books, 2000), 20. Further references to this work will be given in the body of the text in brackets with a "p." or "pp." to indentify the pages.

7. Richard D. E. Burton, "The French West Indies *à l'heure de l'Europe,*" in *French and West Indian,* 3–4.

8. Patrick Chamoiseau, *Chronique des sept misères* (Paris: Gallimard, 1986).

9. Beverly Ormerod, "French West Indian Writing Since 1970," in *French and West Indian,* 170–71. In addition to the work of Glissant and Placoly, Ormerod cites Jeanne Hyvrard's three novels of 1975–1977 (*Les Prunes de Cythère, Mère la mort, La Meurtritude*) as typical of this trend. She also points to Maryse Condé's 1976 novel about post-independence Africa, *Heremakhonon,* as equally concerned with the problems of cultural identity, in this instance in relation to the search for African roots.

10. Édouard Glissant, *Malemort* (Paris: Éditions du Seuil, 1975), 124. " . . . la saccade du corps soudain cambré dans l'impossibilité de dire quoi que ce soit."

11. Walter Benjamin, *Illuminations,* trans. Harry Zorn (London: Pimlico, 1999), 91.

12. Édouard Glissant, *Le discours antillais* (Paris: Éditions Gallimard, 1997), 173.

13. Richard Price, *The Convict and the Colonel: A Story of Colonialism and Resistance in the Caribbean* (Boston: Beacon Press, 1998), 173.

14. Édouard Glissant, *Caribbean Discourse: Selected Essays,* trans. J. Michael Dash (Charlottesville: University Press of Virginia, 1989), 102.

15. Glissant, *Le discours antillais,* 298–99. " . . . avec la standardisation des enterprises . . . avec l'importation de tous les produits naturels ou fabriqués . . . le créole en fait, dans la logique du système, *n'a plus de raison d'être.* Une langue *dans laquelle* on ne fabrique plus rien (si on peut ainsi dire) est une langue menacée. Une langue folklorique."

16. Glissant, *Caribbean Discourse,* 198.

17. Ibid., 207.

18. Frantz Fanon, *The Wretched of the Earth,* trans. Constance Farrington (London: Penguin, 2001), 195.

19. Glissant, *Caribbean Discourse,* 208–09.

20. Karl Marx, *Capital. Vol. 1,* trans. Ben Fowkes (London: Penguin, 1990), 165–66.

21. On the issue of the emergence of what feels like a perpetual present under late capitalism, see Fredric Jameson, "Marx's Purloined Letter," *New Left Review,* 4 (July-August 2000): 103, 108.

22. Karl Marx, *Economic and Philosophic Manuscripts of 1844,* trans. Martin Milligan (Mineola and New York: Dover Publications Inc., 2007), 106.

23. Ibid.

24. Ibid., 107.

25. E. San Juan, Jr., "Art Against Imperialism, For the National Struggle of Third World Peoples," in *Ruptures, Schisms, Interventions: Cultural Revolution in the Third World* (Manila: De La Salle University Press, 1988), 130.

26. Amilcar Cabral, "The Weapon of Theory," in *Revolution in Guinea: Selected Texts,* trans. and ed. Richard Handyside (New York and London: Monthly Review Press, 1969), 102.

27. Glissant, *Le discours antillais,* 633. "Quand, dans une société, les rapports de production et d'échange (qui «déterminent» des rapports de classes) sont *dominés* par un facteur extérieur, les rapports de classes à leur tour en sont obscurcis, deviennent factices *quant au lien social,* c'est-à-dire que la société donnée devient incapable de trouver en elle-même les «motifs» de son évolution."

28. Ibid., 627.

29. Ibid., 655.

30. J. Michael Dash, *The Other America: Caribbean Literature in a New World Context* (Charlottesville and London: University Press of Virginia, 1998), 12.

31. Mimi Sheller, *Consuming the Caribbean: From Arawaks to Zombies* (London and New York: Routledge, 2003), 188.

32. Ibid., 191.

33. Antonio Benítez-Rojo, *The Repeating Island: The Caribbean and the Post-modern Perspective,* trans. James E. Maraniss (Durham and London: Duke University Press, 1996), 4.

34. Ibid., 81.

35. Ibid.

36. Ibid., 176.

37. Ibid., 167.

38. Fernando Coronil, "Transculturation and the Politics of Theory: Countering the Center, Cuban Counterpoint," Introduction, *Cuban Counterpoint: Tobacco and Sugar,* trans. Harriet de Onís (Durham and London: Duke University Press, 1995), xli.

39. Fernando Ortiz, *Cuban Counterpoint: Tobacco and Sugar,* trans. Harriet de Onís (Durham and London: Duke University Press, 1995), 98.

40. Ibid., 100–01.

41. Ibid., 101.

42. Ibid., 4, 98.

43. Coronil, "Transculturation and the Politics of Theory," xxvii.

44. Ibid., xxviii.

45. Ibid., xxx.

46. George Lamming, "Caribbean Labor, Culture, and Identity," in *The Birth of Caribbean Civilization: A Century of Ideas about Culture and Identity, Nation and Society,* ed. O. Nigel Bolland (Kingston: Ian Randle Publishers, 2004), 621.

47. Walter Rodney, *A History of the Guyanese Working People, 1891–1905* (London and Kingston: Heinemann Educational Books, 1981), 179.

48. However, Rodney emphasizes that in the nineteenth century, "the existing aspects of cultural convergence were insufficiently developed to contribute decisively to solidarity among the working people of the two major race groups." See *A History,* 179.

49. On this point, see Rex Nettleford, "National Identity and Attitudes Towards Race in Jamaica," in *The Birth of Caribbean Civilization,* 465–66.

50. E. K. Brathwaite, *The Development of Creole Society in Jamaica, 1770–1820* (Oxford: Clarendon Press, 1971), 311.

51. James Millette, "Decolonization, Populist Movements and the Formation of New Nations, 1945–70," in *General History of the Caribbean. Vol. V: The Caribbean in the Twentieth Century,* ed. Bridget Brereton (Paris, London and Oxford: UNESCO and Macmillan, 2004), 215.

52. Brathwaite, *The Development of Creole Society,* 311.

53. Glissant's analyses in *Le discours antillais,* for example, underscore that if creolization is to aid in the construction of an emancipated cultural identity, it can only do so as part of a wider socio-political project, since to treat cultural practice independent of its material context, is to fail to grasp the enabling (or in the case of Martinique, disabling) conditions under which it operates. Thus, with reference to Martinique, he warns that when a population lacks control over the socioeconomic structuration of its own reality, cultural practice will become reified and hollow; hence, it is necessary to confront and transform these socioeconomic conditions, if the emancipatory potential of certain cultural practices and forms is not to be short-circuited. See, in particular, the section "Un discours éclaté," and especially the essay "Théâtre, conscience du people," in *Le discours,* 465–721.

54. Shalini Puri, *The Caribbean Postcolonial: Social Equality, Post-Nationalism, and Cultural Hybridity* (New York: Palgrave Macmillan, 2004), 32.

55. Bernabé, Chamoiseau, and Confiant, *Éloge de la créolité,* 27. "La Créolité c'est *«le monde diffracté mais recomposé»,* un maelström de signifiés dans un seul signifiant: une Totalité."

56. Glissant, *Le discours antillais,* 627.

57. Coronil, "Transculturation and the Politics of Theory," xxx; Price, *The Convict and the Colonel,* 173.

58. Criticisms along these lines have been made of the work of Chamoiseau and his fellow Créolistes. See, in particular, Richard Price and Sally Price, "Shadowboxing in the Mangrove"; and Richard D. E. Burton, *"Ki Moun Nou Ye?* The Idea of Difference in Contemporary French West Indian Thought," *New West Indian Guide,* 67 (1993): 5–32.

59. Patrick Chamoiseau, *Biblique des derniers gestes* (Paris: Gallimard, 2002), 185.

60. Édouard Glissant, *Poetics of Relation,* trans. Betsy Wing (Ann Arbor: University of Michigan Press, 1997), 150.

Chapter 8

West Indian Plays and Caribbean Masculinity

An Assessment of Black Jacobins, Ti Jean and his Brothers, Pantomime, *and* Moon on a Rainbow Shawl

Dennis Gill

INTRODUCTION

Drama is an artistic representation of life, but it also concentrates life, focuses it, and holds it up for examination. Unlike prose fiction and many forms of poetry, which require a range of significant reading competencies from participants, the situations in drama have already been read and sequenced by the director, and the audience's responsibility is primarily that of interpreting the action being lived out before them. For this reason, drama has always been one of the most engaging and lucid art forms for communicating feelings, situations, and ideas to audiences.

Understandably, then, while drama has remained primarily a major source of entertainment, it has also been conceptualized and used by societies as a cultural and ideological contact zone, whereby audiences are often consciously and unconsciously invited to participate in political and ideological discourse. Marxist critics, such as Terry Eagleton, have, in fact, suggested that drama (like other literary forms) is charged with ideology and is potentially a very influential agency for the transmission of ideology.[1] Within the postcolonial climate of the Anglophone Caribbean, there also seems to be a view that West Indian dramatists should be using their craft, not only to delight Caribbean audiences, but also, in a cultural and an ideological sense, for the purpose of reconstructing the colonial mindset. For Trinidadian playwright Errol Hill, West Indian drama should address the disunity created by the colonial past and "knit together . . . [the] fragmented confused society . . . our large working class elements with the better educated middle and upper class segments of our population; the poor and the powerful."[2] While for theorist Rob Canefield, it should "become a process of signification, a cultural 'contact zone' through which [the] community reinvents itself via a dialect between actor and audience and author/director."[3]

However, Barbadian novelist George Lamming, regarded by some as the "conscience of the Caribbean," does not only see West Indian Drama as a potential catalyst for self-analysis and cultural and social reformation among Caribbean peoples, but suggests that West Indian drama, along with the novel, are already at the vanguard and are getting the society "to look at itself and [examine] how it feels and how it thinks."[4] This chapter endorses Lamming's view and submits that West Indian Drama has assumed a crucial role in the ongoing discourse of Caribbean masculinity, by bringing clarity and new perspective to some of the more complex ideas often encoded in the more densely textual, academic discourses associated with Caribbean masculinity. I have taken a sample of four West Indian plays of the 1930s to the1970s, and examined how these plays may be applied to postcolonial theories, particularly to some of the key ideas encoded in Franz Fanon's *Black Skin, White Masks,* and Aime Césaire's *Discourse on Colonialism.*[5] The plays in this sample— C. L. R. James' *Black Jacobins,* Derek Walcott's *Ti Jean and his Brothers* and *Pantomime,* and Errol John's *Moon on a Rainbow Shawl*—address the motif of Caribbean masculinity in a very precise way.[6] Moreover, they share with Fanon's *Black Skin, White Masks,* and Césaire's *Discourse* a common interest in exploring the impact of colonialism on Caribbean masculinity.

This essay does not include the contributions of any Caribbean women playwrights, but the omission should not be regarded as an attempt to silence or ignore the significant contributions of groups such as Sistren to the discourse of Caribbean masculinity. Rather, the absence is due mainly to the fact that a primary goal of this chapter is to have Caribbean men to speak for themselves on the subject of Caribbean manhood, and, at the same time, to give us the opportunity to assess whether these male subjects reaffirm patriarchy in these plays, or are attempting to reform and redefine the perception of masculine.

Fanon's theory delineates that Caribbean male subjects are conditioned over time, through rigorous colonial indoctrination, to see the "white mask," which Fanon uses symbolically to represent a Western model of masculinity based on conquest and control, as the only form of acceptable manhood. Applying his background in psychiatry to strengthen his case, Fanon contends that while theories in classical psychoanalysis hold that mental illnesses usually begin with childhood trauma which is repressed, and later reappears as neuroses, psychosis, or other psychic disturbances, that in the case of Caribbean men, the catalyst for this trauma is the rejection of the colonizer/former colonizer and his world. Fanon surmises, therefore, that in the case of Caribbean males, the Jungian notion of the "collective unconscious . . . is purely the sum of prejudices, myths, collective attitudes of a given group."[7]

Furthermore, by applying his understanding of the underlying psychological and neurological factors that enable humans to acquire language, Fanon argues that the requirement by European colonizers for Caribbean peoples to master the standards of their languages to be deemed "civilized," has resulted in a form of schizophrenia among Caribbean subjects. Fanon contends that subjects who successfully acquire the colonizer's language develop a form of pathological alienation and self-division, since their learning of the new language involves their assumption of the civilization of the colonizer's world (the thinking, feeling, and being of that world), as well as their rejection of the world of their "fellows." Hence, Fanon submits that since they do not ever feel accepted in the colonizer's world, and also lose communion with the world of their fellows, they ultimately acquire a state of "non-being."[8]

Like Fanon, Césaire's sociological argument is that there is a correlation between "colonization" and "civilization," and that the operations of colonialism manifest a "decadent," "stricken," and a "dying" civilization. Césaire envisions colonialism, like capitalism, as reducing colonized males and females to function as instruments of production or to a state of "thingification." He therefore perceives it as a policy to keep Caribbean people in a perpetual state of dependency, and "cunningly" install fear in "millions of men," who have "been taught an inferior complex to tremble, kneel, despair, and behave like flunkeys."[9] In essence, these two theorists see colonialism as being destructive to both the colonized and the colonizer. They see it as castrating colonized males and creating within them a psyche which sees "black = ugliness, sin, darkness, immorality." They also envisage the philosophy of power and domination as destroying the humanity of the colonizer. For Fanon, the colonizer becomes alienated and dysfunctional because of the patriarchal mindset, and therefore, "to be human" they become slaves.[10] While, for Césaire, colonization resurrects the latent, atavistic traits, and "works to decivilize the colonizer, to brutalize . . . degrade . . . awaken him to buried instincts, to covetousness, violence, race hatred and moral relativism."[11]

JAMES AND THE POSTCOLONIAL SELF-HATRED

C. L. R. James in *Black Jacobins* provides useful insights on the binary, postcolonial arguments presented by Fanon and Césaire. James examines the St. Domingue Revolution of 1791–1804, and enacts the postcolonial situation in the immediate aftermath of the only successful slave revolt in the Caribbean. While the play in itself is set in the Francophone Caribbean, it is written from the point of view of a playwright from the Anglophone Caribbean, and is therefore apt for this discussion, since it informs us on the wider cause and effect relation between the operations of colonialism in the Caribbean, constructs of masculinity, and forms of political leadership. Like Fanon and Césaire, James advances the theory that colonialism, like capitalism, perpetuates a class structure, one which empowers the dominant ruling classes at the expense of the oppressed classes. James elects to utilize the epic theatre model, which is ideal for engaging an audience in discourse on the subject of the St. Domingue Revolution. The episodic structure of the play, it's loosely connected scenes, the symbolic use of characters, the fact that some of the actors serve as narrators and storytellers, as well as the reality that no attempt is made to conceal the fact that we are viewing a performance, are distinct epic theatre characteristics. This form of drama proves to be very effective in illustrating the Manichean-type class structure in the newly independent society, which both Fanon and Césaire have linked with colonialism.

Through the use of dialogue among the working class, which functions as both a reportage and social commentary on the state of the revolution, James informs the audience that although the oppressive French leaders may have been removed, the legacy of an oppressive class structure is still rigidly entrenched in the newly liberated St. Domingue. He uses the interplay between the aides of the leaders of the revolution, Dessalines, Moise, Christophe, and Toussaint, to draw attention to the Manichean structure that has been retained. There are no longer the "Big whites," "Small whites," "free backs," and "slaves," but in the new system there is Toussaint, the generals, their aides, the working class, freed slaves, and somewhere waiting in the wings, the mulattos who have mixed loyalties. The focus has shifted in the postcolonial from White Colonial dominance to a form of Black Colonial supremacy, whereby black elitist males are now in positions of power, demonstrating the same ruthless control over lesser men and women in society. In this regard, Césaire's theory of colonialism giving way to capitalism, and creating relations of domination and subordination, actually walks on stage.

The scene from *Black Jacobins* below parodies the concept of change under a colonial capitalist structure. It illustrates, somewhat amusingly, that while the cast of leading actors in political governance may have changed from white to black, the script regarding the way in which Caribbean men perceive leadership remains unchanged. Leadership is about control. It is about valorizing the male ego, and remains a way of asserting vertical superiority and dominance over the lives of the masses.

Marat:	All this goddam furniture to be moved. This is work for slaves.
Max:	They ain't got no more slaves.
Marat:	All right. Not slaves, but fellas to do heavy work. I am a soldier. I am free. What is the use of being free and having to move the piano. When I was a slave I had to move the piano. Now I am free I have to move the piano.
Max:	You used to move the piano for M. Bullet. Now it is General L'Ouverture.
Marat:	The piano is still a piano and as heavy as hell (pp. 391–92).

With the entrance of Mars Plaisir, the valet of Toussaint L'Ouverture, James now turns his attention towards addressing the postcolonial argument that the legacy of a history of colonial supremacy has resulted in the oppression, dehumanization, exploitation, and degradation of Caribbean men. He uses the interplay, in the episode below between Plaisir and the aides of the generals of newly independent Haiti (formerly St. Domingue) to address the question: how has a legacy of a repressive colonial class structure entrenched in capitalism impacted on the perception of the self, and the interpersonal relationships among Caribbean subjects at the varying strata in society?

Mars Plaisir: Now, on behalf of my General, General L'Ouverture, this room must be ready in ten minutes. You know what the General is about time. Tell them where to put the things—Jacques and Jean. Or maybe, Marat, they now have new names too?

Orleans:	Yes, I have a new name. I am now the Duke of Orleans.
Mars Plaisir:	(*Good-humoredly*) Good. You are a Duke.
Orleans:	Duke of Orleans.
Mars Plaisir:	Orleans. And you . . . Jacques?
Max:	My name is Robespierre. Maximillian Robespierre. Call me Max.
Mars Plaisir:	Marat, Max, and Orleans . . . Ten minutes. (He exits) (p. 392)

Noticeably, the dialogue between Plaisir, Orleans, Max, and Marat is used to get the audience to observe the vertical (top-down) nature of communication between Plaisir and the other three soldiers. Plaisir, as aide or valet to Toussaint, has more clout than the two officers. Plaisir's tone is not only superior, but contemptuous; the type postcolonial theory would associate with the colonizer. This is particularly noticeable in his sneering question with reference to the new names that the soldiers have assigned themselves: "Or maybe, Marat, they now have new names too?" And later, his final order, "Marat, Max and Orleans . . . Ten minutes," emerges as an authoritative gesture that reminds the officers and the audience alike that the rank and file are still perceived as the marginalized "other" in the new social stratification, of the revolution.

Fanon, more than likely applying Nietzsche's theory that a history of resentment often results in a contemptible attitude within the psyche of those who have experienced it, has suggested that colonialism has led to a form of self-hatred among Caribbean males who have been dominated.[12] The above episode seems to also shed light on this theory. Plaisir seems to be displacing the resentment which has characterized his colonial past unto the other soldiers he deems to be now as inferior to himself. He now lives out the desire to be the colonizer, which he would have only experienced vicariously in the era before the revolution. The three soldiers, for their part, appear void of a sustainable form of identity, even under black leadership, within a colonial framework. They appear more like caricatures, rather than empowered men under a liberating political system. Max has taken on the alias Maximillian Robespierre, a stalwart in the French Revolution of 1789, while his fellow officer, Orleans, has assumed the name the Duke of Orleans, a member of the French dynasty. James, through this scene, also makes the point that the self-division within Caribbean men ultimately leads to divisions and disunity within their societies. Since James depicts these characters as being representative of the larger society, the self-naming does not only signal a form of schizophrenia within the soldiers, but also manifests the erosion of the unity of the revolution with one section of the society favoring a republic, and the other leaning towards establishing a colonial monarchy in the newly formed Haiti.

It may, however, be James' portrayal of Toussaint that is the most significant offering to the postcolonial discourse of Césaire and Fanon on the subject of Caribbean masculinity. By offering Toussaint on stage, arguably as a tragic figure, and symbolically presenting him as the heart of the revolution, James essentially dramatizes some of the problems associated with colonialism and black leadership in the postcolonial Caribbean. Fanon has stated that, as Caribbean subjects acquire the colonizer's language, they also assimilate the culture and value systems, and gain a degree of acceptance. He further submits that in the process, they become alienated and dislocated from their cultural roots and lose "self."[13] Through Toussaint, James explores the phenomenon of the emotional and psychological estrangement that colonialism has enacted upon the Caribbean subject, as well as how the acquisition of the colonizer's language and culture has had a paradoxical relationship in the rise and fall of this subject.

James concedes that it is through the knowledge of the colonizer's language, and an understanding of the culture embedded in that language, that Toussaint emerges as leader of the black republic. Toussaint is introduced to us in the prologue reading alone with his wife close by, far away from the action of the slave revolt. James uses this scene symbolically to suggest a distance between the field slaves, who are at the vanguard of the revolution against colonialism, as against the privileged reading house slave, who is a distant observer to the struggle. However, by having the triumphant field slaves unanimously place the mantle of leadership upon Toussaint, the playwright subtly suggests that though the slaves have freed themselves in a physical sense, they are still psychically chained to the notion that leadership requires knowledge of the colonizer's language and culture.

Moreover, James asserts that the Caribbean leader's knowledge of, and critical awareness of the colonizer's language, mindset, and culture, are crucial to his political survival in a world dominated by colonial empires. In fact, *Black Jacobins* implicitly suggests that Toussaint's background in the language and modus operandi of the colonizer have significantly contributed to his becoming a self-confident, shrewd leader, capable of outmaneuvering the French, British, and Americans in the artifice of political diplomacy. In one scene, we see the Toussaint masquerading as the naive noble savage, swearing loyalty to Spain and convincing the Spanish general that he is "one of the purest spirits that can be found in these Godforsaken islands" (p. 395). Then, after being advised of the abolition of slavery in France by Moise, he promptly has the Spanish general arrested (p. 397). Additional evidence of his knowledge of the operations of colonial politics is also seen in his skilful handling of the mulatto uprisings and his duplicitous relationships with the British, French, and Americans. In dealing with the mulattoes, Toussaint wisely engages the services of his mulatto general to act as a liaison between the mulatto population and the new leadership. Against the Europeans and Americans, we see his mastery of political espionage. Being fully aware of the limitations of his army, he tempers the temptation towards reckless aggression and arrogance, and instead settles for diplomatic relationships with generals Hédouville, Maitland, and even Bonaparte (pp. 408–09).

Nevertheless, James also provides a visually compelling viewpoint of what Fanon and Césaire have identified as the alienating and psychical complications which may develop in the Caribbean subject as a consequence of the assimilation of colonial values. Toussaint is presented as a tragic hero, whose hamartia is a divided consciousness, and his fall provokes pity, and informs the audience of the cancerous nature of the colonial mindset. Toussaint, who has enjoyed the privileges of being a house slave, appears to be at ease in the world of colonial politics, but he is essentially an alienated man. James establishes this point by symbolically limiting Toussaint's presence on stage to his meetings with his generals, the European and American diplomats, and his mistress, Bullet. The very system of colonial stratification, which appears to have worked in the subject's favor in relation to his ascendancy to political power, has concomitantly exiled him from his people. The episode below serves to emphasize the self-division and pathological alienation in the postcolonial subject, which Fanon and Césaire have linked to the colonial experience.

Bullet:	No, Toussaint, that is over. I have come to say goodbye. I want your permission for a passport to go to Paris. I have spent many years of my life in San Domingo. They have been exciting years. First, the revolution, then the abolition of slavery, and then, you. Now it's over. I want to go.
Toussaint:	But Madame Bullet . . .
Bullet:	(angrily) Do not call me that. If you do I shall call you Commander-in-Chief.
Toussaint:	Forgive me, Louise, but if you go, I shall be left alone. Since I have become Governor, I scarcely have anyone here who I can call a friend. Over the years you have been the only one I can count on (p. 424).

Another significant point of view raised by Fanon that has been endorsed by James in *Black Jacobins* is the theory that Caribbean males perceive white women as symbolic fillers of the psychical breech caused by colonialism. Fanon describes this phenomenon as a race-based attitude, a neurosis whereby Caribbean males view white females as links to the status of the colonizer, and to achieve this status is the objective of Caribbean males.[14] While James reveals the clarity and precision of Toussaint's leadership in his earlier encounters with internal and external opposition when he is not involved with Bullet, he later shows that developing a romantic connection with his former mistress, undermines his role as a leader. He is torn, for example, between naming Moise as his successor and pleasing Bullet (which would please the whites) by distancing himself from his fellow revolutionary. James' depiction of Toussaint as being at his weakest when he is with Bullet is particularly evident in the scene below.

Toussaint:	Louise, forgive me. Here you are offering to give me what I needed so much and all I can do is ask you to undertake a political mission. Louise forgive me, I could not help it.
Bullet:	(smiling) Yes, I know you, Toussaint. You could not help it. But remember, I first came to you for a passport. I wanted to go and now I know that I must go. I wanted to get away from you and as usual, you are doing what I wanted (pp. 430–31).

James shifts focus from Toussaint to Dessalines, and highlights the latter's gradual dehumanization to show the destructive influences of colonialism on the psyche of black males in leadership. James thus directs our attention to the three, critical stages in Dessalines' rise and decline: (1) his rejection of the native cultural and spiritual practices of Voodoo, and his seeking the aid of Marie Jeanne, his mulatto mistress; (2) his quest to be leader of the revolution, which encourages him to turn to the French language and reject the Creole language of his country and people; and (3) his totalitarian, psychopathic leadership, a fulfillment of the desire to become the ultimate mimic man of the colonizers. *Black Jacobins,* therefore, functions specifically to demonstrate the crises which colonialism invokes upon the Caribbean male psyche, as well as the dehumanizing characteristics of the colonial brand of masculinity. More significantly, it provides us with concrete frames of reference in the form of men in leadership positions, whose lives have been influenced by colonialism, such as Toussaint and Dessalines. In this regard, the play opens us to a deeper, more intimate reading of the postcolonial theories of Fanon and Césaire.

PRE- AND POST-INDEPENDENCE CARIBBEAN MAN IN WALCOTT'S PLAYS

The next phase of this discussion interrogates the usefulness of Derek Walcott's *Ti Jean and his Brothers* and *Pantomime* to the discourse of masculinity. Through these plays, I attempt to illustrate Fanon and Césaire's notion that the philosophy of colonialism is destructive to colonizer as well as colonized. The two plays, which are over twenty years apart, are separated by the pre- and post-independence periods, and therefore present the opportunity to do a comparative analysis of Walcott's views on both periods.

Ti Jean stands out as one of most significant dramatizations of the nature and operations of colonialism, and is certainly one of the few plays to explore the complications that the philosophy of colonialism has imposed on the lives of the colonized and colonizer. Walcott, through his symbolic embodiment of colonialism in the character of the Devil, has used the stage to bring across a deeper understanding of colonial authority. The Devil, like colonialism, is interpreted as being paradoxical in nature, in that, while he/it has assumed a form of global omnipotence and omniscience, he/it lacks the power and knowledge to experience humanity. From the onset, Walcott stresses that the Devil or colonial authority is imprisoned by the very power used to destroy others. In the episode below, this external conflict between the Devil and subjects, as well as the Promethean conflict within the Devil himself, are revealed.

Bolom: The devil my master
                Who owns half the world,
                In the kingdom of night,
                Has done all that is evil
                Butchered thousands in war,
                Whispered his diseases
                In the ears of great statesmen,
                Invented human justice,
                Made anger, pride, jealousy,
                And weakened prayer,
                Still cannot enjoy
                Those vices he created.
                He is dying to be human (p. 33).

Like Milton's *Paradise Lost,* Walcott's shows the Devil as an object of contempt and subject of pity. His tragic flaw lies in his inability to feel, a bastion of colonialism whose albatross is the very same philosophy which has made him/it powerful, has damned him/it to inhuman immortality. Walcott perceives an inner tension within the colonial authority figure, in which he seeks to dominate, but also desires the humanity of the subjects he oppresses. Fanon describes this conflict as the struggle "to meet the human level."[15] Walcott expresses agreement with both Fanon and Césaire that colonialism is a dehumanizing mask, but one which inadvertently feeds on its subjects' humanity.[16]

In his portrayal of the Devil in the mask of Papa Bois, Walcott focuses mainly on the operations of what Octave Mannoni has alluded to as the "Prospero Complex," a view supported by Fanon that colonialism summons within the colonizer a providential, paternal, culturally superior desire to colonize subjects, and keep them in a state of childhood dependency.[17] Walcott conveys, through the Devil's action, that colonialism is variable and transferrable, and is now operating through the mythical Caribbean folk character depicted in Papa Bois. However, the playwright moves away from the folk narrative and presents Papa Bois in a fallen state where he has become alienated from, and an adversary of, both the creatures in the forest and the trees. He now operates as an appendage of colonialism and a predator of humanity, no longer playing his traditional, folk role of warning friends against hunters, but being controlled by colonialism, and functioning now as a hunter, luring human creatures to their deaths.

Papa Bois engages with some key colonial strategies which have impacted the Caribbean male. Markedly, Bois assumes the role of the authoritative "other," who determines the ego of the two Caribbean sons at the mirror stage of their development. Walcott suggests that the colonial authority figure replaces the caregiver in the context of Caribbean male subjects, and that this forms the basis on which later identifications of the subjects are made, and determines the scope of Caribbean masculinity. Walcott translates this complex, theoretic in the interplay between Papa Bois and Gros Jean, as shown below:

Gros Jean:	(advances calmly) What you would say is the quickest way?
Old Man:	The quickest way to what?
Gros Jean:	To what counts in life
Old Man:	What counts in the world is money and power (p. 37).

Strikingly, Papa Bois (the Old Man) has taken on the role of the wise father figure and Gros Jean, in the presence of the colonial authority figure, appears to be functioning at the stage of infancy. Like an impetuous child he enquires, "What you would say is the quickest way?" Bois perpetuates the hegemonic masculinity of the colonizer, which is centered on "money and power." Later in the same scene, Walcott illustrates the same caretaker/child dichotomy by having the Old Man feign weakness and toy with Gros Jean. Gros Jean, the Caribbean subject, lifts the Old Man in the air, a process which creates within Gros Jean the illusion of invincibility, but which, in the final analysis, demonstrates the real power of the Old Man, who mystifies the naïve Caribbean subject, who has convinced him into submitting to the role of the passive slave of capital on the sugar plantation. "With your arm of iron, the first thing to kill is wisdom?" the Devil instructs, and the infantile subject responds, "That's right, papa" (p. 37). The image presented by the colonizer holds a great attraction to Gros Jean, the child. Having slain wisdom, the Caribbean subject's perception of masculinity is centered exclusively on brawn and being led, in this case by the colonial authority figure on the sugar plantation. Gros Jean joins other Caribbean men in enduring colonial subjugation and exploitation.

Walcott also suggests that colonialism goads the colonial authority to systematically destroy the Caribbean subject, but which is also causing the colonizer to decay both physically and morally. We see the fleas feasting on the Old Man's flesh, and hear him acknowledge to Gros Jean that, "the flesh of the earth is rotting" (p. 37). Later, Walcott has the Old Man pause midway through his song of celebration over the Caribbean subject, to shed light on the pathetic state of his life as a colonizer: "Ah well, there's wood to cut" (p. 38).

Walcott uses the episode between Papa Bois and Mi Jean to direct the audience's attention towards the role of pre-independence (colonial) education in the formation of hegemonic masculinities among Caribbean male subjects. James, in presenting Toussaint, has shown colonial education as having a dual, paradoxical influence, in that it contributes to a form of self-division, and helps to shape a warrior psyche, one which is capable of holding a revolution. Walcott focuses more on the failure of colonial education to help Caribbean males to develop self-confidence, independent thinking, and common sense. He exemplifies the view of Kenyan novelist, Ngugi Wa Thiong'O, who joins Fanon and Césaire in arguing that colonial education annihilates the beliefs and capacities of people, and drives them to identify with things removed from themselves.[18] Walcott shows how through colonial education, the Caribbean male is made to identify with the Sambo construct, which encourages him to accept exploitation and to suffer silently. He has Mi Jean deconstruct the chapters of his "book," one chapter of which muzzles Mi Jean with maxims such as "wise is dumb" and "debate is just a hook." A mist is placed over Mi Jean's analytical vision through the use of negative instancing, which identifies historic figures such as Socrates, who have paid with their lives for daring to question "why" (p. 47). A profound form of pathological alienation is imposed on the subject, and makes him deaf to his social reality—the suffering of Caribbean subjects and their lack of self-expression. Colonial subjects are incapable of disrupting colonial authority because of the colonial context.

Through Gros Jean's interplay with the plantation owner, we see the Devil with sardonic delight manipulating the Caribbean subject and getting him to direct his power at himself and other suffering colonial subjects. Hence, we find that Gros Jean, rather than using his "arm of iron" as a weapon of resistance, he functions as a submissive slave to the plantation owner. This form of hegemony is not the same straightforward one implied by Antonio Gramsci.[19] Walcott also sees it as enrolment, wherein its exercise is aided by convincing and cajoling Caribbean subjects into believing that they want what the colonizers' wants. Gros Jean carries out the role of the "boy" assigned to him by the colonizer with zealous demeanor, though he performs a series of trifling, unachievable tasks, namely the "counting the numbers of cane leaves" and the "collecting fireflies." The colonizer completes the castration by stripping Gros Jean of his name, taunting him about his invisibility with colonial aliases such as "Joe," "Mac," "Charley," and "Hubert," until the subject self-destructs. Walcott dramatizes the destruction with an explosion at the end of the scene (pp. 41–42).

Walcott goes to great lengths to exemplify the ills of the colonial education through Mi Jean's ignorance and incompetence, but achieves this end through using Mi Jean to foil both the creatures in the forest and the Devil. Mi Jean lacks the nobility and profundity of the creatures of nature, and seems to be at the basic stage of the creole continuum. He is torn between the creole he "thinks" in and the colonial standard towards which he aspires. At the syntactic level, he seems to be inadequate in the colonizer's dialect and "is dying" to articulate in the standard. To the creatures he remarks, "Gros Jean was one man. I is the next," while to the Devil he retorts, "You can't get me into no argument! I have brains, but won't talk." Gros Jean's incompetence in the semantic dimension of the colonizer's language is also noticeable in his use of malapropism: "lustiferous" as against "lascivious" (pp. 44–45).

Homi K. Bhabha asserts that colonial discourse wants the colonized to be an inferior prototype of the colonizer—similar but not identical.[20] Noticeably, Walcott's dramatization of Mi Jean involves the subject in the receipt of a colonial education which is almost the same, but not quite the same as the plantation owner's. Mi Jean has not even been allowed to fully master the colonizer's language. The tiny "book" he carries encapsulates the narrow curriculum which he has been permitted to experience from the colonial status quo. Unlike West Indian writers of Walcott's generation, who at least "knew the literature of Empires, Greek, Roman, British through their essential classics," and possessed the linguistic and literary tools to create, Mi Jean is a harmless shadow of the Devil, a generic stereotype of the "educated" Caribbean male, who has an education but the depth of which is limited.[21] Mi Jean, daft academically, therefore appears lost in both of his worlds. Among the colonized, he is a fisherman by trade, who "fishes without bait," and is thus alienated from the wisdom of his mother and nature's creatures in the forest. In the other world of the colonizer, Mi Jean is a philosopher, tied to a role of inferiority and servitude to the plantation owner, and exiled from the world of common sense (pp. 28–29).

Brazilian psychologist, Paulo Freire, has argued that education can either be used to bring about conformity or as a means by which men and women deal critically and creatively with reality, and discover how to participate in the transmission of the world.[22] Walcott, through Mi Jean, posits a consensus, postcolonial position that the colonial education has been designed to get Caribbean subjects to blindly conform to colonial standards, in order to maintain the colonial status quo. Hence, Mi Jean's "education" has not trained him to think outside of the "book." In fact, Walcott suggests, through Mi Jean's obsession with the book, that the education system institutes a form of mental slavery over some Caribbean male subjects, denying them the ability and scope to question or to change things. Subsequently, the plantation owner suggests that the goat may be more intelligent than Mi Jean, and lacking the critical thinking skills to resolve even practical problems associated with his manhood, Mi Jean erupts in anger, loses both his temper and his life (p. 52).

As seen in *Ti Jean,* Walcott's focus in *Pantomime* is the contact between colonizers and colonized, but set in post-independence Trinidad and Tobago. Walcott makes his male characters interchange roles from the classic Daniel Defoe novel, *Robinson Crusoe.* He reaches conclusions about colonialism which show a philosophical shift from his presentations in *Ti Jean. Pantomime* was staged in 1978, when the post-independence milieu of the Anglophone Caribbean pushed Walcott into what Bhabha has classified as the "Third space of Enunciation," which places emphasis on the interdependence rather than domination between colonizer and colonized.[23] Walcott's use of the meta-theatrical device is crucial to *Pantomime* and the creation of the third space, and necessary in Walcott's view for the discourse of Caribbean masculinity. Meta-theater challenges theater's claim to be realistic, but also makes us aware of life's uncanny likeness to art. Essayist Stuart Davis has also observed that meta-theater calls attention to the theatricality of life, and marks those boundaries that conventional dramatic realism would hide.[24] Walcott's use of it creates a forum for discourses on the impact of colonialism and imperialism on Caribbean masculinity.

The first space identifiable is the use of the stage for the instilling of colonial values. Drama, in this regard, is working in partnership with colonialism. Harry Trewe emerges as a potential director/actor, and it is noticeable from the onset that there are reminders of neo-colonialism emanating from him. The fact that he is an Englishman and hotelier, qualifies him to be a ruthless remnant of the colonialism. He is a retired English actor, who is now acting as a capitalist attempting to lure tourists into his hotel. In this hotel, this burlesque colonial empire, there is only one servant whose name is Jackson, a retired Calypsonian. Trewe himself is convincing as a castaway, a marooned Englishman escaping a haunting, tragic past. He says, "I've no idea I'd wind up in this iron position of giving orders, but if the new script I've been given says: HARRY TREWE, HOTEL MANAGER, then I'm going to play Harry Trewe, Hotel Manager to the hilt, dammit" (p. 108). The Crusoe pantomime therefore gives Trewe an opportunity to act the part and be the part and exercise a power that he lacks. It also gives him the opportunity to experience, vicariously, the power of re-enacting the colonial master/slave relationship—to function as Crusoe, to become the symbol of Western civilization and power, to make poor Jackson his Man Friday, the colonial Sambo.

The second space is that which Rob Canefield describes "as an ontological space upon which the foundational ideologies and systems of representation play leading roles."[25] This is a stage where drama is employed by Caribbean subjects as a means of deconstructing colonial images, and reconstructing new images of Caribbean peoples. This is also a stage through which the Caribbean seeks a catharsis for the pent up anger its peoples have been carrying for centuries. Drama, in this context, is more than merely a pantomime or light story intended for the entertainment of audiences. Walcott's Jackson, for sure, cannot see the re-enactment of colonialism in the vein of Walter Pater's "art for the sake of art."[26] Rather, he advocates a Marxist/postcolonial model, whereby drama is an instrument, one used for interrogating the colonial discourse. Jackson, therefore, challenges the directorship of Trewe, who seeks to reinstate the colonial script and to have him, like Man Friday, show all the signs of subjection, servitude, and submission:

> For three hundred years I served you . . . served you breakfast in . . . in my white jacket on a white veranda, boss, bwana, effendi, bacra, sahib . . . in that sun that never set on your empire I was your shadow, I did what you did, boss, bwana, effendi, bacra, sahib . . . that was my pantomime. Every movement you made your shadow copied . . . and you smiled at me as a child does smile at his shadow's helpless obedience (p. 112).

The lines are indicative of the arguments of postcolonial theorists. They reflect the bleak and brutal history of servitude and exploitation. At the psychological level, colonialism is portrayed as keeping Caribbean males as subjects, and in a stage of childhood, where they function as the harmless shadows of the colonizer, and, like the Sambo, always smiling in helpless obedience. As a consequence, this second space of drama has emerged as a menacing form of mimicry, which Jackson proceeds to explain to Trewe:

> But after a while the child does . . . say to himself, that is too much obedience
> But the shadow don't stop, no matter if the child stop playing the pantomime,
> And the shadow does follow the child everywhere . . . he cannot get rid of it, no
> Matter what . . . that is the power and black magic of the shadow . . . until
> It is the shadow that start dominating the child, it is the servant that start
> Dominating the master . . . and that is the victory of the shadow boss (pp. 112–13).

Jackson places a postcolonial spin on Jacques Lacan's theory of the mirror image. Whereas Lacan presents the child (or in the context of postcolonial discourse, the colonized subject) as a mere impotent image, or shadow of the guardian (colonizer), Jackson sees the role play at this second space as being shifted to one where the shadow of the colonized now becomes what Bhabha refers to as a "threatening menace" to the colonizer.[27]

Nevertheless, implicit is a point of view that neither the first space (where the focus has been on the colonizer seeking atonement for his guilt by validating the presence of colonialism in the Caribbean) or the second (where the focus has been on the colonized seeking emancipation from his anger over his state of oppression which imprisons him) have resulted in the emergence of more humanizing constructs of masculinity. Walcott prescribes a mediatory form of interplay between the colonizers and the colonized, which are designed to get the two groups through a process of role reversals, to at least begin the process of breaching the chasm created by the colonial past, and, in the process, heal their respective manhood. Bhabha refers to this process as "hybridity," which "reverses the colonial disavowal, so that the other denied 'knowledges' enter upon the dominant discourse and estrange the basis of its authority . . . its rules of recognition."[28]

Walcott suggests, through the trading of places, that there is a correlation between the manifestations of constructs of masculinity and the roles subjects are assigned to play. For instance, Jackson, the Caribbean subject, is playing the role of Crusoe, who seeks to enforce upon Trewe, who now plays the role of the colonized, the very process of colonization, which has been historically enforced upon Caribbean subjects. We see manifestations of narcissism, superiority, and inhumanity in Jackson, while he is wearing the mask of Crusoe. In the scene below, he exercises cultural superiority, treats the colonized as invisible, and uses his language to name and exercise authority over the colonized subject's world:

(Slams table)
Pantamba!
(Rattles beach chair)
Backaraka! Backaraka!
(Drops cup)
Banda karan!
(Puts his arm around Harry, points at him)
Subu!
(Faster, pointing)
Masz!
(Stamping the floor)
Zohgoooor!
(Rests his snoring head on his closed palms)
Oma! Omaaaa!
(Kneels looking skyward. Pauses, eyes closed)
Boora! Boora!
(Meaning the world. Silence. He rises) (p. 116)

The above scene also echoes Fanon's point that the Caribbean male seeks to trade places with the white authority figure of his colonial past. At the same, it suggests that we may be dealing with universal issues regarding masculinity and power. Arthur Brittan identifies "Masculism" as a universal construct, which justifies and naturalizes male domination.[29] Walcott is still justified in believing that both colonizers and colonized need to experience the interplay to understand themselves first, and then each other.

The reversal of roles aids the discourse of colonial representations. While Trewe has bragged about being a liberal, Walcott shows that, like Crusoe, he has a deep-rooted cultural prejudice regarding Christianity. While his liberalism allows him to play the role of the colonized European subject, it will not permit him to put African Gods on the same stage with the God of Christianity (p. 126). However, Walcott uses Jackson to get Trewe to see the ambivalence of his own religion, and the problem with binary labels, such as *barbaric* and *civilized*. Jackson points him to the paradoxical relationship between Christianity's Holy Communion and so-called paganism, lures him into acknowledging that both may be said to involve the savage and canni-balistic practices. Trewe has to reach a stage in his evolution as a man where he can acknowledge vulnerability and humanity, through acknowledging ambivalence within his culture. Jackson's rebellion functions as the inciting force, which helps the Englishman to introspect and gradually change into a better person. Jackson's refusal to read Trewe's lines and his rewriting of his script becomes symbolic of the postcolonial artist at work, deconstructing the script of colonial discourse.

Jackson's rewrite must, therefore, have the "parrot" drown in Trewe's bathroom, in order for Trewe to start to experience life. However, the parrot, which seemingly represents the submissive, subservient Caribbean male, is not a catalyst for the humanization of the colonizer. To the contrary, it is the Caribbean subject's challenging of Trewe's script that serves as the dramatic incitement, which leads Trewe to eventually confront his tragic past. Jackson taunts Trewe by posing with the pictorial representation of the Englishman's wife. Bearing in mind that Trewe's wife is a symbolic representation of the anger and grief the subject feels, Jackson's gesture is one of the most brazen forms of insubordination. It is, however, this moment which triggers off Trewe's anagnorisis, and instructs him to confront his past in the same way that the brazen, colonial subject (Jackson) has chosen to confront him. It is at that moment that Walcott has Trewe attack the representation of his wife with an ice pick, making a dramatic statement that, for humane masculinities to emerge, representations which imprison their sensibilities must be first destroyed (p. 125).

Pantomime offers a discourse which shows that men can work through their differences through art—in this sense, reversed role play. Being the other, we better understand ourselves and others; we can identify and challenge representations that stand in the way of our understanding of ourselves and others. We find Trewe, his rage having subsided, being able to revisit his past through more objective eyes, and who is in a better psychological state to now rewrite his relationships both with his wife and Jackson. Jackson has also, through this dialogue with Trewe, rewritten his relationship with Trewe. It is no longer a binary one where he is possession and Trewe is his master. Rather, he now re/emerges as a Calypsonian, the practitioner of a musical form that gives him the entitlement to continue re/writing the neo-colonial script, as it was manifested in post-independence Trinidad and Tobago.

MALE RELATIONSHIPS AND FATHERHOOD IN *MOON ON A RAINBOW SHAWL*

So far, the plays examined have been silent on the impact of constructs of Caribbean masculinity on women in the Caribbean. The same cannot be said of Errol John's *Moon on a Rainbow Shawl*. The play contends that the preoccupation of West Indian males with the pursuance of hegemonic masculinities is resulting in the "death" of West Indian women. Subsequently, John suggests that West Indian men may very well be experiencing a paradoxical relationship with patriarchy. On the one hand, they are the oppressed victims of patriarchy; while on the other hand, they are appendages of patriarchy, oppressing West Indian women. John examines this concept through the relationships between Charlie and Sophia, Ephraim and Rosa, and Ole Mack and Rosa.

Charlie is the microcosm of the policy of exclusion that the colonial establishment has instituted against West Indians on racial grounds. He is indicative of the black Caribbean male, who dares to challenge the operations of the colonial status quo, and who has to be whipped into recognizing his status as a nonbeing. Because Charlie dares to question the discriminatory practice of providing white West Indian cricketers with superior accommodation, he is barred from international cricket for life. However, while John seems to elicit empathy from the audience for the West Indian subject in relation to his plight, and generates feelings of rage towards the colonial status quo for its racist and repressive policies, the playwright makes us question Charlie's refusal to find a job to support his family. The playwright is critical of his leaving of his wife, Sophia, who is relegated to "wearing" the "mother's shoes" as well as the "father's shoes" in order to support the family (p. 23). John's views in this regard are antithetical to Merle Hodge's, who, in her article, "The Shadow of the Whip," has suggested that the psychical scars of a history of slavery and colonialism may have made West Indian men powerless to assume the responsibilities of manhood.[30] Rather, John is adamant that some West Indian men need to remove the albatross of the colonial victim from around their necks, and adapt a revolutionary approach by demonstrating real warrior-hood through owning their responsibilities in their households and society. In fact, the playwright suggests through Charlie that when some West Indian men choose to play the role of hapless victims that they wittingly/unwittingly function as appendages of colonialism in the furtherance of the exploitation of West Indian women.

Inherent in this portrayal of the dynamics of the marital relationship between Charlie and Sophia is a point that marriage is a re-enactment of slavery for black West Indian women, since they are exploited at the domestic, physical, sexual, and even economic levels by idealistic, non-working men. The playwright makes us experience Sophia's fatigue, her frustrations, and fears for the future of Esther, who seeks a responsible father, who will give her the opportunity to move from being "a tin whistle" in an urban Trinidadian ghetto, to a "trumpet" in a more liberated world (p. 18). We also feel Sophia's anguish, as she witnesses her husband operate at the stage of infancy, too proud to work outside of cricket, but willing to cry out to an indifferent colonial "Father," who is only prepared to supply him with alcoholic beverages at parties held at the American base to facilitate his alcoholism. As we experience Sophia's tragic plight, we recognize that John is echoing the concerns of West Indian women writers and academics that Caribbean women are being doubly marginalized—at one front by the colonial landlord and at the other by the men in their lives. No other point is this better felt in the play as when it becomes clear that Charlie will be jailed for taking a shortcut solution to his financial woes, by robbing Ole Mack's store, and his Sophia is left to spend the remainder of her life slaving to support the family.

In the next relationship between Ephraim and Rosa, John examines the absent father syndrome in urban Trinidad, and the catastrophic consequences it is having on West Indian females. Sigmund Freud has suggested, in the theory of the Oedipus complex that the presence of a father authority figure is crucial for the son to realize an empowering and sustainable form of manhood.[31] John's treatment of the characterization of Ephraim seems to concur with Freud. He suggests that the psychical breach caused by the absent father has helped to create constructs of masculinity, which generate inferiority, alienation, restlessness, callousness, and self-centeredness within some Caribbean male subjects. In the case of Ephraim, who has had to endure the psychological trauma of growing up without both parents, the situation is even more compounded, and the subject seems to develop both distrust in relationships as well as a deep-seated anger and resentment for the social inequalities of life.

Ephraim's locates his anger and restlessness in the socio-economic structure, which has given the capitalist landlord, Ole Mack, the authority to exploit his tenants, while having them endure inhumane conditions, and the right to restrict his (Ephraim's) role to being that of a trolley driver. This explanation certainly helps us to understand his anger for Ole Mack and the colonial status quo. It does not, however, explain nor does it validate the anger and gross insensitivity that Ephraim shows towards Rosa, on learning that the eighteen-year-old is carrying his child, or why he chooses to leave her to raise a child alone to escape to an uncertain future in Great Britain. John seems to therefore suggest that the absence of fathering has resulted in the formation of dysfunctional constructs of masculinity among men, who have not themselves experienced fathering, and who are psychologically inadequate to function as fathers.

John does not only direct our attention to colonialism and the psychical problems it has triggered among Caribbean men in relation to fathering, he also points us to the plight that the male discontent creates for women. As in the case of Charlie, the playwright challenges the male response to colonialism and the absence of fathering, and points us to Rosa, who has grown up as an orphan with the nuns, and unlike Ephraim, has not even benefitted from the love of a grandmother. In addition, like other Trinidadian women, she has also had to cope with colonial challenges as well as manage with the abuse from Caribbean males, who displace their frustrations and anger with the colonial authority on her. John, therefore, suggests that the Caribbean male responses to the issues related to colonialism often turn them into oppressors of Caribbean women, and seems to be urging male-centered discourses to be cognizant of the plight of Caribbean women.

CONCLUSION

What have I been able to achieve in this chapter? Firstly, it has illustrated that the plays in this sample have been for decades raising the consciousness of Caribbean audiences on Caribbean masculinity. It also suggests that West Indian drama, if and when applied to the discourse of Caribbean masculinity, can provide a visually informative and entertaining medium through which larger audiences can become involved in the discourse of regional masculinity. In addition, it indicates that there are male artists who are questioning and challenging the operations of patriarchy in the Caribbean. However, while this collection of plays suggest that some attention is being paid to the plight of Caribbean women, there still appears to be a need for a greater effort to be made to present women characters in a more realistic way in male-centered texts. Finally, this chapter contends that a greater effort needs to be made towards applying West Indian fiction to theoretical discourse.

Notes

1. Terry Eagleton, *Criticism and Ideology: A Study in Marxist Literary Theory* (London: Verso, 1976), 62.

2. Errol Hill, "From the Emergence of a National Drama in the West Indies," in *Twentieth Century Theatre: A Sourcebook of Radical Thinking,* ed. Richard Drain (London: Routledge, 1995), 311.

3. Rob Canefield, "Theatralising the Anglophone Caribbean, 1492 to the 1980's," in *A History of Literature in the Caribbean,* ed. Arnold A. James (New York: John Benjamin, 1994), 285.

4. "Damning Lamming: Lamming speaks with writer Knolly Moses about his concerns for the region," *Panmedia,* http://www.panmedia.com.jm/archive/features/lamming.htm, Accessed on July 10, 2010.

5. See Franz Fanon, *Black Skin, White Masks* (New York: Grove Press, 1968), and Aime Césaire, *Discourse on Colonialism* (Paris: Monthly Review Press, 2001).

6. See C. L. R. James, "Black Jacobins," in *A Time and a Season,* ed. Errol Hill (Kingston: University of the West Indies Press, 1996), Derek Walcott, "Ti Jean and his Brothers," in *Plays for Today,* ed. Errol Hill (Port of Spain: Longman, 1985), Derek Walcott, "Pantomime," in *Remembrance & Pantomime: Two Plays,* Derek Walcott (New York: Farrar, Strauss and Giroux, 1980), 90–170, and Errol John, *Moon on a Rainbow Shawl* (London: Faber and Faber Ltd., 1958). Note that all quotes from these plays appear in brackets in the text of the essay and the page numbers are shown after a "p." or "pp."

7. Fanon, *Black Skin, White Masks,* 188.

8. Ibid., 8.

9. Césaire, *Discourse on Colonialism,* 177, 22.

10. Fanon, *Black Skin, White Masks,* 192, 8.

11. Césaire, *Discourse on Colonialism,* 129.

12. Fanon, *Black Skin, White Masks,* 12.

13. Ibid., 17, 18.

14. Ibid., 13, 63.

15. Ibid., 11.

16. Césaire, *Discourse on Colonialism,* 21.

17. Octave Mannoni, quoted in Fanon, *Black Skin, White Masks,* 84.

18. Ngugi wa Thiong'O, *Decolonization of the Mind: The Politics of Language in African Literature* (London: Heinemann, 1986), 3.

19. See Antonio Gramsci, *Selections from the Prison Notebooks* (London: Lawrence and Wishart, 1971).

20. Homi K. Bhabha, *Location of Culture* (London: Routledge, 1989), 86.

21. See Derek Walcott, "What the Twilight Says," in *Dream on Monkey Mountain and Other Plays,* Derek Walcott (New York: Farrar, Strauss and Giroux, 1970), 4.

22. Paulo Freire, *Pedagogy of the Oppressed* (New York: Continuum, 1993), 34.

23. Bhabha, *Location of Culture,* 114.

24. The definition of "Metatheatre" was originally created by Stuart Davis for his Shakespeare Class at Cornell University in the Spring of 1999. See the following website for more details: www.spiritus-temporis.com/metatheatre/works-cited.html—United States.

25. Canefield, "Theatralising the Anglophone Caribbean," 296.

26. Walter Pater, "Arts for Arts' Sake," *Encyclopedia Britannica Online,* http://www.britannica.com, Accessed on July 10, 2010.

27. See Jacques Lacan, "The Mirror Stage," in *A Critical and Cultural Reader,* eds. Anthony Easthope and Kate McGowan (Westport: Greenwood Press, 1993), 71–76; see also Bhabha, *Location of Culture,* 85–92.

28. Bhabha, *Location of Culture,* 114.

29. Arthur Brittan, *Masculinity and Power* (New York: Basil Black, 1989), 3.

30. Merle Hodge, "The Shadow of the Whip," in *Is Massa Day Dead? Black Moods in the Caribbean,* ed. Orde Coombs (New York: Doubleday and Anchor, 1974), 115.

31. Judith Worell, *Encyclopedia of Women and Gender: Sex Similarities and Differences* (New York: Academic Press, 2001), 530.

Chapter 9

A "Coolitudian" Caribbean Text

The Trajectory of Renewal in David Dabydeen's **Our Lady of Demerara**[1]

Shivani Sivagurunathan

INTRODUCTION

The demise of slavery in the early to mid nineteenth century in the Caribbean did not result in the dissipation of its legacy. Instead, it remained looming on plantation society because cheap labor in the forms of servitude akin to slavery was needed to maintain the production level of the plantations for the preservation of European consumerism in an age of burgeoning consumption.

Even as agitations against the slave trade were made evident in as early as the seventeenth century by the American Quakers and Methodists, later on by the Society for the Abolition of the Slave Trade (1787–1806) led by their main spokesmen William Wilberforce, Thomas Clarkson, and Granville Sharp, the Anti-Slavery Society (1823–39) headed by Thomas Fowell Buxton, and, of course, supported by the numerous slave revolts, the horrors of slavery did not deter the aspiration for more exploitation of labor. Thus, when Apprenticeship, a form of labor control designed to aid the planters in the switch from slavery to the employment of free labor, ended in 1838, another device for the perpetuation of the plantation economy, primarily the sugar plantations, in the colonies mainly in the West Indies, South Africa, and Mauritius, was created: East Indian coolie indentureship.

Some of the coolies managed to return home to India after several years of hard labor, but the majority of them remained within their locations and sought to build lives amidst complex social conditions. The coolies brought with them unique cultural traits, which distinguished them from other communities, and this resulted in the exclusion of Indians from the mainstream of national, cultural, and political issues. It is precisely for this reason that the Indo-Mauritian poet, Khal Torabully, coined the poetics of "coolitude," a concept that repositions the coolie in the national imaginary, be it in the Caribbean, Africa, or Asia.

Khal Torabully's concept of coolitude begins with the recuperation of the term *coolie*. Its negative connotations have served, both then and now, to define Indians and their descendents through the degradation of their past, the humiliation of their servitude. The retrieval of the word coolie is vital precisely because of its dark history.

The founding text of coolitude is Torabully's 1992 collection of poetry, *Cale d'Etoiles Coolitude,* which is divided into three sections: "The Book Metissage," "The Book of the Voyage," and "The Book of Departure." The nature of the division is cyclical, so that the pivot of the poetic experience is "The Book of Voyage," which illuminates the centrality or the point of origination of the discourse of coolitude: the voyage. Recollection of the journey that transformed Indians into coolies is the first step towards reconstituting the coolie and his/her descendents in a multicultural society.

Collective memory is integral, but not to the point of exclusion, where the dialectics of a plural environment is neglected at the expense of an established identity. What should ensue, once the act of re-membering has begun, is the acknowledgement of other co-existing social and cultural elements. It follows that the definition of coolitude is "a complex and dynamic one, in which, depending on the social, historical, and cultural context, a single aspect may at any time be highlighted, but which should not, in any circumstances, lead to an exclusive vision of identity."[2] Thus, in bringing out hitherto underrepresented racial elements, the concept of multiculturalism achieves its ideal of inclusion and cohabitation in its most effective form. The course of highlighting is never complete, and along with it is the process of a never-ending identity construction, which forms one of coolitude's prime approaches to the interplay of racial referents: "Coolitude is a process of identity construction which takes into account the impossibility of putting a full stop to this task, and not essentially a philosophy where the meaning is predetermined."[3] The spirit of coolitude is clarified through its emphasis on disengaging the binaries of Self and Other, so that what prevails is a constant connection with "otherness," a Baroquian insistence on crossings and "impurities" in a vision where self and other interchange and engages in new webs of relationships.[4]

In this essay, I explore the concept of coolitude in relation to David Dabydeen's novel, *Our Lady of Demerara,* which I argue is a fundamentally coolitudian text, while being, at the same time that it emphasizes the coolie element, an undeniably Caribbean piece of work. These two elements are utilized by Dabydeen to disclose the various means through which the process of social and cultural rejuvenation can begin within the Guyanese context.

THE TEXT'S MOTIVATION

In *Our Lady of Demerara,* Dabydeen's concern is with the *place* of indentureship as a historical event and coolies as subjects of this event in the context of the wider world and in *relation* to other elements. His philosophy echoes the great Caribbean theorists Wilson Harris, Édouard Glissant, and Antonio Benítez-Rojo, who explicate the chaotic, detour-ridden, paradoxical, and asymmetrical inclinations of Caribbean society that cannot simply adhere to static groupings, racial, or otherwise. In this sense, it is more than anything else a Caribbean novel, as it recognizes the fragmentation, instability, isolation, uprootedness, and cultural heterogeneity of Guyana. By delving both in form and content into pre-Columbian beliefs and Hindu notions of reincarnation, which suggest continual rehearsals, Dabydeen highlights at once the link between Aboriginal faith and the faith of the migrants, and points towards a revisionary method, while highlighting spiritual connections in the space of the colonial web. Thus, the novel itself performs the details of coolitude, by promoting opacity, which refuses an easy classification of social elements, through an understanding that coolies remain referents among other social referents, in the construction of mosaicness, and as part of the complex of colonial relations.

The polarization of faith and place, which occurs in the novel through the mobilization of spiritual beliefs and physical life, opens up new spaces that are not only regenerative, but also redemptive. Importation of religion into the Caribbean suggests isolation from the material environment, but the combination of faiths, both colonialist and indigenous, intertwined with the natural world, results in sentiments of hope, thus indicating that Dabydeen is not only exposing the nature of Caribbean life in its cultural, religious, spiritual, and natural dimensions, but also defining the restitutive potential in the Guyanese environment, which becomes especially evident in the dense interior of the country. The kaleidoscope of spirituality that binds space and non-space promotes the non-reductionist, spatial linkage in the novel's "continuum of cross-cultural womb of space."[5]

In effect, the mobilization of fragments occurs. It is largely a result of the polarization of faith and place: geographical connections are made through space dispersals and re-connections, where personalities and identities, associated with land and place, are reversed, replayed, and rediscovered, thus alluding to the ceaselessness of identity, its constant deferral. These fragments of moments and personalities suggest the structure of mosaicness in the colonial web of the novel, involving places of Dabydeen's own multilayered identity (Guyana, India, England).

The novel exemplifies the second facet of coolitude's tenets, which attempts to release itself from a bondage to India. The initial stages of coolitude emphasize a reliving of the voyage across the *kala pani,* an assessment of the poetics of migration, and a restitution of the space of the "Fall."[6] The second half of coolitude's agenda, however, insists on the relation of coolies to "otherness," and the way in which plural societies formulate themselves and build up notions of interaction and relationality. Torabully states that "coolitude as a living process shows that, while adhering to Indianity as a major set of references, one should also put this in contact with other visions of the world . . . this implies that the attitude to identity can no longer be thought of alongside the narrow visions of atavistic desires."[7] Thus, coolitude has to leave its first stage for the climax or the end result of its poetics, which is the inclusion of the rest of society into its celebration and renewal of the coolie. Torabully explains that the way in which this can be done is to address and expose the opacities in post-plantocratic societies, which he has placed under the rubric of "baroque poetics." The pragmatism of the colonial system of labor, disallowed the proliferation and chaos of differences to be acknowledged, hence, he states that "baroquism, by its 'impure,' multiple, mosaic consistence, enables [the] coexistence of opacities."[8] The notions of "impurities," chaos, and opacities appear in the discourse of several Caribbean theorists as well, namely Benitez-Rojo, Glissant, and Harris.[9] Thus, *Our Lady of Demerara* also has to be read within the theoretical context to which it belongs, where such ideas are central to its foundations. The importance of applying coolitude to the novel is, firstly, because it *is* a coolitude text, and secondly, because it discloses Dabydeen's approach to the perception of race and history, and his conscious departure from an obsession with the coolie in order to conceive the bigger picture of society and the world.

In view of the coolitude baroquism of the novel, which involves issues such as chaos, repetitions, rehearsals, and renewals, various themes overlap, so as to create a constant intermingling, where few clear-cut separations are able to be made. Fragments are often treated holistically, and several notions form the essence of the novel, so that they are able to appear under different headings. Therefore, themes such as *reincarnations* and *cross-culturalities,* *rhythm,* and *chaos,* repeat themselves in the present study, indicating their centrality to the novel's philosophy.

RHYTHM AND CHAOS

Benitez-Rojo's advice for reading Fernando Ortiz's essay "Contrapunteo" is applicable to *Our Lady of Demerara* as well, because the spirit behind both texts, which is very Caribbean in nature, seems unitary: "read it as a dialogic and uncentered text, in whose plurality of voices and rhythms the most varied disciplines and the most irreconcilable ideologies come forward along with enunciations that correspond to two very different forms of understanding, of knowing."[10] The notion of knowledge is interrogated at this point, because any secure definition becomes problematic in the context of a specifically Caribbean interpretation of what constitutes the realm of knowing and of understanding. When Jacques Lyotard defines two kinds of knowledge as being "scientific" and "narrative," Benitez-Rojo associates the latter type of knowledge with societies that are "underdeveloped in the epistemological, theoretical, technological, industrial, imperialist, etc. senses." In short, it belongs to "Peoples of the Sea," or those who define themselves through maritime associations implicit with a distinct rhythm.[11]

This rhythm, in a Caribbean context, is a polyrhythm, typified, as Benitez-Rojo states, by the "presence of several rhythmic sources: Indo-america, Africa, Asia, and Europe." He makes a distinction between the white rhythms, which "articulate themselves in a binary fashion," and the "copper, black, and yellow rhythms," which belong to "Peoples of the Sea" and are characterized as "turbulent and erratic, [appearing] as eruptions of gases and lava that issue from an elemental stratum, still in formation; in this respect they are rhythms without a past, or better, rhythms whose past is in the present, and they legitimize themselves by themselves." This division of meaning does not separate the two rhythms, for they work within the same rhythmic system, one that is essentially a *mestizaje*, which produces a space that is not a synthesis of differences, but an insoluble meeting of divergences. Thus, Benitez-Rojo defines the Caribbean novel as a *mestizo* text with layers of texts inbuilt within its general structure, resembling the nature of Caribbean society, which he describes as "an unpredictable society that originated in the most violent currents and eddies of modern history where sexual and class differences are overlaid with differences of an ethnographic nature."[12] Effectively, such a society is chaotic by nature, continually undetermined with interchangeable elements perpetuating the dynamics of human relation.

However, despite the apparent anarchy of those social complexities, there remain "constants," or in the language of Chaos Theory, "strange attractors," which indicate regularities within supposed disorder.[13] Benitez-Rojo's reading of Caribbean life in the context of Chaos Theory is done through the conviction that "Caribbeanness" is a social and not a cultural construct, formed by its own peculiar rhythm and within which differences in the Caribbean coexist "in the forms of the ritual sacrifice and directed toward all of the senses [and this gives] pan-Caribbean cultures a way of being, a style that is repeated through time and space in all its differences and variants."[14] This repetition, allegorized with the principle of entropy in Chaos discourse, eventuate a difference at every point of recurrence, and brings forth various points of energy at various times, so that some dimension is always highlighted without exclusion or prejudice.

Resembling Benitez-Rojo's formulations is coolitude's notion of "spotlighting," which brings to the forefront previously neglected elements in a cyclical fashion, thus producing a continual reverberation that never tires. Benitez-Rojo analogizes this repetition rooted in chaos to the spiral chaos of the Milky Way "that sketches in an 'other' shape that keeps changing, with some objects born to light while others disappear into the womb of darkness; change, transit, return, fluxes of sidereal matter." Furthermore, the Antilles physically correlates to its metaphorical inferences of chaos, bridging "'in a certain way,' South and North America, that is, a machine of spume that links the narrative search for El Dorado with the narrative of the finding of El Dorado; or if you like, the discourse of myth with the discourse of history; or even, the discourse of resistance with the language of power."[15] Thus, its geographical functions enter into its cultural, historical, and mythical discourse, presenting what Wilson Harris has called a cosmic space-time, which contains, as Marina Camboni writes, the "spiritual legacy of historical pasts and the potential of the new, alive with the regenerative energy of the physical universe."[16] Time becomes infinite, or where dialogic communication between disparate points in space and time occurs and reoccurs, in a process of infinite rehearsal.

PLACE, SPACE, AND FAITH

In view of the preceding definitions and considerations, *Our Lady of Demerara* is an explicitly *mestizo* text. In other words, it is from beginning to end a Caribbean novel, promoting, and embodying at the same time the rhythm of the "Peoples of the Sea" to display the way in which Caribbean society is and operates. Its form and context are carefully woven together to propound the chaos of Guyanese life with its implications of place, landscape, people, vegetation, its beasts, and myths. And the novel appears to create, or rather, re-create the "great Caribbean machine," a reinvention of the Sugar Machine to accommodate the fractal existence caused by colonialism. In the body of this machine is the convergence of what Benitez-Rojo describes as "cosmogonies, mythic bestiaries, remote pharmacopoeias, oracles, profound ceremonies, and the mysteries and alchemies of antiquity."[17]

Self-consciously positioning the novel at the borderline between myth and history, Dabydeen invites the reinvention of time, where it attempts to fuse the freshness of the living moment with notions of belief and the past through "The Infinite Rehearsal"—Wilson Harris' concept which is mentioned at the very start of the novel, along with quotations by historical figures about Amerindian and Hindu faith, thus alluding to the restitution of history through spiritual remembrance. However, it is not simply a recovery of history that is evident in the novel. In fact, history becomes less important as the text progresses. What becomes more pronounced is the life of the landscape, the correspondence between myth and place, word and flesh. The landscape, Derek Walcott states in his Nobel Lecture, contains history's memory: "It is there in Antillean geography, in the vegetation itself. The sea sighs with the drowned from the Middle Passage, the butchery of its aborigines, Carib and Aruac and Taino, bleeds in the scarlet of the immortelle, and even the actions of surf on sand cannot erase the African memory, or the lances of cane as a green prison where indentured Asians . . . are still serving time."[18] Thus, because history is already embedded in the natural world, it is this natural world, which freshly exists in the present moment, that needs to be considered and understood. Instead of "evocations," Walcott asks, "why not 'celebrations of real presences?'"[19] The real presences signify the reality of a place and its people, its natural life, architecture, villages, and so on.

Therefore, in *Our Lady of Demerara,* when Lance arrives in Guyana, hoping to conduct an historical excavation of the Priest's life, it is the physicality of the city that first strikes him, with its "bombast of signs" and which then leads him to believe that the "National Archive promised much, if one believed the hugeness of the signboard announcing its existence" (p. 76). Of course, the historical documentations of the Archive paled in comparison to the building's tangible presence. The reason for this is simple, as Manu explains to Lance: "You can't blame we. We too shame to remember and when we do, we just feel guilt and anger" (p. 78). This historical humiliation is obliterated by the struggle to live and survive: "People were too occupied with the immediate grind of living to contemplate the past, much less preserve its records" (p. 78). Survival, which stems from the desperation that poverty induces, is what typifies the cities of the Antilles, says Walcott, and what makes history or the recording of history, negligible. He writes in his essay "The Caribbean: Culture of Mimicry?" "in the Caribbean, history is irrelevant, not because it is not being created, or because it was sordid; but because it has never mattered.

What has mattered is the loss of history, the amnesia of the races, what has become necessary is imagination as necessity, as invention."[20] Besides, ghosts of the past have already formed part of the present. In the novel, references to the Amazonian jungle are filled with historical inferences. It was where, we are told, Walter Raleigh went in search of "the fabled city of gold and its great chieftain El Dorado" (p. 77). In subsequent years, many foreign adventurers followed in his footsteps, dying from "disease or hostile native arrow," indicating the conflict of culture, race, and environment. Hence, "the jungle interior of the country was littered with the bones of foreigners" (p. 77). The question of place and its relation to its inhabitants becomes important, as is the interconnection between the people within the geometrical foundations of place. The jungle, with its proliferation of life and lack of discrimination for its victims, visitors, or denizens, compels Manu to inform Lance that, "All-body here is foul, we is one spirit, no high or low, top or down, all is thief or abductor or bugger-man" (p. 79). In other words, the interior of the country, with its ambiguity, sinister density, and cornucopia of organisms, living or dead, equalizes everything and everyone, and becomes a place suitable for the birth and perpetuation of cross-culturalities.

Cross-culturalities, defined by Harris as necessarily different from the notion of the "alter-ego" (which indicates a split rather than an overlap), is particularly suited to the history of South America, which is, he insists, a history that is never final and never locatable in a defined linearity.[21] This trait eventuates from the fact that numerous expeditions into the hostile interiors of the South American landscape have been made, some with knowledge of their outcome and others with a mysterious absence or disappearance of bodies and people, thus creating a constant possibility of re-enactment and reinvention of those adventures. This is why, Harris says in an interview with Marina Camboni and Marco Fazzini, the character Donne in his novel *Palace of the Peacock,* dies three deaths because "you have to look at Donne, you have to bring Donne back, you have to see Donne as not a finished creature. He appears to have been finished and yet he animates the thing afresh . . . each death may imply a different journey, a different possibility in terms of his life. So, there is an unfinished aspect to Donne's life which allows us to look beyond Donne, to look through Donne into a future that we cannot locate exactly, yet it bears on the language, it bears on our language, it animates our language, it opens up all sorts of possibilities which are not static. You can see composite realities at work."[22]

It is this very "unfinished aspect" that Dabydeen puts forth in the novel in his approach to perceiving the Guyanese condition, both in its natural and human life. The existence of spirits within the soil and the waters of the jungle implies the ceaselessness of life, the continual engagement between the living and the dead, as well as a blurring of this distinction when the spirits, supposedly properties of the dead, perform functions of the living, as Manu once again informs Lance: "The river full of jumbie from the past which suddenly appear and shine in the mud like silver fish, sunlight flick off the glass so they look as if they living" (p. 87). The jungle, then, is a place that combines, adds, and fuses, incapable of negation or subterfuge. In this sense, it is a positive space that accepts rather than rejects, despite its violent history of excavation and murder. In fact, it is the very viciousness of the past that gathers in the natural environment to form a composite reality that undermines temporal sequence. The harrowing aspect of the past re-forms itself through the present reality of the river, "when tide low all kinda tings does wash up, as if the riverbed convulse and cough up what does choke it. Sometimes knives and guns, sometimes pieces of chain wrapped round bones, and when you put them together you get a picture of long-time Negro slave people breaking chain and running away from plantation, and whiteman chasing them all the way in the bush, but when whiteman go to catch them, they jump into the river and prefer to drown" (p. 86). Voices of the past, which include that of the Negro, the white plantation owners, as well as the Dutch, Spanish, and English soldiers, resurface on the waters of the river to consolidate the interconnectedness of these racial and cultural aspects of present Guyanese life, from which the memory of the past cannot be extricated, because this past within which death is a prominent feature, where wars, plunder, slave rebellions, and coolie riots typify its nature, is not quite the past, but a living reality, tied to the "living landscape," another Harrisian notion.

The "living landscape" suggests that the interior life, which includes the life of the landscape, the riverscape, and the skyscape, is integral to the reality of place. This interior life is not passive. Instead, it bubbles with resonance and possesses its own pre-discursive language, one that Harris equates to an open book, which is to be read with an inner eye. Its language moves beyond the purely textual to accommodate music and silence as well, performed by its implicit orchestra, "when consciousness sings through variegated fabrics and alternations of mood, consonance as well as dissonance, unfathomable age and youth, unfathomable kinships," to create linkages beyond the issue of linearity or logic.[23] Hence, in *Our Lady of Demerara*, Manu's description of the Arawakian belief in sudden changes, or leaps in one's condition, from one form to the other, without a supposedly rational explanation for this metamorphosis, ties in with the idea of the "unfathomability" that the living landscape produces: "Arawak people different from we—they believe in gods who can change you when you still living, not bothering to wait until you die.

One moment you are a man planting your cassava quietly, when badam-bam-bam! Arawak gods send a spirit . . . turn you into a howler-monkey" (p. 106). It is this notion of the extra-human interfering with human life that creates the mystery of place, an indefinable aura surrounding its apparent tangibility, which then crosses binaric formations in order to emphasize the existence of cross-culturalities.

Hence, as Lance contemplates, Christian dichotomies, such as Man/God, Son/Father, Whore/Virgin, Flesh/Word, Earth/Heaven, and Sin/Salvation, cannot have meaning in Aboriginal faith, and consequently in the lives of those who reside within that Aboriginal context, for, as Harris writes in his essay "Letter from Francisco Bone to W. H.," "the mixed people of African or Indian or European or Chinese descent who live in modern Guyana today are related to the Aboriginal ghosts of the past" (p. 50). This is a strongly cooli-tude ethic in its correlation of all racial elements, thereby creating composite identities, rather than ones entrenched in the rigidity of roots. Torabully high-lights that "one of the aims of coolitude is . . . to foster a larger community of vision encompassing the experiences of people of African descent and foster-ing interaction with later immigrant groups . . . [such as the] coolies."[24] And to push this point of African/Indian intermingling further, by reconsidering the influence of Aboriginal existence on every aspect of modern Guyanese life, is an attempt to create a "whole," or, rather to piece together fragments in order to recreate that "whole." Walcott's analogy of this process is the gluing together of a broken vase, where the vestige of the cracks has more meaning and love than when the vase was whole, which indicates the labor of recon-struction, and the creative energy associated with it.[25]

Furthermore, on the subject of faith, the echoes of Hindu notions of rein-carnation with the Arawakian concept of rebirth, conjoin these communities in their refusal of Western either/or paradigms, for as Manu states, "nothing ever dead-dead for true," hence indicating the cyclical nature of things, as well as an idea of time that conflicts with the Western one (p. 91). Torabully suggests that the reason for writing *Cale d'Etoiles* in a cyclical fashion was because "its cyclical aspect echoes the cyclical vision Oriental peoples have of time and history."[26] The crucial consideration of this temporal uniqueness is centered on the physical environment, for it is only then, when faith and the landscape fuse and complement one another, that the process of restitution can begin and succeed. For the importation of religion in the Caribbean, par-ticularly Christianity, which clashed not only with Aboriginal spiritual life, but also with that of its immigrants, culminated, as Victoria Carchidi writes, "in an alienation from the physical life of the Caribbean."[27] In *Our Lady,* the Priest's attempt to instill Christian rationality in the lives of the Arawaks, Africans, and Indians, would have simply led to confusion. As he gradually absorbs the essence of the Guyanese interior, Lance, who goes to Guyana to seek redemption through the Priest's text, begins to understand the futility of the Priest's missionary work, believing that "nothing he said would have made sense to them," because the apertures of faith between the cultures were too great (p. 107). Spirituality had to be directly connected to lived experience, and not to doctrines invented in places and times disjointed from the present moment. Any attempt to force a borrowed spirituality onto a race or a culture that could not possibly relate to it, would result in the appearance of "lacunae . . . in which new spiritual practices begin to emerge, practices that draw syncretically not only on established European religious traditions but also on African and other cultural beliefs."[28] Thus, the Priest's efforts have to be rewritten, his doctrine of faith reconsidered, this time with the very syncretic outlook that it once denied. Part II of the novel is this retextualization of spirituality, while the novel, as a whole, is a comment on the necessity of this rewriting, with its division into two sections, the first written in a social realist mode, the latter in the fragmented and chaotic fashion of Arawakian/ Hindu belief systems, explicitly drawing a line between the two sections to indicate the clash of spiritualities.

However, as the title of the novel indicates, the entire text is a fusion of spiritual systems, rather than a purely postcolonial resistance to cultural and historical imposition, where "Our Lady" signifies both the Virgin Mary of Christianity and the Great Arawak Mother of Aboriginal belief, thus creating an ambiguity to her identity, and her residence in Demerara points to the specificity of Dabydeen's intentions: to display the spiritual origination of Guyana through religious dialogue. In this way, "Our Lady" is the psychical space of redemption, one of the poetic spaces under which El Dorado or Utopia are also categorized. In this space, as Benitez-Rojo states, "antagonisms that separate Self from Other must be reconciled," for these are the very colonial ideologies that have to be confronted and consequently dissolved— ideologies that have perpetuated the division between subject and object, which are based on the type of binary distinctions that Lance considers to be useless in the Guyanese context.[29] The true quest then, is not the actual expedition into the jungle's interior, or into a material El Dorado, but involves a metaphorical *leap beyond*, as Fazzini has termed it, where the physical and the psychical are considered simultaneously, creating an experience close to a spiritual revelation.[30]

This "leap beyond," Dabydeen seems to advocate, can only be done through a proper lens. For perception through the wrong lens creates a wall between the pre-leap and post-leap spaces. This is why, Lance states, Father Jenkins could not communicate with the Arawaks: "He had looked at life through his lens, with superficial eyes" (p. 109). And Lance's success at rewriting the Priest's manuscript is attributed to Samaroo, who gave him not only the manuscript, but also "a Hindu lens through which to read it [which] offered glimpses into the processes of regenerating one's self, of being born anew and in multiplicity . . . fissure, crack, abortion and rupture took place in one's lifetime, but from these could emerge utterly different redemptive conceptions of one's self" (pp. 111–13). It is this Hindu lens that aids Lance's understanding of the magic of the Arawaks, thus creating a palimpsest of faiths from which to view the entirety of society. The novel's analogy of this layering, which resembles Walcott's "vase analogy," is that of the gluing of the fragments of an eggshell without hiding its cracks. Father Harris tells the narrator, "Always leave a memory of the original . . . the memory of the original only comes when you see the breakage," thus suggesting that nothing of the past can ever be covered or ignored, that even as one celebrates the Great Arawak Mother, one has to also acknowledge the Virgin Mary, Kali, and other female religious figures within the collective of Guyanese society (p. 159). It is apt then for Lance, as an abuser of women and as a motherless Englishman, to be the one on this trajectory of rediscovering the "Mother" and the spiritualities of a place so geographically remote from him, yet historically proximate, in order to piece together the fragments of a broken connection between Britain and her colonies, which was once only typified by cultural and economic colonialism, without the lateral historical implications of imperialism. For every element in this phenomenon forms a web, where the former contributes to the latter's structure. Lance, then, symbolizes the importance of not only reassessing the culture of the colonized, but that of the colonizer as well, where a mirroring of influences exposes the inseparability of cultures, which then leads to the necessity of seeing these cultures, formed out of histories, as subject to perpetual reassessment, because their constant movement implies constant possibilities.

THE INFINITE REHEARSAL

Dabydeen introduces a suitable metaphor for this interconnectedness, where one is able to deduce the continual revisitation of history. The eggs that Lance's mother in Part II miraculously receives to feed her son symbolize, through their spherical shape, Harris' "unfinished genesis of the imagination," which refers to the incompletion of history, and the interplay of elements within a globular structure.[31] The sphere is the archetypal shape, whose center resists direct perception, and whose roundness displays qualities of indeterminacy, where overlapping and interpenetration occur. Thus, it provides indeterminate solutions and possibilities, and is the space where binaries collapse. The whore and the virgin meet in the figure of Lance's mother, declared by him to be the former, but her almost biblical dedication to her son brings her closer to the virgin. Hence, even as she is already a rehearsal of Beth in Part I, she perpetuates the mobility of her personality by making the separation of qualities impossible, thereby creating possibilities. This reincarnation also alludes to a racial reconfiguration, with Beth in Part I in denial of being quarter-Indian, but in Part II made to accept the challenges of interfusion.

While Dabydeen does not explicitly comment on the ideal conduct of race relations, he does so in an implicit way, often through poetic or metaphorical means, so as to avoid any dogmatic inclinations concerning the issue. Thus, rather than preach integration, Dabydeen displays it. A clear example of this is in the multiracial Arawak family that Lance encounters in the jungle, which once again alludes to the jungle as a space of redemption and fusion. The Arawak woman's children "were all slightly different in appearance. There were hints, in the shapes of their noses, in the texture of their hair, in the various tints of their skin, of a history of cross-breeding. Hindus, Africans and even the odd Chinese . . . What was remarkable was the seeming harmony of this mongrel community" (pp. 104–05). They represent the composite identity that Harris, Benitez-Rojo, and Torabully speak of as being crucial in the Caribbean make-up, although they most often refer to it in cultural rather than biological terms. Torabully states that "the composite identity is assumed there to be a root conjoined with another root (the root of the other), without a predatory or central root, thus leaving identity open to *la relation* or the fact of bringing into the relation another component," and this is the very identity that Torabully puts forth in his poetics.[32] As coolitude first propounds an acknowledgement of the coolie, his migration, voyage, trials, and tribulations, it ultimately insists on the relationality of fragments, its creolization, rather than essentialization. In other words, "coolitude attempts to break away from the danger in constructing a rhizome-identity based on *one* interpretation or *one* component . . . it points towards multiple identities in a dynamic interaction, in a 'dialectic of mutations,'" which then creates the image of the bastard through promiscuous interplay.[33] In the novel, Dabydeen's obsession with whores, prostitutes, out of wedlock pregnancies and abortions, alludes to his acceptance of this promiscuity as part and parcel of the process of, as Torabully would have it, cross-cultural vagabondage.

This cross-culturalism, however, does not remain spatially contained within Guyana. Part I of *Our Lady* exists to provide a cultural cartography of Part II, which involves Coventry, Ireland, India, and finally Guyana, where all four meet in dialogue. This mongrel web is materialized through the rehearsals of personalities in Lance's rewritten manuscript. Coventry characters are reinvented through the Arawakian and Hindu scope of reincarnation, discussed earlier in order to draw the type of connections necessary for the configuration of cross-culturalities. Thus, characters such as Rohini/Corrine, Miriam,

Geoff, Lance, and Beth replay themselves, with elements added to their identities, to indicate the ceaselessness of identity construction, another crucial point in coolitude's aesthetics. Of course, this ceaselessness relates back to the notion of the composite identity, wherein several elements amalgamate and the ability for these components to vary causes this identity to continually change, thereby creating a sense of continuity, despite the ongoing alterations in composition. This incessancy, which is not subjected to time, although time remains a factor within its process, resembles the taxonomical classification propounded by Michel Foucault, through pre-Darwinian evolutionists such as Bonnet, Maupertuis, Diderot, Robinet, and Benoit de Maillet. Rather than a succession of beings, where one overtakes another, these organisms survive in interdependency, through a common journey "towards the perfection of God." Thus, this "evolutionism" is not based on an individual selfishness, but "is a way of generalizing the principle of continuity and the law that requires that all beings form an uninterrupted expanse."[34] In other words, time and space form a continuity that creates an infinity, whose ultimate goal is the perfection of the entirety, in this case, the entirety of beings on the taxonomical table, and in the case of the novel, the entirety of the characters, their countries, races, cultures, and societies within the connective web mentioned earlier, whose function resembles that of the taxonomical table of the natural world.

Another aspect of "evolutionism" negates any kind of temporality in order to "reveal, one after the other, the squares that, when viewed together, will form the continuous network of the species," which again harks back to the notion of an endless relation between beings. Resemblances between seemingly far-fetched organisms indicate how taxonomia works: these partial identities are the marks "revealed in the present, of one and the same living being, persisting through all the upheavals of nature and thereby filling all vacant possibilities offered by the taxonomic table."[35] Thus, as Benoit de Maillet states, the resemblance between the wings of a bird and the fins of a fish exists because birds once belonged to "the original waters of the earth," and therefore, like Father Harris' advice to the young Priest, the memory of the original remains somewhat intact.[36] And it is Father Harris who states, mirroring Maillet's formulation on the interconnectedness of beings, that "all are bound together in *one* process of living, immeasurably various as it is" (p. 216). Immediately after this declaration, Father Harris begins to re-member the conjoining of the bones of Stephen Yardley, Mark Yardley, Christopher Reece, and John Taylor, who were "on the surface different men but identical in the foundation of an earthen grave," a thought that calls up not only the notion of intertwining characters, but also the aforementioned bones of the foreigners in the jungle, whose presence feeds into and affects the lives of the living, in one chain of osmosis-like exchange (p. 216). Rehearsals then, are not trite repetitions, but a dialogue between selves on the taxonomical table, always readjusting positions, always incomplete in Father Harris' *"one process of living"* (p. 216).

Despite the continuity of this process, its movements are not categorically logical, consisting, as it does, of innumerable particles, miscarried differences and variations, so that combinations become complex and the ways in which elements combine are varied and unpredictable, and this then denies a linear explanation of continuity. Hence, Father Harris asks, "Why should we always want things to follow, a, b, c, why always want things to make sense, to make a sequel and a finished story?" (p. 214). His rhetorical question outlines the novel's philosophy of leaps and chaos, rehearsals and reincarnations, but with a firm belief in the fundamental connectivity of these seemingly disparate events and characters. Effectively, it becomes simple enough for Father Harris to see how Sarah and Alice together form a kind of continuum: "[Sarah] would play Alice, become Alice, and he, Father Harris, had witnessed Alice's past in the evolving of Sarah's future" (p. 206). In Part I of the novel, no connection seems to have been made between Alice and Sarah, but in Part II, their link creates a new portal not just into a reinvention of character, but an apparent system of order. This order, however, is not explicit where points are connected in succession of one another, in the kind of linear fashion that Father Harris dismisses. Instead, it is of a chaotic nature, undetermined only because its cause of determination is too complex to be identified. In reference to Chaos Theory, Ian Stewart writes in his book *Does God Play Dice?* that chaos can be defined as "stochastic behavior occurring in a deterministic system, [in other words], lawless behavior governed entirely by law."[37] This law, however, is impossible to detect because it refuses predictability, famously exemplified by the "butterfly effect" concept, which explicates that the fluttering of a butterfly's wings in one place results in a storm elsewhere. Thus, while Alice and Sarah may have been so disjointed in Part I where any kind of linkage between them would have seemed absurd, Part II offers them an opportunity for some kind of commonality. Why Alice and Sarah, and not Beth and Alice, or Sarah and Beth, does not really need an explanation, or, perhaps, put quite simply, it cannot be explained, just as the randomness of movement of the whorls of cigarette smoke cannot be explained after a certain point (a common example given by exponents of Chaos Theory).

While Father Harris embraces ideas of reinvention, connectivity, the philosophical, and the poetic, his adversarial twin, Father Wilson, represents the other end of the scale, with his science of taxidermy and his insistence that "mist off a goat's horns was mist off a goat's horns was mist off a goat's horns was not the Virgin" (p. 211). His approach to the anatomy of organisms differs from Father Harris,' in that he favors a rational and pragmatic study of the animals that he stuffs. And when Father Harris refers to the young Priest as a poet and a philosopher after his "discovery" that both the moth and the German cockroach had chitinous teeth, Father Wilson exclaims, "There's no philosophy to the being of an ant, no poetry in the way it crawls over rotting food. Modern science describes its mechanics, anything else is medieval mysticism," thus making explicit the division in their ways of thinking (p. 215). Although they are split, Father Harris' philosophy that "all are bound together in *one* process of living, immeasurably various as it is," would suggest that both Father Wilson and Father Harris are interminably bound together, and the space within which their distinctions are dissolved is ultimately the same space of redemption, where Christian dichotomies such as the ones mentioned in the Old Testament which the novel alludes to—Saved/Damned, Jews/Gentiles, We/Them, Birds/Insects, Men/Fish—are finally annihilated (p. 216). In other words, it is also the poetic space of "Our Lady" that Lance and the other characters are attempting to find and inhabit.

This space ensures not difference, but resemblance, and accommodates the mythical, the fantastical, the odd, as well as the ordinary. For, as Foucault states, in order to maintain the continuum of seemingly different objects, one has to allow into this order, the symbol of difference, which he characterizes as the "monster," as well as the symbol of resemblance, which is the "fossil." The monster represents the missing pieces or the background of the taxonomical scheme of which the fossil is explicitly a part. Thus, Foucault writes, "against the background of the continuum, the monster provides an account . . . of the genesis of differences, and the fossil recalls, in the uncertainty of its resemblances, the first buddings of identity."[38] What is important in Foucault's statement is the contribution of both elements, antitheses of one another, like Father Wilson and Father Harris, to the epistemological foundations of perceiving the natural world. In relation to the novel, this monster/fossil symbology can be suitably applied to the way in which the odd/mysterious/shameful (monster) corresponds with the normal/conventionally historical (fossil). In fact, *Our Lady* is littered with such correspondences: Beth's racial heritage, where her Indian coolie blood signifies the "monster" within the "fossil" of her English middle-class upbringing, Father Harris' lack of "logic" as the "monster" in the "fossil" of Father Wilson's established Cartesian rationality, and Arawakian magic as the "monster" within the "fossil" of Christian tradition. This is Dabydeen's attempt at acknowledging the "monster," of intermingling it with the "fossil," so as to reject each one's isolation, again another coolitude point.

For Torabully, bringing out silenced elements in society, whether in terms of race, class, or culture, is very much at the pivot of coolitude's poetics and politics. Thus, the historical demonization and neglect of coolies, within their respective societies, has made it necessary for the coolitudinization of their condition. In other words, it is imperative to bring them to the forefront of society, first to be acknowledged, and then to be equalized with the other elements within the society's plural context. For Dabydeen, the true healing of not just the coolie's condition, but that of the other races in Guyana, and the way in which their interaction occurs, can only be performed through an understanding of how pre-Columbian life correlates with the post-Columbian one, hence the structure of the novel.

THE REDEMPTIVE LANGUAGE

Apart from the structure, another restitutive technique that Dabydeen employs is that of language, an aspect in the regenerative process that is unavoidable, perpetually propounded as it is by postcolonial theorists, and in relation to the Caribbean context, language is one of the most available forms of resistance. Glissant states that the lack of language in the region is linked to two factors: firstly, the community's history of slavery and indenture, which led to a silencing of their past, and secondly, the socioeconomic situation. The repression of the past, he writes, erodes language, and the alienation from the physical reality of the environment results in an inadequate language to express the community's communication with the land. Effectively, things are externalized in words, and new modes of articulation appear, or rather the creolization of language begins. Glissant writes that "creolization offers a different framework, within which the lack of language and the subject's relation to language cease to be relevant because language has become so fluid and diverse that it can no longer be seen as having any role in the constitution of subjectivity."[39] Thus, language upholds its own consciousness and becomes a thing with unlimited potential to generate variations of thoughts, sentiments, and notions, and as Harris puts it, the language of fiction is especially suited for these kinds of alternations because it is a "living language." This living language "composes, within the artist, an interior unpredictable dialogue that gives rise to variables within the language of the Imagination and a ventriloquism of Spirit."[40] It is equipped with a transcendental quality that crosses bridges and creates new ones.

Coolitude propounds the centrality of language to the excavation of history and the reformation of the coolie's place in society. Torabully writes of how language has caged him and his people within the structures of colonial labor. Thus, he states that "language . . . [is] a potent source of relations to the world, to a new universe, or reconnecting to one's humanity in fact, [and] is among the most important spheres of resistance to plantocratic or colonial societies, specially from people who 'left' their aesthetic universe, their symbolical status in language, as they were treated as objects or sub-human entities."[41]

In view of the history of language, where its significance has changed from being a mode simply in which to mark the world, to its representative role for the Classics and its signifying one for the modern world, the reassessment of language is crucial. For, as Foucault writes in reference to what language has become, "the profound kinship of language with the world . . . was dissolved . . . [the] uniform layer, in which the *seen* and the *read,* the visible and the expressible, were endlessly woven, vanished too. Things and words were to be separated from one another."[42] Thus, the association between the "thing" and the "word" needs to be reformulated, re-birthed, in order to create a fresh perception of the world, where language cannot simply be relegated to a construction whose only role is to signify. Dabydeen constantly attempts to build bridges between word and flesh, subject and object, and he does so not only to surpass those binaries, but also to indicate the special rhythm that materializes from the construction of such bridges. For instance, Manu's relationship with the natural life of the jungle is defined in one sense by the musical linguistics of imitation: "'Pi-pi-you. Pi-pi-you,' he called out imitating the whistle of a bird . . . 'Listen you hear that? Crat-crat-cratak-crat-cratak. Is a crow, what we call blanbie-bird'" (p. 89). The sounds of the jungle have been translated into a rhythmic language that can only baffle Lance, who is alienated from the jungle's environment. This rhythmic language is, before anything else, performative, and indicates "the march of Nature," according to Benitez-Rojo, and its very rhythm creates the effect of the words, which are, of course, invented ones in line with the noises of the jungle.[43] Thus, although the words may not have discursive meaning, they have an intuitive one that relates directly to the physical world.

In fact, the entire novel is a comment on language as a means of redemption. Part II exists as a doubly-written text, firstly by Dabydeen, and secondly by Lance, where articulation provides a gateway into finding out "what is" or "what might be." The Priest's story, which was "broken and haphazard," and littered with "cryptic lines, gnomic paragraphs, obscure notes, doodles, impossible puns," had to be decoded, as it were, and reinvented in a new language, in order for Lance to depart in peace (p. 94). Thus, the rewritten manuscript symbolizes, even as it exists as a thing in its own right, the amalgamation of the imagination and language to produce possibilities that materialize in the ceaseless rehearsals of characters. This alludes to the fact that characters can always be rewritten, recreated, reformed. In other words, alternatives are always available, as the novel seems to be suggesting all along. For, from the very start of *Our Lady of Demerara,* certain words are given substitutes in brackets. The substitutes are ironic indications of not double meanings, but secret sentiments that expose the malleability of the spoken word: "Astonished" is followed by "(admonished)," "antiquity" by "(iniquity)," "admiration" by "(abomination)," and "client" by "(cunt)" (pp. 3, 5, 61).

Even Lance's journey to Pillar is foreshadowed by a linguistic tone. His first introduction to Pillar is through the innumerable scrawling of the word "Pillar" in the Priest's manuscript, "with variations like 'rape,' 'liar,' 'pillage,' 'lap,' 'lip,'" thus preparing him for the violent history of the place, which he receives from Manu (p. 108). The anagrams, which bear some light on the reality of Pillar, suggest the transference of language to physical life.

It is possible to deduce, following the discussions above, that *Our Lady of Demerara* works as a performative text, never content to remain still. In fact, one can even imagine a rewriting of the novel, a ceaseless project of exploration and renewal, with characters and events never tiring of the process of becoming.

CONCLUSION

Through the facets of rhythm and chaos, place, faith, and space, the infinite rehearsal and language, Dabydeen demonstrates how the complexities and imperfections of Guyanese life are the very means through which reality is assessed and restitution can begin. By horizontalizing diverse elements, he creates a space for the relayed spotlighting of components, so that the Caribbean mosaic is revealed in which the coolie, just as much as the slave and the aboriginal, is located. The poetics of coolitude, as well as a distinctly Caribbean perspective of mobility and opacity, underscore how cultural and historical interplay within society exists both on subtle and explicit levels, and by bringing this process to the forefront, the realization of multiplicity already contributes towards the project of redeeming the past.

Notes

1. David Dabydeen, *Our Lady of Demerara* (West Sussex: Dido Press, 2004). All quotes from this novel appear in brackets in the text of this chapter, with the page numbers shown after a "p." or "pp."

2. Marina Carter and Khal Torabully, *Coolitude: An Anthology of the Indian Labor Diaspora* (London: Anthem Press, 2002), 150.

3. Ibid., 155.

4. Baroquian in this context refers to Torabully's usage of the term in relation to the racial, cultural, and social interactions within diasporic spaces. Ibid., 172.

5. Wilson Harris, *Selected Essays of Wilson Harris: The Unfinished Genesis of the Imagination,* ed. A. J. M. Bundy (London: Routledge, 1999), 7.

6. *Kala pani,* which literally means "dark waters," refers to the crossing of the seas by Hindus, which was banned because this was believed to result in the loss of one's caste. See Carter and Torabully, *Coolitude,* 25.

7. Ibid., 194.

8. Ibid., 174.

9. See, for example, Antonio Benítez-Rojo, *The Repeating Island: The Caribbean and the Postmodern Perspective,* trans. James E. Maraniss (Durham and London: Duke University Press, 1992); Celia M. Britton, *Édouard Glissant and Postcolonial Theory: Strategies of Language and Theory* (Charlottesville and London: University Press of Virginia, 1999); and Harris, *Selected Essays of Wilson Harris.*

10. Benitez-Rojo, *The Repeating Island,* 158.

11. Ibid., 167.

12. Ibid., 25, 26, 27.

13. Ian Stewart, *Does God Play Dice?: The New Mathematics of Chaos* (London: Penguin, 1997), 17.

14. Benitez-Rojo, *The Repeating Island,* 79–80.

15. Ibid., 6, 4.

16. Marina Camboni, "Resisting Fearful Symmetry: Wilson Harris' Bridges of Language," in *Resisting Alterities: Wilson Harris and Other Avatars of Otherness,* ed. Marco Fazzini (Amsterdam: Rodopi, 2004), 14.

17. Benitez-Rojo, *The Repeating Island,* 17.

18. Derek Walcott, *What the Twilight Says* (New York: Farrar, Straus and Giroux, 1999), 81.

19. Ibid., 68.

20. Derek Walcott, "The Caribbean: Culture of Mimicry?" in *Critical Perspectives on Derek Walcott,* ed. Robert D. Hamner (Boulder: Lynne Rienner Publishers, 1997), 53.

21. Fazzini, *Resisting Alterities,* 23.

22. Ibid., 57–58.

23. Harris, *Selected Essays,* 44.

24. Carter and Torabully, *Coolitude,* 143.

25. Walcott, *What the Twilight Says,* 69.

26. Carter and Torabully, *Coolitude,* 157.

27. Victoria Carchidi, "'Heaven is a Green Place': Varieties of Spiritual Landscape in Caribbean Literature," in *Mapping the Sacred: Religion, Geography and Postcolonial Literatures,* eds. Jamie S. Scott and Paul Simpson-Housley (Amsterdam and Atlanta: Rodopi, 2001), 182.

28. Ibid., 182.

29. Benitez-Rojo, *The Repeating Island,* 193.

30. Fazzini (ed.), *Resisting Alterities,* 57.

31. Ibid.

32. Carter and Torabully, *Coolitude,* 152.

33. Ibid., 172.

34. Michel Foucault, *The Order of Things: An Archeology of the Human Sciences* (London: Tavistock Publications, 1974), 151, 152.

35. Ibid., 152–53.

36. Ibid., 153.

37. Stewart, *Does God Play,* 17.

38. Foucault, *The Order of Things,* 157.

39. Britton, *Édouard Glissant,* 51.

40. Harris, *Selected Essays,* 199.

41. Carter and Torabully, *Coolitude,* 173.

42. Foucault, *The Order of Things,* 43.

43. Benitez-Rojo, *The Repeating Island,* 17.

Chapter 10

Beyond the National

Cross-Culturalism in the Art of the Jamaican Painter Karl Parboosingh

Claudia Hucke

INTRODUCTION

On August 6, 1962, Jamaica entered a new historical stage in which it became fully independent after centuries of slavery and colonialism. Under the nationalist demands of the immediate post-independence period, the new country committed itself to molding an anti-colonial cultural identity, and, at the same time, aspired to become a modern and internationally visible nation. This chapter seeks to unearth some of the challenges Jamaican artists encountered during this period of redefinition, when much of the art, along with its discourse, was self-referential, addressing questions of identity, and the direction of art in a postcolonial society.[1] At the same time, however, Jamaican visual artists were also engaged in cross-cultural dialogues that presented them with novel, aesthetic possibilities to form a hybrid art, one that went beyond the national.

The generation of artists that emerged around independence tried to find their place in an increasingly globalized world. Widely traveled and highly educated abroad, they brought to Jamaica influences from Europe, North America, Latin America, and Africa. These experiences of temporary exile, relocation, and displacement, to use Paul Gilroy's words, were significant for the direction and character of Jamaican art.[2] Based on a case study of the painter Karl Parboosingh, I hope, in this chapter, to demonstrate the dichotomy between nationalism and internationalism in the direction taken in Jamaican art. This dichotomy, I believe, was reflected in a multitude of tensions, for example, between authenticity and cultural mutation, folk and modern, and state and individual.

PARBOOSINGH: THE MAKING OF AN ARTIST

Karl Parboosingh (1923–1975), trained in New York, Paris, and Mexico City, was an artist who embodied the spirit of a new hybrid art around independence, perhaps more than any other individual. Together with Barrington Watson and Eugene Hyde, he founded the Contemporary Jamaican Artists' Association (CJAA), the leading artists' group on the island from 1964 until the early 1970s. The art critic Norman Rae described Parboosingh as an "ebullient, irrepressible Bohemian artist, quicksilver in temperament, readily forgivable."[3] Fiercely independent and often provocative in his public behavior, Parboosingh primarily saw himself as an artist and intellectual. Stylistically, Parboosingh could transition from Fauvism and Expressionism to pure abstraction. In order to reveal the multicultural influences that characterize Parboosingh's work, I would like to first take a closer look at his semi-abstract work *House of Dread* (Illustration 10.1).

Painted in 1975, the year of his death, *House of Dread* illustrates major developments in post-independence Jamaican art, in particular, the iconographic concern of many artists with the island's history and social structure, the use of modern stylistic devices, but also the artists' search for their own individual visual languages.

Formally, *House of Dread* consists of geometric, mostly vertical green, yellow, and red color fields that are framed by thick, black outlines, out of which grow grotesque and at times zoomorphic creatures. Even though not clearly identifiable, the central figure in *House of Dread* is a stylized cat, a recurring motif in Parboosingh's oeuvre since the mid-1950s. A bracket-like structure grows from the cat's back and due to its red "teeth," it is reminiscent of a screaming mouth. To the left and right, as well as above, additional brackets and enclosures of various sizes and forms populate the canvas. On the right hand side, they further create a human-like figure with a head, neck, and two long limbs; in the negative space that they create are more stylized forms such as dots and a star. The artist plays with our understanding of negative and positive space. The negative areas between the extremely elongated legs of the central figures and its green, yellow, and red coloring—similar to the remaining fields in the same colors—become the positive stripes of the Ethiopian flag that was adopted by the Rastafarian Movement.[4]

The painting's title is ambiguous, as it suggests a multi-level reading. As a whole, it references a Rastafarian community called House of Dread in downtown Kingston that was a popular hang-out spot for adherents during the 1960s, and also boasted a football team with the same name. Parboosingh was interested in Rastafari because he believed it embodied a strong revolutionary spirit that provided the philosophical underpinning of the 1960s' youth

Illustration 10.1: Karl Parboosingh, *House of Dread*, 1975, Bank of Jamaica Collection, Kingston, Jamaica. The Karl Parboosingh Estate.

rebellions, including black consciousness. Especially in the aftermath of Haile Selassie's 1966 visit to Jamaica, Rastafarianism gained a great deal of momentum on the island, increasing in the context of the government's ban of black writers who were believed to have communist and black power associations, and the ensuing Rodney Riots in 1968.[5] Parboosingh, regarded as a rebel in the Jamaican art scene, was never himself identified as a Rastafarian, but he accompanied his son, Paris, a member of the movement, to meetings in the early 1970s.[6] Works such as *Communion with the Elders* (c.1973) and *Man with Abeng* (c.1972–73), suggest that Parboosingh had a strong interest in Rastafarianism. The first part of the title of *House of Dread* also references the different groups amongst Rastafarians that are called *houses*, while the second part invokes an image of the typical Rastafarian hairstyle known as *dread*locks.

To understand the *House of Dread* fully, we have to take into consideration the artist's biography. Parboosingh was born as Karl Coy in Highgate, St. Mary, rural Jamaica, in 1923, and was educated at the traditional (elite) high schools of Calabar and Wolmer's. His father was a Scottish foreman at a sugar estate, and "twenty to thirty years older than his wife," a Jamaican of probably partly Indian descent.[7] Karl was raised by his grandmother after his mother, Gladys Coy, moved to New York and worked her way up from a factory worker to become "the first colored person to open a dress salon in the Silk Stocking District of New York," in today's Upper East Side.[8] At nineteen, Karl joined his mother in New York, where, exposed to her love of fashion and the city's museums and galleries, he began to show an interest in the visual arts:

> I didn't start out as a painter. As a matter of fact . . . my introduction to art was through music which I started at the age of three at St. Hilda's in Brown's Town. I continued playing violin up to the time when I left Jamaica. Up to that time I had never painted. I was 19 years old and I had never seen paintings in oil as a matter of fact. I was completely ignorant of the existence of painting and ignorant of the professional standard of a painter and I discovered on my very first visit to America that—I just felt an instinctive attraction when I saw the galleries and paintings in the museums. I immediately persuaded my mother to send me to art school and to discontinue the violin.[9]

Parboosingh belonged to the last generation of artists who were forced to study overseas, due to the lack of an art academy in Jamaica prior to the 1962 establishment of the Jamaica School of Art and Crafts, as a full-time, diploma-granting institution. Before studying art, however, Parboosingh had joined the American Army, and seven months after he completed his military training, World War II ended and he volunteered to join the United States Military Occupational Force in Panama.[10] There, Parboosingh started sketching and drawing seriously, and this period was most likely the start of his interest in Latin American culture, which he would further explore during his time as a student in Mexico a few years later.

Parboosingh said that one of the reasons he became an artist "was the influence of the poetry of the Jamaican-born Harlem Renaissance poet Claude McKay who I discovered while I was in America . . . his poetry gave me a great feeling and sense of dedication to Jamaica by its clearness and I really saw what I had to do from reading his poems."[11] McKay and Parboosingh shared experiences. Both were Jamaicans who had lived abroad, for example. Yet, unlike the poet who was based in the United States for most of his adult life, and became a significant figure in the Harlem Renaissance, Parboosingh created his major artistic contributions while in his homeland of Jamaica.[12] McKay dealt with the experience of exile in his poems (see "I Shall Return").[13] Parboosingh, on the other hand, had a longing to actively contribute to Jamaican life, and "to be a Jamaican artist."[14] The search for identity in McKay's poems, however, was also revealed in Parboosingh's later paintings.

Around the time when he entered the army, Karl Parboosingh changed his last name from Coy to Parboosingh. Several explanations have been offered for his decision to make the change, but his son, Paris, explains that,

> Parboo and his brother Gene and their mother, a dressmaker, lived in New York. My grandmother had her studio on the corner of Lexington Avenue and 11th. Street. She could only afford to send one of her children to school and decided to send Gene which caused annoyance by Karl who then, in protest, changed his name from Coy to Parboosingh. Parboosingh was a name from his mother's side of the family in Highgate.[15]

Another convincing story states that "one of the main reasons was that Parboosingh (taken from his aunt's married name) immediately identified him as an artist from an exotic country. And this was advantageous in those days."[16]

After he left the army in 1948, Parboosingh began his studies, which were financed by the G.I. Bill of Rights at the Art Students' League in New York under George Grosz (1893–1959) and Yasuo Kuniyoshi (1893–1953). The immediate post-war years were a significant time in the development of American art: with the rise of Abstract Expressionists, such as Jackson Pollock, Willem de Kooning, and Mark Rothko, New York became the art capital of the Western hemisphere. Yet, the influence of the New York School would not become visible in Parboosingh's work until much later. As a student, he mingled, instead, with musicians in Greenwich Village; numerous pencil or ink drawings in his sketchbook capture cello, piano, and saxophone players, and express his fondness for jazz. His first wife, Phoebe, recalled that "Music was very important to him, and he knew all the jazz artists in the Village—Charlie Parker, Max Roach, Kenny Clarke, Lester Young. He often said that if he had been born in the United States, he would have been a jazz musician, which was the black tradition."[17]

This statement illustrates Parboosingh's conflicted outsider status—he was black, had served in the American army, yet he did not identify himself as African American. Sometimes, he attended functions of Black Awareness groups, including a meeting of Garveyites, but Phoebe pointed out that "this was not a driving force in his paintings."[18] The star in the lower half of *House of Dread* could be construed as a reference to the Black Star Line, Garvey's shipping company, but Parboosingh was never a radical *black* artist with a strong sense of Garvey's Pan-Africanism in his work. Instead of a black nationalism, Parboosingh believed in an open form of nationalism that included influences from other cultures. In this attitude, he offered an alternative to the almost purely Afrocentric and folk-based version of Jamaican culture promoted after independence, one of the advocates being Edward Seaga, who was Minister of Development and Welfare. Development in Parboosingh's world required the support of a culture that had internal as well as external influences.

In 1949, Parboosingh married the white American Phoebe Wick, a fellow student at the Art Students' League in New York. The couple moved to Paris later that year, where their son, named Paris, was born on Bastille Day in 1950.[19] Whereas New York provided Parboosingh with the foundation of his artistic training, and a taste of the bohemian lifestyle, he became more interested in the exploration of formal and stylistic concerns while in the French capital. He took classes at the Centre d'Art Sacré, and worked with Georges Rouault (1871–1958) and Fernand Léger (1881–1955).[20] Rouault's stained glass windows would be particularly influential on Parboosingh. He recalled that he "hoped to be able to transfer to canvas the color effects of stained glass windows."[21] The mosaic-like effect of stained glass that Parboosingh replicated, suggests that he viewed Jamaican society as multilayered in its ethnic and cultural composition. This is evident especially in later works, such as *The Palette,* which he finished around 1973 (Illustration 10.2).

The influence of Matisse in this French period seems to have been even stronger. Parboosingh's rejection of realism expressed by large fields of non-naturalistic, unmodulated colors, and the black outlines in *The Lamps* (c. early 1950s), clearly reference the French artist's Fauvist style, the simplification of which derived from studies of African carvings. In his later years, Parboosingh returned to Fauvist influences, as seen, for example, in the flat coloring, the two-dimensionality, and the black outlines in *House of Dread.* Overall, Paris evoked in Parboosingh an understanding of himself as a bohemian artist, rooted in the European Modernist tradition, as shown in his 1951 *Self Portrait* (Illustration 10.3). Referencing the artistic language of Western modernism has been popular in Jamaican art since the 1920s and 1930s, when Edna Manley and her circle increasingly fed on influences from Post-Impressionism, Cubism, and other European avant-garde movements that they often combined with a local iconography.

It took a voyage to Mexico to awaken in Parboosingh the idea of a socially conscious art that went beyond formal studies, and included cultural references to his environment. On a visit to Italy, he was exposed to frescoes by the Proto-Renaissance artists Giotto and Cimabue, which triggered his interest in wall painting, a passion that was greatly enhanced by his studies of mural technique at Mexico City's Instituto Politécnico Nacional.

Illustration 10.2: Karl Parboosingh, *The Palette*, c.1973, Paris Parboosingh Collection, Kingston, Jamaica. The Karl Parboosingh Estate.

Parboosingh's teacher, José Gutiérrez, and his meetings with the great muralists Diego Rivera (1886–1957) and David Alfaro Siqueiros (1896–1974), had a profound impact on him. In post-revolutionary Mexico, especially during the 1920s and 1930s, paintings on public walls became a significant way to educate the people about the country's history and indigenous culture. When Parboosingh was in Mexico in the early 1950s, the new campus of the Universidad Nacional Autónoma de México, the Ciudad Universitaria, was being constructed, and the students were asked to work on mural projects there alongside Siqueiros and Rivera.[22] One senses Parboosingh's admiration for the muralists, not only for their art, but also for their political involvement and

Illustration 10.3: Karl Parboosingh, *Self Portrait*, 1951, Paris Parboosingh Collection, Kingston, Jamaica. The Karl Parboosingh Estate.

social standing in his description of their fame: "Man, those muralists were treated like movie stars. When they walked out in the streets, people would greet them as Maestro! You see, apart from the fact that they were involved in all aspects of art, they had all fought in that b[lood]y revolution."[23] This experience made Parboosingh recognize the potential of art as an educational and nation-building tool.

In contrast to the celebrated status of artists in Mexico, Jamaican artists during the 1950s were still struggling for recognition among a broader section of the population. Whilst the circle around Edna Manley had started to introduce more indigenous subject matter into painting and sculpture, in an effort to push the emergence of the nationalist movement from the 1930s, there was not much public art on the island. With the exception of some colonial monuments, most art works were restricted to the limited number of galleries that existed at that time. It does not come as a surprise that Parboosingh faced difficulties when he returned to Jamaica in 1952, ambitious to use art as a medium "for the social message to be painted."[24] What he perceived as the timidity of Jamaicans, however, frustrated him "because at that time, Jamaica being a Colonial country, very few people were actively coming out and saying what was supposed to be said."[25] When he showed the anti-colonialist series, *Give us our Heritage* (1952), in his first one-man show at the Institute of Jamaica, for example, Parboosingh was disappointed by the reception and felt that the paintings were rejected as too revolutionary. In response, he "took up an axe and chopped to shreds" forty of the works, and left Jamaica once again to spend the next four years mainly in New York.[26]

The relationship with his wife, Phoebe, ended during this time, and Parboosingh resettled permanently in Jamaica in March 1956. In the same year, he married Seya, a Lebanese-American poet, who would soon become a successful painter in her own right. Back in Jamaica, he embarked on what he had been passionate about since Mexico: mural painting. As part of the government's scheme for the encouragement and development of art, for example, Parboosingh painted the walls of new government buildings. One mural was at the chief minister Norman Manley's office at 24 East Race Course, Kingston.[27] Another one depicting coffee pickers was at the Ministry of Agriculture.[28]

A number of one-man exhibitions introduced the artist to a wider Jamaican audience, and gallery owner, Christopher Hills, used these opportunities to emphasize Parboosingh's importance to the rise of modern art in Jamaica at this time.[29] In the catalogue for the 1956 Myrtle Bank show, for example, Hills wrote that when he was visiting Greenwich Village in New York City, he found Parboosingh's "name being passed around the tables and night-spots as one of the coming painters."[30] Hills also said that,

> This exhibition is important in the history of art in Jamaica, for here we are not dealing with the artist who paints the pretty pictures we might see on chocolate boxes, and which are so much admired for their technical excellence. . . . Parboosingh is the first artist in Jamaica who has saved expressionist painting from fancy and daydreaming, and brought it down to the roots of aesthetics, or the root of life itself.[31]

One of Parboosingh's dreams was to have a place like Greenwich Village or Paris in Jamaica, where people could enjoy art, listen to poetry, and meet for drinks. In the early 1960s, he proposed a project called Coyaba in Port Henderson, some twenty kilometers outside of Kingston.[32] The Coyaba artists' colony was supposed to "provide a meeting place and opportunities for participation of West Indians and visiting groups in a varied programme of cultural, social and educational activities."[33] Seya Parboosingh pointed out the significance that her husband's experience in Mexico had for this project:

> He was doing it primarily because he loved art and he knew the importance it had in his life. He had lived and gone to school in Mexico, and Mexicans love their art. That flabbergasted him. The Mexicans respected their artists; they didn't do that in Jamaica yet. That fuelled his desire.[34]

During an explanatory meeting at the Ministry of Development, Karl Parboosingh and Vivian Blake, who was chairman of the Coyaba Organizing Committee, outlined plans for the construction of ten resort cottages for vacationers, and an equal number of studio cottages for artists.[35] Seya Parboosingh recalled that, "[Karl] thought Jamaica being a tourist place and having all this art and believing in it, it would be good to set up an art colony, which would also be a resort, a pretty place for people to visit."[36] The idea to connect art and tourism was popular at a time when the tourism sector was becoming more and more relevant for Jamaica's economy. Indeed, it was hoped that Coyaba would become a new major attraction for the culturally inclined traveler. John Bertram wrote in the *Daily Gleaner* that,

> Karl Parboosingh's inspiration, the Coyaba Cultural Resort Village is worthy of mention since not only is it the first of its unique kind in Jamaica, but also since its potentialities are or should be enormous, certainly as an attraction to the many thousands from the North and South American continents as well as from the other islands of the Caribbean, who are interested in the arts, music and all things cultural out of Coyaba, a special "Mecca" on a small scale which should add enormously to the attractions which this island already has to offer the overseas visitor.[37]

The "Cultural and Recreational Centre" known as Coyaba was supposed to boast a theatre, an auditorium, galleries, a restaurant, and a nightclub "with a colorful West Indian atmosphere," along with arts and crafts shops, a library, a "cine-club," and swimming pool, marina, chapel, and promenades.[38] Parboosingh did not only want to create facilities for the visual arts, but also for the performing arts. Plans were made to provide local organizations with space to hold cultural performances, and to invite foreign artists and offer cultural exchange fellowships.

The government of Jamaica "had agreed in principle to negotiate a 99 year loan on 25 acres of land in Port Henderson dependent on approval of plans, specifications, estimates and proposals for financing the project."[39] Despite the government's support regarding the location, finding funding for Parboosingh's elaborate plans, estimated at about £450,000, was difficult. The *Daily Gleaner* pointed out that the project relied solely on "voluntary contributions" from individuals and corporations.[40] In the end, Coyaba did not materialize. Seya explained that the failure was mainly due to Jamaican party politics: "It almost happened, but the government that was behind it [the People's National Party (PNP) under Norman Manley] lost power [in the 1962 elections], and the other one [the Jamaica Labor Party (JLP)] dropped the idea."[41]

While Coyaba had failed, some of the ideas behind it, such as the fusion of the fine arts with the performing arts, and the attention to community work, would later be incorporated into the CJAA. As a founding member of this private artists' group—one that was independent and received no state sponsorship—Parboosingh became known to a wider audience, even though he had exhibited in Jamaica since the mid-1950s. The group, a heterogeneous collection of artists, contributed to the visibility of art in society through exhibitions open to the general public, through educational programs, and through mural projects. Many of their works referenced Jamaican themes, but their stylistic range included both representational and abstract art. The key players were the three founders: Barrington Watson, Eugene Hyde, and Karl Parboosingh—all of whom, after studying overseas, returned to Jamaica around the time of independence to help with the shaping of the island's artistic landscape.

Watson, educated at the London Royal College of Art, was the most conservative of the three, having gained a reputation as a skilful painter of figures and portraits. Eugene Hyde was educated in the United States, and had a strong background in graphic design. Hyde had been influenced by the New York School, and next to Milton Harley, he is still regarded as one of Jamaica's first abstract artists. The CJAA's gallery became the leading platform for local and international artists, and represented a new, modern direction in the art of the island. Their synthesis of international focus, modern and diverse formal languages, and national consciousness, distinguishes them from the older generation, including Edna Manley and her circle, and also from the folk art movement that was supported by Edward Seaga.

HOUSE OF DREAD: A CLOSER LOOK

With this information in mind, let us take a closer look at *House of Dread*. The various geometric compartments or *rooms* that comprise the painting can be read as symbols of the fragmentation of Jamaican society. For, even after independence, and due to its history of slavery and colonialism, Jamaica was a fractured society with deep economic, social, and political inequities amongst its people. The nationalist movement at the time of independence tried to fuse the population of former slaves, former slave masters and colonial masters, and former indentured laborers, into one cohesive community.[42] The project reached one of its high points in the 1930s, when its leadership, drawn from mainly the educated middle class, advocated a change in the culture from its over reliance on Britain, to one that emphasized more the Afro-Jamaican traditions of the majority of the population.

The second meaning of the word *dread* is fear, which we could possibly interpret biographically as Parboosingh's personal anxiety; the various grotesque faces that turn into demons, which haunt and literally attach themselves to the cat that is possibly embodying the artist. Hindu iconography can help to decipher the demons. *Shiva-Lingam,* the symbol of the masculine creator of the Hindu goddess *Shiva,* resembles the forms in *House of Dread* on the top left and right hand side of the painting. It represents the male sex *lingam* being enclosed by the female *yoni.* Despite Parboosingh's Christian upbringing, his mother's partially Indian background seems to have triggered his interest in Hinduism. The signs could well be read as sexual demons, especially when taking into consideration the symbol of the stylized cat. The cat, which in European art history is often associated with female sexuality—as in Edouard Manet's *Olympia* (1863)—embodies a hyper-masculine symbol in Amerindian art, where cats are seen as the ultimate hunters and masters of the night, hence representing primitive male instincts.[43] Other biographical hints from Parboosingh's environment support the sexual demon thesis further. For example, a sketch by Parboosingh's friend, Ed Scott, which shows the emasculated artist standing on mountains of breasts, while playing the violin with a bottle of rum. The writing next to the artist says, "Play on—brother."

The existence of a semi-abstract painting such as *House of Dread* could not be taken for granted in Jamaica until the mid to late 1960s. For abstract or semi-abstract artists, such as Parboosingh, it was difficult to be accepted during a time when nationalist principles dominated the art of the island, and cultural policies celebrated self-taught artists such as Kapo as prototypes of a truly indigenous and Afrocentric Jamaican culture. The desire to define an authentic art is not a new phenomenon in the art of nations undergoing development. Mark Stevens provocatively stated that, "The more they [artists from the so-called developing world] become like us [artists from the so-called developed world], the less they will be able to paint like themselves."[44] Stevens implies that authenticity in the art of developing countries is measured by the degree of divergence from the canons in developed countries. Substantiating this statement, Jamaican post-independence cultural policy utilized the alleged, unspoiled nature of self-taught artists to demarcate an authentic culture for the island. In this cultural nationalism, claims were made of a special spiritual connectedness between folk artists and Africa, the ancestral homeland of most Jamaicans. These claims were made in spite of the diversity of the Jamaican population, as heard in its national motto: "Out of Many, One People."

Most notably, the Minister of Development and Welfare of the first, post-independence government, Edward Seaga, himself a trained anthropologist, identified Kapo's work and that of other "folk" artists as "inherently afro-centric—even though those artists had never been to Africa . . . had no experience with Africa. And what they produced was very much an afro-type art. And so what this did it started the indigenous art movement."[45] Seaga insinuates an innate bond between what he calls "folk artists" and "Africa."[46] In Seaga's opinion, "inherently Afro-centric," not "distinctively Caribbean" or Jamaican, is the equivalent of "indigenous." In Paul Gilroy's understanding, the policy enunciated by Seaga reflects an "aspiration to acquire a supposedly authentic, natural, and stable 'rooted' identity."[47] The premise of this "aura of Caribbean authenticity," however, was to deny the process of cultural amalgamation that had taken place during centuries of colonialism.[48]

Inside of Jamaica, self-taught artists gained increasing support from public institutions and private collectors after independence. Officially, the Jamaican self-taught artists were elevated as signifiers of a new Jamaican cultural identity. The suspicion that the fabrication of a "primitive" and "afro-centric" Jamaican folk culture appealed to foreign audiences more than to local ones, surfaced from time to time in the media. The island's self-taught or folk artists were generally perceived outside of Jamaica as more *authentic* than academically trained artists. A German journalist emphatically wrote about David Miller's wooden sculptures, which were known for their distinct African facial features. "Here you feel clearly the strange," wrote the journalist, "the peculiar of a different world."[49] Jamaican artists themselves have expressed that "mostly foreigners . . . appreciate what we do. They know it is something new and they appreciate it."[50] The art critic, Andrew Hope, has also claimed that self-taught artists appealed "mainly to foreigners, Americans especially, who like to adopt a patronizing attitude towards our art."[51]

Abstraction, on the other hand, was considered an international movement, and faced opposition due to concerns about its inability to fulfill the "role of art" as an instrument of social change, especially in the forging of a new nation.[52] In an environment in which many expected art to contribute to the process of nation-building, there was the perception that abstract artists "tend[ed] . . . to be less concerned about the creation of a Jamaican art per se," and had a greater interest in "seek[ing] refuge in a more emphatic identification with the international art world."[53] Another concern was that their art was "meaningless" because it did not fully represent Jamaica.[54] It could not contribute to social change in a country it did not represent. This view received the support of the academic community. One of its important voices at the time, Elsa V. Goveia, who became a professor of history at the University of the West Indies in Jamaica, wrote that she regretted that some of the painters in the Caribbean "tend to think in terms of abstract art rather than in terms of painting which can be socially influential."[55]

ABSTRACT ART IN JAMAICA: ROOTS AND REJECTION

The first artist who had a fully abstract exhibition in Jamaica was Milton Harley. Born in 1935 in Kingston, Harley moved to the United States with his family eight years later. Like Parboosingh, he served in the American army and entered the Pratt Institute in 1958, from which he graduated with a Bachelor of Fine Arts. In 1961, Harley moved back to Jamaica "to find [his] roots."[56] But this was hard to do in an environment where, as Norman Rae has noted, "most people still prefer[red] a landscape" that could "reproduce what they think is exactly the scene they see with their own eyes."[57] Harley's abstract paintings were regarded as "curiously out of place."[58] The fashionable art style during his student-days in New York was Abstract Expressionism. Harley remembers that, "When I returned to Jamaica from New York I brought back all these ideas of painting from the New York School in particular, where I saw shows of the giants like Robert Motherwell, Franz Kline, Willem de Kooning. I had met most of the artists there and was part of the movement there."[59]

Thetis (c.1960) was done during this time in New York, and reflects the all-over painting style and the emphasis on the form over subject that characterizes Abstract Expressionism (Illustration 10.4).[60] Thick, spontaneous brush strokes create uneven and overlapping fields of mute colors in varying shades of grays, blues, and beige. Black lines, seemingly quickly drawn, accentuate some of the areas on the canvas. The title, which is based on the Greek sea nymph *Thetis,* one of the fifty *Nereids,* was chosen after the painting was finished, and does not have any apparent significance to the image. When I asked Harley whether he ever felt any responsibility to be a "Jamaican painter" who produced "Jamaican art," his reply was "No, never. I just painted what I felt."[61] His subjects were not particularly Jamaican either, he explained, as "a lot is based on Greek mythology [and] Zen Buddhism."[62] And when I asked if coming back to Jamaica changed his art, Harley replied, "Not really."[63]

During the opening of a 1963 exhibition by Harley, Rex Nettleford encouraged artists to be inspired by their immediate environment, so that their works

Illustration 10.4: Milton Harley, *Thetis*, c.1960, Private Collection. Milton Harley.

of art become expressions of Jamaica's culture, but at the same time, Nettleford advised, Jamaica should expect not to isolate itself culturally, but allow communication with the world outside to take place. According to Nettleford, "It is one of the paradoxes of nation building that a country is never more international than when it becomes a nation."[64] Some of the leading figures of the Jamaican art establishment at the time revolted against the idea of allowing external trends to influence Jamaican art, and launched an attack against abstraction, in particular. Edna Manley, for example, cautioned the Jamaican art scene of the immediate post-independence period not to fully embrace international trends, for it was not ready for such influences. This was while Manley had also claimed that she would "defend to the very death the right of a man to paint a picture which is plain black on plain black."[65] In the interview, which took place in 1968, Manley said that,

> at this stage in West Indian history where there is so little expression of our image, where we are desperately in need of something that widens our horizons about ourselves, that we must not allow ourselves to be swept away by the modern trends and discourage the people who can add to the sum total of one might almost say the record of us as we are. . . . [W]e have such a thin heritage, such a short history.[66]

It is clear that Manley saw contributing to the development of country and region the duty of Caribbean artists. The abstractionist is out of place in this kind of environment, where art is expected to serve nation-building. As a rule, abstractionists would "tend . . . to be less concerned about the creation of a Jamaican art per se," and would "seek refuge in a more emphatic identification with the international art world."[67] It is important to understand that figures such as Manley were from an older generation of artists, whose nationalism was both personal and political. She had been influenced by the anti-colonial labor struggles and political protests during the 1930s. Her husband went into politics and was a founder of the PNP, one of the major political parties in modern Jamaica, and later Chief Minister and Premier. So, while Manley had given strong support to allowing artists freedom of expression, her goal was to promote "Caribbean" images as part of an iconographic struggle against colonization. Her ultimate aim was to build a nation that was new, and in her view, this required an imagery that was not abstract.

As for Parboosingh, his own increasing interest in abstraction (particularly important towards the end of his life)—as epitomized in *House of Dread* and the mural at A. D. Scott's Olympia International Art Centre (1974)—was also inspired by his friendship with Aubrey Williams (1926–1990). The latter was a Guyana-born artist and a founding member of the London-based Caribbean Artists' Movement (CAM). Parboosingh was greatly influenced by the collaboration with Williams, especially by his Amerindian-inspired art.[68] Williams even referred to Parboosingh as "my dear brother, who I still consider as the greatest artist Jamaica has ever produced."[69]

Parboosingh had experimented with and shown abstract works from as early as 1964.[70] He was aware that "there still isn't much room for such hedonistic philosophies as art for art's sake in Jamaica."[71] He would recall "that not much of the public [was] prepared to accept art which primarily celebrate[d] the adventures available for the eye à la abstract art."[72] The friendship with Williams certainly multiplied his interest in abstraction and caused a significant change in his style, even though not all of Parboosingh's works in their joint shows were abstracts. Before he had met Williams, Parboosingh's abstracts were evocative of stained glass windows—non-anthropomorphic shapes and black, straight, and irregular lines accentuating the bright color fields of greens, yellows, reds, and blues. Examples of this style are *Biblical Landscape* (before 1970) and *The Palette*. The collaboration with Williams between 1973 and 1975 generated a shift in Parboosingh's formal language. His works became more linear and the color fields cleaner and without tonal value. He introduced a highly personalized symbolism of grotesque creatures, as seen in *House of Dread*.

It can be argued that due to Williams' influence, Parboosingh's abstraction at least partially originates from indigenous Caribbean art. Yet, while a formal similarity can be seen between the brackets in *House of Dread* and those on Taìno sculptures, like the *Beaded Zemi* from the Dominican Republic, it seems more likely that Parboosingh consciously chose the *Lingam* symbol, rather than the decorative Taìno patterns—especially when one takes into consideration other strongly sexual symbols in Parboosingh's oeuvre from this period.

Untitled, a work depicting a stylized black cat in front of a bright orange background, repeats the *lingam*-type symbol on the lower right. Under the cat's arched body, forming a *yoni,* is a vertical phallus, which has entered the negative space of the cat, turning it into the positive space of a vagina. The cat is here associated with the Western idea of lust and sexuality, rather than the "hyper-masculine" denotation of the Amerindians. Similar motifs are also utilized in Parboosingh's mural at Olympia, *Red, Green, Yellow and Black* (1974). The mural's title reveals the original color scheme and is proof of Parboosingh's dedication to a Jamaican (Rastafarian) theme. As part of recent restoration efforts, the green has been replaced by blue, and the yellow by orange, thereby depriving the work of its color symbolism.

Pages from Parboosingh's sketchbook, probably studies for *House of Dread* and the Olympia mural, reveal his fascination with open forms, as well as with grotesque and stylized figures (Illustration 10.5a). Often, the gaping develops out of the creatures' bodies, as seen in the mouths, and one or more circles or phallic-like objects occupy their negative spaces, as shown in the black and white study (Illustration 10.5b). This rearranging and combining of stylized parts to depict different creatures and patterns is related to aspects of Amerindian art, and so are the emblematic forms. The grimacing faces in *House of Dread,* the Olympia mural, and the sketches could be imitations of the fierce expressions of some stylized anthropomorphic Taìno faces.[73]

Interestingly, despite his studies in Mexico and its rich pre-Columbian history, Parboosingh only began to appropriate some formal vocabulary of America's indigenous peoples after developing a friendship with Aubrey Williams. In contrast, Milton Harley, who also spent time studying in Mexico in the 1960s, was immediately drawn to the Toltec-Mayan imagery and culture. His abstract Mayan series, including *Mayan I,* is a response to Amerindian sites such as Teotihuacan, which he visited while he was a student at the Instituto Allende in Mexico City. In both Harley and Parboosingh, the Amerindians inspired an abstract or semi-abstract visual language that extended their relevance into the present. The interest in Mexican culture is another largely unexplored part of Caribbean modernism, one that broadens the usual focus on African and European influences.[74] Indeed, African stimuli that went beyond his interest in the Afrocentric Rastafarian religion appear absent from Parboosingh's oeuvre. While he traveled widely, he never visited Africa.

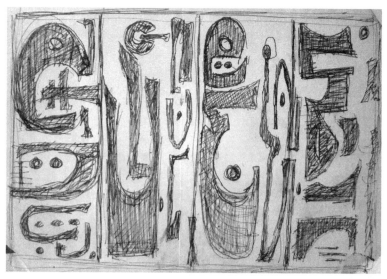

Illustrations 10.5a and 10.5b: Karl Parboosingh, n.d., Pages from his Sketchbook, Paris Parboosingh Collection, Kingston, Jamaica. The Karl Parboosingh Estate.

In addition to abstraction, Parboosingh shared a passion for murals with Aubrey Williams. The Guyanese artist's 1970 mural at Timehri International Airport, Guyana, filled with Carib and Arawak symbols, was one of the first outdoor murals in the Caribbean.[75] In 1974, Parboosingh himself exclaimed to an interviewer:

> Man, I would like to do more murals, to see more art work, all over the place ... look at that g ... airport, not a nothing to welcome people to this country. In Mexico the art is everywhere for everyone to share, and the artists also work in the theatre, designing costumes, backdrops, they illustrate books, record covers, the whole thing.[76]

As this statement articulates, Parboosingh's vision was to integrate the arts much more into the everyday lives of people and also to fuse visual arts with other forms of art. The synthesis of painting, architecture, and drama was realized when Parboosingh was commissioned to paint a mural at the Barn Theatre in 1967, a playhouse at 5 Oxford Road, Kingston.[77] Consisting of four panels, the *Dance Macabre* features grotesque black creatures—dancers with various odd body shapes seemingly swinging their limbs. They all have semicircular heads and straight white lines drawn irregularly across their bodies. The occasional green, red, or blue color splashes break up the rigid forms. The mural that now forms part of the Wallace Campbell collection was fitted under the stage roof, which meant that it provided a permanent backdrop to the performances. Its semi-abstract black figures foreshadow the artist's later works, such as *Flight into Egypt* and *House of Dread,* both done in the 1970s.

Stylistically different is the representational Wilton Gardens mural (1970), commissioned by the Ministry of Housing, and part of its rehabilitation project in the low-income community in West Kingston (Illustration 10.6).[78] Done in acrylic on three large panels of pre-stressed concrete, Parboosingh's first large, outdoor mural was painted in a warehouse, and then mounted in the Wilton Gardens community park.[79] Wilton Gardens, or "Rema," as it is commonly called by its residents, is a housing complex that was built by the JLP in 1963 to replace a conglomeration of shacks. The two- and four-story high-rises were arranged around a courtyard and constructed from prefabricated concrete slabs. Piped water, electricity, and sewage facilities were big improvements in the living conditions of the residents. The building of the Wilton Gardens complex bolstered support for the JLP among the residents, and following the victory of the PNP in the 1972 general elections, "the Rema enclave became a political flashpoint. ... Rema's location in a PNP-controlled constituency became an irritant to newly victorious hardliners determined to contain if not eliminate this JLP presence in their midst."[80]

The ensuing violence stands in sharp contrast to Parboosingh's nostalgic mural, describing life in a traditional Jamaican village. In the center, an embracing couple and their child look directly at the viewer, while waving a Jamaican flag.[81] The family is behind a variety of Jamaican plants on the street, surrounded by ackee, orange, and banana trees. A woman selling coal pots, yabbas, and fruits is sitting on the ground towards the right of the couple and to the left of a goat.[82] In the background, a pushcart vendor is selling iced drinks, and a fisherman is tending his nets. To their right, a donkey is grazing in front of a traditional, wooden, country house elevated on stilts. Young girls are resting on the ground, and other children seem to be on their way to school. The right foreground depicts a man wearing a straw hat who is carrying a hoe on his shoulder.

Parboosingh used a similar man in another painting, *Man with a Hoe,* in which the man is the main feature. Having emerged from the village scene, he is now in the fields brandishing the same tool that he will presumably use to dig-up the soil or remove weeds. Other workers are in the background. The farmer could be a tribute to Parboosingh's Mexican experience and his mentor, Siqueiros. In fact, there is a stylistic similarity between Parboosingh's farmer and the revolutionaries in Siqueiros' *From the Dictatorship of Porfirio Diaz to the Revolution—The Revolutionaries* (1957–1965). While Parboosingh has replaced their rifles with an agricultural tool, the forward movements and determined, confident expressions are certainly comparable.[83]

The atmosphere of the Wilton Gardens mural is tranquil and picturesque like a rural paradise. According to a newspaper review, Parboosingh had said that he "strived to show aspects of Jamaican life—small-time commerce, agricultural activity, family life."[84] Is this the Jamaica that Parboosingh envisioned or dreamed of? While references to the Mexican muralists in terms of the socialist glorification of the workers and farmers can be made, Parboosingh's painting gives a romanticized image. In this mural, Jamaica is not a modernizing country that is characterized by struggles between the old and new, or between continuity and change. Rather, it is a place that thrives on the traditional and natural environment, one that is self-reliant and where the people are contented with the abundance of fruits and vegetables, a place where citizens go about their daily business without worry and strife. The pastoral backdrop of this mural represents the non-urban character of parts of Jamaica. Its nationalism is also represented in the rural life of the folk who are depicted as the real or authentic Jamaicans.[85] In a curious way, this contrasts with the idea of modernity that was promoted by the CJAA.

Possibly a climax of the Jamaican mural movement was the 1974 opening of the Olympia International Art Centre. Engineer and art patron, A. D. Scott,

Illustration 10.6: Wilton Gardens Mural, 1970, Kingston, Jamaica.

the man responsible for the opening of the Centre, had envisioned it as a home and studio space for artists. Scott invited leading Jamaican artists and the Guyanese Aubrey Williams to paint the exterior and interior walls of the building on Old Hope Road in Kingston. Radiating from its large, central gallery were twelve self-contained sub-galleries, which were later transformed into apartments for the artists.[86] Many of the walls in this complex were covered with murals created by Parboosingh, Carl Abrahams, Leonard Ferguson, Aubrey Williams, and Barrington Watson.[87] Ralph Campbell supplied the painted landscapes on the doors. Most of the murals in Jamaica at that time had materialized because the artists had taken the initiative, or because of private patronage, and only occasionally were murals commissioned by the government. This was a significant difference from the Mexican situation, where the Muralist movement had benefited from considerable government support. Parboosingh himself had been involved in the production of only a small number of murals in Jamaica, and his political views were certainly less clearly defined than those of the strong leftist Muralists in Mexico, such as Rivera.

Parboosingh held his last major solo-show at the Olympia in 1974, the same year that the Art Centre opened, and passed away on March 18, 1975.[88]

CONCLUSION

Karl Parboosingh displayed in his work diverse stylistic and iconographic interests, the foundations for which were laid early on in his career. He had participated in a Jamaican art scene that was full of optimism, and which was conscious of the importance of its place in the future of the country. The colonial ties had been broken by independence in the early 1960s and artists had begun to embrace a new self-awareness—a feeling of individuality when possibilities began to seem endless—and a sense of entitlement.

Parboosingh and his contemporaries negotiated a place in a Jamaica that was at a historic crossroads in its development. At the same time, they were adamant that they would not place restrictions on themselves. They would not be limited by any aspect of life in the old or new Jamaica. Those artists who were involved in the CJAA resisted the demands to produce nationalist, "authentic" Jamaican art during the immediate post-independence period. Instead, they drew on foreign influences and personal experiences which they gathered while they were abroad. They made themselves part of the international art world, and in this respect, they provided an alternative to the politically-driven, stridently Afrocentric folk art that was being promoted in Jamaica. Nationalism and internationalism clashed in the immediate post-independence era, and that contestation was a defining moment in the development of modern Jamaican art.

Parboosingh provided examples of how ideas about art travel across cultures. He managed to merge international and local endeavors, which diversified his technique and made it transnational. But it was also national in another sense, since Parboosingh painted for himself and used abstraction to pursue his own agenda to create authentic works of arts. He exemplifies the kind of artist that Kobena Mercer has in mind when discussing the modern art world as a "'contact zone'—a social space . . . where disparate cultures meet, clash and grapple with each other."[89] Before his life ended, Parboosingh had combined a range of cultures in his art. These included the Amerindian, Hindu, and Mexican cultures, the modernism of Early Modern European art, and Rastafarianism from Jamaica. Parboosingh created a complex and personal visual language, one that was a potpourri of stimuli, as seen in *House of Dread,* a work that echoes the racially and culturally diverse history of Jamaica and the wider Caribbean. Parboosingh demonstrated his ability to merge influences, and to create art that went beyond the national.

Notes

1. Parts of this essay are based on my dissertation, "Picturing the Postcolonial Nation: (Inter)Nationalism in the Art of Jamaica, 1962–1975," PhD Dissertation (Hamburg: University of Hamburg, 2009).

2. Paul Gilroy, *The Black Atlantic: Modernity and Double Consciousness* (Cambridge: Harvard University Press, 1993), 18.

3. Norman Rae, "A Line from the Tower of Bable," *The Gleaner,* c.1980. This article was taken from the Parboosingh Clipping File, College Library, the Edna Manley College of the Visual and Performing Arts, Kingston.

4. Green symbolizes the sacred motherland of Africa, yellow or gold the wealth of the country, and red the blood that was shed during slavery. While the shade black is not a part of the Ethiopian flag, it is found in the Jamaican flag and the flag of Marcus Garvey's pan-Africanist organization, the Universal Negro Improvement Association. In both cases, black refers to the black people and their attempt to unify and form a nation.

5. The so-called "Rodney Riots" took place in Kingston in October 1968, after the Jamaican government banned the Guyanese historian and University of the West Indies (UWI) lecturer Walter Rodney from returning to the country. Reputedly a black power activist, Rodney was prevented from resuming his job at the Mona campus of UWI. He was accused of associations with Communist regimes as well. In protest, students left the university and marched onto the streets of Kingston, where they were met by security personnel. Several people were killed before the marching stopped.

6. Paris Parboosingh, Interview with the author, March 31, 2009, Kingston.

7. Ibid.

8. Gladys Coy, quoted in Heather Royes, "Karl Parboosingh—The Early Years. Youthful impressions that lasted a lifetime," *The Jamaica Daily News,* February 1, 1976, 4.

9. "'The Fine Arts'—discussed by Edna Manley, Karl Parboosingh and Robert Verity," *Caribbean Quarterly: "The Arts"* 14, nos. 1 and 2 (1968): 63–76.

10. Parboosingh, when stationed in Panama, was attached to the Department of Information and Education, Caribbean Defense. During that time, he took a course in art at the National Institute of Panama. See Rudolph Dunbar, "Parboo Singh—the artist," *Daily Gleaner,* October 2, 1952, 6.

11. Ibid.

12. The Harlem Renaissance, or the New Negro Movement, was a revival of African American artistic and intellectual life that took place mainly in Harlem, New York, during the 1920s.

13. Excerpt from Claude McKay's "I Shall Return":
I shall return to loiter by the streams
That bathe the brown blades of the bending grasses,
And realize once more my thousand dreams
Of waters rushing down the mountain passes.
I shall return to hear the fiddle and fife
Of village dances, dear delicious tunes
That stir the hidden depths of native life,
Stray melodies of dim remembered runes.

14. Before leaving France, Parboosingh had a joint exhibition with his wife at the Galerie Placide.

15. Paris Parboosingh, Interview with the author. For a period starting in the 1950s, Karl Parboosingh dropped his first name, took Parboo as his first name and Singh as his family name. See "Parboo Singh and Seya. 'International' Painters Visit," *Evening Chronicle,* Allentown, PA, June 19, 1959.

16. Royes, "Karl Parboosingh—The Early Years," 4.

17. Ibid.

18. Ibid.

19. See "Young Couple Succeeds in International Art," *New York Amsterdam News,* July 7, 1951.

20. In his later years, Léger also designed mosaics and stained glass windows. These can be found at the Central University of Venezuela in Caracas, among other places.

21. See Ronald Moody, "Parboo Singh," *Exhibition Catalogue,* London, 1951. Clipping in Parboosingh's scrap book, private collection, Kingston.

22. "Parboosingh talks with Christine Craig. Mexico," publisher and date unknown. Clipping in Parboosingh's scrap book, private collection, Kingston.

23. Ibid.

24. "'The Fine Arts'—discussed by Edna Manley, Karl Parboosingh and Robert Verity," 63–76.

25. Ibid.

26. "West Indians seen as new, vital people," *Trinidad Guardian,* September 22, 1971.

27. The mural at what is today the Ministry of Finance at East National Heroes Circle, Kingston, was the first in a series of commissioned art works for new government office buildings, part of the government's scheme for the encouragement and development of the arts.

28. The coffee picker mural was unveiled at the end of June 1956. See John Hearne, "Faithful to the things he has to do," *Daily Gleaner,* July 2, 1956, 12.

29. Parboosingh's major one-man shows were at the Tower Isle Hotel (September 1956) and the Myrtle Bank Hotel (December 1956). The show at the latter was held December 1–15, and was hung by Hills Galleries and included twenty works on canvas, woodcuts, etchings, and Parboosingh's "commercial work." See *Jamaica Times,* December 8, 1956.

30. Christopher Hills, "Introduction. Parboosingh show," Myrtle Bank Hotel, Kingston, December 1956. Clipping in Parboosingh's scrap book, private collection, Kingston.

31. Ibid.

32. The name "Coyaba" is a combination of his birth name, Karl Coy, and the Arawak word for heaven, *Kuyaba.*

33. "'Coyaba'—No longer a dream. Plans for cultural village outlined," *Daily Gleaner,* February 12, 1961, 20.

34. Seya Parboosingh, Interview with the author, October 10, 2005, Kingston.

35. "'Coyaba'—No longer a dream," 20.

36. Seya Parboosingh, Interview with the author.

37. John Bertram, "Industry and Commerce," *Daily Gleaner,* July 2, 1961, 9.

38. "'Coyaba'—No longer a dream," 20.

39. Ibid. The architectural consultant was Edgar Tafel who had worked with Frank Lloyd Wright on the famous Pennsylvania house, Falling Waters, between 1935 and 1939. Tafel visited the Coyaba site in April 1961 and met with various government officials. See "Personal Mention by Kitty Kingston. Coyaba consultant leaves," *Daily Gleaner,* May 1, 1961, 16.

40. "'Coyaba'—No longer a dream," 20. To raise funds, the Coyaba Committee organized a "benefit dance and auction" on April 21, 1961 at the Caymanas Country Club. See "'Coyaba' dance at Caymanas," *Daily Gleaner,* April 17, 1961, 20.

41. Seya Parboosingh, Interview with the author.

42. See Benedict Anderson, *Imagined Communities* (London and New York: Verso, 2006).

43. I thank Lawrence Waldron, Art Historian from St. John's University, New York, for pointing this out.

44. Mark Stevens, "Black Magic," *Newsweek,* September 18, 1978, 69. Quoted in Gerald Alexis, "Caribbean Art and Culture from a Haitian Perspective," *Caribbean Visions—Contemporary Painting and Sculpture,* Exhibition catalogue, Art Services International (1995), 62.

45. Edward Seaga, Interview with the author, January 31, 2007, Kingston.

46. In her 1985 article, Patricia Bryan connects the works of Jamaica's self-taught artists to traditional African art. See Patricia Bryan, "Towards an African Aesthetic in Jamaican Intuitive Art," *Arts Jamaica* 3:3, 4 (July 1985): 2–11. For a similar thesis, also see Edward Brathwaite, "Art and Society. Kapo—A Context," *Jamaican Folk Art,* Institute of Jamaica (c.1970s).

47. Gilroy, *The Black Atlantic,* 30.

48. Ibid., 31.

49. For a debate on the extent to which enslaved Africans were able to reproduce their African cultures in the New World, see David Scott, *Conscripts of Modernity: The Tragedy of Colonial Enlightenment* (Durham: Duke University Press, 2004); John Thornton, *Africa and Africans in the Making of the Atlantic World, 1400–1800* (Cambridge University Press, 1998); Sydney Mintz and Richard Price, *The Birth of African-American Culture: An Anthropological Perspective* (Boston: Beacon, 1992); Stuart Hall, "Negotiating Caribbean Identities," in *New Caribbean Thought: A Reader,* eds. Brian Meeks and Folke Lindahl (Kingston: University of the West Indies Press, 2001), 24–39.

50. Wilhelm Hambach, "Liebenswertes Jamaika. Flensburger Mäzen organisierte eine interessante Schau/Bis zum 28. August im Städtischen Museum der Rumstadt zu sehen," *Flensburger Tageblatt,* August 3, 1963.

51. B. G., "Exciting Art of the Rastafarians," *Sunday Gleaner Magazine,* February 22, 1970, 10.

52. Andrew Hope, "Art View. Art for the Masses," *Sunday Gleaner Magazine,* May 16, 1982.

53. Edwin Todd, "Abstract Art, The Avantgarde and Jamaica," *Jamaica Journal* 4, no. 4 (December 1970): 33. The American art critic, Clement Greenberg, advocated abstraction as the culminating moment of modernism, a position that was widely held in the Western world until the 1960s and was supported by the success of the New York School. See Clement Greenberg, "Modernist Painting," in *Modern Art and Modernism: A Critical Anthology,* eds. Francis Frascina and Charles Harrison (Boulder: Westview Press, 1983), 5–10.

54. Edmund B. Gaither, "Introduction," *Jamaican Art since the Thirties,* Exhibition catalogue, Spelman College, Atlanta (November 9—December 10, 1969).

55. Elsa Goveia was speaking at the first conference of the Caribbean Artists Movement in London in September 1967. Her talk was entitled the "Socio-Cultural Framework of the Caribbean." See Anne Walmsley, *The Caribbean Artists Movement, 1966–1972: A Literary and Cultural History* (London and Port of Spain: New Beacon, 1992), 99f. Aubrey Williams reacted strongly to Goveia's remarks because he was worried about the "prevalent conception that good art, working art, must speak, it must be narrative." Williams is also quoted in Walmsley, *The Caribbean Artists Movement*, 101.

56. Milton Harley, Interview with the author, May 2, 2005, Kingston.

57. Norman Rae was critiquing an exhibition by the realist painter Lloyd van Pitterson at the Contemporary Jamaican Artists' Associations Gallery in Kingston. He observed that van Pitterson's paintings "sell more readily than many more exciting or more original works from other studios." See Norman Rae, "Paintings by Pitterson. Popular work," *Daily Gleaner,* October 22, 1966, 22.

58. The author compared Milton Harley's works to those of the "only two absolutely natural primitive painters [Kapo and Benjamin Campbell]" in a Festival exhibition at the Contemporary Jamaican Artists' Association's Gallery, Kingston, in August 1967. See J. E. B., "Fine Art exhibition. Good-to-middling," *Daily Gleaner,* August 5, 1967, 24.

59. Milton Harley, Interview with the author.

60. The literature on Jamaican art lists 1963 as the date for Harley's *Thetis.* The artist insists, however, that he completed the work before his return to Jamaica in 1961. The medium of *Thetis* is oil on canvas, but Harley switched to acrylic paint after he moved back to Jamaica because he developed allergies against the lead then added to white oil paints.

61. Milton Harley, Interview with the author.

62. Ibid.

63. Ibid.

64. "'The artist should work to the pulse of Jamaica'—Rex Nettleford at Harley exhibition," *Daily Gleaner,* March 16, 1963, 19.

65. "'The Fine Arts'—discussed by Edna Manley, Karl Parboosingh and Robert Verity," 63–76.

66. Ibid.

67. Gaither, "Introduction," *Jamaican Art since the Thirties.*

68. Aubrey Williams employed, for example, forms that he saw in Pre-Columbian Guyanese petroglyphs and his exposure to the Warrau people as an agricultural scientist. See Rasheed Araeen, "Excerpts from 'Conversation with Aubrey Williams,'" in *Aubrey Williams,* ed. Reyahn King (Liverpool and London: National Museums Liverpool and October Gallery, 2010), 10–33.

69. Aubrey Williams quoted in Anne Walmsley, *The Caribbean Artists Movement,* 219.

70. See J. T. B. ad, *Life Magazine,* May 29, 1964, 76. This ad features a photograph of the opening of Karl Parboosingh's 1964 solo show in Ocho Rios, St. Ann, Jamaica.

71. Clyde Burnett, "Spelman Visitor: He Paints a Bright Future for Art in Colorful Jamaica," *The Atlanta Journal,* November 20, 1969.

72. Ibid.

73. For a detailed discussion of Taìno art, refer to Ricardo Alegria and Jose Arrom, *Taìno: Pre-Columbian Art and Culture from the Caribbean* (New York: Monacelli, 1998).

74. The sculptor Edna Manley also visited Mexico during the 1960s. Petrina Dacres identifies stylistic similarities between Olmec sculptures and Manley's *Paul Bogle* monument and points to the practice of glorification of heroes that can be seen in both the Mexican muralist movement and Manley's work. See Petrina Dacres, "Modern Monuments: Fashioning History and Identity in Postcolonial Jamaica," PhD Dissertation (Atlanta: Emory University, 2008).

75. *Timehri* is an Amerindian word meaning "mark of the hand" or "hand of God." See Wilson Harris, "Aubrey Williams," in *Selected Essays of Wilson Harris: The Unfinished Genesis of the Imagination,* ed. Andrew Bundy (London and New York: Routledge, 1999), 222–25. The *Timehri* murals at Guyana's Timehri airport, four external and one internal, depict Amerindian motifs: *Tumatumari, Kamarau, Kaietuma, Maridowa, Itiribisi.* See Anne Walmsley, *The Caribbean Artists Movement,* 277.

76. "Parboosingh talks with Christine Craig. Mexico."

77. For reviews of the Barn Theatre mural, see "Parboo meets challenges of building structure," *Daily Gleaner,* November 26, 1967; Archie Lindo, "'Ask Your Mama.' Players all 'Tip-Top,'" *The Star,* September 27, 1967. The panels of this mural are now part of the Wallace Campbell collection.

78. For reviews of the Wilton Gardens mural, see "Parboosingh's first big outdoor work. Concrete Mural for Wilton Gardens. 'Lovely, very all right' say admiring workmen," Publisher unknown, September 27, 1970. Clipping in Parboosingh's scrap book, private collection, Kingston. See also "'Creative Adornment to Public Areas,' by the Features Editor," *Sunday Gleaner,* November 29, 1970,8.

79. A sketch of the painting is in the collection of Paris Parboosingh, Kingston.

80. For a discussion of the politics affecting Kingston's inner city communities, see Obika Gray, *Demeaned but Empowered: The Social Power of the Urban Poor in Jamaica* (Kingston: University of the West Indies Press, 2004), 178f.

81. As there was no flag in the sketch, Parboosingh possibly decided to highlight the nationalist nature of the mural which was, after all, commissioned by the government.

82. *Yabbas* are traditional African earthenware vessels that were made popular in Jamaica by the potter Cecil Baugh in the 1930s.

83. On the Wilton Gardens mural, also see "Creative Adornment to Public Areas," *Daily Gleaner,* November 29, 1970, and "Old Sanitary Convenience Site, Munitions Dump—Base for City's largest Public Mural," *The Star,* November 13, 1970.

84. "Parboosingh's first big outdoor work."

85. I thank Rivke Jaffe, Social Anthropologist at Leiden University, The Netherlands, for pointing this out.

86. See Neville Garrick, "$750,000 art complex to be [?]," *Jamaica Daily News,* May 15, 1974.

87. Barrington Watson's mural, *Our Heritage,* runs the entire inner circumference of the top floor of the Olympia International Art Centre. Carl Abrahams' mural, *International Invitation,* is placed at the entrance to the Centre. Leonard Ferguson's *Children in the Mist* is located on the western wall of the central office. Karl Parboosingh's *Our Flag* (alternatively referred to as *Red, Yellow, Green and Black*) stretches around the art supply store. A. D. Scott's sculpture, *Man has Many Dimensions,* is installed outside of the building on the lawn close to Old Hope Road. Until 1978, the Center had a very active exhibition schedule and an artists-in-residence program. It further housed A.D. Scott's private collection which was one of the most important collections of Jamaican art anywhere. See David Boxer, "Introduction," *A. D. Scott: Art Patron and Collector,* Exhibition catalogue (Kingston: National Gallery of Jamaica, June 12—July 16, 1988). Today, Olympia still operates as a gallery with occasional exhibitions and an art shop.

88. "Faith, life, work: by Parboosingh," *Jamaica Daily News,* October 14, 1974. The exhibition with forty-eight works was opened from October 7–31, 1974. Some of the paintings on show included *Mary, Jesus and Joseph, Sermon on the Mount, Natty Dread, Youth with Spliff* and *Bathers in the River.*

89. Kobena Mercer, "Cosmopolitan Contact Zones," in *Afro Modern: Journeys Through the Black Atlantic,* Exhibition catalogue, eds. Tanya Barson and Peter Gorschlüter (Liverpool: Tate Liverpool, 2010), 41. The term *contact zone* was coined by Mary Louise Pratt. See Mary Louise Pratt, "Arts of the Contact Zone," *Profession 91* (New York: MLA, 1991), 33–40.

Chapter 11

Reggae as a Rastafari Poetic of Disenchantment

Eldon V. Birthwright

INTRODUCTION

Jamaican popular culture in general, and the idiom of Reggae music in particular, represent a communal mode of resistance. That is, resistance to oppression, marginalization, and class prejudice, as well as resistance to social injustices, and the various other forms of closure that exist in any society. Tricia Rose has made sure to carefully point out that a profound and recurring pattern of activity among oppressed peoples throughout history is to be found in their use of language, dance, and music, which often mock those in power and are used to express rage and produce fantasies of subversion—seen especially under social conditions in which sustained, frontal attacks on powerful groups are both strategically unwise and often successfully contained.[1]

The movements of colonial dissension of the nineteenth and twentieth century, for example, have been about little other than what the existentialist movement has called the "heroic" attempts to affirm values based on the assertion of self in the public sphere. Jurgen Habermas, for instance, argues that the public sphere is pre-eminently that realm in which private individuals gather together as a public to mainly make use of their ability to engage critically with authority and its judgments.[2] Perhaps nowhere is this assertion of self seen as more pronounced than in the idiom of Jamaican popular culture, and in particular in Reggae music. And since this popular culture has found legitimacy in challenging some of the very same reasons that it was previously derided—the scale of its social impact and its attractiveness to *unschooled* audiences—this has made it central to any understanding of social discourse and society in general.

255

This argument is not new. Rose re-articulates this line of reasoning and goes a step further to explain that such cultural responses to oppression are not safety valves used to challenge and sustain the machines of oppression, but are agents that produce communal bases of knowledge about social conditions and interpretations of these conditions. Both serve as the cultural glue that fosters community resistance.[3] Robert Birt, who seems to support Rose's view, argues that every struggle for human liberation is invariably a struggle for a liberated identity.[4] Birt's argument, for the most part, is reflective of the Rastafari struggle to liberate themselves, the wider Jamaican society, and that group that the Rastafari considers the "community of sufferers." These are the African peoples in Africa and her diasporas. (A note on my grammatical treatment of Rastafari: Because Rastafari adamantly opposes "isms" and the like, I do not use terms such as "Rastafarian" or "Rastafarianism." Instead, "Rastafari" is used to denote the subculture and is also used as a noun denoting a member of the subculture, and as an adjective denoting the qualities of the subculture. My treatment is similar to that of Becky M. Mulvaney.)[5]

In this essay, I treat the Rastafari movement as one of psychic liberation, or a process of metamorphosis in which the old self is discarded and the colonized, oppressed individual, who has been conditioned by his/her position of *inferiority,* acquires a new concept of *him/her*self and a new understanding of the inequalities in society.[6] My aim is to show that Rastafari thus represents a continuation of the emancipation process, a sort of "re-engineering of blackspace," which, according to Erna Brodber, describes in part the development of a philosophy and a set of creeds, myths, and ideologies—the "pegs" on which to hang social and spiritual life, and the construction of experiential frames of reference within which blackness can be *re*defined.[7] Klaus de Albuquerque has added that once the Rastafari has liberated him/herself from the old stereotype and the position of dependency, he/she can then go on to forge a new identity.[8] I will argue therefore that the Rastafari movement, through the Reggae idiom, challenges not only the Caribbean, but also the entire Western World to come to terms with the history of oppressive slavery, the consequences of white racism, and the permanent thrust for dignity and self-respect that is being undertaken by black people all over the world.[9]

THE RELIGIO-POLITICAL THRUST OF THE RASTAFARI MOVEMENT

Arguably, it is the Rastafari movement as a religious construct within the Jamaican social imaginary that has devoted the most theological and ideological space to the delegitimizing of imperial/colonial domination.[10] The ideology of Rastafari has, over time, become the single most influential ideological force in Jamaican society, attacking the traditional Christian concept of self-less love and redemptive suffering, while presenting a new way of asserting personhood. According to Rex Nettleford, one should approach the study of the phenomenon of Rastafari as an integral part of the larger aspect of black religious nationalism, religious folk revivalism, and Jamaican peasant resistance to the plantation economy and state.[11]

Revolutionary political thought alone, rooted in European philosophy, could not liberate the minds of black people, and so there was need for a black component in the narrative of liberation. The notion of a black value system taking into account the political, social, economic, spiritual, and emotional crises faced by black people in the Modern West was crystallized in the Rastafari movement as a by-product of a long history of consistent opposition to an oppressive world created by Euro-America. This oppositional subculture has grown from the suicidal jumps from aboard slave ships, through frequent rebellions during slavery, to the option for a challenged existence in the hills and Free Villages of Jamaica during the immediate post-emancipation period from 1834 to about 1865. The opposition continued through the struggles of the 1930s, culminating in the acquisition of Universal Adult Suffrage in 1944, followed by the struggle for social justice that ran concurrently with the Civil Rights Movement in the United States, leading to Jamaica's political independence from Britain in August 1962, and the struggle for a national consciousness thereafter.

Rastafari personifies and illuminates all of these struggles. Its belief system, according to Leonard Barrett, is comprised of six essential tenets and all of which inspire its adherents to challenge the establishment in an ongoing fight to overcome a complexity of oppressions ranging from the persistent ideologies of colonialism, slavery, and imperialism, to poverty, social injustice, and political misrepresentation in modern Jamaica. According to Barrett, the Rastafari firmly believe and advocate that:

1. Haile Selassie is the living God.
2. The black person is the reincarnation of ancient Israel, who, at the hand of the white person has been in exiled in Jamaica.
3. The white person is inferior to the black person.
4. The Jamaican situation is a hopeless hell. Ethiopia is heaven.
5. The Invincible Emperor of Ethiopia is now arranging for expatriated persons of African origin to return to Ethiopia.
6. In the near future blacks shall rule the world.[12]

In his 1966 "Treatise on the Rastafarian Movement," Ras Samuel Brown, himself a Jamaican Rastafari elder, argued that struggle was crucial to the Rastafari culture, and, in fact, was its essence and basis. This struggle was not only to protest oppressive situations, but also, and more importantly, to establish alternatives. As freedom should have replaced slavery, as Universal Adult Suffrage should have replaced political disenfranchisement, and as independence should have replaced external and internal dependency, so too did the Rastafari see the effective replacement of a range of oppressions with its own ideological codes of belief. Speaking specifically about this plan of action, Brown stresses that,

> unlike all orders of religion, the culture of Rastafari was not handed down from father to son as the people of Christendom. We who have perused the volumes of history know that in this 20th century a king would arise out of Jesse's root, who should be a God (Almighty) for his people, and a liberator to all the oppressed of the earth. We the Rastafarians who are the true prophets of this age, the reincarnated Moseses, Joshuas, Isaiahs, Jeremiahs, who are the battle-axes and weapons of war, we are those who are destined to free not only the scattered Ethiopians (Black man), but all people, animals, herbs and all life forms.[13]

Barrett in his seminal 1988 work, *The Rastafarians: Sounds of Cultural Dissonance,* also argues that one of the reasons for the success of the Rastafari movement in the Caribbean in general stems from the fact that most Caribbean youngsters have only known a life of emptiness, poverty, and lack of opportunity. Rastafari presents them with a level of hope and with the possibility of overcoming existential angst and the absurdities of life. Rastafari has, in fact, consistently asked a question that has always been uncomfortable in Caribbean history: where do you stand in relation to blackness?[14]

RASTAFARI INFLUENCE ON REGGAE MUSIC

Over time, as Rastafari has taken on an ontology (a way of being), a cosmology (a way of thinking about the world), and an epistemology (way of knowing or getting to know things through the world), the idiom of Reggae music has become the main conduit through which Rastafari ideological frames have been crafted, articulated, and spread to the world. As Rastafari has made the quantum leap that all ideologies and social movements must make in terms of defining its own God, its own identity, and its own destiny, the movement has become a progenitor of the most conscious part of a people's struggle: the search for spiritual emancipation. This is due, in part, to the fact that Rastafari is strongly rooted in the concept of human dignity and in the rehabilitation of peoples of African descent following what might be considered 500 years of obscenity: that is, slavery, dispersal, and colonialism, racism and its attendant realities, and social injustice.

The idiom of Reggae—as a mode of resistance within the social consciousness of "subordinate" classes—is significant in that it allows for a clarification of a major debate in both Marxist and non-Marxist literature. That debate centers on the extent to which elite groupings in any given society are able to impose their own image of a just social order, not simply on the behavior of non-elites, but on their consciousness as well.[15] The Reggae idiom debunks the notion that the underclass is totally reliant on the elite groups of society for ideas which inform their consciousness, their sense of self, and further discounts the notion that the underclass is incapable of generating abstract thought. In one sense, the practitioners of Reggae are heirs to the rebellious Caliban—carrying on the struggle to map on the terrain of the imagination a space for the memories, struggles, sacrifices, and hopes of the multitudes.

My use of the Caliban reference is simply meant to highlight, in the words of Glyne A. Griffith, "the colonizer/colonized power relationship at the tactical level where the force of discourse is unequally distributed between subject and object, selfhood and otherness." Caliban represents the colonized, while Prospero is representative of the colonizer, and I am here drawing specific reference to Caliban's challenge to Prospero, in which Caliban judges and uses his name (the *noun*) as a grammatical and imperialist tool, while Prospero who refers to this same name in the form of a *verb*, also uses it indirectly to affirm his own imperialist selfhood.[16]

Music and politics have long been tied, one influencing the other in often subtle ways. Musicians and songwriters all over the world have put their talents to serve social causes, for instance, or to express political statements and voice the plight of the oppressed: in short, to challenge hegemony.[17] In the context of this chapter, hegemony is by all means Gramscian. It is interpreted through the lens of Raymond Williams, who shows that Antonio Gramsci, in articulating his concept of hegemony, argues that societies have an overarching, dominating—if not domineering—mainstream that is internalized in the consciousness of governments, industry, subcultures, and individuals as ideology. Musicians writing songs to oppose any one of these structures and their ideologies are challenging the hegemony which these support as well.[18]

Slobin, 1993 has also argued that Gramscian hegemony "is not monolithic." In other words, "There is no Board of Directors that monitors hegemony daily, adjusting and fine-tuning it. It can be formal and informal, explicit and implicit, conscious and unconscious, bureaucratic and industrial, central and local, historical and contemporary." Slobin further states that "hegemony is not uniform; it does not speak with one voice. It is complex, often contradictory, and perhaps paradoxical. Hegemony is contrapuntal: there are alternative and oppositional voices in this cultural figure that effect and shape the 'themes.'"[19] Protest music, such as Reggae, therefore take on many permutations in order to challenge hegemony, which itself is multisided.

If we argue, like Patrick Hylton does, that cultural poems spring from the history and experiences of the people who develop them, then we can advance the argument that Calypso and Reggae are products of the historical experiences of Africans in the Caribbean. While these as media of expression of both protest and sentiments have taken varying forms, it is noteworthy that, like the content of Black American Jazz and Blues, Calypso in Trinidad and Reggae in Jamaica also reflect the same message: a reaction to the exploitation and oppression of enslaved African people and their descendants in the New World.[20] Ethnomusicologist Samuel A. Floyd argues that Black popular music in the New World also functions in the capacity of "cultural memory," drawing from and critiquing the experiences of slavery and colonialism in such a way that the music has come to represent what Anthony Bogues, invoking Habermas, calls a "Black public sphere."[21] This Black public sphere was not society's official stage, but existed as an alternative space alongside the official one that served to critique and offer alternative voices in opposition to extant conversations.

The lyrical content of Reggae focuses on most aspects of the human experience, stretching across the existential continuum from suffering to deliverance. Inasmuch as the music makes special reference for the most part to the Jamaican situation, issues of the Modern West are also addressed, giving the music universal significance. With this in mind, the music of Reggae is not just representative of cultural memory, but of social memory as well.[22] Bogues cites Erna Brodber who makes the point that "the appeal of music and of words set to music is indeed universal, but its function is more central in communities which depend primarily on the human body for the transmission of messages from person to person and from generation to generation."[23] It is important here to remember that Jamaica evolved as an oral rather than a scribal culture, and this meant that the rhetorical power of music as a site for contesting existing hegemonic discourse was especially poignant.

The rhetorical power of Bob Marley's music, for example, addresses issues of suffering and injustice which bear significance not only to the marginalized peoples of Africa and her Diaspora, but to all those who are oppressed and heavy laden. This, of course, is not entirely new or unique to the Caribbean; the rhetorical power of music concerned even Plato. Music as a form of political power is addressed in *The Republic* in these terms:

> But one law our guardians must keep in force, never letting it be overlooked and guarding it with more care than all the rest. This law keeps new ways in music or gymnastics out of the state which has its fixed and reasoned order. When men say, "the new song has the most attraction," it may be thought that we are

talking not about new songs but about new ways of making them, and so new ways might seem to be given approval. But new ways are not good and these words are not to be taken as saying that they are. We have to keep new sorts of music away from us as a danger to society because forms and rhythms are never changed without producing changes in the most important political forms and ways.[24]

If placed in conversation with Marley, one could see Plato agreeing with the musician because, although the Socratic suspicion of "new forms" strikes the contemporary reader as somewhat reactionary, Plato's judgment of the medium directly notes the intentional and explicit use of music to influence political praxis.[25]

Plato dichotomizes the use of music's power as either legitimately maintaining social and political order, or illicitly disrupting that order to initiate change. According to *The Republic,* political leaders were warned to be very careful about the music that they allowed to be produced and listened to within the territory of their jurisdiction. Keith Negus argues that "such a view has been shared by numerous state officials since Plato and has continued to be asserted throughout the twentieth century, when there have been several attempts to ban certain types of music—not for aesthetic reasons, but because of their potential to connect with ideas and struggles for political change."[26] Negus cites the case of the Stalinist era Soviet Union, in which stringent restrictions were imposed on composers, with many having their music tampered with or banned from performance since music, according to these regimes, had to communicate the "correct" message to the workers. Negus highlights the case of Dimitry Shostakovich, who had to rewrite the endings of his symphonies because they were not optimistic enough by official Soviet standards. Another case in point is Chile in the mid-1970s after Augusto Pinochet seized power. One of his first cultural policies was to ban the use of Quena flutes and the Charango: instruments and songs that had become associated with popular opposition movements. The ban was meant to ensure that peasants, marginalized folk, and those who felt oppressed by Pinochet's regime did not have an outlet to express their disaffection.[27]

In the case of slave societies in the British West Indies, the drum was banned because the planter class feared the subversive capabilities of the instrument. Additionally, the government of Kenya has also, on occasion, banned Reggae songs which it considered to be politically subversive or simply too radical, songs having the capability of challenging the government's *hegemony* and inciting social action. In the case of Jamaica, it has been policy to ban songs seen as adversarial to the political elite. In 1988, for example, amidst economic and social crises, the government banned the song "Price Gone Up," which was an entrant in the National Festival Song Competition, on the grounds that its stirring critique of the government's fiscal policies served to promote social discord.

One hundred and thirty years after Emancipation from slavery, at the time of Reggae's birth, Jamaican blacks, especially the working class, were still socially and economically alienated, and were yet to achieve the sense of socio-political and economic fulfillment which Emancipation had promised. The socio-economic realities of the descendants of slaves around 1968 had not changed much, with the exception of the 17 percent browns (mixed persons) and 4.8 percent blacks who were able to acquire some amount of wealth and a better status.[28] This reality made the experience of slavery contemporary with the continued devaluing of black society. As a consequence, the notion of slavery and suffering as engaging experiences of marginalized Jamaicans became an ongoing motif in the idiom of Reggae. "Do you Remember the Days of Slavery?" asked Reggae singer Burning Spear, in an effort to remind Jamaicans of the past, which to the listeners was also encouragement to move forward. Spear also did the songs "Slavery Days," "The Invasion," "Jordan River," and "Marcus Garvey Words" in order to refocus attention on the slavery motif. Each song was arranged to first embrace the listener with tension and apprehensions, and then to release the listener with hypnotic repetition.

It is important to consider that Reggae music was first and foremost, though not exclusively or universally, a counter-cultural practice with deep roots in modes of religious transcendence and political opposition. There existed and still exists in the musical genre a significant and relatively sophisticated dialogue between opposing political ideologies and metaphysics, which characterized or characterizes the relationship between the musical form and the established Jamaican polity. The music features in the class struggle in a conscious and sometimes organic way, which stemmed from the fact that many issues related to the Jamaican experience—social injustice, oppression, class prejudice, and economic inequality—were not aired and were still undefeated. The music therefore became the vehicle through which these issues were articulated.

Here, one can draw reference to a number of early Reggae tunes, most notably Delroy Wilson's 1975 hit, "Better Must Come." In articulating the social concerns of the masses (masses here is used advisedly), Wilson sings about life being momentarily difficult, but he obtains reassurance from the notion that "he has not sinned more than anyone else, and that there is a God," so better must come for him one day.[29] In the case of the musical idiom, a social reality is created through language, rhythm, and tone, providing rhythmic freedom in place of social freedom, and linguistic wealth in place of pecuniary wealth. The importance of linguistic freedom points to the role of music in enacting in dramatic form the creative potential of marginalized Jamaicans, in addition to healing psychic wounds.

As political critique, Reggae music attacked the dominant classes and acquired the role of promoting political and social consciousness, oftentimes going beyond parochial boundaries. In some cases, the music even embraced what might be considered as revolutionary/subversive activity. Take, for example, Bob Marley's 1976 song, "Crazy Baldheads," in which he suggests that the "crazy baldheads"—who in this case represent the forces of oppression—are chased out of town, so as bring to an end their reign of oppression.[30] In his usual anti-establishment mode, Marley is lamenting social injustice and inequality. Baldheads are part of the Reggae idiom's "establishment" (and Reggae is anti-establishment), who take advantage of the poor descendants of slaves. In this case, the poor are being instructed to rise up and claim what is rightfully theirs by removing the establishment. The establishment represents the Babylonian system, which in the rhetoric of Reggae is the corrupt, hierarchical structure, "*the* system" that incorporates church and state, and all of their attendant evils.[31]

There is much anti-Babylonian sentiment in the Reggae idiom. This in part is due to the Rastafari ideological infusion into the music, "with Babylon becoming an overarching Rastafari metaphor for western societies, containing within the one icon, notions of materialist greed, European imperialism and racism, wicked and sinful lifestyles—but also implying a counter-force of escape, redemption, repatriation to a home of peace, justice and plentitude expressed in the trope of mount Zion."[32] The acceptance of the counter-discourse and the liberating possibilities of Rastafari in the political arena, have helped to strengthen the political commentary/message in the music. The circulation of Reggae, according to Horace Campbell, was part of a deliberate attempt by the Rastafari community to present their message to the wider Jamaican community and to the black world.[33] By the end of the 1960s, the influence of Rastafari on the development of Jamaican popular culture manifested itself in terms of the most serious Reggae artistes becoming adherents to the ideology of Rastafari.[34]

Rastafari, the oppositional Jamaican subculture for which Bob Marley served as musical spokesperson, developed, codified, and disseminated its central concerns and philosophies almost entirely through the medium of music. Arguably, the late 1960s was a period of "pressure build up," with the general populace becoming increasingly disillusioned, similar to the sentiments of the 1950s. The difference between the 1950s and 1960s, however, was that Independence (which took place in 1962 in Jamaica) was proving to be a disappointment. Independence was supposed to signal the development of a nationalist agenda structured around cultural symbols and rites. This was not proving to be the case, as the elite, who controlled economic power, embraced Euro-American notions of high culture, and so the masses expressed their disgruntlements in the music.

It is important to note that such sentimental expressions of frustration and subversion did not require literacy to act as a medium of communication. It was a direct communiqué through Reggae, once there was the technology to promote the form.

IDIOMS OF RAGE AND PROTEST IN 1972 AND 1976

The 1972 elections in Jamaica represented a revolutionary change in the social imaginary of the Jamaican polity. Not only were the elections being contested without the founding fathers of the two major political parties, but the sudden impulse that ran through the nervous system of the generations of the 1960s that was to emerge as Black Power, was a focal point of the elections. Additionally, economic crises, chaos, nihilism, and the widening gap between the rich and poor, which manifested itself in class prejudice, were all issues affecting the national psyche. Based on trends associated with Jamaican political culture, one can assume that Jamaicans, after ten years under the Jamaica Labor Party (JLP), were ready for political change.[35]

The JLP was perceived as insensitive to the needs of the general population, especially the marginalized, and was seen as attempting to distance itself from the rising tide of Black Power. The Caribbean appropriation of Black Power as it was to manifest in Jamaica, according to Walter Rodney, meant three things: "(1) the break with imperialism which is historically white racist; (2) the assumption of power by the black masses in the islands; [and] (3) the cultural reconstruction of society in the image of the blacks."[36] The JLP government's handling of the Rastafari brethren in Jamaica in general, and then Walter Rodney in particular, resulting in the Rodney Riots of 1968, served to further alienate the government from the people.

Ralph Gonsalves, reflecting on the Rodney Riots, argues that the JLP government of Jamaica was planning for several weeks to get Walter Rodney out of the country, but wanted his removal to be an official act of the University of the West Indies. Following the summoning of the vice-chancellor of the University by the minister of home affairs, Roy McNeill, to meet with the cabinet on October 14, 1968, and the vice-chancellor's position that he had no reasonable grounds to terminate Rodney's contract with the University, but that the government could initiate such a termination, a decision was taken by Prime Minister Hugh Shearer to ban Rodney while he was outside of the country attending a conference of the Black Writer's Congress in Canada. On arrival in Jamaica on October 15, Rodney was refused re-entry into Jamaica (Rodney had Guyanese citizenship) and was confined to the aircraft. The

University students, acting in solidarity with Rodney, arranged for a peaceful march on the offices of the prime minister and the minister of home affairs the following day, October 16. Shearer, in retaliation, instructed the police to stop the demonstrations at whatever cost, resulting in serious injury to both students and faculty. Following the end of the student's march, unemployed workers and youths turned the protest into one about inequality, class prejudice, and social justice. The result was looting and damages estimated at over J$1 mill.[37]

In 1968, independent Jamaica was six years old. Unemployment was estimated to be approximately 30 percent. Along with this, 67 percent of the workforce earned less than J$10 per week. In addition, there were nearly 100 strikes in Jamaica that year. Housing, social services, and social legislation were highly inadequate, and the two political parties and their affiliated trade unions seemed more and more undemocratic and unresponsive to the needs of the people. Evident in the society was a Eurocentric cultural bias, as well as open racism against the 90 percent black section of the population. Rodney had perceived the Rastafari movement as a major force in the efforts towards freeing and mobilizing black minds, and shared with the Rastafari brethren the view that African history should serve as a focal point in the liberation process. Accordingly, Rodney wrote that:

One of the major dilemmas inherent in the attempt by black people to break through the cultural aspects of white imperialism is posed by the use of historical knowledge as a weapon in our struggle. We are virtually forced into the invidious position of proving our humanity by citing historical antecedents; and yet the evidence is too often submitted to the white racists for sanction. The white man has already implanted numerous historical myths in the minds of black peoples; and those have to be uprooted, since they can act as a drag on revolutionary activity in the present epoch. Under these circumstances it is necessary to direct our historical activity in the light of two basic principles. Firstly the effort must be directed solely towards freeing and mobilizing black minds. There must be no performances to impress whites, for those whites who find themselves beside us on the firing line will be there for reasons far more profound than their exposure to African history. Secondly, the acquired knowledge of African history must be seen as directly relevant but secondary to the concrete tactics and strategy which are necessary for our liberation. . . . If there must be proving [sic] of our humanity it must be by revolutionary means.[38]

Rodney's rhetoric was seen as a threat to national security, as well as a threat to the old guard which was intent on maintaining the status quo. The government of the day had "never come across a man who offer[ed] a greater threat to the security of this land than does Walter Rodney."[39]

Reggae practitioners, as part of a revived national consciousness, undertook the task of articulating and echoing the sentiments of the masses. In 1968, the Pan-Africanist Reggae group known as The Ethiopians, chronicled the feelings of the general public in their song "Everything Crash." In the song, The Ethiopians highlighted the strike action taken by firemen, watermen and telephone men, as evidence of the country heading toward a state of ruin. This song became almost an anthem for the opposition People's National Party (PNP), in their attempt to highlight the inadequacies and insensitivity of the ruling JLP, as well as their effort to mobilize mass support for their social justice and Black Power platform. The result was the banning of this and several other songs, which seriously criticized the JLP government and which it considered subversive.

Among the songs banned by the government were The Wailers' "Fire, Fire," and "Small Axe"—the latter of which said: "If you are the big tree / [then] I am the small axe / waiting to cut you down"—and the Abyssinians' "Declaration of Rights." Here, we see how music was being regulated according to a very particular rationality and logic, one aimed at quite specific, pragmatic, and utilitarian goals, which, in turn, were informed by predetermined ideas about the importance of music for history and cultural identity, and a belief that the influences of music could be controlled through the regulation of its production and consumption.[40] Reggae in its textual and performative moments sought to challenge the Jamaican society to face existential contradictions in its "Out of Many, One People" national motto—the quintessentially defining site of Jamaican citizenship after independence— and the reality of race, class, and social injustice. Reggae, therefore, became a counter-statement and a challenge to common sense understandings of the Jamaican status quo as it existed then.

There is a point of convergence here with Lawrence Grossberg's observation that "music works 'at the intersection of the body and emotions,' and in so doing can generate 'affective alliances' between people, which in turn can create the energy for social change that may have a direct impact on politics and culture." Keith Negus, who cites from Grossberg's 1992 work, *We Gotta Get Out Of This Place,* puts forward his own argument on music as a politically affective form of communication. Grossberg further argues that the affective empowerment that is generated from the music can provide the potential for hope and political change. For Grossberg, "such empowerment is increasingly important in a world in which pessimism has become common sense, in which people increasingly feel incapable of making a difference."[41]

For the 1972 watershed elections, the PNP, after realizing the capacity of music to provide the Jamaican people with a vision of the future, based on the "politics of fulfillment," rather than the "rational" teleology of orthodox liberal politics, utilized the Reggae genre to create affiliations, alliances, understandings, as well as what can be described as forms of Black Power rationality, which mobilized the people into one accord and held them steadfast to the belief that social conditions would ultimately improve. In Delroy Wilson's song, "Better Must Come," Wilson highlights the fact he constantly tries to succeed but oppressive forces seem to get in the way, nevertheless, he is hopeful that because there is a God, his position of suffering will ultimately change for the better.[42] The PNP also utilized Peter Tosh's "Dem Ha Fi Get A Beatin" to send the message of the need for change in Jamaica House (the Prime Minister's office). Here, Tosh likened the reign of the JLP to 400 years of slavery and oppression, calling for an end to such *obscenity*.[43] The opposition PNP won the 1972 elections by a landslide, winning thirty-seven of the fifty-seven parliamentary seats.

That politicians of the day would use the Reggae genre to gain mass appeal marks a significant milestone in Jamaican political culture, as the "popular experience" became co-opted into partisan politics. For the 1972 elections, the PNP had also appropriated and popularized Max Romeo's "Let the Power Fall on *I*," a song that created an almost Biblical image/aura for the Michael Manley (the leader of the PNP) persona.[44] It is interesting to note that in 1976, Max Romeo, disillusioned and disappointed with the Manley regime, chided Prime Minister Manley in his song "No, Joshua No," which criticized the PNP government in that later period. This act of public chiding irritated the PNP directorate, who had previously seen Romeo as an ally and, as a result, Romeo "voluntarily" departed Jamaica for California. As critique against the Manley government, Ernie Smith, a JLP grassroots activist and musician, also released in 1976 the song "Jah Kingdom Gone to Waste," which was used by the JLP in the 1976 general elections.[45] The fact that Smith had to also run off to Miami before the elections were held in 1976 is not only indicative of him "talk[ing] too much," but more so a realization of the vast political power of Jamaican Reggae music. The use of the Reggae form to gain political mileage was a PNP invention within the Jamaican political culture, even though from as early as 1925, political candidates in Trinidad had special Calypsos composed for use in political campaigns.

The use of music as a means to garner political appeal was so far reaching that Anita Waters makes a claim that the "PNP carried the Jamaican custom of music at mass party meetings several steps further. . . . Rather than incorporating a bit of music into one's political meeting, the PNP kept their political speeches to a bare minimum," and focused on the message in the music.[46] Clancy Eccles, a Reggae musician employed by the PNP during the period leading up to the 1972 elections, stated that "As singers, we knew we were more powerful than the politicians. The people hear us on the radio every day. If Manley gets lazy don't believe we won't start hitting on him."[47] The PNP, which had not held power since 1962, used music to appeal to the masses and to evoke a desire for change by promoting the party as the nationalist party of Jamaica. It is as a result of this use of Reggae that the music itself further engaged and later became a more crucial conduit for discourse and ideology.[48]

Having had what could be best described as a roller-coaster first term, the PNP-led government attempted to regain the confidence of the people as it sought a second term in office. The PNP attempted to further *manipulate* public discourse and institute its ideology of Democratic Socialism, both of which it did by further soliciting the music of the Reggae genre.[49] Following the 1972 elections, the PNP, in 1974, reaffirmed its support and practice of Democratic Socialism while the opposition JLP became more pro-capitalist. The PNP, in fact, extended state ownership of vital sectors in the economy, such as banking, utilities, and bauxite, a move widely viewed by the opposition as a flirtation with communist ideology. The Manley government's strengthening of ties with the Soviet Union, Eastern European states, and with Cuba, strengthened this view held by the opposition. There were also visible internal struggles within the ranks of the PNP itself, as some of the party stalwarts expressed that they were dissatisfied with the public image of the party, as it related to relations with Cuba and the Soviet Union.

The situation got worse for the PNP as by late 1975, violent crimes were on the increase in Jamaica, resulting in the Manley government taking the decision to have joint military/police detachments patrolling sections of the inner city areas of primarily the island's capital, Kingston. By January 1976, political and gang warfare were on the rise. There were several fires in the inner city areas, the Embassy of the United States was stoned, and the Peruvian ambassador was killed. At the same time, the country seemed to be in a state of denial as the Chief Justice-led Commission of Enquiry into the "random and wanton acts of violence" concluded that the violence did not "fit into the known pattern of partisan political violence."[50] As far as the PNP was concerned, the acts of violence represented the effort of the opposition JLP to destabilize the country and topple the government. There was widespread belief that the anarchy was also partly CIA induced, part of the effort of the United States government to protect its sphere of influence from the threat of communism. Although the Jamaican elections were constitutionally due in February 1977, the government decided to call early elections. On November 22, 1976, Manley announced that general elections would be held on December 15 of that year, with Nomination Day as early as November 29.

The PNP's campaign for the 1976 elections was along the lines of its achievements during its first term: promotion of black consciousness, more specifically, Pan-Africanism, socialist idealism, a nationalist agenda, and amelioration from social inequalities. Again, it was the Reggae musicians who had the responsibility of promoting the government's ideological positions in song. Even though, in many cases, the musicians were simply articulating their everyday experiences, the politicians again appropriated the popular form and used it as a medium for transporting and transplanting their own ideas. By the time the 1976 elections came around, socialism had become a popular theme within the Reggae idiom, as was evidenced in the number of songs with socialism as a motif. Take, for example, The Ethiopians' "Socialism Train," which posited socialism as a viable political option, and urged the "masses" to embrace the tide of socialism. It is not exactly clear when this song was released. Musicologists tend to suggest that it was a month or two before the 1976 elections, while some people disagree, claiming that the song had been around from as early as 1974, after Manley had reaffirmed the policy of Democratic Socialism. Interviews in the Jones Town area of Kingston seem to suggest that the song had at least been around before 1976. In any case, that song and others were used to promote Manley's socialist agenda, including Max Edwards' "Social Living," released circa 1975, in which the songwriter encourages the country to stand up for socialism, as he makes the bold claim that socialism as an ideological force was articulated by Marcus Garvey.[51]

But it was not only the PNP that was making use of Reggae music and cultural symbols as part of the political imagination. The JLP, realizing the importance cultural idioms, had, in the face of the success of the PNP in the 1972 elections, not only employed musicians, but also incorporated motifs associated with Rastafari into its campaign. Following the defeat of the JLP in 1972, Hugh Shearer had resigned as leader of the party, more as a result of internal party struggles than as a consequence of the loss. Edward Seaga, who was to become leader of the party, announced that he was going to retire from active politics, but returned six months later to a coronation by delegates from Tivoli Gardens. Seaga had been deeply involved in promoting Jamaican culture from the 1960s, and was already knowledgeable of the various ways that his party could incorporate and make use Reggae music in their political campaign. The JLP's use of popular cultural forms, coupled with the economic woes caused by a destabilization of the country and its economy by internal as well as external forces, as well as propaganda machines promoting the fear that Jamaica was about to go the political route of Cuba, and a general nihilism experienced by many individuals, resulted in the PNP losing much of its popular support. Ernie Smith, who had sung "Let the Power Fall on *I*," one of Manley's theme songs for the 1972 elections, released "Jah Kingdom Gone to Waste" in 1976, harshly criticizing the Manley government. Smith, in his song, highlighted the shortage of food, the political chaos, and the fact that the Manley government had taken on the cloak of the oppressors, thus sending the country into ruin.

The fact that Smith would turn on the PNP, after having been a party loyalist, is indicative of Clancy Eccles' point that, "as singers we know we are more powerful than the politicians."[52] Smith included in his song "Let the Power Fall on *I*" lines that represent the belief that the musician's loyalty is first and foremost to his/her constituent listeners and their collective experiences, and not to the politician, and that Reggae music, with its Rastafari infusion, is part of the radical, subversive, consciousness-raising discourse, which uses poetics in the unending fight against tyranny and oppression.

CONCLUSION

To conclude, I must reiterate the fact that in the 1980s, the JLP, fearing the potency and mass appeal of the Reggae form, resorted to banning Reggae songs which were critical of its policies. The PNP had also adopted the same approach, but not openly as policy, since Ernie Smith, who did break ranks with the PNP, also left the country. Reggae's fight against tyranny and oppression had not ended with the 1976 elections; the elections and the results merely set the stage for a greater and deeper Rastafari infusion into the Reggae form, as a most potent critique of the Jamaican social, economic, and political reality.

Notes

1. Tricia Rose, *Black Noise: Rap Music and Black Culture in Contemporary America* (Hanover, New Hampshire: Wesleyan University Press, 1994), 99.

2. Jurgen Habermas, *The Structural Transformation of the Public Sphere* (Cambridge: MIT Press, 1989), 29.

3. Rose, *Black Noise*, 99–100.

4. Robert Birt, "Existence, Identity, and Liberation," in *Existence in Black: An Anthology of Black Existential Philosophy,* ed. Lewis Gordon (New York: Routledge, 1997), 205.

5. Becky M. Mulvaney, "Rhythms and Resistance: On Rhetoric and Reggae Music," PhD Dissertation (Iowa City: University of Iowa, 1985), 5.

6. Klaus de Albuquerque, "Millenarian Movements and the Politics of Liberation," PhD Dissertation (Blacksburg: Virginia Polytechnic Institute and State University, 1976), 5.

7. Erna Brodber, "Re-engineering Blackspace," Paper presented at the Caribbean Conference in Honor of Prof. Rex Nettleford (Kingston: University of the West Indies, Mona, 1996), 8.

8. Albuquerque, "Millenarian Movements," 5.

9. Horace Campbell, *Rasta and Resistance: From Marcus Garvey to Walter Rodney* (Trenton: Africa World Press, 1987), 1.

10. Paget Henry, "Rastafarianism and the Reality of Dread," in *Existence in Black,* 157.

11. Rex Nettleford, *Caribbean Cultural Identity: The Case of Jamaica* (Kingston: Institute of Jamaica, 1978), 187–88.

12. Leonard Barrett, *The Rastafarians: Sounds of Cultural Dissonance* (Boston: Beacon Press, 1988), ix.

13. Samuel Brown, "Treatise on the Rastafarian Movement," *Journal of Caribbean Studies,* vol. 6, no. 1 (1966): 1.

14. Barrett, *The Rastafarians,* ix.

15. James C. Scott, *Weapons of the Weak: Everyday Forms of Peasant Resistance* (New Haven: Yale University Press, 1985), 305.

16. Glyne A. Griffith, *Deconstruction, Imperialism, and the West Indian Novel* (Kingston: University of the West Indies Press, 1996), 48, 51.

17. See Mark Slobin, *Subcultural Sounds: Micromusics of the West* (Middletown: Wesleyan University Press, 1993), see especially page 23.

18. Raymond Williams, *Marxism and Literature* (Oxford: Oxford University Press, 1970), 108–14.

19. Mark Slobin, *Subcultural Sounds,* 23.

20. Patrick Hylton, "The Politics of Caribbean Music," *Black Scholar Magazine,* vol. 6, no. 5 (1975): 36.

21. Samuel A. Floyd, *The Power of Black Music in History* (Oxford: Oxford University Press, 1995), 8; Anthony Bogues, *Black Heretics, Black Prophets: Radical Political Intellectuals* (New York: Routledge, 2003), see especially pages 187–205, which is Chapter 7: "Get Up, Stand Up: The Redemptive Poetics of Bob Marley."

22. Bogues, *Black Heretics,* 194.

23. Erna Brodber and J. Edward Greene, "Reggae and Cultural Identity in Jamaica," Working Paper No. 35, Institute of Social and Economic Research, Kingston, 1988, 3.

24. Plato, *The Republic,* trans. I.A. Richards (London: Keagan Paul, 1948), 424.

25. For further explanation of Plato's views on the social impact of music, see Mulvaney, "Rhythms and Resistance," p.11. According to Mulvaney, "Plato [also] argued that the social effects of music also went unnoticed because it appeared to be a rather innocent aspect of 'play.'" See also Keith Negus, *Popular Music in Theory: An Introduction* (Hanover: Wesleyan University Press, 1997), 200.

26. Negus, *Popular Music,* 200.

27. Ibid.

28. For a statistical breakdown of the socio-economic indicators of Jamaican society around 1968, see Carl Stone and Aggrey Brown (eds.) *Essays on Power and Changes in Jamaica* (Kingston: Jamaica Publishing House, 1977), 131.

29. Here I have used the interpretation of the song offered by Brodber and Greene in "Reggae and Cultural Identity in Jamaica," 14.

30. Bob Marley, "Crazy Baldheads," *Rastaman Vibration,* 1976.

31. A subsidiary meaning of the word *Babylon* refers to the police as an agent of *the* system.

32. Joe Pereira, "Babylon to Vatican: Religion in the Dancehall," ICS, University of the West Indies, Kingston, 1997, 1.

33. Campbell, *Rasta and Resistance,* 126.

34. Horace Campbell points out that the artistes who were spearheading the development of the musical culture were so uncompromising in their identification with Africa that in 1969, representatives from the ruling Jamaica Labor Party and opposition leader Michael Manley of the People's National Party made pilgrimages to Ethiopia in an effort to keep abreast with this new cultural consciousness. See Campbell, *Rasta and Resistance,* 128.

35. See Ralph Gonsalves, "The Rodney Affair and Its Aftermath," in *Caribbean Quarterly,* vol. 25, no. 3 (September 1979).

36. Walter Rodney, *The Groundings With My Brothers* (London: Bogle-L'Ouverture Publications, 1969), 28.

37. Gonsalves, "The Rodney Affair," 1–24. Gonsalves was president of the Guild of Undergraduates at the Mona campus of the University of the West Indies and offers in this article a comprehensive account of the Rodney Affair which had erupted in 1968.

38. Rodney, *The Groundings,* 51.

39. See Ralph Gonsalves' account of the Minister of Home Affairs, Roy McNeill's address to the House of Representatives, Jamaica, *circa* September 1968, in *Caribbean Quarterly,* vol. 25, no.3 (September 1979), 1–24.

40. Negus, *Popular Music,* 202.

41. Ibid., 220–21.

42. Delroy Wilson, "Better Must Come" (1971). Lyrics transcribed from the album *Tougher Than Tough: The Story of Jamaican Music,* producer Chris Blackwell (Island Records, 1993).

43. Peter Tosh, "Dem Ha Fi Get a Beatin" (c.1971).

44. Max Romeo, "Let the Power Fall on I" (1972).

45. Ernie Smith, "Jah Kingdom Gone to Waste" (1976).

46. Anita Waters, *Race, Class and Political Symbols* (New Brunswick: Transaction Books, 1985), 117.

47. Clancy Eccles, cited in Brodber and Greene, "Reggae and Cultural Identity in Jamaica," 26.

48. Discourse itself is an important component of nationalism, which implies social interaction, language, and a network of communication. As such, it includes the accepted boundaries and conditions of public discussion: that is, the prevalent framework of the topics of social communication. Ideology, on the other hand, differs from discourse in that "an ideology is a normative theory of action"; and "Ideologies 'explain' prevailing social conditions and provide individuals with guidelines for how

to react to them." See Stephen M. Walt, *Revolution and War* (Ithaca: Cornell University Press, 1996), 25. Ideology, therefore, represents a subset of discourse. Discourse defines what *can* be thought, while ideology is normative and defines what *should* be thought and said. Ideologies exist within the boundaries of meaning determined by discourse, while the latter remains the framework for knowledge and practice. This idea is influenced by Mark Ashley and Jasen J. Castillo, "Why Nationalism? Elites, Discourse, and the Perception of Threat in States," Occasional Paper prepared for the Workshop on Nations and Nationalism, Department of Political Science, University of Chicago, October 1997.

49. Waters, *Race, Class,* 144.

50. John Stephens and E. Stephens, *Democratic Socialism in Jamaica* (Princeton, NJ: Princeton University Press, 1986), 133.

51. See Max Edwards' "Social Living" circa 1975 and Derrick Morgan's "People's Decision," 1976.

52. Eccles in Brodber and Greene, "Reggae and Cultural Identity in Jamaica," 26.

Select Bibliography

This bibliography contains only published primary sources and published and unpublished secondary sources. For all the others, see the notes at the end of each chapter.

PART I—HISTORY

CHAPTER 1

Aching, Gerard. *Carnival and Popular Culture in the Caribbean: Masking and Power* (Minneapolis: University of Minnesota Press, 2002).

Benn, Denis. *The Caribbean: An Intellectual History* (Kingston: Ian Randle Publishers, 2004).

Bolland, O. Nigel. *The Birth of Caribbean Civilization* (Kingston: Ian Randle Publishers, 2004)

Brathwaite, Edward Kamau. *The Development of Creole Society in Jamaica 1770–1820* (Kingston: Ian Randle Publishers, 2005 [1974]).

Brereton, Bridget. "Contesting the Past: Narratives of Trinidad and Tobago History," *New West Indian Guide* vol. 81, nos. 3 & 4 (2007): 169–96.

———. "John Jacob Thomas: An Estimate," *Journal of Caribbean History,* vol. 9 (1977): 22–42.

———. "The Reform Movement in Trinidad in the Later 19th Century," Unpublished paper delivered at the 1973 Association of Caribbean Historians Conference at the University of the West Indies, St. Augustine, Trinidad and Tobago.

Comins, D. W. D. *Note on Emigration from India to Trinidad* (Calcutta: Bengal Secretariat Press, 1893).

Driggs, Seth. *The Freemason's Guide or, Pocket Companion* (Port of Spain: The Author, 1819).

Evans, Eric J. *The Forging of the Modern State: Early Industrial Britain, 1783–1870* (London: Longman/Pearson, 1996).

Green, William. "The Creolization of Caribbean History: The Emancipation Era and a Critique of Dialectical Analysis," in *Caribbean Freedom, Economy and Society from Emancipation to the Present,* eds. Verene Shepherd and Hilary Beckles (Kingston: Ian Randle Publishers, 1993).

Harris, Wilson. *The Selected Essays of Wilson Harris,* ed. Andrew Bundy (London: Routledge, 1999).

Higman, B.W. *Writing West Indian Histories* (London: MacMillan, 1999).

Hobsbawm, Eric. *The Age of Capital, 1854–1875* (London: Abacus, 2001).

Hurbon, Laennec. "Ideology," in *General History of the Caribbean, Volume VI: Methodology and Historiography of the Caribbean,* ed. B.W. Higman (London: UNESCO and Macmillan Educational, 1999).

Leland, John. *Hip: The History* (New York: Harper Perennial, 2005).

Look Lai, Walton. *Indentured Labor and Caribbean Sugar: Chinese and Indian Migrants to the British West Indies, 1838–1918* (Baltimore: Johns Hopkins University Press, 2003).

Martin, Tony. "African and Indian Consciousness," in *General History of the Caribbean: Volume V: The Caribbean in the Twentieth Century,* ed. Bridget Brereton (London and Paris: UNESCO and Macmillan, 2004).

Morton, Sarah. *John Morton of Trinidad: Journals, Letters & Papers* (Toronto: Westminster, 1916).

Naipaul, V.S. "Introduction," in *East Indians in the Caribbean: Colonialism and the Struggle for Identity,* eds. Winston Dookeran and Bridget Brereton (New York: Kraus International Publications, 1982).

Ramcharitar, Raymond. "Tourist Nationalism in Trinidad," in *New Perspectives on Caribbean Tourism,* eds. Marcella Daye, et al. (New York: Routledge, 2008).

Ridley, Jasper. *The Freemasons* (London: Arcade, 1999).

Roberts, J.M. *The Mythology of the Secret Societies* (London: Secker & Warburg, 1972).

Rohlehr, Gordon. *My Strangled City and Other Essays* (Port of Spain: Longman, 1992).

———. *The Shape of that Hurt and Other Essays* (Port of Spain: Longman, 1992).

Thomas, Donald. *The Victorian Underworld* (London: John Murray, 1998).

Sharpe, Jim. "History from Below," in *New Perspectives on Historical Writing,* ed. Peter Burke (London: Polity, 2001).

Singh, Sherry-Ann. "The *Ramayana* and Socio-Religious Change in Trinidad, 1917–1990," PhD Dissertation, University of the West Indies, St Augustine, 2005.

Smith, William Adam. "Advocates for Change within the Imperium: Urban Colored and Black Upper Middle Class Reform Activists in Crown Colony Trinidad, 1880–1925," PhD Dissertation, University of the West Indies, St Augustine, 2000.

Tikasingh, Gerad. "The Establishment of the Indians in Trinidad, 1870–1900," PhD Dissertation, University of the West Indies, St Augustine, 1976.

Torres Salliant, Silvio. *An Intellectual History of the Caribbean* (New York: Palgrave Macmillan, 2006).

Tripathi, B.D. *Saddhus of India: The Sociological View* (Bombay: Popular Prakashan, 1978).

Vertovec, Steven. *Hindu Trinidad: Religion, Ethnicity, and Socio-Economic Change* (London: Macmillan, 1992).

Yelvington, Kevin. "Introduction," in *Trinidad Ethnicity,* ed. Kevin Yelvington (London: Macmillan, 1998).

CHAPTER 2

Bacchus, M. K. *Utilization, Misuse and Development of Human Resources in the Early West Indian Colonies from 1492 to 1845* (Ontario: Wilfred Laurier University Press, 1990).

Burnard, Trevor. *Mastery, Tyranny, and Desire: Thomas Thistlewood and His Slaves in the Anglo-Jamaican World* (Chapel Hill: University of North Carolina Press, 2004).

Campbell, Carl. *Colony & Nation: A Short History of Education in Trinidad & Tobago, 1834–1986* (Kingston: Ian Randle Publishers, 1992).

Craton, Michael. "Forms of Resistance to Slavery," in *General History of the Caribbean, Vol. III: The Slave Societies of the Caribbean,* ed. Franklin W. Knight (London and Basingstoke: UNESCO/Macmillan, 1997).

Dallas, R. C. *The New Conspiracy Against the Jesuits Detected and Briefly Exposed* (London: Printed for James Ridgeway, 1815).

Fergus, Howard A. *A History of Education in the British Leeward Islands, 1838–1945* (Kingston: The University of the West Indies Press, 2003).

Firth, C. H. and Rait, R. S., eds. *Acts and Ordinances of the Interregnum, 1642–1660, Vol. 1* (London: Published by His Majesty's Stationary Office, 1911).

Gordon, Shirley C. *A Century of West Indian Education* (London: Longman, Green and Co., 1963).

———. "Schools of the Free," in *Before and After 1865: Education, Politics and Regionalism in the Caribbean,* eds. Brian Moore and Swithin Wilmot (Kingston: Ian Randle Publishers, 1998).

———. "The Negro Education Grant 1835–1845: Its Application in Jamaica," *British Journal of Educational Studies* 6, no. 2 (1958): 140–50.

Hall, N. A. T. "Education for Slaves in the Danish Virgin Islands, 1732–1846," in *Education in the Caribbean, Historical Perspectives,* ed. Ruby Hope King (Kingston: Faculty of Education, University of the West Indies, 1987).

Harmar, Samuel. *Vox Populi, or Glostersheres Desire* (London: Printed for Thomas Bates, 1642).

Hartlib, Samuel. *Considerations Tending to the Happy Accomplishment of England's Reformation* (London: Publisher unknown, 1647).

Hickeringill, Edmund. *Jamaica Viewed, 3rd. ed.* (London: B. Bragg, 1705 [1661]).

Macqueen, James. *The West India Colonies; the Calumnies and Misrepresentations Circulated Against Them by the Edinburgh Review, Mr. Clarkson, Mr. Cropper, Etc.* (London: Baldwin, Cradock, and Joy, 1824).

Morgan, Kenneth. *The Birth of Industrial Britain: Social Change, 1750–1850* (Harlow: Pearson Education, 2004).

Patterson, H. Orlando. *Slavery and Social Death: A Comparative Study* (Cambridge and London: Harvard University Press, 1982).

———. *The Sociology of Slavery: An Analysis of the Origins, Development and Structure of Negro Slave Society in Jamaica* (Rutherford, Madison and Teaneck: Fairleigh Dickinson University Press, 1975).

Rippingham, John. *Mr. Rippingham's Tracts upon Education in General, including a Statement of the Principles and Modes of Education in England and Scotland: with Especial Consideration upon the Present State of Education in Jamaica* (Kingston: Printed by George Worrall Struper, 1818).

St. Pierre, Maurice. *Anatomy of Resistance: Anti-Colonialism in Guyana, 1823–1966* (London and Basingstoke: Macmillan, 1999).

Sheridan, Richard B. "The Jamaican Slave Insurrection Scare of 1776 and the American Revolution," *The Journal of Negro History* vol. 61, no. 3 (July 1976): 290–308.

Turner, Mary. "Planters Profits and Slave Rewards: Amelioration Reconsidered," in *West Indies Accounts: Essays on the History of the British Caribbean and the Atlantic Economy in Honor of Richard Sheridan,* eds. Richard B. Sheridan and Roderick A. McDonald (Kingston: The Press, University of the West Indies, 1996).

Wilberforce, William. *An Appeal to the Religion, Justice, and Humanity of the Inhabitants of the British Empire, in Behalf of the Negro Slaves in the West Indies* (London: J. Hatchard and Son, 1823).

CHAPTER 3

Benjamin, Harold. "The saber-tooth curriculum," in *The Curriculum: Context, Design and Development,* ed. R. Hooper (Milton Keynes: Oliver and Boyd, Edinburgh and Open University Press, 1971).

Campbell, Carl. *Colony and Nation: A Short History of Education in Trinidad and Tobago* (Kingston: Ian Randle, 1992).

Dent, H. C. *The Educational System of England and Wales* (London: University of Oxford Press, 1963).

———. *The Training of Teachers in England and Wales, 1800–1975* (London: Hodder and Stoughton, 1977).

"Education," http://www.mongabay.com/reference/country_studies/caribbean—islands/HISTORY.html, Accessed on May 29, 2010.

Fergus, Howard A. *A History of Education in the British Leeward Islands, 1838–1945* (Kingston: University of the West Indies Press, 2003).

Freire, Paulo. *Education for Critical Consciousness* (New York: Crossroad Publishing, 1974).

Gamoran, Adam. "Standards, Inequality and Ability Grouping in Schools," *Briefings* no. 25 (September 2002).

Gordon, Shirley. *A Century of West Indian Education: A Source Book* (London: Longman, 1963).

Gunther, Dawn E. "Performance on the Common Entrance Examination of all aged schools in Jamaica," MA Dissertation, University of the West Indies, St. Augustine, Trinidad, 1984.

Kerckhoff, Alan C. "Effects of Ability Grouping in British Secondary Schools," *American Sociological Review* 51, no. 6 (1986): 842–58.

Lawton, John and Silver, Harold. *A Social History of Education in England* (London: Methuen and Co., 1973).

London, N. A. "Policy and Practice in Education in the British West Indies during the late Colonial Period," *History of Education* 24, no. 1 (1995): 91–104.

Norwood Report, *Curriculum and Examinations in Secondary Schools Report of the Committee of the Secondary School Examinations Council appointed by the President of the Board of Education in 1941* (London: HMSO, 1943).

Ortmayr, Norbert. "Church, Marriage and Legitimacy in the British West Indies (Nineteenth and Twentieth Centuries)," *History of the Family* 2, no. 2 (1997): 141–70.

Thompson, Benita E. "An Investigation into Certain Psychosocial Variables and Classroom Disruptive Behaviors among Barbadian Secondary Schools," PhD Dissertation, University of the West Indies, Cave Hill, Barbados, 2007.

Turner, Ralph H. "Sponsored and Contest Mobility and the School System," *American Sociological Review,* 25, no. 6 (1960): 855–67.

USAID Economic and Social Database, 2007, http://qesdb.usaid.gov/lac/index.html, Accessed on April 28, 2008.

Warrican, S. Joel. *Hard Words: The Challenge of Reading and Writing for Caribbean Students and their Teachers* (Kingston: Ian Randle Publishers, 2005).

Whyte, Millicent. *A Short History of Education in Jamaica* (London: Hodder and Stoughton, 1977).

World Bank. "World Bank, School and Work: Does The Eastern Caribbean Education System Adequately Prepare Youth For The Global Economy? SKILL CHALLENGES IN THE CARIBBEAN: Phase I Report (2007)," http://siteresources.worldbank.org/INTOECS/Resources/OECSReportSchoolandWork Nov5.pdf., Accessed on June 2, 2010.

CHAPTER 4

Bisnauth, Dale. *History of Religions in the Caribbean* (Kingston: LMH Publishing, 2006).

Brathwaite, Edward Kamau. *The Development of Creole Society in Jamaica, 1770–1820* (Oxford and New York: Clarendon Press and Oxford University Press, 1978).

Bridges, G. W. *A Sermon Delivered in the Parish of St. Ann, Jamaica, before the Worshipful Masters, the Officers, and Brethren of the Seville Lodge of Free and Accepted Masons, on the 4th November 1827* (Falmouth, Jamaica: Printed for the Seville Lodge by Alex. Homes, 1827).

———. *Alpine Sketches* (London: Printed for Longman, Hurst, Rees, Orme, and Brown, 1814).

———. *A Voice from Jamaica; in Reply to William Wilberforce, Esq. M.P.* (London: Longman, Hurst, Rees, Orme, Brown, and Green, 1823).

———. *Dreams of Dulocracy* (London: Whitmore, 1824).

———. *Emancipation Unmask'd in A Letter to the Right Honorable The Earl of Aberdeen, Secretary of State for the Colonies* (London: Edward Churton, 1835).

———. *Outlines and Notes of Twenty-Nine Years* (London: Published Privately, 1862).

———. *The Annals of Jamaica, Vol. 2* (London: Frank Cass and Company Limited, 1968 [1828]).

———. *The Statistical History of the Parish of Manchester; in the Island of Jamaica* (Jamaica: Wakefield Press, 1824).

Bryan, Patrick. "Aiding Imperialism: White Baptists in Nineteenth-Century Jamaica," *Small Axe* no. 14 (September 2003): 137–49.

Burnard, Trevor. "A Failed Settler Society: Marriage and Demographic Failure in Early Jamaica," *Journal of Social History* vol. 28, no. 1 (Autumn 1994): 63–82.

———. *Mastery, Tyranny, and Desire: Thomas Thistlewood and His Slaves in the Anglo-Jamaican World* (Chapel Hill: University of North Carolina Press, 2004).

———. "Powerless Masters: The Curious Decline of Jamaican Sugar Planters in the Foundational Period of British Abolitionism," The Elsa Goveia Memorial Lecture, presented at the University of the West Indies, Mona, Jamaica, March 2010.

Dubois, Laurent. *A Colony of Citizens* (Chapel Hill: University of North Carolina Press, 2004).

Geggus, David. "The Enigma of Jamaica in the 1790s: New Light on the Causes of Slave Rebellions," *The William and Mary Quarterly* vol. 44, no. 2 (April 1987): 274–99.

Goveia, Elsa V. *A Study on the Historiography of the British West Indies to the End of the Nineteenth Century* (Mexico: Instituto Panamericano de Geografia e Historia, 1956).

Hall, Douglas. *In Miserable Slavery: Thomas Thistlewood in Jamaica, 1750–86* (Cave Hill, Barbados: University of the West Indies Press, 1999).

Hannavy, John. ed. *Encyclopaedia of Nineteenth-Century Photography, Vol. 1: A–I* (London: CRC Press, 2008).

Hart, Richard. *Slaves Who Abolished Slavery Volume 2: Blacks in Rebellion* (Kingston: Institute for Social and Economic Research, University of the West Indies, 1985).

Hutton, Joseph E. *A History of the Moravian Church* (Grand Rapids: Christian Classics Ethereal Library, 2000 [1909]).

James, C. L. R. *Black Jacobins* (New York: Vintage Books, 1989).

Lambert, David. "The Glasgow King of Billingsgate: James Macqueen and an Atlantic Proslavery Network," *Slavery & Abolition* 29, no. 3 (2008): 389–413.

Lindsay, John. *A Few Conjectural Considerations upon the Creation of the Human Race. Occasioned by the Present British Quixotical Rage of Setting the Slaves from Africa at Liberty. By an Inhabitant of Jamaica. The Reverend Doctor Lindsay Rector of St. Katherine's in that Island. St. Jago de la Vega. July 23, 1788,* Unpublished manuscript (London: British Library).

Luckock, Benjamin. *Jamaica: Enslaved and Free* (London: Religious Tract Society, 1846).

Morgan, Kenneth. *Slavery and the British Empire, From Africa to America* (Oxford: Oxford University Press, 2007).

O'Gorman, Frank. *The Long Eighteenth Century: British Political and Social History, 1688–1832* (London: Hodder Education, 1997).

Patterson, H. Orlando. *The Sociology of Slavery: An Analysis of the Origins, Development and Structure of Negro Slave Society in Jamaica* (Rutherford, Madison and Teaneck: Fairleigh Dickinson University Press, 1975).

Phillippo, James Murcell. *Jamaica, Its Past and Present State* (London: John Snow, 1843).

Rousseau, Jean Jacques. *The Social Contract, or Principles of Political Right,* trans. H. J. Tozer (Hertfordshire: Wordsworth Editions limited, 1998).

Shepherd, Verene A. *Livestock, Sugar and Slavery: Contested Terrain in Colonial Jamaica* (Kingston: Ian Randle Publishers, 2009).

Sheridan, Richard B. "The Jamaican Slave Insurrection Scare of 1776 and the American Revolution," *The Journal of Negro History* vol. 61, no. 3 (July 1976): 290–308.

CHAPTER 5

Bartlett, W. H. *Footsteps of Our Lord and His Apostles in Syria, Greece, and Italy: A Succession of Visits to the Scenes of New Testament Narrative* (London: Arthur Hall, Virtue and Co., 1851).

———. *Walks about the City and Environs of Jerusalem* (London, 1843).

Bridges, G. W. "A Wayworn Wanderer," in *Selections from Seventeen-Hundred Genuine Photographs: (Views—Portraits—Statuary—Antiquities.) Taken Around the Shores of the Mediterranean Between the Years 1846–1852. With, or Without, Notes, Historical, and Descriptive* (Cheltenham: no date).

———. *Palestine As It Is: In a Series of Photographic Views, Illustrating the Bible* (London: J. Hogarth, 1858–1859?).

Buerger, Janet E. *French Daguerreotypes* (Chicago: University of Chicago Press, 1989).

Donald, Diana. *Endless Forms: Charles Darwin, Natural Science, and the Visual Arts* (New Haven: Yale University Press, 2009).

Flaubert, Gustave. *Oeuvres completes* Vol. 2 (Paris: Société Les Belles Lettres, 1948).

Harmant, Pierre. "Anno Lucis 1839: 1st. part," *Camera*, no. 5 (May 1977): 39–43.

———. "Anno Lucis 1839: 3rd. part," *Camera*, no. 10 (October 1977): 40–44.

Howe, Kathleen Stewart. *Revealing the Holy Land: The Photographic Exploration of Palestine* (Santa Barbara: Santa Barbara Museum of Art, 1997).

Hughes, John Vivian. *The Wealthiest Commoner: C.R.M. Talbot, M.P., F.R.S. (1803–1890)* (Aberavon, Port Talbot, W. Glam.: [the author] 1977).

Isaacs, Rev. Albert Augustus. *The Dead Sea: or Notes and Observations Made During a Journey to Palestine in 1856–7* (London: Hatchard and Son, 1857).

Jammes, Andre and Janis, Eugenia Parry. *The Art of French Calotype* (Princeton: Princeton University Press, 1983).

Keith, Alexander, D. D. *Evidence of the Truth of the Christian Religion, Derived from the Literal Fulfillment of Prophecy; Particularly as Illustrated by the History of the Jews, and by the Discoveries of Recent Travelers* (Edinburgh: William Whyte and Co., 1848).

Lerebours, Noel-Marie-Paymal. *Excursions daguerriennes: vues et monuments les plus remarquables du globe* (Paris: Lerebours et secretan, 1841–42).

Mackesy, Piers. *The War for America, 1775–1783* (Lincoln and London: University of Nebraska Press, 1993).

Nickel, Douglas R. *Francis Frith in Egypt and Palestine: A Victorian Photographer Abroad* (Princeton: Princeton University Press, 2004).

Nochlin, Linda. "Imaginary Orient," in *Politics of Vision: Essays on Nineteenth-Century Art and Society* (Oxford: Icon Editions, 1989).

Perez, Nissan N. *Picturing Jerusalem: James Graham and Mendel Diness, Photographers* (Jerusalem: The Israel Museum, 2007).

Roberts, David. *The Holy Land. Syria, Idumea, Arabia, Egypt and Nubia. From drawings made on the spot* (London: F.G. Moon, 1842).

Robinson, Edward. *Biblical Researches in Palestine and the Adjacent Regions* (London: John Murray, 1856).

Said, Edward W. *Orientalism* (New York: Vintage Books, 1979).

Salzmann, Auguste. *Jérusalem. Etudes et reproductions photographiques de la Ville Sainte depuis l'epoque judaïque jusqu'a nos jours*. 2 vols. (Paris: Gide et Baudry, 1856).

Schaaf, Larry J. H. *Fox Talbot's The Pencil of Nature, Anniversary Facsimile, Introductory Volume* (New York: Hans P. Kraus, Jr. Inc., 1989).

———. *The Photographic Art of William Henry Fox Talbot* (Princeton: Princeton University Press, 2000).

Schama, Simon. *Citizens* (New York: Knoff, 1990).

Solomon-Godeau, Abigail. "A Photographer in Jerusalem, 1855: Auguste Salzmann and His Times," in *Photography at the Dock: Essays on Photographic History,*

Institutions, and Practices, ed. Abigail Solomon-Godeau (Minneapolis: University of Minnesota Press, 1991).

Stevens, Mary Anne. *The Orientalists: Delacroix to Matisse: European Painters in North Africa and the Near East* (London: Royal Academy of Arts, 1984).

Talbot, William Henry Fox. *Some account of the art of Photogenic drawing, or the process by which natural objects may be made to delineate themselves without the aid of the artist's pencil* (London: R. and J.E. Taylor, 1839).

———. "The Traveler's Camera," *The Literary Gazette and Journal of belles letters, science and art* n. 1871, (27 November 1852): 876.

Taylor, Roger. *Impressed by Light: British Photographs from Paper Negatives, 1840–1860* (New York: Metropolitan Museum of Art, 2007).

Twain, Mark. *The Innocents Abroad, or the New Pilgrims' Progress* (Connecticut: American Publishing Co., 1869).

CHAPTER 6

Beckles, Hilary. "Property Rights in Pleasure: The Marketing of Enslaved Women's Sexuality," in *Caribbean Slavery in the Atlantic World: A Student Reader,* eds. Verene Shepherd and Hilary Beckles (Kingston: Ian Randle Publishers, 2000).

———. *Natural Rebels: A Social History of Enslaved Black Women in Barbados* (New Brunswick: Rutgers University Press, 1989).

Benjamin, Harry and Masters, R.E.L. *Prostitution and Morality: A Definitive Report on the Prostitute in Contemporary Society and an Analysis of the Cases and Effects of the Suppression of Prostitution* (New York: The Julian Press, 1964).

Bland, Lucy. "In the Name of Protection: the Policing of Women in the First World War," in *Women-In-Law: Explorations in Law, Family and Sexuality,* eds. Julia Brophy and Carol Smart (London: Routledge and Keegan Paul, 1985).

Brant, Allan. *No Magic Bullet: A Social History of Venereal Disease in the US Since 1880* (New York: Oxford University Press, 1985).

Bush, Barbara. *Slave Women in Caribbean Society, 1650–1838* (Kingston: Heinemann Caribbean, 1990).

Costello, John. *Love, Sex, and War: Changing Values, 1939–1945* (London: Collins, 1985).

Enloe, Cynthia. *Bananas, Beaches, Bases: Making Feminist Sense of International Politics* (London: Pandora, 1989).

Foucault, Michel. *History of Sexuality* (New York: Vintage Books, 1990).

French, Joan and Ford-Smith, Honor. *Women and Organization in Jamaica 1900–1949* (The Hague: Institute of Social Studies, 1985).

Freud, Sigmund. *Reflections on War and Death* (New York: Moffat, Yard and Co., 1917).

Gopaul-Maharajh, Vishnoo Franklin. "The Social Effects of the American Presence in Trinidad During the Second World War, 1939–1945," MA Dissertation, University of the West Indies, St Augustine, 1984.

Hall, Douglas. *In Miserable Slavery: Thomas Thistlewood in Jamaica, 1750–1786* (London: Macmillan, 1989).

Henriques, Fernando. *Prostitution and Society: Europe and the New World, Vol. 2: Europe and the New World* (London: Maggibbon and Kee, 1963).

Hicks, George. *The Comfort Women* (St. Leonards, NSW: Allen and Unwin, 1995).

Hyam, Ronald. *Empire and Sexuality: The British Experience* (Manchester and New York: Manchester University Press, 1992).

Jefferys, Sheila. "Women and Sexuality," in *Women's History: Britain 1850–1945*, ed. June Purvis (New York: St Martin's Press, 1995).

Kempadoo, Kamala, "Theorizing Sexual Relations in the Caribbean: Prostitution and the Problem of the 'Exotic,'" in *Confronting Power, Theorising Gender: Interdisciplinary Perspectives in the Caribbean*, ed. Eudine Barriteau (Kingston: University of the West Indies Press, 2003).

———. "Continuities and Change: Five Centuries of Prostitution in the Caribbean," in *Sun, Sex and Gold: Tourism and Sex Work in the Caribbean*, ed. Kamala Kempadoo (Lanham: Rowman and Littlefield Publishers, 1999).

Kerr, Paulette. "Victims or Strategists? Female Lodging-house Keepers in Jamaica," in *Engendering History: Caribbean Women in Historical Perspective*, eds. Verene Shepherd, Bridget Brereton, and Barbara Bailey (Kingston: Ian Randle Publishers, 1995).

Levy, Andrea. *Small Island* (London: Headline Book Publishing, 2004).

Morrissey, Marietta. *Slave Women in the New World: Gender Stratification in the Caribbean* (Lawrence: University Press of Kansas, 1989).

Paul Raquel, Amy. "'It isn't love, it's business': Prostitution as Entrepreneurship and the Implications for Barbados," PhD Dissertation, University of California, Los Angeles, 1997.

Phoenix, Joanna. *Making Sense of Prostitution* (New York: St. Martin's Press and Palgrave, 1999).

Purvis, June, ed. *Women's History: Britain 1850–1945* (New York, St. Martin's Press, 1995).

Ramos, Jose Flores. "Virgins, Whores, and Martyrs: Prostitution in the Colony, 1898–1919," in *Puerto Rican Women's History: New Perspectives*, eds. Félix V. Matos Rodríguez and Linda C. Delgado (New York: M.E. Sharpe, 1998).

Rose, Ruth. *The Lost Sisterhood: Prostitution in America, 1900–1918* (Maryland: Johns Hopkins University Press, 1982).

Ross-Frankson, Joan. "The Economic Crisis and Prostitution in Jamaica: A Preliminary Study," Paper for Presentation at the Friedrich Ebert Stiftung and University of the West Indies Symposium on Issues Concerning Women, Department of Economics, University of the West Indies, Mona, 1987.

Rousseau, G. S. and Porter, Roy, eds. *Exoticism in the Enlightenment* (Manchester: Manchester University Press, 1990).

Shepherd, Verene. "'Sex in the Tropics': Women, Gender and Sexuality in the Discourses of Asian Labor Migration to the British Caribbean," in *I Want to Disturb*

My Neighbor: Lectures On Slavery, Emancipation & Post-Colonial Jamaica (Kingston: Ian Randle Publishers, 2009).

Suárez-Findlay, Eileen J. *Imposing Decency, The Politics of Sexuality and Race in Puerto Rico 1870–1920* (London and Durham: Duke University Press 1999).

Walkowitz, Judith. *Prostitution and Victorian Society: Women, Class, and the State* (Cambridge and New York: Cambridge University Press, 1980).

PART II—CULTURE

CHAPTER 7

Benítez-Rojo, Antonio. *The Repeating Island: The Caribbean and the Postmodern Perspective,* trans. James E. Maraniss (Durham and London: Duke University Press, 1996).

Benjamin, Walter. *Illuminations,* trans. Harry Zorn (London: Pimlico, 1999).

Bernabé, Jean, Patrick Chamoiseau, and Raphaël Confiant. *Éloge de la Créolité* (Paris: Gallimard, 1993 [1989]).

Bhabha, Homi K. *The Location of Culture* (London and New York: Routledge, 1994).

Brathwaite, E. K. *The Development of Creole Society in Jamaica, 1770–1820* (Oxford: Clarendon Press, 1971).

Burton, Richard D. E. "*Ki Moun Nou Ye?* The Idea of Difference in Contemporary French West Indian Thought," *New West Indian Guide,* 67 (1993): 5–32.

———. "The Idea of Difference in Contemporary French West Indian Thought: Négritude, Antillanité, Créolité," in *French and West Indian,* eds. Richard D.E. Burton and Fred Reno (London: Macmillan, 1995).

———. "The French West Indies *à l'heure de l'Europe,*" in *French and West Indian,* eds. Richard D. E. Burton and Fred Reno (London: Macmillan, 1995).

Cabral, Amilcar. "The Weapon of Theory," in *Revolution in Guinea: Selected Texts,* trans. and ed. Richard Handyside (New York and London: Monthly Review Press, 1969).

Chamoiseau, Patrick. *Biblique des derniers gestes* (Paris: Éditions Gallimard, 2002).

———. *Solibo Magnificent,* trans. Rose-Myriam Réjouis and Val Vinokurov (London: Granta Books, 2000).

Coronil, Fernando. "Transculturation and the Politics of Theory: Countering the Center, Cuban Counterpoint: Introduction," in *Cuban Counterpoint: Tobacco and Sugar,* trans. Harriet de Onís (Durham and London: Duke University Press, 1995).

Dash, J. Michael. *The Other America: Caribbean Literature in a New World Context* (Charlottesville and London: University Press of Virginia, 1998).

Fanon, Frantz. *The Wretched of the Earth,* trans. Constance Farrington (London: Penguin, 2001).

Glissant, Édouard. *Caribbean Discourse: Selected Essays,* trans. J. Michael Dash (Charlottesville: University Press of Virginia, 1989).

———. *Le discours antillais* (Paris: Éditions Gallimard, 1997).

———. *Malemort* (Paris: Éditions du Seuil, 1975).

Jameson, Fredric. "Marx's Purloined Letter," *New Left Review,* 4 (July-August 2000): 75–109.

Lamming, George. "Caribbean Labor, Culture and Identity," in *The Birth of Caribbean Civilisation: A Century of Ideas about Culture and Identity, Nation and Society,* ed. O. Nigel Bolland (Kingston: Ian Randle Publishers, 2004).

Lazarus, Neil. "The Politics of Postcolonial Modernism," *The European Legacy* 27, no. 6 (2002): 771–82.

Marx, Karl. *Capital. Vol. 1.,* trans. Ben Fowkes (London: Penguin, 1990).

———. *Economic and Philosophic Manuscripts of 1844,* trans. Martin Milligan (Mineola and New York: Dover Publications Inc., 2007).

Millette, James. "Decolonization, Populist Movements and the Formation of New Nations, 1945–1970," in *General History of the Caribbean. Vol. V: The Caribbean in the Twentieth Century,* ed. Bridget Brereton (Paris, London, and Oxford: UNESCO and Macmillan, 2004).

Nettleford, Rex. "National Identity and Attitudes Towards Race in Jamaica," in *The Birth of Caribbean Civilization: A Century of Ideas about Culture and Identity, Nation and Society,* ed. O. Nigel Bolland (Kingston: Ian Randle Publishers, 2004).

Ormerod, Beverly. "French West Indian Writing Since 1970," in *French and West Indian,* eds. Richard D.E. Burton and Fred Reno (London: Macmillan, 1995).

Ortiz, Fernando. *Cuban Counterpoint: Tobacco and Sugar,* trans. Harriet de Onís (Durham and London: Duke University Press, 1995).

Price, Richard. *The Convict and the Colonel: A Story of Colonialism and Resistance in the Caribbean* (Boston, Massachusetts: Beacon Press, 1998).

Price, Richard and Price, Sally. "Shadowboxing in the Mangrove," *Cultural Anthropology,* 12, no. 1 (1997): 3–36.

Puri, Shalini. *The Caribbean Postcolonial: Social Equality, Post-Nationalism and Cultural Hybridity* (New York: Palgrave Macmillan, 2004).

Rodney, Walter. *A History of the Guyanese Working People, 1891–1905* (London and Kingston: Heinemann Educational Books, 1981).

San Juan Jr., E. "Art Against Imperialism, For the National Struggle of Third World Peoples," in *Ruptures, Schisms, Interventions: Cultural Revolution in the Third World* (Manila: De La Salle University Press, 1988).

Sheller, Mimi. *Consuming the Caribbean: From Arawaks to Zombies* (London and New York: Routledge, 2003).

Torres-Saillant, Silvio. *An Intellectual History of the Caribbean* (New York: Palgrave and Macmillan, 2006).

CHAPTER 8

Bhabha, Homi K. *Location of Culture* (London: Routledge, 1989).

Brittan, Arthur. *Masculinity and Power* (New York: Basil Black, 1989).

Canefield, Rob. "Theatralizing the Anglophone Caribbean, 1492 to the 1980's," in *A History of Literature in the Caribbean,* ed. Arnold A. James (New York: John Benjamin Publishing Company, 1994).

Césaire, Aime. *Discourse on Colonialism* (Paris: Monthly Review Press, 2001).

"Damning Lamming: Lamming speaks with writer Knolly Moses about his concerns for the region," *Panmedia,* http://www.panmedia.com.jm/archive/features/lamming.htm, Accessed July 10, 2010.

Eagleton, Terry. *Criticism and Ideology: A Study in Marxist Literary Theory* (London: Verso, 1976).

Fanon, Franz. *Black Skin, White Masks* (New York: Grove Press, 1968).

Freire, Paulo. *Pedagogy of the Oppressed* (New York: Continuum, 1993).

Gramsci, Antonio. *Selections from the Prison Notebooks* (London: Lawrence and Wishart, 1971).

Hill, Errol. "From the Emergence of a National Drama in the West Indies," in *Twentieth Century Theatre: A Sourcebook of Radical Thinking,* ed. Richard Drain (London: Routledge, 1995).

Hodge, Merle. "The Shadow of the Whip," in *Is Massa Day Dead? Black Moods in the Caribbean,* ed. Orde Coombs (New York: Doubleday and Anchor, 1974).

James, C. L. R. "Black Jacobins," in *A Time and a Season,* ed. Errol Hill (Kingston: University of the West Indies Press, 1996).

John, Errol. *Moon on a Rainbow Shawl* (London: Faber and Faber Ltd. 1958).

Lacan, Jacques. "The Mirror Stage," in *A Critical and Cultural Reader,* eds. Anthony Easthope and Kate McGowan (Westport: Greenwood Press, 1993).

Pater, Walter. "Arts for Arts' Sake," *Encyclopedia Britannica Online,* http://www.britannica.com, Accessed July 10, 2010.

Thiong'O, Ngugi wa. *Decolonization of the Mind: The Politics of Language in African Literature* (London: Heinemann, 1986).

Walcott, Derek. "Pantomime," in *Remembrance & Pantomime: Two Plays,* Derek Walcott (New York: Farrar, Strauss and Giroux, 1980).

———. "Ti Jean and his Brothers," in *Plays for Today,* ed. Errol Hill (Port of Spain: Longman, 1985).

———. "What the Twilight Says," in *Dream on Monkey Mountain and Other Plays* (New York: Farrar, Strauss and Giroux, 1970).

Worell, Judith. *Encyclopedia of Women and Gender: Sex Similarities and Differences* (New York: Academic Press, 2001).

CHAPTER 9

Benítez-Rojo, Antonio. *The Repeating Island: The Caribbean and the Postmodern Perspective,* trans. James E. Maraniss (Durham and London: Duke University Press, 1992).

Britton, Celia M. *Eduoard Glissant and Postcolonial Theory: Strategies of Language and Theory* (Charlottesville and London: University Press of Virginia, 1999).

Carchidi, Victoria. "'Heaven is a Green Place': Varieties of Spiritual Landscape in Caribbean Literature," in *Mapping the Sacred Religion, Geography and Postcolonial Literatures,* eds. Jamie S. Scott and Paul Simpson-Housley (Amsterdam and Atlanta: Rodopi, 2001).

Carter, Marina and Torabully, Khal. *Coolitude: An Anthology of the Indian Labour Diaspora* (London: Anthem Press, 2002).

Dabydeen, David. *Our Lady of Demerara* (West Sussex: Dido Press, 2004).

Fazzini, Marco, ed., *Resisting Alterities: Wilson Harris and Other Avatars of Otherness* (Amsterdam: Rodopi, 2004).

Foucault, Michel. *The Order of Things: An Archeology of the Human Sciences* (London: Tavistock Publications, 1974).

Harris, Wilson. *Selected Essays of Wilson Harris: The Unfinished Genesis of the Imagination,* ed. A.J.M. Bundy (London: Routledge, 1999).

Stewart, Ian. *Does God Play Dice?: The New Mathematics of Chaos* (London: Penguin, 1997).

Walcott, Derek, "The Antilles: Fragments of an Epic Memory," in *What the Twilight Says,* Derek Walcott (New York: Farrar, Straus and Giroux, 1999).

———. "The Caribbean: Culture of Mimicry?" in *Critical Perspectives on Derek Walcott,* ed. Robert D. Hamner (Boulder: Lynne Rienner Publishers, 1997).

CHAPTER 10

Alegria, Ricardo and Arrom, Jose. *Taìno: Pre-Columbian Art and Culture from the Caribbean* (New York: Monacelli, 1998).

Anderson, Benedict. *Imagined Communities* (London and New York: Verso, 2006).

Araeen, Rasheed. "Excerpts from 'Conversation with Aubrey Williams,'" in *Aubrey Williams,* ed. Reyahn King (Liverpool and London: National Museums Liverpool and October Gallery, 2010).

Barson, Tanya and Gorschlüter, Peter, eds., *Afro Modern: Journeys Through the Black Atlantic,* Exhibition Catalogue (Liverpool: Tate Liverpool, 2010).

Boxer, David. "Introduction," in *A.D. Scott: Art Patron and Collector,* Exhibition Catalogue, David Boxer (Kingston: National Gallery of Jamaica, 1988).

Bryan, Patricia. "Towards an African Aesthetic in Jamaican Intuitive Art," *Arts Jamaica* 3:3, 4 (July 1985): 2–11.

Clifford, James. *The Predicament of Culture: Twentieth-century Ethnography, Literature and Art* (Cambridge: Harvard University Press, 1988).

Dacres, Petrina. "Modern Monuments: Fashioning History and Identity in Postcolonial Jamaica," PhD Dissertation, Emory University, Atlanta, 2008.

Gilroy, Paul. *The Black Atlantic: Modernity and Double Consciousness* (Cambridge: Harvard University Press, 1993).

Gaither, Edmund B. "Introduction," in *Jamaican Art since the Thirties*, Exhibition Catalogue, Edmund B. Gaither (Atlanta: Spelman College, 1969).

Gray, Obika. *Demeaned but Empowered: The Social Power of the Urban Poor in Jamaica* (Kingston: University of the West Indies Press, 2004).

Greenberg, Clement. "Modernist Painting," in *Modern Art and Modernism: A Critical Anthology*, eds. Francis Frascina and Charles Harrison (Boulder: Westview Press, 1983).

Hall, Stuart. "Negotiating Caribbean Identities," in *New Caribbean Thought: A Reader*, eds. Brian Meeks and Folke Lindahl (Kingston: University of the West Indies Press, 2001).

Harris, Wilson. "Aubrey Williams," in *Selected Essays of Wilson Harris: The Unfinished Genesis of the Imagination*, ed. Andrew Bundy (London and New York: Routledge, 1999).

Hucke, Claudia. "Picturing the Postcolonial Nation: (Inter)Nationalism in the Art of Jamaica 1962–1975," PhD Dissertation, University of Hamburg, Germany, 2009.

King, Reyahn, ed. *Aubrey Williams*, Exhibition Catalogue (Liverpool and London: National Museums Liverpool and October Gallery, 2010).

Mercer, Kobena. "Cosmopolitan Contact Zones," in *Afro Modern: Journeys Through the Black Atlantic*, eds. Tanya Barson and Peter Gorschlüter (Liverpool: Tate Liverpool, 2010).

Mintz, Sydney and Price, Richard. *The Birth of African-American Culture: An Anthropological Perspective* (Boston: Beacon, 1992).

Moody, Ronald. *Parboo Singh*, Exhibition Catalogue (London, 1951).

Pratt, Mary Louise. *Imperial Eyes: Travel Writing and Transculturation* (London and New York, Routledge, 1992).

Scott, David. *Conscripts of Modernity: The Tragedy of Colonial Enlightenment* (Durham: Duke University Press, 2004).

"'The Fine Arts'—Discussed by Edna Manley, Karl Parboosingh and Robert Verity," *Caribbean Quarterly: "The Arts"* 14, nos. 1 and 2 (1968): 63–76.

Thornton, John. *Africa and Africans in the Making of the Atlantic World, 1400–1800* (Cambridge University Press, 1998).

Todd, Edwin. "Abstract Art, The Avantgarde and Jamaica," *Jamaica Journal* 4, no. 4 (December 1970): 33.

Walmsley, Anne. *The Caribbean Artists Movement, 1966–1972: A Literary and Cultural History* (London and Port of Spain: New Beacon, 1992).

Williams, Aubrey. "The Predicament of the Artist in the Caribbean," *Caribbean Quarterly: "The Arts"* 14, nos. 1 and 2 (1968): 60–62.

CHAPTER 11

Albuquerque, Klaus. "Rastafarianism and Cultural Identity in the Caribbean," *Revisita Interamericana* 10, no. 2 (Summer 1980): 230–47.

Barrett, Leonard. *The Rastafarians: Sounds of Cultural Dissonance* (Boston: Beacon Press, 1988).

Birt, Robert. "Existence, Identity, and Liberation," in *Existence in Black: An Anthology of Black Existential Philosophy,* ed. Lewis Gordon (New York: Routledge, 1997).

Bogues, Anthony. *Black Heretics, Black Prophets: Radical Political Intellectuals* (New York: Routledge, 2003).

Brodber, Erna. "Re-engineering Blackspace," Paper presented at the Caribbean Conference in Honour of Rex Nettleford, University of the West Indies, Mona, Jamaica, 1996.

Brodber, Erna and Greene, J. Edward. "Reggae and Cultural Identity in Jamaica," Working Paper No. 35, Institute of Social and Economic Research, Kingston, 1988.

Campbell, Horace. *Rasta and Resistance: From Marcus Garvey to Walter Rodney* (Trenton: Africa World Press, 1987).

Floyd, Samuel A. *The Power of Black Music in History* (Oxford: Oxford University Press, 1995).

Griffith, Glyne A. *Deconstruction, Imperialism and the West Indian Novel* (Kingston: University of the West Indies Press, 1996).

Henry, Paget. "Rastafarianism and the Reality of Dread," in *Existence in Black: An Anthology of Black Existential Philosophy,* ed. Lewis Gordon (New York: Routledge, 1997).

Hylton, Patrick. "The Politics of Caribbean Music," *Black Scholar Magazine* vol. 6, no. 5 (September 1975): 23–29.

Negus, Keith. *Popular Music in Theory: An Introduction* (Hanover, NH: Wesleyan University Press, 1997).

Pereira, Joseph. "Babylon to Vatican: Religion in the Dancehall," *Journal of West Indian Literature* vol. 8, no. 1 (1997): 31–40.

Plato. *The Republic,* trans. I.A. Richards (London: Keagan Paul, 1948).

Rodney, Walter. *The Groundings With My Brothers* (London: Bogle-L'Ouverture Publications, 1969).

Rose, Tricia. *Black Noise: Rap Music and Black Culture in Contemporary America* (Hanover, New Hampshire: Wesleyan University Press, 1994).

Scott, James C. *Weapons of the Weak: Everyday Forms of Peasant Resistance* (New Haven: Yale University Press, 1985).

Stone, Carl and Brown, Aggrey, eds., *Essays on Power and Changes in Jamaica* (Kingston: Jamaica Publishing House, 1977).

Walt, Stephen M. *Revolution and War* (Ithaca: Cornell University Press, 1996).

Waters, Anita. *Race, Class and Political Symbols* (New Brunswick: Transaction Books, 1985).

Index

abolition acts, xvii, 6, 37, 44, 54, 88, 92, 96, 98–99, 102–103, 105, 189–190, 205

Abrahams, Carl, 247

Africa, xx, 206, 209, 227, 239, 245, 249n4, 256, 260, 265; art, 232, 239, 245, 251n46, 253n82; beliefs, 197, 213; descent, 9, 13, 26, 136, 159, 160, 174, 178n9, 211, 214–15, 217, 231, 239, 249n12, 251n46, 256, 257, 258, 260, 272n34; enslaved, 39, 99, 129, 172, 251n49

Afro-national, 26;

Afronationalist, 18, 19

agriculture, 62, 69, 161, 235

air force, 132

Algeria, 114, 162. *See also* George Wilson Bridges

alienation, 6, 28, 162, 166, 167, 169, 185, 190, 194, 201, 214, 221

allies, 48, 141;

allied forces, 141

amelioration, 41, 42, 48, 88, 90, 94, 97, 99, 269

America. *See* The United States

American, 4, 8, 9, 10, 13, 17, 189, 190, 201, 205, 230, 231, 232, 235, 236, 239, 240, 249n12, 251n53, 260, 264.
See also North American *and* South American

American Revolution, 17, 92

Anderson, Benedict, 7

Anglican Church, xvi, 88. *See also* Chapter 2, 62; conduct of clergy, 42, 101–102; contribution to slavery, xvi; in Jamaica, xvi. *See also* Chapter 2; involvement in slave instruction, xvi. *See also* Chapter 2

Anglophone, xv, 11, 27, 174, 183, 186, 196

Annales school, 7

anti-colonial, 14, 227, 242;

anti-colonialist, 235

apprenticeship, 77, 78, 79, 103, 205; period of, 103, 203

Arawak, 213, 214, 215, 216, 217, 245; Arawakian, 213, 214, 215, 218, 220

Athens, 114, 115, 120. *See also* George Wilson Bridges

Atlantic, 87, 171

Beckles, Hilary, 51, 129, 130, 149n3

Bell, Andrew, 50. *See also* education

Benítez-Rojo, Antonio, 169, 170, 171, 207, 208, 209, 210, 211, 215, 217, 222

Port of Spain, 13, 16; *Port of Spain
  Gazette*, 21, 22, 23
Port Welfare Authority, 144
postcolonial, xx, 27, 159, 160, 183, 184,
  185, 186, 187, 188, 190, 191, 195,
  197, 199, 215, 221, 227
Price, Richard, 163
profanation, 97
proslavery, xii, 48, 52
Prospero, 13
prostitution, xvii–xviii. *See also* Chapter
  6; and the World War periods, xviii;
  in England, 152n52

racism, 5, 256, 258, 263, 265
Rastafari, xxi, 257, 228, 255, 256, 257,
  258, 263, 264, 265, 269, 270. *See
  also* Jamaica
reggae, xii, xxi, Chapter 11. *See also*
  Jamaica
reincarnation, 207, 208, 214, 217, 218,
  219, 257
Republic. See Plato
resistance, xvi, xxi, 5, 6, 13, 18, 25, 37,
  51, 52, 70, 100, 105, 171, 176, 194,
  210, 215, 221, 222, 255, 256, 257,
  259. *See also* slave resistance
revolution, 17, 39, 91, 92, 185, 186,
  188, 189, 190, 191, 194, 234, 246,
  272n48; revolutionary, 17, 92, 174,
  190, 201, 228, 235, 246, 257, 263,
  264, 265; post-revolutionary, 233
Rivera, Diego, 232, 233, 247
Rodney, Walter, 174, 180n48, 249n5,
  264, 265, 266;
Rodney affair/riots/protest, 229, 249n5,
  272n37
Rome, 17, 120
Romeo, Max, 267
Rousseau, Jean Jacques, xvii; influence
  on George Wilson Bridges, xvii,
  92–93; social contract. *See* the social
  contract

Salzmann, August, 117, 120, 125n31
Seaga, Edward, 232, 237, 239, 269

Senior, Bernard, 52. *See also* George
  Wilson Bridges and James Macqueen
sexuality, xviii, xix, 4, 8, 20, 29, 32n15,
  130, 131, 132, 134, 135, 238, 243;
sexual exploitation, 129, 132, 133,
  150n17, 201
sexual freedom, 9, 24, 25, 137, 147,
  151n41
sexual health, 140
sexual relations, xviii, 3, 21, 129, 130,
  131, 133, 137, 140, 141, 145, 147,
  148
Sheller, Mimi, 169
Shepherd, Verene, 104, 129
ship, 23, 42, 45, 115, 135, 137, 140,
  145, 146. *See also* slave ship
shipment, 42, 43, 45
Sicily, 114, 115
Silver, Harold, 73, 76–77. *See also* John
  Lawton.
Sinclair, Upton, 4
Siqueiros, David Alfaro, 232, 233, 246
slave act, 88, 98
slave instruction, Chapter 2. *See also*
  Anglican Church
slave registration, 89, 98
slave resistance, 37, 48–54, 55n2
slave ship, 257
slave trade, 6, 88, 98, 99, 100, 205
Smith, Adam, 26
Smith, Ernie, 267, 270
Smith, Faith, 12, 27
the social contract, 88–95
Social Purity Organization
  (Association), 133, 142, 143, 147
South America, 210, 212, 227, 236
spirit license, 136
stereotype, 25, 133, 134, 195, 256;
  gender, 133, 134, 195; racial, 25, 256
subaltern, 129, 164, 169
subculture, 8, 256, 257, 259, 263
subordination, 186
subversion, 255, 264
sugar, 39, 170, 172, 193, 205, 210, 229
sugar revolution, 39
Sunday marketing by slaves, 51, 58n46

The Contributors

Dr. Dalea Bean is an Assistant Lecturer at the Regional Coordinating Unit of the Institute for Gender and Development Studies, University of the West Indies, Jamaica, where she coordinates the undergraduate Diploma Program and works with the Graduate Studies Program. She holds a PhD from the University of the West Indies in History. Her research is on the impact of World Wars I and II on Jamaican women, on women and gender in Caribbean history and culture in general, and on gender relations in the hotel industry in Jamaica.

Dr. Eldon V. Birthwright is Assistant Professor of English and African American Studies at Louisiana State University, Baton Rouge. He is a graduate of the University of the West Indies, University of Chicago, and Emory University where he completed his PhD. His research covers the nineteenth century and twentieth century, and focuses on African American Literature. He also does work on the literature and culture of Anglophone Caribbean.

Prof. Trevor Burnard is Professor of History at the University of Melbourne and has held the position of Professor of the History of the Americas at the University of Warwick, where he was also head of the Department of History. He is a widely respected historian of the Caribbean and Americas in general, and his research which focuses on the period of slavery has produced a number of publications that have appeared in several international journals. He is the author of the critically acclaimed monograph, *Mastery, Tyranny, and Desire: Thomas Thistlewood and his Slaves in the Anglo-Jamaican World.*

Dr. D. A. Dunkley holds a PhD in history from the University of Warwick. He is also a graduate of the University of the West Indies, Jamaica, where he currently teaches in the Department of History and Archaeology. His research interests are the history of slavery, freedom, and the Christian Church in the Americas. He also does research on nationalism, identity, and politics in the Post-Independence Caribbean. He is the author of a forthcoming book on the Anglican clergy in the Caribbean to be published by Lexington Press.

Mr. Dennis Gill has taught in Guyana, St. Lucia, and the British Virgin Islands at the secondary and tertiary levels, and is a graduate of the Universities of Guyana, Warwick, and the West Indies. Through his research he has examined the place of Caribbean literature in the discourse on masculinity, and has presented papers at major conferences on this subject. He is currently a columnist for the BVI Standpoint in the British Virgin Islands and has been a frequent guest on radio programs in that country. He is also currently pursuing his PhD in literature at the University of the West Indies in Barbados.

Dr. Claudia Hucke is a Senior Lecturer in Art History at the Edna Manley College of the Visual and Performing Arts in Jamaica. Her doctoral dissertation on "Picturing the Postcolonial Nation—(Inter) Nationalism in the Art of Jamaica, 1962–1975" was completed at the University of Hamburg, Germany. Her research discusses Jamaican visual arts in the immediate post-independence period, in addition to the relationship between art and nation-building. Her other research interests are the African Diaspora art of the Caribbean in general and North America.

Dr. Coreen J. Leacock is a Lecturer in the School of Education at the University of the West Indies, Barbados, where she also carries out the duties of Academic Coordinator for the Joint Board of Teacher Education, the teacher certifying body for the Eastern Caribbean. She holds a PhD in Education from the University of Cambridge, and her research interests include the teaching and learning of mathematics, technology use in education, and small state issues in education.

Mr. Russell Lord is a PhD candidate in Art History at the Graduate Centre, City University of New York, and the Jane and Morgan Whitney Fellow in the Department of Photographs at the Metropolitan Museum of Art in New York City. He has written on nineteenth-century and twentieth-century photography for international journals, and is the author, along with Larry Schaaf, of the monograph study, *Joseph, Vicomte Vigier: Voyage dans les Pyrénées 1853.* His research focuses on early photography and its relationship to painting and printmaking.

Dr. Michael Niblett is a post-doctoral researcher at the Centre for Caribbean Studies, University of Warwick. He has taught in the university's Centre for Translation and Comparative Cultural Studies, and in the Comparative American Studies Department. Currently he is working on a project funded by the Leverhulme Trust on Caribbean literature and the environment. He has published articles on Caribbean literature and is the co-editor of *Perspectives on the "Other America": Comparative Approaches to Caribbean and Latin American Culture.* A monograph, *The Caribbean Novel Since 1945,* is forthcoming with the University Press of Mississippi.

Dr. Raymond Ramcharitar holds a PhD from the University of the West Indies. His doctoral thesis on "The Hidden History of Trinidad: Underground Culture in Trinidad, 1870–1970" was an ambitious rewriting of the official Trinidadian historical narrative and a critique of Caribbean historiography. He has also written the first book-length study of the Trinidadian media entitled *Breaking the News: Media and Culture in Trinidad,* and has books of poetry and fiction, including The Island Quintet, which was nominated for the Commonwealth Writers' Prize for Best First Book (Canada and the Caribbean) in 2010.

Dr. Shivani Sivagurunathan is a Senior Lecturer in English Literature at University Putra in Malaysia. She completed her PhD in Comparative Literature at the University of Warwick. Her research articles have appeared in *The Oxford Companion to Black British History and Coral Identities: Essays on Indo-Caribbean Literature,* and she is currently working on a book about the poetics of "Coolitude" with the Indo-Mauritian poet, Khal Torabully.

Dr. Benita P. Thompson is a Program Coordinator in the Open Campus of the University of the West Indies. She has a PhD in Education and training in History and Sociology. She has extensive experience in teaching, having taught for over twenty-five years in the primary school system. Her research includes adolescent deviant behavior, the performance of primary and secondary students, and the evaluation of technology use in schools. Her current research examines the Human Resource Needs in Tertiary Education in the Caribbean.

Dr. S. Joel Warrican, a Lecturer in the School of Education, University of the West Indies, Barbados, is currently on secondment to the Government of St. Vincent and the Grenadines in the post of Director of the St. Vincent and the Grenadines Community College. He holds a PhD in Education (Language and Literacy) from the University of Cambridge, and has published a number of research articles on issues in education in the Caribbean, and is the author of *Hard Words: The Challenge of Reading and Writing for Caribbean Students and their Teachers.*